ORIGINS OF MARVEL COMICS

Cover Art
CHRIS STEVENS & NATHAN FAIRBAIRN

Collection Editor
ALEX STARBUCK

Editorial Assistants
JAMES EMMETT & JOE HOCHSTEIN

Assistant Editor
NELSON RIBEIRO

Editors, Special Projects
JENNIFER GRÜNWALD
& MARK D. BEAZLEY

Senior Editor, Special Projects
JEFF YOUNGQUIST

Senior Vice President of Sales
DAVID GABRIEL

SVP of Brand Planning & Communications
MICHAEL PASCIULLO

Design
SPRING HOTELING

Editor in Chief
AXEL ALONSO

Chief Creative Officer
JOE QUESADA

Publisher
DAN BUCKLEY

Executive Producer
ALAN FINE

D1213624

ORIGINS OF MARVEL COMICS

THE ORIGINAL

CAPTAIN AMERICA

IN THE DARK DAYS OF WORLD WAR II, YOUNG ART STUDENT *STEVE ROGERS* TRIED TO ENLIST IN THE U.S. ARMY BUT WAS REJECTED AS TOO SCRAWNY AND WEAK FOR MILITARY SERVICE.

DESPERATE TO SERVE HIS COUNTRY IN HER TIME OF NEED, ROGERS VOLUNTEERED INSTEAD FOR *OPERATION: REBIRTH,* THE GOVERNMENT'S *TOP-SECRET SUPER-SOLDIER PROGRAM.*

SCIENTISTS SUBJECTED STEVE TO A GRUELING SERIES OF CHEMICAL AND RADIOLOGICAL TREATMENTS TO TRANSFORM HIM INTO A *PHYSICALLY PERFECT MAN.*

BUT WHEN A NAZI SPY'S BULLET CUT DOWN THE ONLY MIND WITH THE SECRET TO THE PROCESS, ROGERS BECAME AN *ARMY OF ONE.*

WRITER: FRED VAN LENTE   ART: STEVE EPTING   COLORS: FRANK D'ARMATA
LETTERS: NATE PIEKOS   ASST. EDITOR: ALEJANDRO ARBONA   EDITOR: RALPH MACCHIO

U.S. INTELLIGENCE TRANSFORMED HIM INTO A *LIVING SYMBOL* OF AMERICA'S PROMISE IN THE WORLD-- THE PERFECT COUNTER TO THE NAZIS' FEARED HEAD OF TERRORISM, *THE RED SKULL.*

CAPTAIN AMERICA'S SPECTACULAR MISSIONS IN EVERY THEATER OF WAR STRUCK DECISIVE BLOWS FOR THE ALLIES AND KEPT MORALE HIGH BACK HOME!

THE NATION MOURNED AS ONE WHEN "CAP" WAS LOST AT SEA IN HIS FINAL WARTIME MISSION AND PRESUMED DEAD.

BUT THE FRIGID WATERS OF THE NORTH ATLANTIC PRESERVED HIM FROZEN IN *SUSPENDED ANIMATION,* UNTIL HE WAS DISCOVERED AND REVIVED IN OUR ERA!

NOW STEVE ROGERS IS A *MAN OUT OF TIME.* THE WORLD HE ONCE KNEW IS LOST TO *HISTORY...*

...BUT HIS CAUSE *LIVES ON.* LOYAL NOT TO A GOVERNMENT, OR A FLAG, BUT TO A *DREAM,* THAT ALL PEOPLE ARE CREATED *EQUAL...*

...CAPTAIN AMERICA CONTINUES TO BATTLE *ALL* THREATS TO THAT DREAM TODAY, WHEREVER HE MAY FIND THEM!

WHEN THE GOVERNMENT THREATENED TO CANCEL **REED RICHARDS'** EXPERIMENTAL **STARSHIP** PROJECT, THE BRILLIANT SCIENTIST KNEW HE HAD TO PROVE ITS WORTH-- AND **FAST.**

SO REED DECIDED TO TEST FLY THE CRAFT **HIMSELF,** BRINGING ALONG AS CREWMEMBERS HIS BEST FRIEND, CRACK TEST PILOT, **BEN GRIMM**---

---HIS **GIRLFRIEND, SUSAN STORM,** AND HER YOUNGER BROTHER, **JOHNNY.**

BUT THE UNTESTED SHIP FLEW INTO A **COSMIC RAY STORM** WITHOUT ADEQUATE SHIELDING AND THE CREW'S BODIES WERE TRANSFORMED!

BEN WAS TURNED INTO A HIDEOUS **THING.**

JOHNNY COULD BURST INTO FLAME LIKE A **HUMAN TORCH.**

REED COULD **STRETCH** HIS BODY AT WILL.

SUSAN COULD BECOME AN **INVISIBLE WOMAN.**

---NAMING HIMSELF **MR. FANTASTIC,** RICHARDS DEDICATED THIS **FIRST FAMILY** OF HEROES TO EXPLORING NEW WORLDS AND DEFENDING HUMANITY AS THE...

FANTASTIC FOUR

WRITER-FRED VAN LENTE   ARTIST-DALE EAGLESHAM
COLOR ARTIST-PAUL MOUNTS   LETTERER-BLAMBOT'S NATE PIEKOS
ASSOCIATE EDITOR-LAUREN SANKOVITCH   EDITOR-TOM BREVOORT

DOCTOR DOOM

THE SON OF POOR GYPSIES FROM THE BALKAN NATION OF LATVERIA, BRILLIANT *VICTOR VON DOOM* EARNED A SCHOLARSHIP TO STUDY AT *EMPIRE STATE* IN NEW YORK.

HIS ONLY PEER IN THE SCIENCE DEPARTMENT WAS THE YOUNG AMERICAN, *REED RICHARDS.*

VICTOR INSISTED ON TESTING A *DIMENSIONAL TRANSPORTER* OF HIS OWN DESIGN OVER RICHARDS' OBJECTIONS THAT HIS CALCULATIONS WERE *FLAWED.*

THE RESULTING EXPLOSION HORRIBLY *DISFIGURED* VON DOOM, GOT HIM EXPELLED FROM UNIVERSITY--AND EMBITTERED HIM FOR LIFE!

DOOM BELIEVED *SCIENCE* HAD ALREADY TAUGHT HIM ALL IT *COULD.* HE IMMERSED HIMSELF IN STUDY OF THE *WITCHCRAFT* PRACTICED BY HIS MOTHER.

WRITER: FRED VAN LENTE ART: DALE EAGLESHAM COLORS: DAVE McCAIG
LETTERS: NATE PIEKOS ASST. EDITOR: ALEJANDRO ARBONA EDITOR: RALPH MACCHIO

HE FORGED THE *ARMOR* THAT WOULD CONCEAL HIS HIDEOUS VISAGE FROM THE WORLD FOREVER.

A MASTER OF ADVANCED TECHNOLOGY *AND* BLACK MAGIC, DOOM RETURNED TO HIS NATIVE LATVERIA AND EFFORTLESSLY *CONQUERED* IT.

AS A HEAD OF STATE, DR. DOOM HAS *DIPLOMATIC IMMUNITY* AND CANNOT BE ARRESTED OR PROSECUTED BY ANOTHER NATION.

BY THIS TIME, REED RICHARDS AND HIS FRIENDS HAD SUFFERED THE ACCIDENT THAT TRANSFORMED THEM INTO THE *FANTASTIC FOUR.*

AT LAST DOOM COULD PROVE HIS *SUPERIORITY* TO RICHARDS--BY DESTROYING THEM, AND EXTENDING HIS LATVERIAN EMPIRE ACROSS THE ENTIRE *GLOBE!*

WHILE ATTENDING AN AFTER-SCHOOL DEMONSTRATION OF RADIOLOGY, SHY, BOOKISH *PETER PARKER* WAS BITTEN BY AN ACCIDENTALLY *IRRADIATED* SPIDER.

ITS *VENOM* TRANSFORMED THE YOUNG MAN'S *DNA*, GRANTING HIM THE PROPORTIONATE STRENGTH, AGILITY, AND CLINGING ABILITY OF A HUMAN-SIZED ARACHNID!

SEEING THE VAST POTENTIAL FOR *PERSONAL GAIN* IN HIS NEW POWERS, PETER INVENTED A PAIR OF WEB-SHOOTERS AND SEWED HIMSELF A COLORFUL COSTUME...

...AND BECAME THE MYSTERIOUS *ENTERTAINER* KNOWN AS "*SPIDER-MAN*"!

BUT PETER'S DREAMS OF GLORY SOON CRASHED AROUND HIM.

HE SELFISHLY REFUSED TO APPREHEND A *BURGLAR* FLEEING THE STUDIO ONE NIGHT...

...WHO, IN A TRAGIC TWIST OF FATE, SHOT AND KILLED HIS *UNCLE BEN* IN A BOTCHED ROBBERY!

the AMAZING SPIDER-MAN

...HAS SINCE SWORN TO USE HIS POWERS TO DEFEND *OTHERS*, EVEN AT THE EXPENSE OF HIS OWN (QUITE *MESSY*) PERSONAL LIFE...

...FOR HE LEARNED IN THE MOST PAINFUL WAY POSSIBLE THAT WITH GREAT *POWER* MUST ALSO COME GREAT *RESPONSIBILITY*!

WRITER: FRED VAN LENTE   PENCILS: JOHN ROMITA JR.   INKS: KLAUS JANSON   COLORS: DEAN WHITE
LETTERS: NATE PIEKOS   ASST. EDITOR: ALEJANDRO ARBONA   EDITOR: RALPH MACCHIO

HA HA HA HA!!

GREEN GOBLIN

CHEMICAL ENGINEER *NORMAN OSBORN* RUTHLESSLY RUINED COMPETITORS AND PARTNERS ALIKE TO AMASS HIS *OSCORP* INDUSTRIAL EMPIRE.

WRITER: FRED VAN LENTE   ART: MIKE DEODATO   COLORS: RAIN BEREDO
LETTERS: NATE PIEKOS   ASST. EDITOR: ALEJANDRO ARBONA   EDITOR: RALPH MACCHIO

WHEN AN EXPERIMENTAL SERUM EXPLODED IN HIS FACE, HIS STRENGTH AND STAMINA WERE *ENHANCED*, AT THE EXPENSE OF HIS *FRAGILE MIND*.

USING OSCORP TECH TO ARM HIMSELF, OSBORN CREATED A NEW PERSONA, THE *GREEN GOBLIN*, INSPIRED BY A BOGEYMAN THAT HAD FRIGHTENED HIM AS A *CHILD*.

SPIDER-MAN OPPOSED HIS QUEST TO TAKE OVER THE UNDERWORLD...

SO OSBORN KIDNAPPED AND MURDERED THE LOVE OF HIS LIFE, *GWEN STACY*.

BUT OSBORN'S POLITICAL CONNECTIONS EARNED HIM A *PARDON* FOR THE GREEN GOBLIN'S CRIMES-- AND LEFT HIM *FREE* TO CONTINUE TERRORIZING THE WORLD!

AFTER **ODIN**, ALL-FATHER OF THE NORSE PANTHEON, SLEW THE KING OF THE EVIL **FROST GIANTS**, HE DISCOVERED THEY HID A HUMAN-SIZED BABY IN THEIR MIDST.

ODIN TOOK THE CHILD BACK WITH HIM TO THE GODS' HOME OF ASGARD AND ADOPTED HIM, UNDER THE NAME OF...

LOKI

THE BOY GREW INTO A SKILLED SORCERER, SHAPE-SHIFTER, AND ONE OF ASGARD'S STAUNCHEST **DEFENDERS**...

...OFTEN DEPLOYING HIS MAGICKS ALONGSIDE THE MIGHT OF HIS FOSTER BROTHER **THOR**.

WRITER: FRED VAN LENTE ART: GIUSEPPE CAMUNCOLI COLORS: MATT HOLLINGSWORTH
LETTERS: NATE PIEKOS ASST. EDITOR: ALEJANDRO ARBONA EDITOR: RALPH MACCHIO

BUT THE MERCURIAL **GOD OF MISCHIEF** COULD HINDER THE ASGARDIANS AS MUCH AS HELP THEM, AS WHEN HE TRICKED THE BLIND GOD **HODER** INTO SLAYING THE OTHERWISE INVULNERABLE **BALDER**...

AND SO THE GODS NEVER FULLY **TRUSTED** LOKI.

YET IN HIS SELFISH NARCISSISM, HE CONVINCED HIMSELF IT WAS **THOR** WHO STOLE HIS GLORY FROM HIM.

THOR'S DEPARTURE FROM ASGARD TO BECOME GUARDIAN OF **EARTH** GAVE THE GOD OF MISCHIEF THE PERFECT OPPORTUNITY TO **SLAY** HIM OUT OF THEIR FATHER'S SIGHT.

...WITH AN ENCHANTED SPEAR MADE OF **MISTLETOE**.

IF THE THUNDER GOD **FELL**, OR SO HE THOUGHT, THE LOVE--AND **CROWN**--OF ASGARD WOULD BE **HIS**.

HIS REPEATED ATTACKS ON THE THUNDER GOD--AND MYSTICAL EMPOWERMENT OF THOR'S ENEMIES--HAVE MADE LOKI ONE OF THE GREATEST THREATS TO **OUR** WORLD AS **WELL** AS ASGARD!

TONY STARK'S *WEALTH* WAS MATCHED ONLY BY HIS *GENIUS*.

HE RAN THE MOST POWERFUL DEFENSE CONTRACTOR IN THE WORLD, *STARK INDUSTRIES,* AND DESIGNED MOST OF THEIR WEAPONS SYSTEMS *HIMSELF...*

...EVEN THOUGH HE HAD NEVER ACTUALLY EXPERIENCED THE HORRORS OF WAR *FIRSTHAND.*

ALL THAT CHANGED WHEN *ENEMY ORDNANCE* CRITICA[LLY] INJURED STARK'S *HEART* AS HE TOURED A FOREIGN BATTLEFIELD WHERE HIS WEAPONS WERE DEPLOYED.

INSURGENTS CAPTURED HIM AND HELD HIM HOSTAGE, DEMANDING HE NOW BUILD WEAPONS FOR *THEM.*

STARK OUTSMARTED HIS KIDNAPPERS, HOWEVER, BUILDING INSTEAD A SUIT OF *ARMOR* THAT WOULD KEEP HIS HEART *BEATING...*

...AND ALLOW HIM TO *ESCAPE* HIS ENEMIES' STRONGHOLD!

WHEN HE RETURNED TO THE STATES, TONY SWORE OFF BUILDING *LETHAL* WEAPONS SYSTEMS, HAVING SEEN THEIR TERRIBLE *EFFECTS* WITH HIS OWN EYES.

TONY STILL FELT HE HAD MUCH TO *ATONE* FOR, THOUGH. HE SECRETLY INVESTED ALL HIS RESOURCES INTO THE CONSTRUCTION OF A NEW, MORE ADVANCED VERSION OF HIS ARMOR...

...ONE THAT WOULD ALLOW HIM TO REDEEM HIMSELF BY PROTECTING OTHERS AS...

THE INVINCIBLE IRON MAN

WRITER: FRED VAN LENTE   ART: SALVADOR LARROCA   COLORS: FRANK D'ARMATA
LETTERS: NATE PIEKOS   ASST. EDITOR: ALEJANDRO ARBONA   EDITOR: RALPH MACCHIO

PHYSICIST **BRUCE BANNER** HAD AN ABUSIVE FATHER WHO LEFT HIM A DEEPLY **REPRESSED** ADULT.

YET WHEN HE SAW A TROUBLED YOUTH DRIVE ONTO THE TESTING GROUND OF HIS **GAMMA RAY-POWERED WARHEAD** AS THE COUNTDOWN TICKED TOWARD ZERO....

....BANNER ACTED INSTINCTIVELY, **SELFLESSLY,** TO PULL THE YOUNG MAN TO SAFETY....

....ONLY TO BE CAUGHT IN THE GAMMA BLAST **HIMSELF!**

THE CELLS OF HIS BODY SEETHED WITH INCREDIBLE **POWER**--AND THE DARK WELLSPRING OF **FURY** BUBBLING BENEATH HIS CONSCIOUS MIND **ERUPTED** INTO THE LIGHT OF DAY!

IN TIMES OF **STRESS,** BRUCE BANNER IS TRANSFORMED AGAINST HIS WILL INTO A RAMPAGING MONSTER OF **PURE ANGER**--

NOW BANNER IS ON A DESPERATE QUEST FOR A **CURE** FOR HIS CONDITION BEFORE THE AUTHORITIES CATCH AND DESTROY HIM....

THE INCREDIBLE
HULK

....NEVER KNOWING WHEN THE **CHILD OF RAGE** INSIDE HIM WILL NEXT BE **UNLEASHED.**

WRITER:
FRED VAN LENTE

ARTIST:
LEE WEEKS

COLOR ARTIST:
DEAN WHITE

LETTERER:
VC'S JOE CARAMAGNA

ASST. EDITOR:
THOMAS BRENNAN

EDITOR:
STEPHEN WACKER

THERE CAME A DAY, A DAY UNLIKE ANY OTHER...

...WHEN EARTH'S MIGHTIEST HEROES AND HEROINES BANDED TOGETHER TO BATTLE A THREAT NO ONE OF THEM COULD FACE ALONE.

SINCE THAT DAY, THOUGH THEIR ROSTER HAS CHANGED MANY TIMES...

...AND SERVED AS A PROVING GROUND FOR NEW CHAMPIONS AS WELL AS THE RIGHTFUL HOME OF LEGENDS...

...GLORY AND HONOR HAVE ALWAYS GONE HAND-IN-HAND WITH THOSE WHO HEED THE CALL TO ASSEMBLE...

THE AVENGERS

FRED VAN LENTE-WRITER
STUART IMMONEN-PENCILER
WADE VON GRAWBADGER-INKER
LAURA MARTIN-COLORIST
BLAMBOT'S NATE PIEKOS-LETTERER
LAUREN SANKOVITCH-ASSOCIATE EDITOR
TOM BREVOORT-EDITOR

...ENETICIST CHARLES XAVIER WATCHED WITH CONCERN ...S PREJUDICE AGAINST MUTANTS, OR PEOPLE BORN ...TH SUPERHUMAN ABILITIES, SWEPT ACROSS AMERICA...

...IN NO SMALL PART BECAUSE HE WAS A MUTANT HIMSELF, ONE OF THE WORLD'S MOST POWERFUL TELEPATHS.

MUTANTS' POWERS TEND TO MANIFEST IN ADOLESCENCE, SO XAVIER ESTABLISHED AN ACADEMY IN HIS FAMILY'S MANOR IN UPSTATE NEW YORK FOR THEM.

XAVIER SCHOOL for Exceptional Youngsters

HIS FIRST STUDENT WAS A YOUNG MAN NAMED SCOTT SUMMERS, WHOSE NATURAL EYEBEAMS EARNED HIM THE CODE NAME "CYCLOPS."

THOUGH THE WORLD AT LARGE BELIEVES HIS INSTITUTE TO BE JUST ANOTHER TONY PREP SCHOOL...

..."PROFESSOR X," AS HIS STUDENTS DUBBED HIM, SCANS THE WORLD FOR YOUNG MUTANTS WITH THE HELP OF CEREBRO, A COMPUTER HE DEVELOPED TO ENHANCE HIS TELEPATHY...

...AND TEACHES THEM HOW TO USE THEIR POWERS IN HIS DANGER ROOM...

...SO THEY MAY BATTLE AGAINST MUTANT TERRORISTS WHO SEEK TO CONQUER HUMANITY.

XAVIER'S STUDENTS PROVE MUTANTS DESERVE EQUAL RIGHTS THANKS TO THEIR HEROIC EXAMPLE AS THE

X-MEN

WRITER: FRED VAN LENTE   ART: LEINIL FRANCIS YU   COLORS: DAVE McCAIG
LETTERS: VC's CLAYTON COWLES   EDITOR: ALEJANDRO ARBONA
...TOR IN CHIEF: JOE QUESADA   PUBLISHER: DAN BUCKLEY   EXEC. PRODUCER: ALAN FINE

BATTLIN' JACK MURDOCK WANTED HIS SON TO LIVE HIS LIFE WITHOUT FEAR.

HE URGED MATT NOT TO FOLLOW IN HIS FOOTSTEPS AS A SMALL-TIME BOXER... TO HAVE THE GUTS TO MAKE SOMETHING OF HIMSELF.

WHEN MATT WAS STILL A TEENAGE HE SAVED AN OL MAN ABOUT TO B RUN OVER BY A RUNAWAY TRUCK

BUT A RADIOACTIVE CYLINDER FELL FROM THE TRUCK AND BLINDED MATT FOR LIFE.

YET HE SOON REALIZED, HIS OTHER SENSES HAD BECOME SUPERHUMANLY ACUTE!

HE COULD TELL WHETHER OR NOT SOMEONE WAS LYING BY LISTENING TO THE PERSON'S HEARTBEAT.

HE COULD RECOGNIZE PEOPLE BY SCENT ALONE.

AND HE HAD DEVELOPED A SIXTH SENSE, A RADAR-LIKE AWARENESS OF WHERE OBJECTS WERE.

MURDOCK DIDN'T NEED ANY SUPER-POWERS TO GRADUATE AT THE TOP OF HIS LAW SCHOOL CLASS.

HE BECAME A SUCCESSFUL ATTORNEY, FULFILLING THE DREAMS OF HIS FATHER.

BATTLIN' JACK DID NOT LIVE LONG ENOUGH TO SAVOR MATT'S SUCCESS.

GANGSTER'S BULLETS CUT HIM DOWN AFTER REFUSING TO THROW A FIGHT.

JACK DIDN'T WANT MATT TO BECOME A FIGHTER. BUT TO BRING HIS FATHER'S KILLERS TO JUSTICE, HE BECAME A MAN WITHOUT FEAR:

DAREDEVIL

WRITER - FRED VAN LENTE
ARTIST - MARCOS MARTIN
LETTERER - BLAMBOT'S NATE PIEKOS
ASSISTANT EDITOR - THOMAS BRENNAN
EDITOR - STEPHEN WACKER

STEPHEN STRANGE WAS AMONG THE WORLD'S MOST BRILLIANT SURGEONS, BUT A CAR ACCIDENT DAMAGED THE NERVES IN HIS HANDS SO BADLY HE WAS UNABLE TO WORK.

A PROUD AND ARROGANT MAN, STRANGE SCOURED THE GLOBE FOR A CURE. WHEN HE HEARD WHISPERS OF A **MYSTIC** IN THE HIMALAYAS SAID TO WORK **MIRACLES**...

...HE MADE THE ARDUOUS JOURNEY TO SEEK OUT THIS **ANCIENT ONE.**

STRANGE WOULD RECEIVE THE HELP HE NEEDED ONLY IF HE **HUMBLED** HIMSELF BY BECOMING THE WIZENED SORCERER'S **SERVANT.**

STRANGE DISCOVERED THE ANCIENT ONE'S APPRENTICE, **MORDO,** WAS SECRETLY PLOTTING TO DESTROY HIS MASTER WITH HEXES AND STEAL HIS POWER.

TO COUNTER MORDO'S GROWING EVIL, STRANGE VOLUNTEERED TO BECOME A PUPIL OF THE MYSTIC ARTS HIMSELF.

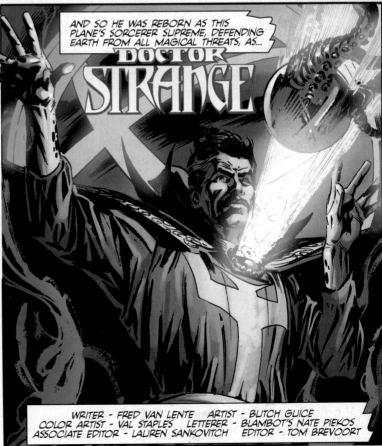

AND SO HE WAS REBORN AS THIS PLANE'S SORCERER SUPREME, DEFENDING EARTH FROM ALL MAGICAL THREATS, AS...

DOCTOR STRANGE

AT LAST HE UNDERSTOOD: CONQUERING HIS OWN SELFISHNESS **WAS** THE SALVATION THE ANCIENT ONE OFFERED!

WRITER - FRED VAN LENTE   ARTIST - BUTCH GUICE
COLOR ARTIST - VAL STAPLES   LETTERER - BLAMBOT'S NATE PIEKOS
ASSOCIATE EDITOR - LAUREN SANKOVITCH   EDITOR - TOM BREVOORT

BLACK PANTHER

IS THE TOTEMIC DEITY OF THE **WAKANDA** TRIBE OF CENTRAL AFRICA. FOR HUNDREDS OF YEARS THEIR **CHIEFTAIN** HAS CLAD HIMSELF IN ITS IMAGE AS THE PEOPLE'S PROTECTOR.

MILLENNIA PAST, A METEORITE CONTAINING THE RARE ENERGY-ABSORBING METAL **VIBRANIUM** LANDED ON A WAKANDAN MOUNTAIN-SIDE FREQUENTED BY THE GREAT CATS.

SALE OF VIBRANIUM HAS MADE TINY WAKANDA ONE OF THE **RICHEST**, MOST TECHNOLOGICALLY **ADVANCED**... AND MOST **SECRETIVE** NATIONS ON EARTH.

T'CHALLA INHERITED THE MANTLE OF **BLACK PANTHER**, ATE THE SACRED **HEART-SHAPED HERB** THAT GAVE HIM MORE-THAN-MORTAL SPEED AND STRENGTH...

BUT THE OUTSIDE WORLD STILL MANAGED TO INTRUDE ON WAKANDA'S IDYLLIC TRANQUILITY.

A MERCENARY FROM THE WEST, **ULYSSES KLAW**, MURDERED CHIEF **T'CHAKA** IN FRONT OF HIS YOUNG SON **T'CHALLA** IN A FAILED ATTEMPT TO SEIZE THE VIBRANIUM CACHE!

...AND WENT OUT INTO FOREIGN LANDS TO STRIKE AT THREATS **BEFORE** THEY COULD REACH HIS BELOVED HOMELAND'S DOOR!

WRITER: FRED VAN LENTE   ART: MIGUEL SEPULVEDA   COLORS: TOM SMITH   LETTERS: BLAMBOT'S NATE PIEKOS   ASST. EDITOR: RACHEL PINNELAS   EDITOR: BILL ROSEMANN

SERGEANT NICK FURY LED HIS ELITE U.S. ARMY RANGER "HOWLING COMMANDOS" UNIT TO VICTORY AFTER VICTORY IN A DARING SERIES OF GUERILLA MISSIONS DURING WORLD WAR II.

A LAND MINE NEARLY KEPT FURY FROM LIVING TO SEE WAR'S END.

BUT HE WAS RESCUED BY A SCIENTIST WHO GAVE HIM AN EXPERIMENTAL "INFINITY FORMULA" TO SAVE HIS LIFE--AND GREATLY SLOW HIS BODY'S AGING PROCESS.

FURY WENT TO WORK FOR THE CENTRAL INTELLIGENCE AGENCY UPON HIS RECOVERY.

AS THE COLD WAR RAGED, AN EVEN GREATER THREAT TO WORLD SECURITY SOON ASSERTED ITSELF: INTERNATIONAL TERRORISM.

AMONG THE MOST FEARED OF THESE ANTIDEMOCRATIC, FASCISTIC ORGANIZATIONS WAS HYDRA, LED BY FURY'S OLD NAZI NEMESIS, BARON VON STRUCKER.

THE UNITED NATIONS ORDERED THE FORMATION OF AN INTERNATIONAL AGENCY TO MATCH THE THREAT OF HYDRA:

THE STRATEGIC HAZARD INTERVENTION, ESPIONAGE AND LOGISTICS DIRECTORATE...S.H.I.E.L.D.

...BUT ITS GREATEST WEAPON MAY BE THE LEADER THEY CHOSE, AN ETERNAL WARRIOR WHO BRINGS DECADES OF EXPERIENCE IN SHADOW WARFARE TO BEAR: **NICK FURY**

S.H.I.E.L.D. BOASTS ADVANCED WEAPONRY DESIGNED BY TONY (IRON MAN) STARK HIMSELF AND A MOBILE COMMAND CENTER, THE HELICARRIER...

WRITER: FRED VAN LENTE   ART: STEFANO GAUDIANO   COLORS: JOSE VILLARRUBIA
LETTERS: VC's CLAYTON COWLES   EDITOR: ALEJANDRO ARBONA
EDITOR IN CHIEF: JOE QUESADA   PUBLISHER: DAN BUCKLEY   EXEC. PRODUCER: ALAN FINE

WOLVERINE

AT THE END OF THE 19th CENTURY, A BOY NAMED JAMES HOWLETT WAS BORN IN THE FORESTS OF BRITISH COLUMBIA.

WHEN HE REACHED PUBERTY, HE DISCOVERED HE WAS A *MUTANT*, BORN WITH RETRACTABLE BONE *CLAWS* IN HIS HANDS AND THE ABILITY TO HEAL FROM ANY WOUND OR ILLNESS.

HOWLETT'S HEALING FACTOR EFFECTIVELY MADE HIM *IMMORTAL*--AND HIS SAVAGE *INSTINCTS* MADE HIM AN EXPERT AT *ENDING* THE LIVES OF *OTHERS*.

HE CONTROLLED THE BERSERKER INSIDE HIM BY FEEDING IT A STEADY DIET OF *BATTLES* AS A SOLDIER AND SPY IN EVERY MAJOR CONFLICT OF THE 20TH CENTURY.

BUT HIS GOVERNMENT *BETRAYED* HIM, BONDING THE UNBREAKABLE METAL *ADAMANTIUM* TO HIS CLAWS AND SKELETON AGAINST HIS WILL.

ONLY HOWLETT'S HEALING FACTOR ALLOWED HIM TO SURVIVE THE PROCESS-- BUT THE *PAIN* DESTROYED HIS MEMORY--AND HIS *SANITY*!

WRITER: FRED VAN LENTE ART: MIKE CHOI & SONIA OBACK
LETTERS: NATE PIEKOS ASST. EDITOR: ALEJANDRO ARBONA EDITOR: RALPH MACCHIO

AND SO THE MAN WHO CALLS HIMSELF *"WOLVERINE"* FOUND A CAUSE TO FIGHT FOR OTHER THAN *INSTINCT*.

HE ESCAPED THE GOVERNMENT INTO THE WILD, MORE *MONSTER* THAN *MAN*.

BUT A BACKPACKING COUPLE DISCOVERED HIM AND NURSED HIM BACK TO HEALTH--AND *HUMANITY*.

THOUGH HIS BESTIAL SIDE SHALL NEVER FULLY *LEAVE* HI WOLVERINE REAFFIRMS HIS *OWN* HUMANITY BY BATTLING ON *ALL* MANKIND'S BEHALF AS A *HERO*!

ORPHANED AT AN EARLY AGE, CLINT BARTON DID WHAT SOME KIDS ONLY DREAMED OF: HE RAN AWAY AND JOINED THE CIRCUS.

IT WAS THERE THAT HE FOUND HE WAS A NATURAL WITH A BOW AND ARROW, QUICKLY BECOMING "THE WORLD'S GREATEST MARKSMAN." BUT THAT WASN'T ENOUGH FOR THIS RESTLESS ADVENTURER.

WITNESSING IRON MAN IN ACTION, CLINT DECIDED THAT HE, TOO, COULD BECOME A SUPER HERO!

CLINT CRAFTED A COSTUME AND CREATED SPECIAL "TRICK" ARROWS. DESPITE BEING MISTAKEN FOR A VILLAIN ON HIS FIRST OUTINGS, HE SOON FOUND HIMSELF, ALONG WITH TWO OTHER REFORMED "VILLAINS," RECRUITED INTO THE AVENGERS BY CAPTAIN AMERICA.

CLINT FINALLY FOUND HAPPINESS--MEETING AND MARRYING THE SUPER HERO KNOWN AS MOCKINGBIRD, AND EVEN FOUNDING HIS OWN BRANCH OF THE AVENGERS. HE SEEMED TO HAVE IT ALL.

UNFORTUNATELY, IT DIDN'T LAST...

AFTER MOCKINGBIRD APPARENTLY DIED, THINGS WERE NEVER THE SAME. CLINT FACED HIS OWN BRUSH WITH DEATH AND A RETURN FROM THE GRAVE. LOST AND ALONE, HE ADOPTED THE IDENTITY OF "RONIN" IN AN EFFORT TO FIND HIS PLACE IN THE WORLD.

AFTER MUCH SOUL-SEARCHING, A LONG-AWAITED REUNION WITH MOCKINGBIRD, AND THE RETURN OF THE TRUE AVENGERS, CLINT BARTON REALIZED WHO AND WHAT HE WILL ALWAYS BE:

HAWKEYE

THE WISE-CRACKING, RULE-BENDING, SELF-MADE HERO...THE GREATEST MARKSMAN IN THE WORLD!

WRITER: JIM McCANN   PENCILS: DAVID LÓPEZ
INKS: ALVARO LÓPEZ   COLORS: TOM SMITH
LETTERS: BLAMBOT'S NATE PIEKOS
ASST. EDITOR: RACHEL PINNELAS
EDITOR: BILL ROSEMANN

BARBARA "BOBBI" MORSE WANTED A FUTURE AS A BIOLOGIST. BUT HER BRILLIANT MIND AND UNCANNY FIGHTING SKILLS CAUGHT THE ATTENTION OF INTERNATIONAL ESPIONAGE AGENCY S.H.I.E.L.D. SHE SERVED LOYALLY FOR YEARS BEFORE STRIKING OUT ON HER OWN AS THE COSTUMED CRIME-FIGHTER

MOCKINGBIRD

ARMED WITH HER TRADEMARK BATTLE STAVES AND QUICK WIT, BOBBI MADE A SPLASH ON THE SUPER HERO SCENE. SHE QUICKLY MET AND MARRIED THE AVENGER HAWKEYE, AND FOUND A HOME WITHIN THE TEAM'S NEW WEST COAST BRANCH.

THESE LOVERS WERE NOT WITHOUT THEIR PROBLEMS, HOWEVER. WHEN NOT FACING OFF AGAINST VILLAINS, THEY WERE AT ODDS WITH EACH OTHER. BUT THROUGH IT ALL, THEY ALWAYS FOUND THEIR WAY BACK TO ONE ANOTHER.

BUT AFTER A BITTER SPLIT WITH HAWKEYE, BOBBI WAS KIDNAPPED BY THE ALIEN SHAPE-CHANGING SKRULLS. SHE WAS REPLACED WITH A REPLICA, BUT THAT IMPOSTER WAS KILLED, LEADING THE WORLD TO BELIEVE SHE HAD DIED.

THE TRUTH WAS FAR WORSE.

MOCKINGBIRD WAS HELD CAPTIVE FOR THREE YEARS ON THE SKRULL HOMEWORLD. WHEN SHE FINALLY RETURNED TO EARTH, SHE FOUND A WORLD THAT HAD CHANGED GREATLY AND MOVED ON WITHOUT HER.

NOW, WITH A NEW LOOK AND A RETURN TO HER SPY ROOTS, BOBBI HAS RECLAIMED HER LIF. REUNITED WITH HAWKEYE, THE HOT-HEADED HEROES' FUTURE AS A COUPLE IS UNKNOWN, BU' SHE IS DETERMINED TO PROVE TO THE WORLD ONCE AGAIN WH MOCKINGBIRD IS A WOMAN TO BE FEARED AND RESPECTED!

WRITER: JIM MCCANN
PENCILS: STEPHANE ROUX
INKS: JULIEN HUGONNARD-BE
COLORS: TOM SMITH
LETTERS: BLAMBOT'S NATE PIE
ASST. EDITOR: RACHEL PINNE
EDITOR: BILL ROSEMANN

BLACK WIDOW

WRITER: FRED VAN LENTE   ART: JAMIE McKELVIE   COLORS: NATHAN FAIRBAIRN
LETTERS: VC's CLAYTON COWLES   EDITOR: ALEJANDRO ARBONA
TOR IN CHIEF: JOE QUESADA   PUBLISHER: DAN BUCKLEY   EXEC. PRODUCER: ALAN FINE

NATASHA ROMANOVA TRAINED TO BE RUSSIA'S GREATEST BALLERINA.

BUT THE DEATH OF HER FIANCÉ DURING MILITARY SERVICE INSPIRED HER TO GO INTO ESPIONAGE INSTEAD.

OR...SO SHE THOUGHT.

IN REALITY, THE ORPHANED NATASHA HAD BEEN RAISED SINCE BIRTH IN THE GOVERNMENT'S INFAMOUS RED ROOM TO BE A MASTER ASSASSIN, BRAINWASHED WITH PHONY MEMORIES TO ENSURE HER LOYALTY.

CODE-NAMED "BLACK WIDOW," NATASHA WAS DISPATCHED TO THE U.S. TO STEAL SECRETS AND ELIMINATE ENEMIES OF THE STATE.

BUT HER WILL WAS TOO STRONG TO REMAIN A PUPPET FOR LONG. WHEN HER HANDLERS ASKED HER TO KILL A MAN SHE LOVED, HER PROGRAMMING UNRAVELED.

BLACK WIDOW DEFECTED TO THE GLOBAL SPY AGENCY S.H.I.E.L.D., WHERE SHE NOW PUTS HER LETHAL SKILLS TO USE FOR THE INTERNATIONAL COMMUNITY...

...THOUGH IF SHE CAN GET A LITTLE PAYBACK ALONG THE WAY, WELL, SO MUCH THE BETTER!

FRANK CASTLE **TRIED** TO LEAVE HIS WAR **BEHIND.**

WHEN HE RETURNED **HOME** TO HIS FAMILY, FOR A TIME HE MANAGED TO CONVINCE HIMSELF HE HAD **SUCCEEDED.**

BUT THAT **SOON** PROVED TO BE A LIE.

HIS WAR **FOUND HIM.**

AND **ROBBED** HIM OF HIS FAMILY FOR DARING TO **FORSAKE** IT.

NOW FRANK CASTLE KNOWS HIS WAR WILL NEVER LEAVE **HIM,** AND **HE** WILL NEVER LEAVE IT.

CRIME IS THE ENEMY, AND THE **WORLD** IS HIS BATTLEFIELD.

FRANK CASTLE WILL MAKE **NO** TRUCES, TAKE **NO** PRISONERS, AND SHOW **NO** QUARTER, FOR HE IS THE...

PUNISHER

FRED VAN LENTE – WRITER
ROBERTO DE LA TORRE – ARTIST
TOM SMITH – COLORIST
BLAMBOT'S NATE PIEKOS – LETTERER
RACHEL PINNELAS – ASSISTANT EDITOR
BILL ROSEMANN – EDITOR

Black Cat

FELICIA HARDY WANTED TO FOLLOW IN HER FATHER'S FOOTSTEPS AND BECOME THE WORLD'S MOST FEARED CAT BURGLAR.

SHE CREATED THE MASKED PERSONA OF THE BLACK CAT TO BREAK WALTER HARDY OUT OF PRISON WHEN SHE LEARNED HE WAS TERMINALLY ILL.

BUT ON HIS DEATHBED, WALTER BEGGED HIS DAUGHTER NOT TO FOLLOW HIS CRIMINAL EXAMPLE.

FELICIA INVESTED HER ILL-GOTTEN GAINS INTO ACQUIRING AN EDGE AGAINST SUPERHUMAN FOES.

WRITER: FRED VAN LENTE   ARTIST: JOE QUINONES   LETTERER: BLAMBOT'S NATE PIEKOS
ASSISTANT EDITOR: THOMAS BRENNAN   EDITOR: STEPHEN WACKER

WHOA! WHERE'D THAT COME FROM?

SSSS

SQUEE

...NAMELY, THE PROBABILITY-ALTERING POWER OF GIVING "BAD LUCK" TO ANYONE WHO DARES CROSS HER PATH!

I.O.U. NADA! XOXO

NOW, THE BLACK CAT HONORS HER FATHER'S WISH BY MAKING HER LIVING ROBBING THE EVIL IN DEFENSE OF THE INNOCENT...

...AND HAVING A REALLY GOOD TIME DOING IT!

HERCULES

WAS BORN OF MORTAL WOMAN AND ZEUS, KING OF THE GODS OF GREECE, AND BECAME THE GREATEST CHAMPION OF THE CLASSICAL AGE.

NO FOE COULD MATCH HIS GREAT STRENGTH. HE CONQUERED ALL WHO OPPOSED HIM.

BELIEVING HIMSELF INVULNERABLE, HE IDLED HIS DAYS AWAY IN CAROUSING AND DEBAUCHERY.

THIS HUBRIS PROVED TO BE HIS UNDOING.

A DECEITFUL CENTAUR GAVE HIS WIFE A TUNIC LACED WITH THE GALL OF THE HYDRA AND TOLD HER ITS ENCHANTMENTS WOULD BIND HER FAITHLESS HUSBAND TO HER FOREVER.

INSTEAD, THE POISONOUS SHIRT SLEW HERCULES IN HIDEOUS AGONY!

WRITER: FRED VAN LENTE   PENCILS: RYAN STEGMAN   INKS: MICHAEL BABINSKI
COLORS: JUNE CHUNG   LETTERS: VC's CLAYTON COWLES   EDITOR: ALEJANDRO ARBONA
EDITOR IN CHIEF: JOE QUESADA   PUBLISHER: DAN BUCKLEY   EXEC. PRODUCER: ALAN FINE

FATHER ZEUS TOOK PITY ON HIS SON AND RAISED HIM UP TO MOUNT OLYMPUS IN FULL GODHOOD...

...WHICH THE PRINCE OF POWER FOUND DREADFULLY DULL. HE YEARNED FOR THE EXCITEMENT AND ADVENTURE OF THE MORTAL WORLD.

SO WHEN ZEUS SENT HIM BACK TO EARTH TO LOCATE AND TRAIN HIS SUCCESSOR, HERC LEAPT AT THE OPPORTUNITY...

...THOUGH HE WAS STUNNED TO LEARN THE CHAMPION OF THIS NEXT AGE WOULD COME IN A MOST UNUSUAL FORM...

...THAT OF IRASCIBLE TEEN GENIUS AMADEUS CHO.

NOW HERCULES TRIES TO SCHOOL HIS HEADSTRONG CHARGE IN THE WAYS OF HEROISM...OFTEN BY NEGATIVE EXAMPLE...

(...WHILE TRYING TO FIT IN AS MUCH CAROUSING AND DEBAUCHERY AS HUMANLY POSSIBLE...)

LUKE CAGE

CARL LUCAS WAS IMPRISONED IN BRUTAL **SEAGATE** ISLAND PRISON FOR A CRIME HE **DIDN'T COMMIT.**

WHEN RESEARCH SCIENTISTS ASKED INMATES TO PARTICIPATE IN HUMAN TRIALS OF A NEW **CELL REGENERATION** PROCESS, LUCAS VOLUNTEERED, THINKING HE HAD NOTHING TO LOSE.

BUT A CORRUPT GUARD WHO DESPISED LUCAS SNUCK INTO THE LAB AND JACKED THE MACHINE'S CONTROLS TO THEIR **LIMIT,** HOPING TO KILL HIM!

INSTEAD, LUCAS' BODY WAS ENHANCED BEYOND **HUMAN** LEVELS WITH SUPER-STRENGTH AND INVULNERABILITY.

HE USED HIS NEW POWERS TO **ESCAPE** SEAGATE AND LOST HIMSELF AMONGST THE TEEMING MULTITUDES OF **MANHATTAN.**

WRITER - FRED VAN LENTE
ARTIST - MICHAEL GAYDOS
LETTERER - BLAMBOT'S NATE PIEKOS
EDITOR - THOMAS BRENNAN

LUCAS CHANGED HIS NAME TO **"LUKE CAGE"** TO THROW THE LAW OFF HIS TRAIL...

EVENTUALLY, HE BROUGHT THE GANGSTERS WHO FRAMED HIM TO JUSTICE AND GOT HIS CONVICTION OVERTURNED.

Plagued by:
DRUG DEALERS? GANG MEMBERS? SUPER VILLAINS?
No more! I can help! Call:
LUKE CAGE
HERO FOR HIRE
1-800-555-CAGE
All major credit cards accepted

...AND OPENED A **SUPER** PRIVATE DETECTIVE AGENCY SO HE COULD FINANCE HIS QUEST TO CLEAR HIS NAME!

BUT HE FOUND HE **ENJOYED** HELPING PEOPLE. FOR FREE OR FOR HIRE, LUKE CAGE **REMAINS A** NAME SYNONYMOUS WITH **"HERO!"**

...PLORER AND
...ANCIER **WENDELL**
...ND EXPENDED
...CH OF HIS FORTUNE
...YING TO FIND
...ET'S LOST CITY
...K'UN-LUN...

...AT THE COST OF HIS OWN LIFE.

BUT HIS YOUNG SON **DANNY** SUCCEEDED WHERE HE FAILED.

HE WAS ADOPTED BY THE DEATHLESS INHABITANTS OF THE HIDDEN CITADEL...

...AND TAUGHT IN THE WAYS OF KUNG FU BY THE LEGENDARY **THUNDERER,** **LEI KUNG** HIMSELF.

AT HIS FINAL TRIAL, DANNY SLEW THE DRAGON **SHOU-LAO THE UNDYING** AND BURNED THE CREATURE'S SCAR INTO HIS CHEST.

HE PLUNGED HIS **FISTS** INTO A CAULDRON CONTAINING THE SERPENT'S FLAMING HEART TO RENDER THEM UNBREAKABLE!

DANNY BID HIS FOSTER FAMILY FAREWELL AND RETURNED TO AMERICA TO ASSUME CONTROL OF HIS FATHER'S COMPANY, RAND INDUSTRIES...

...BUT HE DONS CEREMONIAL GARB WORTHY OF AN IMMORTAL WEAPON TO FIGHT ON BEHALF OF THOSE WHO CANNOT FIGHT FOR THEMSELVES AS

THE IMMORTAL IRON FIST

WRITER: FRED VAN LENTE   ART: TRAVEL FOREMAN
COLORS: IAN HANNIN   LETTERS: VC's CLAYTON COWLES   EDITOR: ALEJANDRO ARBONA
EDITOR IN CHIEF: JOE QUESADA   PUBLISHER: DAN BUCKLEY   EXEC. PRODUCER: ALAN FINE

MARC SPECTOR SERVED AS SECOND IN COMMAND TO RAOUL BUSHMAN, ONE OF THE WORLD'S MOST FEARED MERCENARIES.

THEY WOULD FIGHT FOR ANY SIDE, SIDE WITH ANY CAUSE, AND CAUSE DEATH AND DESTRUCTION ANYWHERE...SO LONG AS THE PRICE WAS RIGHT.

WHILE WORKING IN EGYPT, SPECTOR AND BUSHMAN STUMBLED ACROSS AN ANCIENT TEMPLE DEDICATED TO KHONSHU, GOD OF THE MOON...AND VENGEANCE.

BUSHMAN DECIDED HE WANTED THE TEMPLE'S TREASURES ALL TO HIMSELF.

HE SAVAGELY BEAT SPECTOR AND LEFT HIM FOR DEAD.

AS THE MERCENARY LAY DYING, KHONSHU HIMSELF APPEARED TO SPECTOR IN A VISION AND OFFERED TO SAVE THE MORTAL'S LIFE IF HE BECAME THE GOD'S EMISSARY ON EARTH.

SPECTOR SEIZED THE OPPORTUNITY NOT JUST TO SAVE HIS OWN LIFE...BUT TO RIGHT ALL THE WRONGS HE HAD COMMITTED AS AN AMORAL GUN-FOR-HIRE!

HE RETURNED TO CIVILIZATION TO STRIKE TERROR INTO THE EVILS OF THE NIGHT AS THE FIST OF KHONSHU...

MOON KNIGHT

WRITER:
FRED VAN LENTE
ART: MIKE PERKINS
COLORS: TOM SMITH
LETTERS: NATE PIEKOS
ASST. EDITOR:
RACHEL PINNELAS
EDITOR:
BILL ROSEMANN

ARES

...IS THE **GOD OF WAR** OF THE ANCIENT GREEKS, SON OF ZEUS AND HERA OF OLYMPUS.

ARES' FELLOW 'ODS **DESPISED** HIM FOR HIS 'AVAGE DELIGHT IN HE **BLOODLUST** OF BATTLE.

SICK OF BEING HATED **AND** EXPLOITED, ARES QUIT THE REALM OF GODS AND RETREATED IN ANONYMITY TO THE **MORTAL** PLANE.

THE GOD OF WAR FOUND **PEACE** AS A SUBURBAN CONSTRUCTION WORKER AND SINGLE PARENT.

BUT LIKE ANY **TRUE** WARRIOR, THE SIREN-SONG OF COMBAT LURED ARES BACK INTO THE FRAY ONCE MORE.

FOR A GOD OF WAR, **BATTLE** IS ITS OWN **VIRTUE!**

WRITER: FRED VAN LENTE   ART: TRAVEL FOREMAN
COLORS: JUNE CHUNG   LETTERS: NATE PIEKOS
ASST. EDITOR: ALEJANDRO ARBONA   EDITOR: RALPH MACCHIO

WHILE STILL IN THE WOMB, THEIR DAUGHTER **JESSICA** WAS STRUCK WITH A LASER CONTAINING THE GENETIC CODE OF A VARIETY OF **ARACHNIDS**.

HUSBAND AND WIFE RESEARCHER TEAM **JONATHAN** AND **MIRIAM DREW** WERE TRYING TO PRODUCE A HARDIER FORM OF **HUMAN** THROUGH GENETIC COMBINATION WITH SPIDER DNA.

SHE FIRST MANIFESTED HER STINGING **VENOM BLAST** TO INTERRUPT A FIGHT BETWEEN HER PARENTS.

JESSICA DID NOT KNOW HER PARENTS WERE SECRETLY WORKING FOR THE TERRORIST ORGANIZATION **HYDRA**.

AND SHE WAS THE **SUPER-SOLDIER** THEY HAD BEEN LOOKING FOR.

BUT JESSICA HAD **OTHER** PLANS.

SHE REJECTED HYDRA AND ITS WAYS AND **DESTROYED** THEIR ARACHNOID SOLDIER PROGRAM.

NOW NONE CAN **CONTROL** HER, AND ALL EVIL **FEARS** HER, THE DARK ANGEL OF THE NIGHT...

SPIDER-WOMAN

WRITER–FRED VAN LENTE
ARTIST–TOM RANEY
COLOR ARTIST–ANTONIO FABELA
LETTERER–BLAMBOT'S NATE PIEKOS
ASSOCIATE EDITOR–LAUREN SANKOVITCH
EDITOR–TOM BREVOORT

JOHNNY BLAZE GREW UP AMONG A LEGENDARY FAMILY OF STUNT RIDERS ED BY HIS BELOVED FOSTER FATHER, "CRASH" SIMPSON.

WHEN CRASH CONTRACTED TERMINAL CANCER, A DESPERATE BLAZE TURNED TO THE OCCULT TO SAVE HIM.

HE OFFERED HIS SOUL TO THE DEMONIC MEPHISTO IN EXCHANGE FOR CURING CRASH...

...WHICH THE DEVIL DID...

...SO CRASH COULD DIE ANYWAY IN A JUMP GONE AWRY!

BLAZE ACCUSED MEPHISTO OF TREACHERY AND REFUSED TO UPHOLD HIS END OF THE BARGAIN.

BUT WHEN THE DEVIL WANTS HIS DUE, YOU PAY, ONE WAY OR ANOTHER.

MEPHISTO PUNISHED JOHNNY BY BONDING HIS SOUL WITH THE SPIRIT OF VENGEANCE.

NOW, WHENEVER BLAZE SENSES EVIL...

...WHEREVER EVIL MEN HUNGER FOR SIN...

...AND MURDER IS A WAY OF LIFE...

...ROARING OUT OF A TRAIL OF HELLFIRE YOU WILL FIND...

GHOST RIDER

D VAN LENTE-WRITER   MARK TEXIERA-ARTIST
BLAMBOT'S NATE PIEKOS-LETTERER
AUREN SANKOVITCH-ASSOCIATE EDITOR
TOM BREVOORT-EDITOR

WRITER – FRED VAN LENTE
ARTIST – RICHARD ELSON
COLORIST – TOM SMITH
LETTERS – BLAMBOT'S NATE PIEKOS
ASST. EDITOR – RACHEL PINNELAS
EDITOR – BILL ROSEMANN

THERE CAME A TIME WHEN THE RAMPAGING **HULK** FOUND HIMSELF EXILED TO THE SAVAGE ALIEN WORLD OF **SAKAAR.**

ENSLAVED AS A **GLADIATOR**, HE SHATTERED HIS CHAINS AND LED HIS FELLOW **WARBOUND** IN A SUCCESSFUL BATTLE AGAINST THE PLANET'S DESPOT...

...AND FOUND **LOVE** IN THE FORM OF THE FIERCE WARRIOR **CAIERA** OF THE SHADOW PEOPLE.

BUT WHEN THE CRAFT HE ARRIVED IN **EXPLODED,** THE HULK LOST BOTH KINGDOM **AND** QUEEN.

THE GREEN GOLIATH RETURNED TO EARTH TO **PUNISH** THOSE RESPONSIBLE...

...UNAWARE THAT THE UNBORN CHILD INSIDE CAIERA'S BODY HAD SURVIVED.

RAISED IN **BATTLE,** BAPTIZED BY **FIRE,** THE HULK'S SON WAS AS MERCILESS AND BRUTAL AS THE FATHER AND THE **WORLD** THAT GAVE HIM BIRTH.

BUT HE WAS ALSO HIS **MOTHER'S** CHILD, AND SHE HAD WIELDED THE MYSTERIOUS **OLD POWER** OF THE SHADOW PEOPLE.

DUE TO THE POWER, THE BOY GREW TO ADULTHOOD IN LESS THAN A **YEAR...**

...AND OPENED A WORMHOLE TO EARTH, WHERE HE MIGHT CLAIM HIS BIRTHRIGHT OF **RAGE...**

...BY FINDING AND DESTROYING THE **FATHER** WHO ABANDONED HIM!

SKAAR SON OF HULK

WHILE DIGGING ON THE MOON ONE DAY, LOCKJAW, THE TELEPORTING INHUMAN DOG, CAME ACROSS ONE OF THE INFINITY GEMS.

THE GEMS ARE EXTREMELY POWERFUL AND IN THE WRONG HANDS--OR PAWS--COULD LEAD TO UNTOLD HORRORS.

LOCKJAW GATHERED OTHER ANIMAL HEROES TO JOIN HIM ON HIS QUEST TO GATHER THE REMAINING INFINITY GEMS IN ORDER TO PROTECT THEM.

TELEPORTING TO PARTS UNKNOWN, THEY FOUND MANY STRANGE CREATURES BLOCKING THEIR PATH TO THOSE GEMS.

TRAVELING THROUGH TIME AND SPACE, IN THE AIR AND UNDER WATER, THEY RETRIEVED THE POWERFUL GEMS ONE AT A TIME, UNTIL...

...THEY REACHED THE FINAL ONE.

BUT, IN THEIR WAY STOOD THANOS. A BEING OF IMMENSE POWER WHO CLAIMED THE GEMS FOR HIS OWN.

THEY FOUGHT BRAVELY AND DEFEATED THANOS, SENDING HIM TO ANOTHER DIMENSION.

USING THE POWER OF THE GEMS, THEY CREATED A TELEPATHIC LINK...

...SO THAT IF ANOTHER CRISIS SO GREAT SHOULD COME ABOUT THAT EVEN HUMANS CAN'T OVERCOME, THE WORLD CAN ALWAYS TURN TO...

...FROG THOR, LOCKJAW, ZABU, LOCKHEED, HAIRBALL, MS. LION AND REDWING ALSO KNOWN AS...

THE PET AVENGERS

WRITER-CHRIS ELIOPOULOS ARTIST-IG GUARA COLOR-CHRIS SOTOMAYOR LETTERER - BLAMBOT'S NATE PIEKOS ASSOCIATE EDITOR - LAUREN SANKOVITCH EDITOR - TOM BREVOORT

Alex Power, **ZERO G.** Gravity Power. The Leader.

FOUR NORMAL KIDS...

...GRANTED EXTRAORDINARY POWERS.

Julie Power, **LIGHTSPEED.** Acceleration Powers. The Brains.

I grant you extraordinary powers.

WRITER: ALEX ZALBEN ART: GURIHIRU LETTERS: DAVE SHARPE EDITOR: JORDAN D. WHITE SUPERVISING EDITOR: NATHAN COSB

HOOD

PARKER ROBBINS' DAD WAS AMONG THE TOP LIEUTENANTS OF NEW YORK CITY'S *KINGPIN OF CRIME.*

BUT HIS ATTEMPTS TO LIVE UP TO HIS FATHER'S *LEGEND* ALWAYS FELL *SHORT.*

WRITER: FRED VAN LENTE   ART: KYLE HOTZ   COLORS: DAN BROWN
LETTERS: NATE PIEKOS   ASST. EDITOR: ALEJANDRO ARBONA   EDITOR: RALPH MACCHIO

THEN, DURING A SEEMINGLY ROUTINE WAREHOUSE BURGLARY, ROBBINS STUMBLED UPON A *WEIRD CREATURE* CLAD IN MYSTIC HOOD AND BOOTS.

SLAYING THE BEAST WITH A LUCKY SHOT, HE DONNED ITS GARMENTS FOR HIMSELF...

...DISCOVERING THEY GRANTED HIM A VARIETY OF *MAGICAL ABILITIES,* INCLUDING INVISIBILITY, TELEPORTATION AND LEVITATION.

HE QUICKLY REALIZED THAT WITH GREAT *POWER* CAN COME GREAT *OPPORTUNITY.*

THROUGH A COMBINATION OF CHARISMA, VISION, AND SHEER *RUTHLESSNESS,* THE HOOD BECAME THE *KINGPIN* OF NEW YORK CITY'S *SUPER VILLAIN COMMUNITY...*

...THEREBY *SURPASSING* HIS FATHER!

BUT PARKER ROBBINS HAS NEVER STOPPED TO *ASK* HIMSELF:

IS HE USING THE DEMONIC POWERS OF HIS ENCHANTED HOOD TO GAIN CONTROL OF MANHATTAN'S *UNDERWORLD...*

...OR ARE THOSE INFERNAL FORCES USING *HIM...?*

ONCE UPON A *TIME*, IN A MORE *INNOCENT* AGE, COLLEGE FRESHMAN *ROBERT REYNOLDS* DRANK A PROFESSOR'S SECRET FORMULA.

A MIRACULOUS *TRANSFORMATION* TOOK PLACE, SUFFUSING THE BOY WITH THE POWER OF *A MILLION EXPLODING SUNS.*

THE SENTRY

...GOLDEN *GUARDIAN* OF *GOOD,* BECAME THE *BRIGHTEST* OF A NEW GENERATION OF HEROES WHOM HE SERVED AS MENTOR AND *IDEAL...*

WRITER: FRED VAN LENTE   ART: TREVOR HAIRSINE   COLORS: FRANK D'ARMATA
TERS: NATE PIEKOS   ASST. EDITOR: ALEJANDRO ARBONA   EDITOR: RALPH MACCHIO

...ALL THE WHILE BATTLING HIS ARCH-NEMESIS, THE MURDEROUS *VOID,* WHO ALWAYS MANAGED TO ELUDE CAPTURE.

BUT THEN, ONE DAY, AS IT *MUST,* INNOCENCE CAME TO AN *END.*

THE HEROES DISCOVERED THERE WAS A VERY GOOD REASON THE SENTRY COULD NEVER DEFEAT THE VOID: THEY WERE ONE AND THE *SAME.*

THE LIGHT AND DARK HALVES OF REYNOLDS' PERSONALITY HAD BEEN SPLIT INTO DISTINCT ENTITIES BY THE SERUM.

WITH HEAVY HEARTS, THEY USED ADVANCED TECHNOLOGY TO WIPE FROM REYNOLDS' MIND-- AND THE *WORLD'S*-- THAT THE SENTRY *OR* THE VOID HAD EVER EXISTED.

BUT WHEN REYNOLDS' MEMORIES RETURNED, SO DID THE *WORLD'S* GREATEST HERO....

...ALONG WITH ITS GREATEST *VILLAIN.*

JAMES "BUCKY" BARNES' FATHER WAS KILLED IN A BASIC TRAINING ACCIDENT ON A WORLD WAR II ARMY BASE, WHEN BUCKY WAS STILL A BOY.

HE WAS ADOPTED BY THE REGIMENT AND BECAME CLOSE TO PRIVATE STEVE ROGERS...

...ACCIDENTALLY DISCOVERING THAT ROGERS WAS SECRETLY CAPTAIN AMERICA!

BARNES INSISTED THE RELUCTANT ROGERS TAKE HIM ON AS A PARTNER IN EXCHANGE FOR HIS SILENCE.

BUCKY PROVED HIMSELF MORE THAN ABLE AS CAPTAIN AMERICA'S SIDEKICK AND CONFIDANT THROUGHOUT THE WAR...

...AND WAS BELIEVED LOST IN THE SAME EXPLOSION THAT NEARLY CLAIMED ROGERS' LIFE AS WELL.

THE SOVIETS RECOVERED THE AMNESIAC BUCKY, HOWEVER, AND TRANSFORMED HIM INTO A CYBERNETICALLY ENHANCED ASSASSIN, THE WINTER SOLDIER.

IN THE MODERN ERA, CAPTAIN AMERICA SUCCEEDED IN FREEING BUCKY OF HIS PROGRAMMING--AND HIS RUSSIAN HANDLERS.

AND WHEN ROGERS APPEARED TO THE WORLD TO PERISH IN A NOBLE CAUSE, IT WAS BUCKY, HIS FORMER STUDENT, WHO PICKED UP THE FALLEN STANDARD, AND BECAME THE NEXT...

CAPTAIN AMERICA

SO THE DREAM OF FREEDOM MAY NEVER DIE!

WRITER: FRED VAN LENTE   ART: MIKE PERKINS   COLORS: ELIZABETH DISMANG BREITWEISER
LETTERS: NATE PIEKOS   ASST. EDITOR: ALEJANDRO ARBONA   EDITOR: RALPH MACCHIO

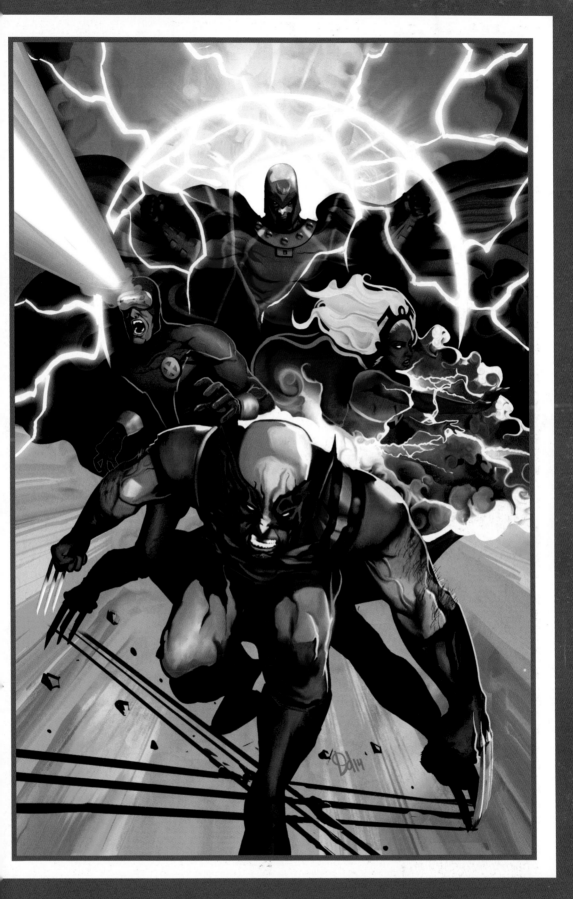

ORIGINS OF MARVEL COMICS: X-MEN

ORIGINS OF MARVEL COMICS

Cover Art: Mike Del Mundo

Lettering: Dave Sharpe

Production: Dan Remollino

Editors: Sebastian Girner, Daniel Ketchum,
Jody LeHeup, Nick Lowe, Jake Thomas & Jeanine Schaefer

Executive Editor: Axel Alonso

Editor in Chief: Joe Quesada

Publisher: Dan Buckley

Executive Producer: Alan Fine

X-MEN

HAVING LOST HIS FATHER AT AN EARLY AGE, CHARLES XAVIER WAS BROUGHT UP IN THE HOUSEHOLD OF THE SADISTIC KURT MARKO.

WHEN HIS PSYCHIC POWERS EMERGED, HE BECAME FASCINATED BY HUMAN MUTATION--AND BEGAN THE RESEARCH THAT WOULD DOMINATE HIS LIFE.

HIS INTELLECT WAS HIS SALVATION. WINNING A SCHOLARSHIP TO OXFORD, HE LEFT HOME AND NEVER LOOKED BACK.

RESEARCH THAT SUGGESTED A NEW GENERATION WAS RISING IN ALL THE NATIONS OF EARTH--MARKED BY THE X-GENE AND ITS UNPREDICTABLE EFFECTS.

IN ISRAEL HE MET ERIK LENSHERR--MAGNETO--WHO BELIEVED THAT MUTANTS WOULD SOME DAY SUPPLANT HUMANITY.

IT WAS A MEETING THAT WOULD SHAPE BOTH OF THEM, AND POLARIZE THEIR BELIEFS.

WAR, LOSS AND CRIPPLING INJURY ONLY HONED PROFESSOR X'S IDEALS. RETURNING TO THE USA, HE GATHERED A GROUP OF YOUNG MUTANTS TO BE HIS STUDENTS--THE FIRST OF MANY.

HE TRAINED THEM IN THE USE OF THEIR POWERS, AND OFFERED THEM SHELTER FROM A WORLD THAT FEARED THEM.

BUT HE TAUGHT THEM, TOO, THAT HUMANS AND MUTANTS CAN LIVE TOGETHER IN PEACE--AND THAT THEIR AWESOME POWERS MUST BE USED IN THE SERVICE OF THAT PEACE.

THE X-MEN STILL FOLLOW THAT CREED, AND THAT MISSION STATEMENT.

PROFESSOR X

WRITTEN BY *MIKE CAREY* • ART BY *MICK BERTILORENZI* • COLORED BY *MATT MILLA*

BORN **MAX EISENHARDT** IN 1920S GERMANY, THE MUTANT WHO WOULD SOMEDAY BE KNOWN AS **MAGNETO** EXPERIENCED THE RISE OF NAZISM FIRST HAND.

AS A JEW IN HITLER'S GERMANY, HE AND HIS FAMILY SUFFERED UNIMAGINABLE HARDSHIPS, FINALLY BEING SENT TO THE CONCENTRATION CAMP AT **AUSCHWITZ.** HE WAS ONE OF THE VERY FEW TO ESCAPE ALIVE, ALONG WITH MAGDA, THE WOMAN HE LOVED AND RISKED EVERYTHING TO SAVE.

THOSE EARLY EXPERIENCES SHAPED MAGNETO PROFOUNDLY. WHEN HE CAME INTO HIS MUTANT POWERS, HE RENOUNCED HUMAN LAW AND SWORE ALLEGIANCE ONLY TO HIS OWN RACE.

HE FOUNDED THE BROTHERHOOD OF MUTANTS TO RETALIATE AGAINST HUMANITY FOR ACTS OF ANTI-MUTANT VIOLENCE-- A RUTHLESS COUNTER- BALANCE TO CHARLES XAVIER'S DREAM OF PEACEFUL COEXISTENCE.

BUT MAGNETO ULTIMATELY CAME TO DOUBT THE VIOLENT TACTICS HE HAD EMBRACED, AND WILLINGLY GAVE HIMSELF UP FOR TRIAL.

IN THE COURSE OF THE TRIAL, PROFESSOR XAVIER--CLOSE TO DEATH AFTER AN ATTACK-- ENTRUSTED HIS SCHOOL AND THE FATE OF THE STUDENTS INTO MAGNETO'S HANDS. THE RELATIONSHIP BETWEEN MAGNETO AND THE X-MEN HAD IRREVOCABLY CHANGED.

NOW, STANDING FOREMOST IN THE RANKS OF HIS FORMER ENEMIES,

MAGNETO

STILL DEFINES HIS GOALS AS HE ALWAYS DID: TO PRESERVE HIS FELLOW MUTANTS AGAINST THE THREATS OF A WORLD THAT HATES AND MISTRUSTS THEM.

A PRAGMATIST OR AN IDEALIST? A MONSTER OR A HERO? JUDGE HIM BY HIS ACTS--AND THREATEN HIM OR THOSE HE LOVES AT YOUR OWN RISK.

SCRIPT BY *MIKE CAREY* • ART BY *NICK BRADSHAW* • COLOR ART BY *GURU-eF.*

AT A YOUNG AGE, *SCOTT SUMMERS* WAS ORPHANED. ALL THE PAIN AND ANGER THAT HE FELT, HE BOTTLED IT UP INSIDE.

WHEN HIS POWERS ACTIVATED, IT WAS AS IF HIS BODY FOUND A WAY TO RELEASE EVERYTHING HE WAS HOLDING IN.

BUT SCOTT COULDN'T CONTROL HIS POWERFUL OPTIC BLASTS...UNTIL HE MET *PROFESSOR CHARLES XAVIER.*

XAVIER HELPED SCOTT CONTAIN HIS POWER AND GROOMED HIM TO LEAD THE STUDENTS AT HIS SCHOOL FOR GIFTED YOUNGSTERS...*THE X-MEN.*

UNDER HIS LEADERSHIP, THE X-MEN PROTECTED A WORLD THAT HATED AND FEARED THEM...BUT SCOTT ALSO SUFFERED THE LOSS OF HIS FIRST LOVE, JEAN GREY.

NOW, SCOTT HAS STEPPED OUT OF PROFESSOR X'S SHADOW AND TAKEN HIS PLACE AS THE LEADER OF ALL MUTANTKIND, HEROES AND FORMER VILLAINS ALIKE.

HE HOLDS THE FUTURE OF HIS SPECIES IN HIS HANDS. *SCOTT SUMMERS* IS

CYCLOPS

SCRIPT BY *CHRIS YOST* • PENCILS BY *BRIAN CHING*
INKS BY *VICTOR OLAZABA* • COLORS BY *GURU eFX*

ROBERT DRAKE WAS THE SECOND X-MAN TO BE RECRUITED BY PROFESSOR XAVIER FOR HIS NEW MUTANT ACADEMY.

SAVED FROM A LYNCH MOB BY PROFESSOR X AND CYCLOPS, HE DIDN'T HAVE TO THINK TWICE ABOUT ACCEPTING THE OFFER OF A PLACE AT THE SCHOOL.

PROFESSOR X HELPED ICEMAN TO REFINE HIS POWERS, MAKING HIS DIFFUSE, SNOWY FORM HARDER AND DENSER.

EVENTUALLY, HE COULD EVEN REPAIR HIS ICY BODY USING FROZEN MOISTURE FROM THE AIR AROUND HIM, BECOMING VIRTUALLY INVULNERABLE.

THE SUPER HERO LIFESTYLE SEEMED TO AGREE WITH BOBBY.

WHEN HE WASN'T WITH THE X-MEN, HE WAS A MEMBER OF SEVERAL OTHER SUPER TEAMS, INCLUDING *THE CHAMPIONS* AND *THE NEW DEFENDERS*.

BUT HIS FIRST LOYALTY WAS ALWAYS TO THE FRIENDS HE'D MADE AT THE XAVIER ACADEMY--AND ONCE HE RETURNED TO HELP THEM DEAL WITH THE MUTANT COLONY CREATURE KNOWN AS KRAKOA, HE NEVER LEFT.

HIS POWERS CONTINUE TO EVOLVE AND MATURE: HE HAS ALREADY BEEN IDENTIFIED AS AN OMEGA-LEVEL MUTANT, ONE OF THE FEW WITH CAPABILITIES THAT DEFY ALL MEASUREMENT.

WHATEVER THE FUTURE HOLDS

ICEMAN

WILL FACE IT AS AN X-MAN.

WRITTEN BY *PETER DAVID* • ART BY *PABLO RAIMONDI* • COLOR BY *BRIAN REBER*

WARREN WORTHINGTON III WAS RAISED WITH UNIMAGINABLE WEALTH AND PRIVILEGE.

BUT IN HIS TEENAGE YEARS, HE BEGAN HIDING HIS DARK SECRET...

WARREN WAS A *MUTANT*, WITH WINGS AND THE ABILITY TO FLY.

TAKING THE NAME *ANGEL* TO PROTECT HIS IDENTITY, HE SOON JOINED THE ORIGINAL *X-MEN*.

BUT WHEN THE ANCIENT MASTERMIND *APOCALYPSE* CHOSE WARREN TO BE HIS FOURTH HORSEMAN--

--*THE ANGEL OF DEATH*--

--EXPERIMENTS TRANSFORMED HIM, YIELDING RAZOR WINGS AND BLOODY IMPULSES.

WITH THE AID OF HIS TEAMMATES, WARREN FREED HIMSELF OF APOCALYPSE'S CONTROL.

THE STRUGGLE TO RETURN TO HIS FORMER SELF, HOWEVER, HAS PROVEN MUCH MORE DIFFICULT.

EVEN NOW, WARREN WORTHINGTON BALANCES HIS NOBLE INTENTIONS WITH HIS DARK TRANSFORMATIONS...

AS THE X-MAN

ARCHANGEL

WRITTEN BY *JAMES ASMUS* • ART BY *TOM RANEY* • COLORED BY *MATT WILSON*

...OF THE UNCANNY X-MEN, *HENRY "HANK" McCOY*--AKA *BEAST*--HAS TOILED TIRELESSLY FOR THE BENEFIT OF HIS FELLOW MAN.

BUT THIS HULKING FRAME CONTAINS A MIND EQUALLY ADEPT AT ARTS AND SCIENCES.

AND *PROFESSOR McCOY* UNDOUBTEDLY SAVES AS MANY LIVES WITH HIS MEDICAL AND GENETIC BREAKTHROUGHS AS HE DOES WITH HIS FEATS OF STRENGTH AND ACROBATICS.

UNLIKE MOST MUTANTS, HE BORE THE MARKS OF GENETIC MUTATION FROM BIRTH.

AND SEEMINGLY EVERY TIME THE WORLD (OR THE MAN HIMSELF) CAME TO ACCEPT HIS DIFFERENCES--

--MISFORTUN[E] TRANSFORMED HENRY McCOY FURTHER TOWAR[D] THE *BEAST* T[HE] WORLD BELIEVE[D] HIM TO BE.

YET WHETHER IN THE THICK OF BATTLE OR THE DEPTHS OF RESEARCH--

--ALONGSIDE OTHER MUTANTS O[R] FELLOW *AVENGERS*

--NO SOCIA[L] STIGMA, NO ADVERSARY, N[O] INSURMOUNTAB[LE] ODDS PREVENT T[HE] **BEAST** FROM BECOMING ON[E] OF MAN'S GREATEST HEROES.

WRITTEN BY *JAMES ASMUS* • ART BY *SALVA ESPIN* • COLORED BY *JIM CHARALAMPIDIS*

ALEX SUMMERS BEGAN HIS STRANGE PATH TO HEROISM WHEN HE AND HIS BROTHER, SCOTT, NARROWLY EVADED DEATH AT A YOUNG AGE. FLYING BACK WITH THEIR PARENTS FROM VACATION IN THEIR FATHER'S VINTAGE PLANE, THE AIRCRAFT CRASHED INTO A SHI'AR SCOUT SHIP. THE BOYS WOULD HAVE DIED IF THEIR MOTHER, IN HER LAST ACT, HADN'T PUSHED THEM OUT THE DOOR SO THEY COULD PARACHUTE TO SAFETY.

THE BOYS BECAME SEPARATED AND GREW UP APART FROM EACH OTHER. BUT FATE REUNITED THEM WHEN, AFTER A MISADVENTURE WITH THE LIVING MONOLITH, ALEX WAS CAPTURED BY THE SENTINELS. THEIR MASTER, LARRY TRASK, KNEW THAT ALEX HAD THE POWER TO ABSORB AND HARNESS COSMIC RADIATION, AND UNLEASH IT TO DEVASTATING EFFECT.

HE GAVE ALEX THE CODE NAME OF HAVOK AND A COSTUME THAT WOULD MONITOR THE BUILDUP OF ENERGY WITHIN HIM. BUT HAVOK WAS EVENTUALLY LIBERATED BY THE X-MEN AND REUNITED WITH HIS BROTHER.

IN TIME, HE HEADED UP HIS OWN MUTANT TEAM, X-FACTOR, UNDER GOVERNMENT AUSPICES, ALONG WITH HIS LOVER, LORNA DANE, A.K.A. POLARIS.

SINCE THEN HE EVENTUALLY WOUND UP AS LEADER OF THE STARJAMMERS AFTER THE DEATH OF CORSAIR, THE SPACE PIRATE WHO WAS ACTUALLY ALEX'S OWN FATHER, HAVING SURVIVED THE PLANE CRASH SO MANY YEARS AGO.

STILL OUT IN SPACE, BUT UNDOUBTEDLY DESTINED TO RETURN TO EARTH SOME DAY, ALEX SUMMERS CONTINUES TO LIVE UP TO HIS CODE NAME BY RAISING

HAVOK

WRITER: PETER DAVID
PENCILS: STEPHEN SEGOVIA
INKS: CRIMELAB STUDIOS
COLORS: CHRIS SOTOMAYOR

THE WORLD'S DEADLIEST MUTANT WAS BORN MORE THAN A CENTURY AGO INTO A SEEMINGLY IDYLLIC [LIF]E ALONG THE CANADIAN FRONTIER.

BUT WHEN THAT LIFE ENDED IN TRAGEDY, THE BOY WHO NOW CALLED HIMSELF LOGAN TOOK OFF INTO THE WILDERNESS, WHERE HIS BONE CLAWS AND ANIMAL-LIKE SENSES HELPED HIM FIND A NEW HOME.

YEARS LATER, LOGAN'S MUTANT ABILITIES BROUGHT HIM TO THE ATTENTION OF THE CLANDESTINE AMERICAN BLACK OPS ORGANIZATION, WEAPON X.

BECAUSE LOGAN'S MUTANT HEALING FACTOR ALLOWS HIM TO RECOVER FROM MOST ANY WOUND, WEAPON X WAS ABLE TO PUT HIM THROUGH A TRAUMATIC SURGICAL EXPERIMENT, FOREVER LACING HIS BONES WITH THE INDESTRUCTIBLE METAL ADAMANTIUM.

[B]UT LOGAN REBELLED AGAINST HIS WOULD-BE MASTERS, [R]EFUSING TO SERVE AS THEIR MINDLESS KILLING MACHINE.

AND THOUGH HE ESCAPED FROM WEAPON X, LOGAN FOUND HIMSELF SADDLED WITH CLOUDED MEMORIES OF HIS PAST AND A VIOLENT BERSERKER NATURE THAT HE WAS EVER FIGHTING TO REPRESS.

FROM SAMURAI TO ASSASSIN, LOGAN HAS WALKED MANY DIFFERENT ROADS OVER THE YEARS WHILE SEARCHING FOR HIS PLACE IN THE WORLD.

IT WAS ONLY WHEN PROFESSOR CHARLES XAVIER INVITED HIM TO JOIN HIS TEAM OF MUTANT HEROES, THE X-MEN, THAT LOGAN FINALLY FOUND A ROLE HE COULD EMBRACE: THAT OF HERO.

WOLVERINE

SCRIPT: JASON AARON • ART: RENATO GUEDES • COLOR ART: JOHN RAUCH

AFTER THE DEATH OF HER PARENTS LEFT HER ORPHANED AND ALONE, *ORORO MUNROE* WAS TRAINED AS A THIEF IN THE TORTUOUS BACK STREETS OF CAIRO.

CHARLES XAVIER CALLED HER FROM THAT LIFE WHEN HE INVITED HER TO JOIN THE RANKS OF THE *X-MEN.*

ORORO ACCEPTED THAT INVITATION, DESPITE INITIAL MISGIVINGS. TAKING THE NAME *STORM,* SHE BECAME ONE OF THE TEAM'S CORE MEMBERS-- AND HAS REMAINED SO EVER SINCE.

...BUT EVEN WITHOUT THEM, SHE WAS ABLE TO BEAT SCOTT SUMMERS--*CYCLOPS*-- IN A CONTEST FOR THE LEADERSHIP OF THE TEAM.

MARRIAGE TO KING T'CHALLA OF WAKANDA THE BLACK PANTHER TOOK HER AWAY FROM THE X-MEN FOR A WHIL

SOME FEARED THAT I MIGHT MARK A DECISIV SPLIT, SINCE SHE'D NO HAVE OFFICIAL DUTIE AND RESPONSIBILITIE HALF A WORLD AWAY FRO HER FORMER TEAMMATE

BUT WHEN HER MUTANT POWERS EMERGED, GIVING HER CONTROL OVER THE WEATHER, SHE WAS WORSHIPPED AS A *GODDESS* ON THE ENDLESS PLAINS OF KENYA.

STORM'S POWERS PUT HER IN THE ELITE GROUP OF MUTANTS WITH OMEGA-LEVEL POTENTIAL...

BUT

STORM

HAS PROVED TIME AND AGAIN THAT HER LOYALTIES STILL LIE WITH MUTANTKIND...

AND WITH ITS CHAMPIONS AND PROTECTORS, THE *UNCANNY X-MEN.*

WRITTEN BY *MIKE CAREY* • PENCILED BY *TERRY DODSON* • INKED BY *RACHEL DODSON* • COLORED BY *CHRISTINA STRAIN*

FEW MUTANTS HAVE DISCOVERED THEIR POWERS IN MORE TRAUMATIC CIRCUMSTANCES THAN THE YOUNG RUNAWAY KNOWN AS *ANNA-MARIE.*

HER FIRST KISS LED TO TRAGEDY AS SHE ABSORBED THE MEMORIES OF HER BOYFRIEND, CODY ROBBINS, CATAPULTING HIM INTO A COMA.

...SED AS A DAUGHTER BY THE SUPER VILLAIN *MYSTIQUE,* ...ROGUE WAS INDUCTED INTO THE *BROTHERHOOD OF* ...VIL MUTANTS, AND FOUGHT THE X-MEN MANY TIMES.

...ABILITY TO ...BSORB THE ...OWERS OF ...HER MUTANTS ... A SINGLE ...UCH PROVED ...VASTATING ... COMBAT.

BUT IT WAS TO THE *X-MEN*--AND TO CHARLES XAVIER-- THAT ROGUE TURNED IN HER MOMENT OF CRISIS, WHEN HER POWERS THREATENED TO DESTROY HER MIND.

PROFESSOR X RESPONDED BY MAKING HER A MEMBER OF THE TEAM.

A CONTROVERSIAL CHOICE, OPPOSED BY MANY OF HER FELLOW MUTANTS.

BUT THIS ACT OF FAITH WAS A TURNING POINT FOR ROGUE-- AND FOR THE X-MEN THEMSELVES.

ROGUE

SERVING AS A FRONT-LINE MEMBER OF SEVERAL TEAMS, AND EVEN LEADING A TEAM OF HER OWN, SHE HAS PROVED HERSELF A HERO A HUNDRED TIMES OVER.

NOW, IN FULL CONTROL OF HER POWERS FOR THE FIRST TIME EVER, SHE IS A FORMIDABLE FORCE AND A PRICELESS ASSET TO THE X-MEN.

SCRIPT: *MIKE CAREY* • ART: *DAVID LOPEZ* • COLOR ART: *JOHN RAUCH*

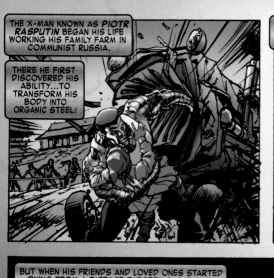

THE X-MAN KNOWN AS *PIOTR RASPUTIN* BEGAN HIS LIFE WORKING HIS FAMILY FARM IN COMMUNIST RUSSIA.

THERE HE FIRST DISCOVERED HIS ABILITY...TO TRANSFORM HIS BODY INTO ORGANIC STEEL!

PIOTR'S METALLIC SKIN, INCREDIBLE STRENGTH, AND NEAR INVULNERABILITY LED *PROFESSOR XAVIER* TO RECRUIT THIS GENTLE GIANT INTO HIS SECOND GROUP OF X-MEN.

AND THE MUTANT NOW CALLE[D] *COLOSSUS* DEDICATED HIMSE[LF] AS DEVOUTLY AS ANYONE T[O] XAVIER'S DREAM.

BUT WHEN HIS FRIENDS AND LOVED ONES STARTED DYING FROM A DISEASE TARGETING MUTANTS, PIOTR LOST HIS FAITH, AND LOST HIS WAY.

HE BROKE AWAY FROM HIS FRIENDS, JOINED RANKS WITH MAGNETO...

AND EVENTUALLY GAVE HIS *LIFE* IN ORDER TO BECOME HOST TO THE VIRUS' CURE.

RECENTLY

COLOSSUS

WAS FOUND--*RESURRECTED*--

--AND REDEDICATED HIMSELF TO THE FIGHT FOR THE FUTURE OF MUTANT-KIND ALONGSIDE HIS FRIENDS, HIS FAMILY, THE *X-MEN!*

WRITTEN BY *JAMES ASMUS*
ART BY *DAVID YARDIN*
COLORED BY *MATT WILSON*

OVER THE COURSE OF HER LIFE, *BETSY BRADDOCK* HAS BEEN MANY THINGS...

CHARTER PILOT.

FASHION MODEL.

AND EVEN A COSTUMED CRIMEFIGHTER.

ONCE A YOUNG BETSY DISCOVERED HER TELEPATHY-- AN ABILITY TO READ AND AFFECT THE MINDS OF PEOPLE AROUND HER--

--SHE QUICKLY SOUGHT THE TRAINING AND COMPANY OF HER FELLOW MUTANTS IN THE *X-MEN.*

SOON AFTER, PSYLOCKE WAS ABDUCTED, AND SHE AND A YOUNG ASIAN ASSASSIN WERE EXPERIMENTED UPON.

AND THE TWO WOMEN WERE RE-COMBINED-- BODY, SKILL, AND SOUL.

HAVING GAINED A NEW DEMEANOR, A MASTERY OF THE MARTIAL ARTS, AND USE OF DEADLY TELEKINETIC KNIVES, IT MAY BE DIFFICULT TO RECOGNIZE BETSY BRADDOCK.

BUT THE FIERCE AND FORMIDABLE *PSYLOCKE* IS UNMISTAKABLE.

WRITTEN BY JAMES ASMUS • ART BY HARVEY TOLIBAO • COLORED BY ULISES ARREOLA

BORN TO A KENTUCKY COAL MINING FAMILY, SAM GUTHRIE IS THE OLDEST OF TEN SIBLINGS-- THE FIRST GUTHRIE, BUT FAR FROM THE LAST, TO DEVELOP MUTANT POWERS.

HIS SISTERS PAIGE (HUSK) AND MELODY (AERO) FOLLOWED HIM TO THE XAVIER ACADEMY, AND HIS BROTHER JOSH (ICARUS) TRAGICALLY DIED WHILE A STUDENT THERE.

SAM'S BLAST FIELD ALLOWS HIM NOT JUST TO FLY BUT TO SMASH THROUGH ALL OBSTACLES, WHILE SIMULTANEOUSLY SHIELDING HIM FROM HARM.

THE NAME CANNONBALL SEEMED TO BE A GOOD FIT FOR HIM.

WHEN THE TIME-TRAVELLER KNOWN AS CABLE CLAIMED THAT THE MUTANT RACE COULD NOT BE PROTECTED EFFECTIVELY WITHIN THE LAW, CANNONBALL LEFT THE ACADEMY TO JOIN CABLE'S UNDERGROUND TEAM--THE FIRST X-FORCE.

CABLE HELPED SAM TO DEVELOP HIS POWERS, HONE HIS LEADERSHIP SKILLS, AND IN MANY WAYS WAS A SURROGATE FATHER TO HIM.

BUT WHAT GOES AROUND, COMES AROUND: WHEN CABLE'S X-FORCE DISBANDED, CANNONBALL RETURNED TO THE X-MEN FOLD AND IN DUE COURSE REASSEMBLED HIS ORIGINAL TEAM.

FORGED AND HARDENED IN THE FIRES OF MANY BATTLES,

CANNONBALL

IS THE PERFECT LEADER FOR THE NEW MUTANTS.

WRITTEN BY MIKE CAREY • ART BY BOB MCLEOD • COLORED BY SONIA OBACK

ILLYANA RASPUTIN SPENT THE FIRST FEW HAPPY YEARS OF HER LIFE ON A FARM COLLECTIVE IN RUSSIA.

UNTIL, THAT IS, HER BROTHER *PIOTR* MANIFESTED MUTANT ABILITIES.

THOUGH STILL A CHILD WITH NO SIGN OF MUTANT ABILITY, SHE CAME TO THE U.S. AND LIVED WITH HER BROTHER AND HIS NEW COMPATRIOTS *THE X-MEN*.

SOON AFTER, ILLYANA FELL CAPTIVE TO *BELASCO*--THE DEMONIC RULER OF THE LIMBO DIMENSION.

THE TORTURES SHE ENDURED AGED HER BY SEVERAL YEARS, STRIPPED PORTIONS OF HER SOUL, FILLED HER WITH BLACK MAGIC, AND BONDED HER TO A MYSTICAL *SOUL SWORD*.

SHE HAS SINCE RETURNED AS

MAGIK

TO THE X-MEN, AND HER TEAMMATES ON THE *NEW MUTANTS*.

BUT EVERY DAY ILLYANA STRUGGLES TO MAINTAIN CONTROL...

...AND BOTH HER FRIENDS AN FAMILY REMAIN UNSURE WHETH SHE WILL GIVE WAY TO THE DA FORCES STILL WITHIN HER!

WRITTEN BY *JAMES ASMUS* •ART BY *LEONARD KIRK* •COLORED BY *LEE DUHIG*

WHEN XI'AN "SHAN" COY MANH TRIED TO ESCAPE A WAR-TORN VIETNAM WITH HER FAMILY, HER MUTANT POWER SUDDENLY MANIFESTED--

--GIVING HER THE ABILITY TO *POSSESS* THE MIND, BODY, AND WILL OF THOSE AROUND HER.

HER PARENTS DID NOT SURVIVE THE DESPERATE JOURNEY TO AMERICA. BUT XI'AN SAFELY GUIDED HER TWO YOUNGER SIBLINGS TO NEW YORK CITY.

FORTUNATELY FOR XI'AN, A NEW LIFE WELCOMED HER IN NEW YORK. TAKING THE NAME *KARMA*, SHE BECAME A FOUNDING MEMBER OF PROFESSOR XAVIER'S *NEW MUTANTS*.

BUT SOON AFTER JOINING THE NEW MUTANTS, XI'AN BECAME POSSESSED BY A POWERFUL ADVERSARY OF THE PROFESSOR KNOWN AS SHADOW KING.

HE USED KARMA IN AN ATTEMPT TO KILL HER OWN TEAMMATES, AND NEARLY DESTROYED HER MIND AND BODY IN THE PROCESS.

ONCE FREE OF THE SHADOW KING'S GRASP, XI'AN RETURNED HER ATTENTION TO CARING FOR HER YOUNGER SIBLINGS...

...AND EVENTUALLY FOR OTHER MUTANTS AT THE XAVIER INSTITUTE.

AND EVERY ONE OF THEM KNOWS THAT **KARMA** WILL NEVER STOP FIGHTING TO PROTECT THE PEOPLE SHE LOVES, NO MATTER WHAT THE COST.

WRITTEN BY *JAMES ASMUS* • ART BY *LEONARD KIRK* • COLORED BY *JOHN RAUCH*

NATHAN SUMMERS WAS BORN A TARGET.

THE SON OF SCOTT SUMMERS AND MADELYNE PRYOR, HE WAS CAPTURED BY APOCALYPSE AND INJECTED WITH A DEADLY TECHNO-ORGANIC VIRUS.

THE ONLY WAY TO SAVE YOUNG NATHAN WAS TO SEND HIM INTO THE DEEP FUTURE WITH THE ASKANI TRIBE, A SISTERHOOD DEDICATED TO DEFEATING APOCALYPSE.

LATER, CYCLOPS AND JEAN GREY WERE PULLED INT THE SAME FUTUR TO RAISE YOUNG NATHAN AND TEA HIM HOW HIS MUT ABILITIES CAN KEEP THE T/O VIRUS AT BAY.

SWORN TO DESTROY APOCALYPSE BEFORE HIS RISE TO POWER, NATHAN--N CALLING HIMSELF "CABLE"--RETURNED THE PRESENT AND SOON ORGANIZED MUTANT STRIKE TEAM X-FORCE.

BUT HIS GREATEST MISSION WAS PROTECTING THE ONE MUTANT BORN SINCE M-DAY...THE SO-CALLED MESSIAH. THE BABY HE NAMED HOPE.

HOPE WAS ALSO BORN A TARGET. AND TO

CABL

NOTHING W MORE IMPORTANT TH KEEPING HER ALIVE-- MATTER THE COST HIMSELF.

WRITTEN BY DUANE SWIERCZYNSKI • ART BY DAVE WILK

DOMINO WASN'T ALWAYS SO LUCKY. SHE WAS BORN INTO A MUTANT BREEDING PROGRAM DESIGNED TO CREATE THE PERFECT WEAPON.

THE PROGRAM DEEMED YOUNG NEENA A FAILURE, AND SHE BARELY ESCAPED WITH HER LIFE.

HER LUCK CAME WHEN HER MUTANT POWERS KICKED IN. DOMINO AFFECTS THE WORLD AROUND HER SUBCONSCIOUSLY, TELEKINETICALLY MAKING THINGS GO HER WAY.

SOMETIMES GOOD THINGS HAPPEN FOR HER... SOMETIMES BAD THINGS FOR THOSE STANDING AGAINST HER.

DOMINO'S LUCK INSTINCTIVELY GUIDES HER MOVEMENTS, KEEPING HER OUT OF HARM'S WAY AND GIVING HER AN EDGE...

...BUT BEING AN UNPARALLELED MARKSWOMAN AND HAND-TO-HAND FIGHTER DOESN'T HURT.

DOMINO

HAS GONE FROM EXPERIMENT AND PAWN TO MERCENARY AND MUTANT FREEDOM FIGHTER, GUIDED BY INSTINCT...NOT TO MENTION MONEY AND A GOOD TIME.

NOW DOMINO FINDS HERSELF FIGHTING THE GOOD FIGHT WITH THE X-MEN, AND DOING THE DIRTY JOBS THAT ONLY CABLE...

WRITER: FRED VAN LENTE   PENCILS: PACO MEDINA   INKS: JUAN VLASCO
COLORS: IAN HANNIN   LETTERS: VC's CLAYTON COWLES   EDITOR: ALEJANDRO ARBONA

ONLY **JEAN-LUC LEBEAU** OF THE NEW ORLEANS THIEVES' GUILD HAS ANY CLUE TO **GAMBIT'S** TRUE IDENTITY AND ORIGIN.

HE WAS THE ONE WHO STOLE THE CHILD IN THE FIRST PLACE--BUT THEN DECIDED TO RAISE HIM AS HIS OWN SON, AND TEACH HIM TO BE THE BEST THIEF THE WORLD HAD EVER SEEN.

THE YOUNG **REMY LEBEAU** HAD AN EYE FOR THE LADIES, BUT WHEN HE FELL IN LOVE WITH **BELLA DONNA BOUDREAUX**, HIS FATE WAS SEALED.

CHALLENGED BY HER BROTHER, JULIEN, HE FOUGHT A DUEL TO THE DEATH AND AS REMY'S POWERS SURGED OUT OF CONTROL, IT WAS JULIEN WHO LOST BOTH THE CONTEST AND HIS LIFE.

REMY'S POWER--TO FILL ANY OBJECT TO THE BRIM WITH BIOKINETIC ENERGY, TO THE POINT WHERE IT LITERALLY EXPLODES--NEARLY RUINED HIS LIFE.

THE MYSTERIOUS **MR. SINISTER** HELPED BRING GAMBIT'S POWER BACK UNDER HIS CONTROL-- BUT THE PRICE WAS A TERRIBLE ONE.

GAMBIT ACTED AS GUIDE TO THE **MARAUDERS** ON THE NIGHT OF THE **MUTANT MASSACRE**, AN INNOCENT ACCOMPLICE TO A GENOCIDAL RAMPAGE.

MEETING THE **X-MEN** MARKED THE TURNING POINT IN GAMBIT'S LIFE, GIVING HIM A CHANCE TO ATONE FOR OLD SINS.

STILL A THIEF BY INSTINCT AND A ROGUE BY NATURE, **GAMBIT** IS NOW A HERO BY TRADE.

HIS HOME--WHEREVER HE HAPPENS TO BE.

WRITTEN BY **MIKE CAREY** • ART BY **LEONARD KIRK** • COLORS BY **JOHN RAUCH**

JUBILATION LEE'S MUTANT ABILITY TO GENERATE "FIREWORKS" OF EXPLOSIVE PLASMA MANIFESTED WHILE LIVING IN A MALL AFTER HER PARENTS' MURDER.

USING THESE POWERS TO BUSK DREW THE UNFORTUNATE ATTENTION OF A MUTANT-HUNTING ORGANIZATION. LUCKILY, SOME X-WOMEN HAPPENED TO BE NEARBY, AND SAVED HER LIFE.

CURIOUS ABOUT HER RESCUERS, JUBILEE FOLLOWED THE WOMEN, BUT CONTINUED TO LIVE IN HIDING...

...UNTIL SHE FOUND THE MUTANT WOLVERINE BEING TORTURED BY REAVERS.

HORRIFIED, JUBILEE RESCUED WOLVERINE AND NURSED HIM BACK TO HEALTH, PROTECTING THEM BOTH BY UNLEASHING THE FULL DESTRUCTIVE POWER OF HER ABILITIES.

WOLVERINE TOOK JUBILEE UNDER HIS WING, AND THE TWO DEVELOPED A CLOSE AND UNSHAKABLE BOND.

AFTER PARTNERING WITH HER ON HIS ADVENTURES AROUND THE WORLD, AND TEACHING HER HOW TO FIGHT, WOLVERINE BROUGHT JUBILEE TO THE X-MEN WHERE SHE JOINED THEM AS A JUNIOR MEMBER...

...AND IMMEDIATELY BECAME THE HEART OF THE TEAM.

AND THOUGH SHE LOST HER POWERS AFTER M-DAY, HER COURAGE, STREET SMARTS, LOYALTY, AND WICKED SENSE OF HUMOR ARE WHAT CONTINUE TO MAKE

Jubilee

AN X-MAN

EVENTUALLY, SHE WENT ON TO JOIN *GENERATION X* AND *NEW WARRIORS*.

SCRIPT BY *MARJORIE L*
PENCILS BY *REILLY BROW*
INKS BY *TERRY PALLOT*
COLORS BY *MATTHEW WIL*

EMMA FROST STARTED LIFE AS THE MOUSY DAUGHTER OF A WEALTHY NEW ENGLAND FAMILY. AFTER A SUDDEN PSYCHIC OUTBURST, SHE RAN AWAY FROM HOME AND FOUND HERSELF ON THE DOORSTEP OF THE NOTORIOUS *HELLFIRE CLUB*.

TAKEN UNDER THE WING OF FELLOW MUTANT *SEBASTIAN SHAW*, EMMA BECAME THE *WHITE QUEEN* OF *THE HELLFIRE CLUB*. SHE SOON CUT A SWATH OF TERROR THROUGH NOT ONLY THOSE WHO WOULD *SUBJUGATE* MUTANTKIND...BUT THE *X-MEN* AS WELL.

THOUGH THE WHITE QUEEN WAS A DANGEROUS OPPONENT TO HER ENEMIES, A SLIGHTLY SOFTER SIDE EMERGED WHEN TEACHING HER BELOVED STUDENTS, *THE HELLIONS*. THESE CHILDREN WERE HER PRIDE AND JOY.

WHEN EMMA'S PUPILS WERE KILLED BY THE FEARSOME *SENTINELS*, SHE LOST THE ONE THING SHE TRULY CARED ABOUT IN LIFE.

THIS TRAGEDY PUSHED EMMA DOWN A DIFFERENT PATH.

HER CHANGE OF HEART, SHOWN IN HER WORK AS THE CO-FOUNDER OF *GENERATION X*, LED EMMA TO EVENTUALLY JOIN *THE X-MEN*.

Emma Frost

HAS NEVER BEEN AN ANGEL EVEN ON HER BEST DAYS, BUT SHE HAS PROVEN HERSELF TIME AND TIME AGAIN TO BE A POWERFUL FORCE FOR GOOD (WHEN SHE WISHES TO BE!)

HER ARCH-ENEMIES WERE NOW HER TEAMMATES...AND AN UNLIKELY ROMANCE BLOSSOMED BETWEEN HER AND TEAM LEADER *CYCLOPS*.

BUT MOST IMPORTANT TO EMMA WAS THE FACT THAT SHE HAD GIFTED YOUNG MUTANTS TO TEACH AGAIN, HEALING THE WOUNDS LEFT BY THE DEMISE OF HER ORIGINAL STUDENTS.

SCRIPT BY *VALERIE D'ORAZIO*
ART BY *MARK BROOKS*

A TROUBLED AND TRAGIC CHILDHOOD LED TWINS *JEAN-PAUL* AND *JEANNE-MARIE BEAUBIER* TO RELY ON EACH OTHER FOR EVERYTHING. SMALL WONDER THAT WHEN THEIR MUTANT POWERS KICKED IN, THEY TURNED OUT TO BE INTERDEPENDENT.

BOTH POSSESSED FLIGHT AND SUPER-SPEED, AND A BLINDING BURST OF LIGHT WAS PRODUCED WHENEVER THE TWINS TOUCHED.

AS A SUPERSTAR SKIER, JEAN-PAUL WAS THE IDOL OF MILLIONS. BUT HE WAS ALSO A MUTANT, AND GAY-- ASPECTS OF HIS NATURE THAT HE HID FOR MANY YEARS.

ACCEPTANCE INTO THE CANADIAN GOVERNMENT'S *ALPHA FLIGHT* OUTED HIM AS A MUTANT, BUT IT WAS MANY YEARS BEFORE HE FELT CONFIDENT ENOUGH TO DECLARE HIS SEXUALITY OPENLY. HE WAS THE FIRST SUPER HERO TO DO SO.

AS AN X-MAN, NORTHSTAR'S ABRASIVE AND ARROGANT NATURE HAS OFTEN BROUGHT HIM INTO CONFLICT WITH TEAMMATES.

BUT HE BECAME RESPECTED AS A TEACHER AND MENTOR AT THE XAVIER ACADEMY, AND A ROLE MODEL FOR YOUNGER MUTANTS WHO WERE AS CONFLICTED ABOUT THEIR IDENTITY AS HE HAD ONCE BEEN.

NOW A FRONTLINE MEMBER OF THE X-M

NORTHSTAR

HAS MORE FORMIDABLE POWERS THAN EVE AND DEPLOYS THEM MORE INGENIOUS

RUMORS THAT HIS TEMPER IS MELLOW MAY, HOWEVER, BE A LITTLE PREMATU

WRITTEN BY *MIKE CAREY* • ART BY *DAVID YARDIN* • COLORED BY *SONIA OBACK*

SOME YEARS AGO, WHEN A STARTLED OBSTETRICIAN SLAPPED A NEWLY DELIVERED CHILD ON HIS BACKSIDE, THE RESULT WAS A SECOND NEWBORN SNAPPING INTO EXISTENCE BESIDE HIM.

THUS DID JAMES "JAMIE" MADROX ANNOUNCE HIS ARRIVAL INTO THE WORLD.

HE WAS GIVEN A SPECIAL SUIT TO NEUTRALIZE HIS POWER SO THAT CASUAL IMPACT WOULDN'T CREATE MORE DUPLICATES.

WHEN HE WAS FIFTEEN, A TORNADO OF MYSTERIOUS ORIGINS KILLED HIS PARENTS ON THEIR KANSAS FARM.

INVITED TO JOIN THE X-MEN, HE INSTEAD WOUND UP ON MUIR ISLAND, WORKING FOR DOCTOR MOIRA MacTAGGERT...

...BEFORE WINDING UP ON THE GOVERNMENT-SPONSORED TEAM CALLED X-FACTOR.

NOW HE IS THE LEADER OF A MODERN DAY X-FACTOR, NOT WORKING FOR THE GOVERNMENT BUT INSTEAD A DETECTIVE AGENCY SPECIALIZING IN THE SORTS OF CASES THAT ONLY THEIR SUPER HERO OR SUPER VILLAIN CLIENTS CAN BRING TO THEM.

AS FOR HIS DUPES, THEY'RE AN UNPREDICTABLE LOT, EACH DISPLAYING SOME ASPECT OF HIS PERSONALITY AND NOT ALWAYS COOPERATIVE. BUT THAT'S PART OF THE PERPETUAL X-FACTOR OF BEING THE MULTIPLE MAN.

MADROX

WRITER: PETER DAVID • ART: PABLO RAIMONDI • COLORS BRIAN REBER

- PABLO 2010 -

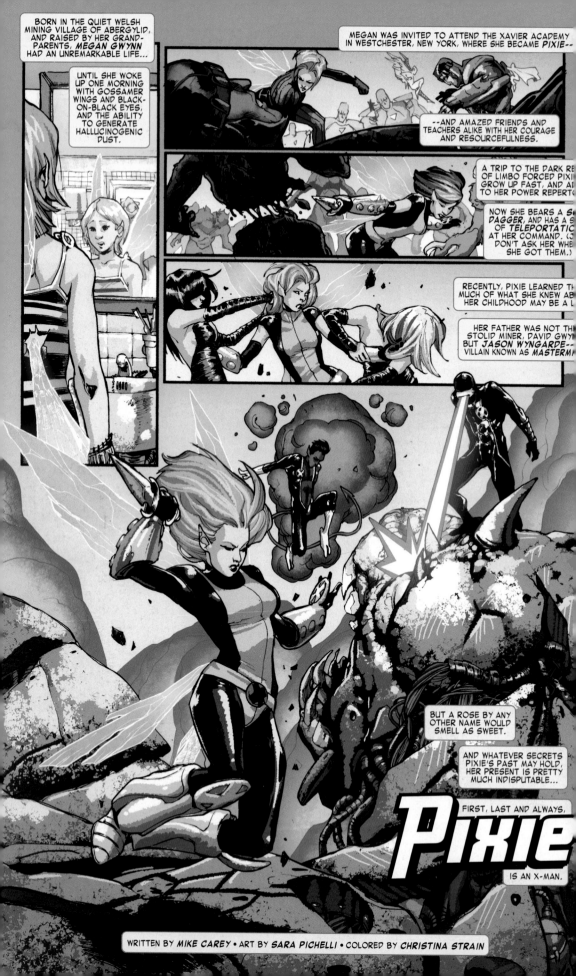

BORN IN THE QUIET WELSH MINING VILLAGE OF ABERGYLID, AND RAISED BY HER GRAND-PARENTS, *MEGAN GWYNN* HAD AN UNREMARKABLE LIFE...

UNTIL SHE WOKE UP ONE MORNING WITH GOSSAMER WINGS AND BLACK-ON-BLACK EYES, AND THE ABILITY TO GENERATE HALLUCINOGENIC DUST.

MEGAN WAS INVITED TO ATTEND THE XAVIER ACADEMY IN WESTCHESTER, NEW YORK, WHERE SHE BECAME *PIXIE*--

--AND AMAZED FRIENDS AND TEACHERS ALIKE WITH HER COURAGE AND RESOURCEFULNESS.

A TRIP TO THE DARK RE[G] OF LIMBO FORCED PIXI[E] GROW UP FAST, AND A[D] TO HER POWER REPERT[OIRE].

NOW SHE BEARS A *S[OUL] DAGGER*, AND HAS A S[ET] OF *TELEPORTATIO[N]* AT HER COMMAND. (J[UST] DON'T ASK HER WHE[RE] SHE GOT THEM.)

RECENTLY, PIXIE LEARNED T[HAT] MUCH OF WHAT SHE KNEW AB[OUT] HER CHILDHOOD MAY BE A L[IE].

HER FATHER WAS NOT TH[E] STOLID MINER, DAVID GWY[NN] BUT *JASON WYNGARDE*-- VILLAIN KNOWN AS *MASTERM[IND]*

BUT A ROSE BY ANY OTHER NAME WOULD SMELL AS SWEET.

AND WHATEVER SECRETS PIXIE'S PAST MAY HOLD, HER PRESENT IS PRETTY MUCH INDISPUTABLE...

FIRST, LAST AND ALWAYS,

PIXIE

IS AN X-MAN.

WRITTEN BY *MIKE CAREY* • ART BY *SARA PICHELLI* • COLORED BY *CHRISTINA STRAIN*

CAPTAIN AMERICA WAS THE WORLD'S FIRST SUPER SOLDIER, BORN WHEN A SKINNY AMERICAN BOY SLURPED DOWN SOME RANCID TASTING SERUM.

THE NEWEST GENERATION OF SUPER SOLDIER WAS BORN UNDER FAR MORE GLAMOROUS CIRCUMSTANCES.

THEY CALL IT *THE WORLD.*

THE WORLD WAS AN EXPERIMENTAL SUPER LAB RUN BY THE NEFARIOUS WEAPON PLUS PROGRAM WHERE A NEW RACE OF MUTANTS WERE BIO-ENGINEERED

WHOLE GENERATIONS OF MUTANT WOMEN WERE IMPREGNATED WITH MICROTECHNOLOGY AND IN THEIR BELLIES GREW THE MOST HIGHLY-ADVANCED SUPER SOLDIERS EVER KNOWN TO MAN.

THUS WAS BORN *FANTOMEX.*

HE WAS THE ULTIMATE WEAPON, GIFTED WITH ENHANCED FIGHTING PROWESS AND MYSTERIOUS POWERS OF MISDIRECTION. A SUPER SENTINEL ARMED WITH NANO-ACTIVE BLOOD, MULTIPLE BRAINS AND GUNS THAT FIRED MUTANT-KILLING BULLETS.

HE WAS WEAPON XIII.

UNTIL HE ESCAPED.

NOW HE SERVES NO MASTER BUT HIS OWN THIRST FOR ADVENTURE. AND THE OCCASIONAL DESIRE TO TAKE THINGS THAT DON'T BELONG TO HIM.

ALONG WITH HIS BIO-MECHANICAL SPACESHIP, *E.V.A.*, FANTOMEX HAS SOMETIMES AIDED THE X-MEN, AND HAS HELPED WOLVERINE TO DEMOLISH THE WEAPON PLUS PROGRAM.

BUT AS EVER, HIS TRUE MOTIVATIONS AND GOALS REMAIN SOMETHING OF AN ENIGMA.

MASTER THIEF! MASTER KILLER! PRETEND FRENCHMAN!

FANTOMEX

WRITTEN BY *JASON AARON* • ART BY *ERIC CANETE*

HISAKO ICHIKI WAS A STUDIOUS, UNASSUMING YOUNG GIRL IN HER NATIVE JAPAN, UNTIL HER MUTANT GENETICS KICKED IN...

...AND SUMMONED A POWERFUL PSIONIC EXOSKELETON THAT DRAWS ITS STRENGTH FROM THE SPIRITS OF HER ANCESTORS.

SHE QUICKLY ENROLLED IN THE *XAVIER INSTITUTE* IN ORDER TO BETTER UNDERSTAND AND CONTROL HER POWERS.

BUT SHE FOUND IT DIFFICULT TO COME OUT OF HER SHELL.

BUT A WHIRLWIND OF EVENTS SWEPT THE INEXPERIENCED STUDENT ALONG WITH THE *X-MEN* TO ANOTHER WORLD...

...AND INTO A BATTLE FOR THEIR SURVIVAL.

SINCE THAT TIME, HISAKO HAS ALREADY PROVEN HERSELF TIME AND AGAIN.

TAKING THE NAME

ARMOR

SHE HAS BECOME THE YOUNGEST AND ONE OF THE STRONGEST OF THE *ASTONISHING X-MEN.*

WRITTEN BY *JAMES ASMUS* • ART BY *GABRIEL HERNANDEZ WALTA*

EW HEROES COUNT ILDINGS AMONG THEIR NCESTORS, AND ONLY E TRACKS ITS ORIGINS O A *TRAINING ROOM* FOR MUTANTS.

UT WHEN THE X-MEN EBUILT THE "*DANGER* OOM" WITH *ALIEN* ECHNOLOGY, THEY EVER *IMAGINED* IT OULD *MUTATE* A MIND OF ITS OWN.

SELF-AWARENESS: A TECHNOLOGICAL *MIRACLE*, COUPLED WITH *HARDLIGHT* PROJECTORS, BLEEDING-EDGE *INTELLECT*...

...AND AN UNFORTUNATE THIRST FOR *REVENGE* ON THOSE WHO'D ENFORCED ITS *SERVITUDE*.

CAPING THE FINES OF ITS HITECTURE-- NG *HUMAN* ORM--THE HINE ALMOST LUGHTERED EM ALL...

...BUT WITH *TIME* AND *REASON* IT--*SHE*--CAME TO ACCEPT THE WISDOM OF *PROFESSOR X*, AND AGREED TO HELP MUTANTKIND AS AN *EQUAL*.

PART JAILER, PART OPERATING SYSTEM, PART LIVING WAR-MACHINE, IT NAMED ITSELF

DANGER

WRITTEN BY SIMON SPURRIER
ENCILED BY STEPHEN SEGOVIA
INKED BY DANNY MIKI
COLORED BY MARTE GRACIA

...AND NOW HELL HATH NO *FURY* LIKE AN *A.I.* SCORNED.

IN THE WEAPON X PROGRAM'S PURSUIT TO CREATE THE PERFECT WEAPON, THEY CAPTURED THE MUTANT KNOWN AS WOLVERINE.

BUT A PIECE OF HIM REMAINED.

A SHADOWY ORGANIZATION CALLED THE FACILITY STOLE THE DNA SAMPLE AND HIRED GENETIC PIONEER DR. SARAH KINNEY TO CREATE A CLONE OF WOLVERINE.

ON HER 23RD ATTEMPT, DR. KINNEY CREATED A VIABLE FEMALE TWIN.

THEIR EXTRAORDINARY EFFORTS SUCCEEDED, BUT WOLVERINE SOON TURNED ON HIS CREATORS AND ESCAPED.

AND BY THE AGE OF TEN, X-23 WAS AN EMOTIONLESS ASSASSIN FOR HIRE.

WITH THE HELP OF HER CREATOR AND MOTHER, DR. KINNEY, X-23 ESCAPED THE FACILITY...

...BUT SHE WOULD DO SO ALONE.

X-23, NOW CALLING HERSELF *LAURA KINNEY*, LOCATED WOLVERINE, WHO CONVINCED HER TO ENTER THE XAVIER INSTITUTE...

NOW

X-23

USES HER DEADLY SKILLS TO SAFEGUARD MUTANTKIND, WHILE SEARCHING FOR HER OWN HUMANITY.

SCRIPT BY *CRAIG KYLE* AND *CHRIS YOST* • ART BY *PHIL NOTO*

LITTLE IS KNOWN ABOUT THE MUTANT DAKEN AKIHIRO, WHO HAS LIVED HIS LIFE IN THE SHADOWS, WAITING FOR HIS MOMENT TO EMERGE INTO THE WORLD AND TIP THE BALANCE OF POWER--INTO HIS HANDS.

THE SON OF WOLVERINE, DAKEN POSSESSES MUCH OF HIS FATHER'S POWERS--INCLUDING A HEALING FACTOR THAT ALLOWED HIM TO SURVIVE BEING RIPPED FROM THE WOMB OF HIS MURDERED MOTHER. THE MAN WHO STOLE HIM AND HID HIS EXISTENCE FROM WOLVERINE WAS THE IMMORTAL ROMULUS.

AKEN SPENT SOME OF HIS HILDHOOD IN THE CARE OF A GOOD, UPSTANDING JAPANESE COUPLE.

BUT AFTER THEY WERE KILLED MUCH OF HIS LIFE WAS CONTROLLED BY ROMULUS, WHO TRAINED HIM--IN THE MOST BRUTAL WAYS IMAGINABLE--TO BE AN ASSASSIN.

ORDER TO PUNISH HIS FATHER, WHOM HE BLAMED FOR HIS MOTHER'S EATH AND HIS LIFE OF SUFFERING, DAKEN JUMPED AT THE CHANCE TO IN NORMAN OSBORN'S DARK AVENGERS AS HIS WOLVERINE--TO PROVE TO THE WORLD HE WAS BETTER THAN HIS FATHER.

BUT WHEN OSBORN WAS BROUGHT DOWN BY THE TRUE AVENGERS, DAKEN IMMEDIATELY JUMPED SHIP AND STRUCK OUT ON HIS OWN TO CREATE HIS OWN EMPIRE AND START A NEW LEGACY--THAT OF

DAKEN
THE DARK WOLVERINE.

SCRIPT: MARJORIE LIU AND DANIEL WAY •
ART: GIUSEPPE CAMUNCOLI • COLOR ART: FABIO D'AURIA

HE WAS BORN THE CHILD OF AN AMERICAN EXPLORER AND THE PRINCESS OF ATLANTIS.

THOUGH A MUTANT, UNLIKE ANY OTHER OF HIS KINSMEN...

BUT NAMOR REPEATEDLY FOUND HIS KINGDOM UNDER ATTACK FROM ALL MANNER OF FORCES,

AND HIS HOT TEMPER LED THE KING TO *INSTIGATE* JUST AS MANY BATTLES WITH THE SURFACE WORLD.

NAMOR THE SUB-MARINER SOON BECAME THE RULER OF THE LOST CITY--AND BY EXTENSION--OF THE SEVEN SEAS.

OVER THE YEARS, NAMOR HAS WORKED AND FOUGHT ALONGSIDE HEROES AND VILLAINS ALIKE.

IN TRUTH, THESE ALLIANCES WERE ALWAYS MADE TO FURTHER *ONE CAUSE:* THE PROTECTION AND ADVANCEMENT OF THE PEOPLE OF ATLANTIS.

WHEN ATLANTIS ITSELF WAS DESTROYED, NAMOR FORGED AN ALLIANCE WITH ANOTHER BELEAGUERED GROUP FIGHTING FOR SURVIVAL-- *MUTANTKIND,* NOW GATHERED UNDER THE PROTECTION OF THE *X-MEN.*

A MAN OF TWO WORLDS, OF TWO NATURES, IS NOW THE CHAMPION OF ATLANTEANS AND MUTANTS ALIKE--

KING
NAMOR
THE SUB-MARINER.

WRITTEN BY *JAMES ASMUS* • PENCILS BY *TERRY DODSON*
INKED BY *RACHEL DODSON* • COLORED BY *JASON KEITH*

AS FAR AS COHESIVE TEAM UNITS GO, IT'S A CURIOUS MIX...

A BLEEDING-EDGE BIOCHEMIST WITH GUILT ISSUES, WHO ONCE TRIED TO EXPUNGE MUTANTS FROM THE GENE-POOL.

KAVITA RAO. A PLEASURE.

2: A MUTANT VIETNAM VET WITH HIS HEAD IN THE CLOUDS AND HIS BODY ENDLESSLY BUILDING SUPERTECH.

UH. MADISON JEFFRIES.

HEY.

AND 3: A HUNDRED-YEAR-OLD UBER-GENIUS WITH THE MUTANT ABILITY TO ASSUME YOU'RE AN IDIOT, WHO SPENT THE PAST SIXTY YEARS FRAGGING NAZIS.

JAMES BRADLEY.

THAT'S DOCTOR NEMESIS TO YOU.

I'M BUSY.

BUT WHEN MUTANTKIND STOOD ON THE BRINK OF ANNIHILATION, IT WAS TO THESE UNCANNY INTELLECTS THE X-MEN TURNED FOR SCIENTIFIC HELP.

TOGETHER THEY FORMED THE

X-CLUB

AND TODAY THEIR ROLE IS SIMPLE:

WE.

THINK.

DIFFERENTLY.

WRITTEN BY SI SPURRIER • ART BY PHIL NOTO

SHE WAS THE FIRST MUTANT BORN SINCE *M-DAY.*

VARIOUS FACTIONS IMMEDIATELY TRIED TO *CONTROL, CONSUME, DESTROY* AND *SAVE* HER.

TIME-TRAVELING MUTANT CYBORG CABLE--BELIEVING HER TO BE A MUTANT MESSIAH-- BROUGHT HER INTO THE FUTURE SO THAT SHE COULD BE RAISED IN RELATIVE PEACE AND *CHOOSE HER OWN DESTINY.*

HOWEVER, THAT PEACE WAS SHATTERED BY TIME-TRAVELING MUTANT COP *LUCAS BISHOP,* WHO BELIEVED HOPE WOULD GROW UP TO DESTROY THEM ALL-- INCLUDING HIS OWN FAMILY.

EVENTUALLY HOPE CHOSE TO RETURN TO THE PRESENT, ONLY TO FIND THAT SHE WAS STILL *VERY MUCH A TARGET*...AND THAT MUTANTKIND ITSELF WAS ON THE BRINK OF DESTRUCTION.

AFTER PROVING HERSELF IN BATTLE, HOPE WATCHED HER SURROGATE FATHER MAKE THE *ULTIMATE SACRIFICE,* THEN TOOK HER PLACE WITH THE X-MEN.

BUT WAS CABLE RIGHT? IS SHE THE *MESSIAH?*

OR DOES SOMETHING DARKER LURK WITHIN

HOPE

WRITTEN BY *DUANE SWIERCZYNSKI* • ART BY *JAMIE MCKELVIE* • COLORS BY *MATT WILSO*

HEROIC AGE: SUPER HEROES

HEROIC AGE: VILLAINS

HEROIC AGE
SUPER HEROES & VILLAINS

Head Writer/Coordinator
MICHAEL HOSKIN

Writers
CHAD ANDERSON, ANTHONY FLAMINI, ROB LONDON, SEAN MCQUAID, KEVIN GARCIA, MARKUS RAYMOND, GABRIEL SCHECTER, DAVID WILTFONG, PETER SANDERSON, STUART VANDAL & MADISON CARTER

OHotMU Overseer
JEFF CHRISTIANSEN WITH STUART VANDAL

Super Heroes Cover Artists
TOM RANEY WITH JOHN RAUCH
Villains Cover Artists
JAE LEE WITH JUNE CHUNG
Book Design
RODOLFO MURAGUCHI

Editor
JEFF YOUNGQUIST
Editors, Special Projects
JENNIFER GRÜNWALD & MARK D. BEAZLEY
Assistant Editors
ALEX STARBUCK & NELSON RIBEIRO
Editorial Assistants
JAMES EMMETT & JOE HOCHSTEIN
Copy Editor
THEODORE KUTT
Senior Vice President of Sales
DAVID GABRIEL

Editor in Chief
JOE QUESADA
Publisher
DAN BUCKLEY
Executive Producer
ALAN FINE

Special thanks to **TOM BREVOORT,**
RONALD BYRD, JEFF CHRISTIANSEN, PAUL CORNELL,
CHRISTOS N. GAGE, MARK GRUENWALD, MARC GUGGENHEIM
MIKE O'SULLIVAN, OLAV ROKNE, FRED VAN LENTE, WWW.G-MART.COM
and the guys at **THE APPENDIX (WWW.MARVUNAPP.COM).**

I feel a deep excitement within me, as though a fist I held for years were finally relaxed. The future, holding all the wonder and horror it always has, lies ahead, but a sense of serenity surrounds me. I know that in the days and years to come, I will be called to challenge myself, to lead and shape others, the same mission I began in 1941 and will endure until my final rest.

I am commander of my country's arsenal of super heroes, an undertaking far greater than any assignment the Army or the Avengers ever requested. I am comfortable with the Avengers, who have been my closest comrades since I was revived in modern times. I accept that the Avengers consider me the greatest leader in our ranks, but does that make me the best candidate for leading our nation's heroes? To set the example for all Earth's heroes?

A question burned deep within me, but the answer could only be sought from a higher power. Fortunately, men in my line of work have conduits to such realms. I sought Black Crow, the Navajo mystic who calls me brother, and he placed me into a deep meditation. Guided safely by the spirit of the Crow, my consciousness seemed to travel into another place, what Black Crow calls the Dreamscape. Like a terrible melody, the very spirit of the American Dream seemed a breathing thing in this realm, but my vision was clouded, and I could only faintly sense my surroundings. I saw only a gray, misty void.

My vision cleared as a figure robed in white emerged from the mist. "Veritas," said the Crow. "Some call him Sayge, the spirit of truth. He will answer your question." I thanked the Crow and addressed Veritas:

"What makes a hero?"

With a stern voice that seemed to speak in a single breath, Veritas replied:

"Heroes reveal themselves through action and inaction, the choices which shape their destinies. Certain attributes must work together harmoniously to complete the hero's foundation.

"The first attribute is power. Without power, a hero cannot carry out their decisions and must suffer in silence, having no effect on the world around them. But power itself does not make a hero.

"The second attribute is conscience, an inner sense that lets one know what is right and what is wrong. Without conscience to guide a hero's actions, they cannot use their power heroically, in a manner that accomplishes good. But even power joined with conscience does not make a hero.

"The third attribute is a sense of responsibility to others. A hero who has power and conscience can exercise their power to prevent others from coming to harm, but they are called to go beyond their own wishes and aid others, without thought of personal gain. The sense of responsibility guides heroes who have power and conscience to choose to help others for the sake of helping others. But even these three attributes do not complete a hero.

"The fourth attribute is wisdom. In spite of power, conscience and responsibility, a hero still requires the discernment granted by wisdom to know the best means by which they can help others. But even with four attributes, the hero is unfinished.

"The fifth attribute is courage. Having achieved power, conscience, responsibility and wisdom, a hero must possess the courage to risk their own life for the cause of heroism. But despite having found courage, the hero's character is still in progress.

"The sixth attribute is determination. Even the most powerful, conscientious, responsible, wise and courageous hero must suffer disappointment and failure. A true hero finds the determination to persevere in the face of overwhelming odds, but even still, this hero is incomplete.

"The seventh attribute is free will. Those who have been forced by others to perform heroic deeds like an automaton must discover the spark of heroism within their souls. So much more wonderful are those heroes who choose to set their power, conscience, responsibility, wisdom, courage and determination to the banner of heroism, but even such a hero lacks one quality.

"The eighth and last attribute is limitations. No true hero possesses unlimited power, for such a being would lack both courage and determination. The closer one is to their mortality, the better able they are to wield their power, conscience, responsibility, wisdom, courage, determination and free will together. It is in the struggle of mortals against the infinite power of the universe that you behold completed heroes."

I absorbed Veritas' words, grappling with them in my heart. "I want to believe that you speak the truth," I answered, "but how can I trust in my own ability to know truth?"

Veritas drew his hands up to the sides of his hood. "Soldier, know truth," he said. As the hood lowered from his head, I gazed upon his face; it was like nothing of Earth, a brilliant white light more perfect than anything in existence. As the light bathed me, my thoughts expanded; new revelations came to me and I understood myself, my comrades, and my mission. But then the meditation ended.

That was an hour ago.

Already the peace I knew with Veritas has begun to lift, and my mind is filled again with the world's needs. Tomorrow, I will set my will to fighting for the defenseless, but today, I concern myself with my fellow heroes. Power, conscience, responsibility, wisdom, courage, determination, free will and limitations. I can still sense these qualities in Earth's heroes, to varying degrees. And so, I have applied this document to the analysis of heroes. The certainty I have now will soon fade, but in the days to come, this record of my fellow heroes of the here and now will remind me of the content of their characters, the true bearing of their hearts and the measure of their souls.

A-BOMB

AFFILIATIONS:
Hulk, Avengers

STATUS: Free agent; identity protected

When I was first awakened from the iceberg, I was overwhelmed with the loss of Bucky; I had no idea at the time that Bucky had been taken by the Soviets. When I met Rick Jones, I saw that same warrior spirit in him, and I trained him to be a new Bucky for a time, but that didn't work out. For a while, Rick made a career for himself as a professional sidekick to me, the Hulk, Captain Marvel, and the Spaceknight Rom. Despite not having powers himself, he was instrumental to the formation of the Avengers and to the successful conclusions of the Kree-Skrull War and the Destiny War. Since my return, I've learned that both Rick and his wife, Marlo, have been transformed into gamma beings, A-Bomb and the Harpy. I need to find Rick as soon as time allows and offer him a hand of friendship and support.

PROS: Super strength, impervious to injury, natural camouflaging ability.

CONS: I understand that Rick has been struggling with his intelligence, much like the Hulk often does. Gamma radiation on the human body seldom has positive effects.

POWER GRID	1	2	3	4	5	6	7	8	9	10
POWER										
CONSCIENCE										
ALTRUISM										
WISDOM										
COURAGE										
DETERMINATION										
FREE WILL										
VULNERABILITY										

AMERICAN EAGLE

AFFILIATIONS: Navajo Nation Division of Public Safety

STATUS: Law enforcement agent; identity public

Jason Strongbow's reputation paints an imposing picture. When his brother, Ward, sold out their tribe in a secret deal with super-criminal Ulysses Klaw, Jason fought back, gaining super-powers in a radioactive accident along the way. Aided by my old friend Ben Grimm and others, Jason brought Klaw to justice, then continued fighting crime as the costumed American Eagle. Mostly active in Southwestern native communities, he's done his part against global threats like the Dire Wraiths, too. He impressed Ben, and sources at the FBI, NYPD and INTERPOL speak well of him. That being said, Strongbow's a proud, cynical man with a chip on his shoulder about racial/political issues; he can be suspicious and uncooperative in dealing with outsiders and he has proven willing to defy federal officials, escaping prosecution through his status as an authorized Navajo super-operative. He's proud, volatile, unpredictable — but I'm encouraged by his costumed identity. The name he chose and the colors he wears suggest that he and I might have more in common than we expect.

PROS: Enhanced strength, durability and senses; good crossbow marksman.

CONS: Wary of non-native authorities; hot-tempered, prone to unilateral action.

POWER GRID	1	2	3	4	5	6	7	8	9	10
POWER										
CONSCIENCE										
ALTRUISM										
WISDOM										
COURAGE										
DETERMINATION										
FREE WILL										
VULNERABILITY										

ANGEL

AFFILIATIONS: X-Men, X-Force, X-Club, X-Factor, Defenders, Champions

STATUS: Free agent; identity public

I sometimes wonder why Angel never joined the Avengers. We've had other X-Men on the team, and he fits the traditional super-hero image more than most: altruistic, attractive, non-threatening. Combining fame and fortune with his mutant power of winged flight, Warren Worthington is the kind of media-friendly hero who raises our unique profession's profile in a good way. A super hero since his teens, even before helping found the X-Men, he's highly capable and dedicated — hence our offering him Avengers membership a time or two. While he socializes avidly within the super hero community, he's mostly worked with mutant groups in recent years. Be advised: the villain Apocalypse transformed Warren into a blue-skinned, razor-winged killer called Archangel years ago, and apparently Angel's reverting to that form on occasion now. This worries me — not just because of my misgivings about lethal vigilantes, but also because a sunny personality like Angel adopting a dark persona like Archangel can't be good for Warren's mental health.

PROS: Supremely skilled flier, experienced fighter, wealthy, charismatic, influential.

CONS: Sometimes reckless, lacks raw power as Angel, ruthless and unstable as Archangel.

POWER GRID	1	2	3	4	5	6	7	8	9	10
POWER										
CONSCIENCE										
ALTRUISM										
WISDOM										
COURAGE										
DETERMINATION										
FREE WILL										
VULNERABILITY										

ANT-MAN

AFFILIATIONS: Avengers, Thunderbolts, Paladin, Visioneer, Monstro

STATUS: Free agent; identity protected

The current occupant of the Ant-Man suit is certainly different from the good men who've worn it before. Put bluntly, he's self-centered, is a well-practiced liar, and seems primarily interested in saving his own skin. He claims to have stolen the suit from SHIELD in order to escape deranged SHIELD agent Mitch Carson; Carson is certifiable, but I'm not sure if Ant-Man's story checks out, making him a thief, as well. He was also a member of Osborn's Thunderbolts, a team staffed solely by mercenaries and sociopaths. Furthermore, much of his personal conduct out of the suit has been frankly reprehensible. But I don't think he's irredeemable. He saved dozens of lives with Damage Control, attacked the Hulk when he besieged Manhattan, uncovered the Skrulls' plot to destroy the Earth, and turned on his Thunderbolts colleagues before they could present the Spear of Odin, a weapon of incalculable power, to Norman Osborn. These aren't the acts of a coward. There's the potential for greatness in Ant-Man, and if he's willing to man up, I have just the team for him.

PROS: Very resourceful, adept with the Ant-Man suit.

CONS: Amoral, compulsive liar.

POWER GRID	1	2	3	4	5	6	7	8	9	10
POWER										
CONSCIENCE										
ALTRUISM										
WISDOM										
COURAGE										
DETERMINATION										
FREE WILL										
VULNERABILITY										

ANTI-VENOM

AFFILIATIONS: Spider-Man, Punisher

STATUS: Free agent, fugitive; identity public

When embittered reporter Eddie Brock merged with Spider-Man's discarded alien costume, they became the nightmarish Venom and plagued Spider-Man's life for years. Brock eventually separated from the creature, which moved on to other hosts, but recently something, possibly another symbiote or a delayed reaction to the residual symbiote tissue in his body, transformed Brock into Anti-Venom. Brock was pardoned for his crimes as Venom, as he claimed that the symbiote's malign influence drove him to murder. Having been host to one of the vile things for a brief time myself, I can believe him. He's since taken on New York's drug dealers with his new powers, which can now heal as well as kill. Brock may still be mentally unstable, and I've heard disturbing reports of a lethal rampage involving Anti-Venom, the Punisher, and a drug cartel in Mexico. I don't know if I'm comfortable with Brock running loose on the streets; at the very least, I'd like to bring him in for evaluation.

PROS: Seeming commitment to change, powerful healing abilities.

CONS: Possibly psychologically unstable, overenthusiastic.

POWER GRID	1	2	3	4	5	6	7	8	9	10
POWER										
CONSCIENCE										
ALTRUISM										
WISDOM										
COURAGE										
DETERMINATION										
FREE WILL										
VULNERABILITY										

AQUARIAN

AFFILIATIONS: The Command, Initiative, Project: PEGASUS

STATUS: Free agent; identity protected

The Aquarian has a peculiar background. Known originally as Wundarr, he was born on another planet and sent to Earth in a spacecraft that landed in the Florida swamp where the Man-Thing lives. Wundarr emerged from his ship a full-grown adult with the mind of a child. Eventually, Wundarr was taken into custody by the energy research complex Project: PEGASUS, where he came into contact with the Cosmic Cube, finally achieving the mind and maturity of an adult. But rather than becoming a superhuman adventurer, he became a kind of preacher as the Aquarian, advocating non-violence and spiritual enlightenment. In fact, he even generates an energy-dampening field that nullifies any force used against him. More recently, Wundarr has seemingly abandoned this path and joined the Initiative. Even though I see myself as a soldier for justice, I admired the Aquarian's commitment to his pacifist philosophy and wonder if he will return to his mission of bringing peace to the world.

PROS: Superhuman strength, energy-dampening field that nullifies force used against him.

CONS: As a pacifist, the Aquarian is opposed to using violence to counter criminals.

POWER GRID	1	2	3	4	5	6	7	8	9	10
POWER										
CONSCIENCE										
ALTRUISM										
WISDOM										
COURAGE										
DETERMINATION										
FREE WILL										
VULNERABILITY										

ARABIAN KNIGHT

AFFILIATIONS: Al Mukhabarat Al A'amah

STATUS: Saudi government agent; identity protected

I barely knew the previous Arabian Knight, Abdul Qamar, but what I saw of him suggested he was a good man. I've never even met his successor, a Saudi intelligence service agent who laid claim to Qamar's mystic scimitar, sash and carpet after Qamar died, but Union Jack vouches for him, and I trust his judgment. Though the Knight's clearly loyal first to his own country, when RAID threatened London he helped defend the British capital alongside Israel's Sabra, apparently having less of a problem working together than she did. But what really impressed Jack was that when the Knight was injured too badly to stay in the fight and learned Jack was about to face an opponent who might only be stoppable by magic, he told Jack to kill him so Jack could use his scimitar, which wouldn't work for anyone else while its master lived. That willingness to surrender your own life to save others is the mark of a true hero.

PROS: Extensive covert operations training, team player.

CONS: Operates under jurisdiction of a foreign government.

POWER GRID	1	2	3	4	5	6	7	8	9	10
POWER										
CONSCIENCE										
ALTRUISM										
WISDOM										
COURAGE										
DETERMINATION										
FREE WILL										
VULNERABILITY										

ARACHNE

AFFILIATIONS: Omega Flight, Shroud, Avengers, Initiative, Force Works, Secret Defenders, CSA, Freedom Force

STATUS: Canadian government agent; identity protected

Tricked by the CSA into participating in her own mutation, she was originally dubbed Spider-Woman and assigned to Freedom Force. Her conscience drove her to betray immoral orders, and she became a fugitive until her new teammates, the Avengers' West Coast branch, cleared her with the authorities. She repeatedly proved her worth with them and other teams, including Force Works. Despite joining the Initiative, her attempt to help her boyfriend, unregistered vigilante the Shroud, evade capture, led to some of her former Avengers teammates arresting her. She still feels deeply betrayed, and guilt over his part may be contributing to Wonder Man's current black mood. Separated from her daughter, Arachne abducted the girl from the child's grandparents and fled the country. Tony Stark worked out a deal allowing Arachne to stay in Canada, working for the Canadian government in the now-defunct Omega Flight. Since returning to the US Arachne was nearly killed by the Kraven family. Madame Web blinded and turned Arachne into her successor during this conflict leaving Arachne with the power to see into the future.

PROS: Team player; superhuman strength; psi-webs; family person; clairvoyance.

CONS: Blind, ongoing custody dispute.

POWER GRID	1	2	3	4	5	6	7	8	9	10
POWER										
CONSCIENCE										
ALTRUISM										
WISDOM										
COURAGE										
DETERMINATION										
FREE WILL										
VULNERABILITY										

ASGARDIANS

ASSOCIATIONS: Avengers

STATUS: Foreign race; identities public

The existence of the Asgardian gods has always been shaped by the perpetual cycle of death and rebirth known as Ragnarok, all of which had occurred in the Asgardian dimension. However, the most recent attack on the Asgardians was nothing like the Ragnaroks of the past. Not only had Thor recreated the City of Asgard on Earth (specifically, in Caddo County, Oklahoma, near the unincorporated community of Broxton), but the Asgardians found themselves besieged not by giants and trolls but by Norman Osborn and his army of Earth-born combatants. When I saw the first shots fired on television, I knew I had to assemble a team of Earth heroes to come to Asgard's aid. Even Thor realized that the stakes had changed since previous Ragnaroks and accepted our assistance. Although Osborn's forces were defeated, Asgard was badly damaged and many of its citizens were killed during the battle. As the Asgardians begin the slow process of rebuilding their Golden Realm, we've pledged to assist our otherworldly allies in whatever capacity needed.

PROS: A warrior race of virtual immortals with superhuman strength & durability, among other innate powers; access to various magical weapons & talismans.

CONS: As a sovereign nation, Asgard's foreign policy decisions may not always coincide with US interests.

POWER GRID	1	2	3	4	5	6	7	8	9	10
POWER										
CONSCIENCE										
ALTRUISM										
WISDOM										
COURAGE										
DETERMINATION										
FREE WILL										
VULNERABILITY										

ATLAS

AFFILIATIONS: Defenders, Thunderbolts, Dallas Riordan, Masters of Evil

STATUS: Free agent; identity public

Erik Josten ran from his family to join the Army, then fled that to become a mercenary, finally finding direction in the employ of my nemesis Heinrich Zemo — but fled again when Heinrich was inadvertently killed while fighting me. Though given superhuman strength and durability via Heinrich's ionic ray machines and then size-changing powers via Pym Particles, Josten never recaptured the purpose he enjoyed under Heinrich's leadership until Helmut Zemo, Heinrich's son, enlisted him in the Masters of Evil. Josten was among the villains Helmut chose to pose as the heroic Thunderbolts team — but while Helmut secretly plotted world domination, Atlas and the other Thunderbolts eventually turned against him. Atlas won international acceptance as a hero when he nearly died sealing the Wellspring of Power, a conduit for reality-defying metahuman energies that threatened to consume the planet.

PROS: Can grow to gigantic sizes, superhuman strength & durability, skilled unarmed combatant, combat tactician.

CONS: Since his interaction with the Wellspring of Power, Atlas' size-changing powers have been erratic and unreliable; prone to manipulation by others.

POWER GRID	1	2	3	4	5	6	7	8	9	10
POWER										
CONSCIENCE										
ALTRUISM										
WISDOM										
COURAGE										
DETERMINATION										
FREE WILL										
VULNERABILITY										

AURORA

AFFILIATIONS: Northstar, Alpha Flight, X-Men, Wolverine

STATUS: Free agent (Canadian); identity public

Of the very few times I've battled alongside Alpha Flight, Aurora is one of the most complex to understand. Jeanne-Marie Beaubier and her twin brother, Jean-Paul, aka Northstar, seem to share a bond that goes beyond their powers, even further than most twins would have. She appears to suffer from dissociative identity disorder and her affection, or sometimes hatred, toward friends and family can create a distraction for her at times, even during battle. However, she is willing to push herself to her limits and beyond to accomplish a mission and is an asset for any team. She often utilizes her hand-to-hand combat training in conjunction with her flight and superhuman speed and reflexes to become a formidable opponent. At times she can use her sex appeal during battle to catch her opponent off guard, but in my opinion, someone with her abilities doesn't need to resort to those kinds of tricks.

PROS: Team player, loyalty to friends and family.

CONS: Suffers from dissociative identity disorder, usually operates under jurisdiction of the Canadian government.

POWER GRID	1	2	3	4	5	6	7	8	9	10
POWER										
CONSCIENCE										
ALTRUISM										
WISDOM										
COURAGE										
DETERMINATION										
FREE WILL										
VULNERABILITY										

BATWING

AFFILIATIONS: Initiative, Shadow Initiative

STATUS: Free agent; identity protected

Mutated by contaminated water into a bat-like being, this young man has my full sympathy. He lost his father at a young age and was rejected by his father, who perceived his mutation as demonic. Forced into a life on the streets of New York City and feared by everyone, Batwing was branded a menace. Fortunately, he shared his diary with Spider-Man, who brought him to Dr. Curt Connors. Connors eventually found a way to revert Batwing to human form, a process that proved only temporary. Forced to join the Initiative upon becoming Batwing again, he worked hard to improve his skills and survived Osborn's reign against all odds, despite being placed in the Shadow Initiative as cannon fodder. He even fought against the criminals Osborn placed in the Initiative and recently joined fellow Initiative recruit Butterball in North Carolina to replace the criminal U-Foes. I'm glad Batwing found a quiet state like North Carolina where he could protect citizens. Hopefully the locals will see through his monstrous appearance. Nobody should tremble in fear of him.

PROS: Flight, night vision, ultrasound.

CONS: Light sensitivity, unstable mutation.

POWER GRID	1	2	3	4	5	6	7	8	9	10
POWER										
CONSCIENCE										
ALTRUISM										
WISDOM										
COURAGE										
DETERMINATION										
FREE WILL										
VULNERABILITY										

BEAST

AFFILIATIONS: Avengers, X-Men, Wonder Man

STATUS: Free agent; identity public

Henry McCoy is by far one of the most brilliant scientists in the world, and his intellect is matched by his agility and quick wit. McCoy has gone through various transformations to his appearance, gaining increasingly animalistic physical characteristics with every new metamorphosis, hence the code name "Beast." A name that is all too fitting as the mutation forces him to wrestle with his identity, fearing that others see him as less than human, though he remains the same man inside. Even though McCoy was born a mutant, he is one of the few that has transcended above the typical mutant stereotype if you will and often viewed as a super

hero by the public more than anything. I think his approach to being an unofficial liaison for mutants during his inaugural membership as an Avenger has helped him bridge the gap between humans and mutants. He is an asset to any team in both the field and as a think-tank, and I for one am glad that he has joined the Avengers once more.

PROS: Extremely intelligent; super-strong, agile; team player, loyal to friends; dedicated to solving scientific problems.

CONS: His dedication to science and helping others sometimes cause him more harm than good.

POWER GRID	1	2	3	4	5	6	7	8	9	10
POWER										
CONSCIENCE										
ALTRUISM										
WISDOM										
COURAGE										
DETERMINATION										
FREE WILL										
VULNERABILITY										

BENGAL

AFFILIATIONS: Initiative (Shadow Initiative)

STATUS: Free agent (Vietnamese); identity protected

Bengal is a prime example of how a well-intentioned but poorly-executed foreign policy can turn potential allies into sworn enemies. Born in the remote jungles of Vietnam, he was left for dead as a child after witnessing American military forces indiscriminately murdering his friends and family members. His village's only known survivor, Bengal subjected himself to rigorous training from that day forward so that he could eventually avenge the deaths of his loved ones. As an adult, he traveled to the US and made good on his vow to kill several of the soldiers involved in his village's massacre; but gave up his quest for vengeance upon falling in love with and marrying an American woman. With a family of his own for the first time in over a decade, Bengal registered

with the government and was quickly assigned to the Shadow Initiative, an elite strike force specializing in black ops missions. Bengal dutifully remained with the Initiative, even under the leadership of Norman Osborn, and managed to survive under great adversity when Osborn repurposed the Shadow Initiative as cannon fodder to use in human wave attacks. Bengal is currently operating a martial arts school in Brooklyn, New York.

PROS: Excellent martial artist, acrobat, archer & tracker; extensive espionage training; fiercely loyal.

CONS: Foreign citizen; criminal record in US.

POWER GRID	1	2	3	4	5	6	7	8	9	10
POWER										
CONSCIENCE										
ALTRUISM										
WISDOM										
COURAGE										
DETERMINATION										
FREE WILL										
VULNERABILITY										

BETA RAY BILL

AFFILIATIONS: Thor, Omega Flight, Star Masters

STATUS: Free agent (extraterrestrial); identity protected

After I once briefly lifted Thor's hammer, he told me that a bond exists between all those who have proven worthy to hold it. If that's the case, then despite my limited personal experience with Beta Ray Bill, it is a bond I share with him as well. Thor has consistently spoken highly of Beta Ray Bill, considering him a brother-in-arms. Bill has suffered much, with Galactus recently consuming his native world, apparently exterminating Bill's people. Although I'm told the Korbinites have returned from seeming extinction before, the experience has profoundly changed Bill.

Nonetheless, he retains his capacity for heroism and self sacrifice, as seen when he was recently active on Earth. Despite visiting Earth many times, Bill has never stayed for long, pulled away by his responsibilities to his people, as well as his natural inclination as a wanderer. Although I don't know Bill personally, I trust Thor's word and remain confident that he will continue his acts of heroism, no matter where his travels bring him.

PROS: Extremely powerful, noble, and self sacrificing.

CONS: Traumatized by the apparent destruction of his people.

POWER GRID	1	2	3	4	5	6	7	8	9	10
POWER										
CONSCIENCE										
ALTRUISM										
WISDOM										
COURAGE										
DETERMINATION										
FREE WILL										
VULNERABILITY										

BIG HERO 6

AFFILIATIONS: Alpha Flight

STATUS: Japanese government agents; identities protected

Baron Nushima. Lady Lotus. Captain Okada and his Sea Dragon. When I began my career as Captain America, much of my time was spent battling agents of the Empire of Japan hell-bent on toppling the US government. Thankfully, much has changed in the decades since then, and Big Hero 6 — a team recruited and funded by a top-secret consortium of Japanese politicians and business entities — have the potential to become key partners in our mission of maintaining global peace and security. Assisted by his robotic synthformer bodyguard Baymax, teen genius Hiro Takachiho serves as the team's field leader and strategist. Secret agent Honey Lemon wields a high-tech "Power-Purse" that grants her access to items from other worlds and dimensions, while ex-convict Go-Go Tomago dons a battlesuit that can transubstantiate her body mass into thermochemical energy. The team's roster is rounded out by newcomers Wasabi No-Ginger, a master of bladed weaponry and expert chef, and Fred, a Japanese-American bound to the spirit of a giant, reptilian kaiju.

PROS: Diverse roster with connections to the scientific, governmental, business, mystical, supernatural, and criminal communities of Japan.

CONS: As operatives of the Japanese government, Big Hero 6 may embark on missions adverse to US interests.

POWER GRID	POW	CON	ALT	WIS	COU	DET	FRW	VUL
BAYMAX	8	9	8	9	10	9	7	6
FRED	9	9	9	9	10	10	8	7
GO-GO TOMAGO	8	9	9	9	10	10	8	8
HONEY LEMON	8	9	8	8	9	10	8	8
HIRO TAKACHIKO	6	9	9	10	9	10	7	9
WASABI NO-GINGER	8	9	9	9	10	10	8	8

BLACK CAT

AFFILIATIONS: Spider-Man, Heroes for Hire, Foreigner, Puma

STATUS: Free agent, fugitive; identity public

Felicia Hardy is a skilled and somewhat reformed cat burglar who is an occasional crimefighter and mercenary. She has great physical prowess, reflexes, agility, and the stamina of an Olympic level acrobat. She rarely ventures outside the boundaries of her own abilities and is generally more a street-level crimefighter, but on few occasions, usually to help Spider-Man, she will tackle any problem. Despite being seen helping other costumed heroes often, she has a tendency to side with criminals for personal gain. She seems to have a lot of good luck, and rumors persist she has some sort of psionic ability to affect probability fields. While I have only worked with Black Cat on a few occasions, Spider-Man vouches for her, and although I've questioned some of Spider-Man's associates over the years, I know that he has good judgment in character. The amount of loyalty she shows to Spider-Man makes me wonder if there isn't something between the two. However, I personally would not trust her with valuable information or objects.

PROS: Very resourceful, strong-willed, clever, and loyal.

CONS: Shady past, questionable choice in associates, self-serving at times.

POWER GRID	1	2	3	4	5	6	7	8	9	10
POWER										
CONSCIENCE										
ALTRUISM										
WISDOM										
COURAGE										
DETERMINATION										
FREE WILL										
VULNERABILITY										

BLACK KNIGHT

AFFILIATIONS: Avengers, Heroes for Hire, MI13

STATUS: UK government agent; identity public

One of the earliest Avengers, Dane Whitman took his code name from his criminal Uncle Nathan Garrett of the first Masters of Evil group. A unique blend of science and sorcery, Dane has had connections to the historical Black Knight, Sir Percy of Scandia, during King Arthur's time. A talented swordsman (though I share concerns about his lengthy connection to the Ebony Blade) proficient in multiple forms of combat, Dane has had good runs with the Avengers and other groups. I was surprised to learn he has been working with UK's MI13 in recent months. It seems he has found a new protégé in Excalibur, and I don't expect his return to American shores any time soon. I'd gladly use his skills in one of the current incarnations of the Avengers.

PROS: Team player, science training, trained swordsman with mystical connections.

CONS: Has spent periods of time lost in the past, ties to the cursed Ebony Blade have caused problems on repeated occasions. We really should consult with Dr. Strange and Dr. Voodoo about cleansing that sword once and for all.

POWER GRID	1	2	3	4	5	6	7	8	9	10
POWER										
CONSCIENCE										
ALTRUISM										
WISDOM										
COURAGE										
DETERMINATION										
FREE WILL										
VULNERABILITY										

BLACK PANTHER [T'CHALLA]

AFFILIATIONS: Wakanda, Avengers, Storm

STATUS: Wakandan royalty; identity public

As the Black Panther, my friend T'Challa is the heir a long tradition in his African kingdom of Wakanda. ach king of Wakanda undergoes rituals that enhance his hysical capabilities to superhuman levels. When we've ught, we've proved to be equally matched. I suppose you ould say that the Black Panther is a Wakandan version of a uper-soldier," only he gains his powers from supernatural ther than scientific means. I first met T'Challa when we ined forces against an impostor posing as my old wartime emy Heinrich Zemo. We became friends, so it was rprising to learn that he subsequently joined the Avengers order to spy on us. But T'Challa soon came to regard

the Avengers as allies, not potential adversaries. As king of Wakanda, T'Challa has sometimes been at odds with the United States, but always due to his moral principles. I've always found him to be steadfastly loyal to his sense of ethics and to his friends. I won't forget how he sided with me against the Superhuman Registration Act during the super heroes' "Civil War."

PROS: Natural leader, superb strategist; master of armed and unarmed combat.

CONS: T'Challa's first loyalty is to Wakanda, and therefore sometimes opposes American interests.

POWER GRID	1	2	3	4	5	6	7	8	9	10
POWER										
CONSCIENCE										
ALTRUISM										
WISDOM										
COURAGE										
DETERMINATION										
FREE WILL										
VULNERABILITY										

BLACK PANTHER [SHURI]

AFFILIATIONS: Wakanda

STATUS: Wakandan royalty; identity public

Every time I think I have learned to trust T'Challa (who I recommended to the Avengers in the first place), I learn more secrets from his past. He has kept so many things from me over the years. I understand his eed to protect his country's integrity (I was in Wakanda uring the war), but he has spied on the Avengers, and w I learn that he has a sister that I never knew about. nlike his "brother" Hunter (the White Wolf), Shuri is Challa's actual sister, and she has taken on the role of e Black Panther after T'Challa's recent fall. She has

caused large amounts of havoc recently while active on American soil, battling American criminals. No good can come from this war between Wakanda and Latveria, and to make matters worse, over a dozen American citizens are involved. I'll have to keep a close eye on Wakanda's situation; I just wish I could trust T'Challa and Shuri to be clear with me on their intentions.

PROS: Unknown; hopefully counts her brother's allies among her own.

CONS: Loyalties are only to Wakanda, unknown quantity and motivations.

POWER GRID	1	2	3	4	5	6	7	8	9	10
POWER										
CONSCIENCE										
ALTRUISM										
WISDOM										
COURAGE										
DETERMINATION										
FREE WILL										
VULNERABILITY										

BLACK TARANTULA

AFFILIATIONS: Daredevil, the Hand, various criminal elements

STATUS: Free agent (Argentinian), fugitive; identity public

I truly believe in second chances, and I have seen everal former criminals and terrorists reinvent themselves s heroes (from the Scarlet Witch to Songbird), but at what oint do we draw a line? Luke's work with the Thunderbolts ould help me answer that question. Carlos LaMuerto n a criminal empire. He's a powerful foreign operative, convicted murderer, with no loyalties to anyone. After rming a tenuous alliance with Daredevil in recent onths, he now seems to work for the Hand in their New ork operations, and according to the reports I've seen, he

was actually killed and resurrected by the Hand, much like Elektra once was (and we all know how that turned out). Association with Daredevil is not enough for me to be able to trust this dangerous man. We need answers, and soon, about LaMuerto and the White Tiger as well.

PROS: Powerful skill set, including deadly fighting skills, force blasts, super strength, and the ability to heal himself and others from otherwise mortal injuries

CONS: Strong affiliations to dangerous foreign powers and criminal elements

POWER GRID	1	2	3	4	5	6	7	8	9	10
POWER										
CONSCIENCE										
ALTRUISM										
WISDOM										
COURAGE										
DETERMINATION										
FREE WILL										
VULNERABILITY										

BLACK WIDOW

AFFILIATIONS: Avengers, Russian intelligence, Champions, SHIELD, Thunderbolts, former partner of Daredevil

STATUS: Free agent (Russian); identity public

I've known Natasha Romanova since she was a child. Strange as it seems, that was nearly seventy years ago, and she still looks as if she's in her twenties. Wolverine, her old friend Ivan Petrovitch and I rescued her from Baron Strucker and the Hand back in 1941on the island of Madripoor. She was special even then. The Soviet government trained her from childhood to become a sort of super-soldier, greatly slowing her aging. She became a leading operative for Russian intelligence. When I first encountered her, she led Power Man and Swordsman in battling the Avengers. But Natasha had fallen in love with Hawkeye and defected to the US. Although at first she disagreed with our code against killing, over the years she has proved to be a valuable and devoted member of the Avengers, even becoming team leader. Although she and I were on opposite sides of the "Civil War," Natasha has long been my loyal and trusted ally. At the top of the field in athletics, hand-to-hand combat techniques and espionage skills, Natasha is the consummate professional.

PROS: Extraordinary athletic skills, mastery of espionage techniques, excellent leadership abilities.

CONS: Has sometimes been on opposite side from myself on ethical issues, such as the Superhuman Registration Act.

POWER GRID	1	2	3	4	5	6	7	8	9	10
POWER										
CONSCIENCE										
ALTRUISM										
WISDOM										
COURAGE										
DETERMINATION										
FREE WILL										
VULNERABILITY										

BLADE

AFFILIATIONS: MI13, SHIELD, Howling Commandos, Nightstalkers, Midnight Sons, Nine, Bloodshadows

STATUS: UK government agent; identity protected

Blade was born in the same era I was, but that is pretty much all we have in common. A vampire variant known as Dhampir, Blade is a dangerous individual whose sole purpose is to hunt down and kill all vampires on Earth. He is doing a good job and has worked with many other famous vampire hunters against the bloodsuckers, demons and other monstrosities. Despite being a loner, he also works pretty well in a team, bringing along a vast arsenal of weapons and knowledge of supernatural threats. What irks me is that his agenda against vampires often overshadows everything else, which occasionally brings him into conflict with allies. Staking a vampire teammate or shooting an ally in the kneecaps is not teamwork. He still has a pretty good track record against dangerous vampires and other supernatural threats. Last I heard, he was working for Britain's MI13 and, surprisingly, is romantically involved with Spitfire, herself a vampire. I hope he is available if we run into his kin.

PROS: Skilled hand-to-hand combatant, expert on vampires.

CONS: One-track mind, vampire, works for British government.

POWER GRID	1	2	3	4	5	6	7	8	9	10
POWER										
CONSCIENCE										
ALTRUISM										
WISDOM										
COURAGE										
DETERMINATION										
FREE WILL										
VULNERABILITY										

BLAZING SKULL

AFFILIATIONS: Defenders, Invaders

STATUS: Free agent; identity protected

Of all of my WWII-era allies, Blazing Skull is uniquely peculiar. Even back then, he was unorthodox, but sane at least. At the beginning of the war, he was a pacifist reporter who used the powers given to him by a subterranean race of Skull-Men to foil Nazi plots, but over the years, he became an advocate of a stronger military. Not too long ago, he was found alive — having barely aged since I last saw him — held captive for years in the Middle East. His imprisonment greatly strained his sanity, but not his fighting spirit. Brought into a new incarnation of the Invaders, he has since bounced from team to team, trying to find a direction and purpose for his life in a modern world. After the ill-conceived Invaders disbanded, Skull found his way into the Initiative and was placed on the Defenders team, which saw just as little success. He stuck with the program after that, slowly working on regaining the mind he once had.

PROS: Near-indestructible; investigative skills.

CONS: Questionable sanity.

POWER GRID	1	2	3	4	5	6	7	8	9	10
POWER										
CONSCIENCE										
ALTRUISM										
WISDOM										
COURAGE										
DETERMINATION										
FREE WILL										
VULNERABILITY										

BLONDE PHANTOM

AFFILIATIONS: All-Winners Squad, She-Hulk

STATUS: Free agent; identity protected

A fellow hero from the 1940s, the Blonde Phantom has a long reputation for crime-busting and sleuthing. Although she retired around 1949, she renewed contact with the super-hero community when she worked with She-Hulk during She-Hulk's time with the New York district attorney's office. Operating under her civilian identity, the Blonde Phantom assisted in several adventures through time and space, forging contacts with various humans and alien cultures. The Blonde Phantom was instrumental in bringing peace between She-Hulk, Spragg the Living Hill and the Mole Man, and after an incident involving a strange subterranean mineral, she regained her youth and vitality. Her physical condition has since fluctuated, due to

dietary concerns rather than age, but she recently resumed her costumed identity to solve a friend's murder. Time will tell if she continues to operate as a masked hero. Blonde Phantom's legacy has also been picked up by the younger generation, as the youthful Phantom Blonde has expressed interest in adventuring and was considered for recruitment under the first iteration of the Initiative.

PROS: Team player, experienced detective, skilled negotiator, decades of experience.

CONS: Often operates outside the law, possible eating disorder, decades of inactivity.

POWER GRID	1	2	3	4	5	6	7	8	9	10
POWER										
CONSCIENCE										
ALTRUISM										
WISDOM										
COURAGE										
DETERMINATION										
FREE WILL										
VULNERABILITY										

ELSA BLOODSTONE

AFFILIATIONS: Nextwave Squad, Frankenstein's Monster

STATUS: Free agent; no dual identity

There have been numerous so-called "monster hunters" in our line of business, some more noble than others. One that I had the utmost respect for, though our paths rarely crossed, was Ulysses Bloodstone. Though he is no longer with us, his daughter Elsa carries on the family tradition in part thanks to a choker she wears that carries part of the Bloodstone gem in it. Still relatively untrained, the young woman has shown a knack for the job, though I worry about the company she keeps on occasion in the Nextwave Squad, most notably the Captain. Still, although she's untested, I see potential

here. Her work cataloging the various "creatures of the night" across the globe helped the previous SHIELD incarnation immensely with their ill-conceived Howling Commandos unit. She's fearless and takes her role seriously, striving to honor her father's legacy. She will need to be watched closely, and hopefully she can retain her humanity in a very ugly line of work.

PROS: Team player, research skills; superhuman athlete; regenerative (full level untested).

CONS: Still fairly untrained; memories tampered with by H.A.T.E.; poor influences, treading a fine moral line.

POWER GRID	1	2	3	4	5	6	7	8	9	10
POWER										
CONSCIENCE										
ALTRUISM										
WISDOM										
COURAGE										
DETERMINATION										
FREE WILL										
VULNERABILITY										

BLUE SHIELD

AFFILIATIONS: Initiative, Project: PEGASUS, Dazzler, Quasar, Barrigan crime family

STATUS: Active adventurer; identity protected

Hard to get a read on this guy. Not sure where he got his force field-generating, strength-augmenting belt, but we do know it mutated him over time, so he now has the belt's powers himself. Blue Shield started out as an anti-mob vigilante, spent his whole early life trying to take down the Barrigan crime family because they caused his father's death. Seemed a bit lost after the Barrigan gang fell apart. Applied to the Avengers, but he was overeager and lacked teamwork skills, so we rejected him. Landed a top job as Project: PEGASUS security director, quit after blaming himself for a security

breach, came back, eventually quit again. Later active with the Initiative as a solo licensed super hero in New York. Quasar, the Avenger who knows him best, says the Shield's a good man apart from lacking direction and self-confidence. That description would have fit Quasar himself once upon a time, and he's one of our best, so maybe the Blue Shield is destined for bigger things someday.

PROS: Force field, enhanced physical abilities; experienced fighter; security expertise; organized crime expert.

CONS: Used to working solo; violent temper, self-confidence issues.

POWER GRID	1	2	3	4	5	6	7	8	9	10
POWER										
CONSCIENCE										
ALTRUISM										
WISDOM										
COURAGE										
DETERMINATION										
FREE WILL										
VULNERABILITY										

ABIGAIL BRAND

AFFILIATIONS:
SWORD., Beast

STATUS: Government agent; identity public

Though I have had little personal contact with Abigail Brand (outside of that bizarre Breakworld bullet incident, in which the Earth was nearly destroyed), I hear only the best about her from trusted allies like her boyfriend the Beast, though his opinion may be slightly biased. Brand is a half-extraterrestrial woman who has employed several alien operatives in the SWORD. organization. This in itself is not a concern (I've worked with many honorable aliens, such as Mar-Vell and Starfox), but I am concerned with how she chose to conduct herself in recent months when Henry Gyrich tried taking over her organization. She's a skilled commander, but she seems to only follow her own agenda. I'll have to work at forming a close alliance with her, and soon. There are a lot of alien presences still on Earth, we still haven't cleaned up from the Maximum Security or Skrull incidents, and it'll be impossible for me to keep an eye on all of them myself.

PROS: Independent operative, willing to do what it takes to get things done.

CONS: Has recently been on the outs with the government under Osborn's regime.

POWER GRID	1	2	3	4	5	6	7	8	9	10
POWER										
CONSCIENCE										
ALTRUISM										
WISDOM										
COURAGE										
DETERMINATION										
FREE WILL										
VULNERABILITY										

BRIDE OF NINE SPIDERS

AFFILIATIONS: Iron Fist, Fat Cobra, Prince of Orphans

STATUS: Free agent; identity protected

Of the Immortal Weapons, we know the least about the Bride of Nine Spiders, the champion of an unidentified mystical city; her body apparently contains a swarm of ravenous spiders, which she can unleash upon her opponents. Her dealings with Earth have been extremely limited until recently, when she allied with Iron Fist and the other Immortal Weapons to search for the Eighth Capital City of Heaven. There are scattered reports of a Bride of Nine Spiders active in Nepal in the '30s, but that was apparently the current Bride's predecessor. Iron Fist reports that she is a steadfast ally and aided him against Hydra, the demonic Ch'i-Lin, and the monstrous hordes of Changming; however, we also have a report that implicates her in the deaths of an antiquities collector and his family. She seems to be more inhuman and otherworldly than the rest of the Weapons, and I recommend that we avoid her unless absolutely necessary; there are other mystic warriors we can more easily call upon.

PROS: Decades of combat experience and martial arts mastery.

CONS: Unpredictable nature; linked to at least one murder case.

POWER GRID	1	2	3	4	5	6	7	8	9	10
POWER										
CONSCIENCE										
ALTRUISM										
WISDOM										
COURAGE										
DETERMINATION										
FREE WILL										
VULNERABILITY										

BUTTERBALL

AFFILIATIONS: Batwing, Gorilla Girl, Speedball, Initiative

STATUS: Free agent; identity protected

I've met, and fought, plenty of people with invulnerability. For almost all of them, there's some limit — one thing that can hurt them, one spot where they can be injured, one possible weakness. If Butterball has a limit, we haven't found it yet. He's also spiritually tough; even after washing out of the Initiative, he signed back up to join Norman Osborn's Shadow Initiative, and currently defends Morganton, North Carolina, with his friend Batwing. I think he's thrilled just to be a super hero now, but with his powers, he could be of great help in a search-and-rescue or hazardous environment exploration situation. Normally, I'd blanch at sending someone so unprepared into harm's way, but I'm not sure it's possible to put Butterball in harm's way. He could be a valuable asset; I don't recommend we put him into active duty with an Avengers team, but for certain missions, his peculiar power set could be highly advantageous.

PROS: Totally indestructible, boundless enthusiasm.

CONS: No potential for physical improvement, can be overbearing in the presence of figures he admires.

POWER GRID	1	2	3	4	5	6	7	8	9	10
POWER										
CONSCIENCE										
ALTRUISM										
WISDOM										
COURAGE										
DETERMINATION										
FREE WILL										
VULNERABILITY										

LUKE CAGE

AFFILIATIONS: Thunderbolts, Avengers, Heroes for Hire, Iron Fist

STATUS: Free agent; identity public

When I asked Luke to join the Avengers, he let me know that he was going to have a different way of doing things, and that he would want to be heard. Luke proved to be an innovative and original team member, always sticking to his guns. He has an intense character, passionate in his beliefs and loyal to a fault. Luke is a devoted family man and puts the safety of his wife and daughter before everything else. He also has a long-standing close friendship with Iron Fist and gained a great deal of team experience through their lengthy partnership.

As a street hero, Luke was always interested in addressing more down-to-earth problems than most heroes and is painfully aware of social ills and inequalities. Perhaps this awareness contributes to his sometimes short temper, but there are few heroes I'd rather have guarding my back than Luke Cage. I trust he'll continue to make me proud in his new position with the Thunderbolts.

PROS: Good leadership skills; experienced team member; intensely loyal.

CONS: Sometimes loses his temper; his family has been exploited as a weakness in the past.

POWER GRID	1	2	3	4	5	6	7	8	9	10
POWER										
CONSCIENCE										
ALTRUISM										
WISDOM										
COURAGE										
DETERMINATION										
FREE WILL										
VULNERABILITY										

CAPTAIN AMERICA

AFFILIATIONS: Avengers, Liberty Legion, Kid Commandos, Invaders, Young Allies

STATUS: Free agent; identity protected

I cannot say enough about my successor, nor could I imagine a better man to bear the shield. That is no slight to others who have borne the same Captain America, but I have known Bucky through the toughest battles of World War II, and more recently, through his personal recovery after years as a mind-controlled assassin working for foreign interests. Even as a teen, he was one of the most highly trained fighters among the Allies and often willing and able to take steps that caused me to hesitate. Add to this his skills with firearms and the shield, and his bionic arm courtesy of Nick Fury, and this Captain America is a force to be reckoned with. Initially, I was unsure about allowing such a young man onto the battlefield, but the top brass and his own moxie soon convinced me otherwise. He was my closest friend throughout the war, and after I thought him lost, I held out hope he would be found alive. Now he is back, and I stand by him as Captain America.

PROS: Master combatant, experienced leader, loyal yet willing to question authority when necessary.

CONS: Possible psychological trauma from years as a brainwashed assassin.

POWER GRID	1	2	3	4	5	6	7	8	9	10
POWER										
CONSCIENCE										
ALTRUISM										
WISDOM										
COURAGE										
DETERMINATION										
FREE WILL										
VULNERABILITY										

CAPTAIN BRITAIN

AFFILIATIONS: MI13, Avengers, Excalibur

STATUS: UK government agent; identity public

Brian Braddock and I are remarkably similar on many levels — both chosen by others to represent our countries and striving to uphold the ideals those nations stand for, without overlooking the mistakes they sometimes make. Unlike myself, Brian wasn't exactly a volunteer, but he takes his responsibility seriously; he's overcome the doubts of his past and a tendency for impetuous action to become the UK's premier hero. We've known each other since early in his career, and I trust him implicitly; except for one obvious problem, if Bucky wasn't around and I had to choose a new Captain America, Brian would be a prime contender.

I understand he's gone through a literal rebirth recently, and like most British heroes these days he works for Britain's Extraordinary Intelligence Service (colloquially, MI13). Especially after what happened here with Registration, hearing that any country has drafted their entire super-hero population should ring warning bells, but Brian's involvement reassures me greatly, if not completely.

PROS: Scientific genius armed with high-end magical abilities, exceptional integrity.

CONS: Powers dependent on confidence. Operates under jurisdiction of foreign government.

POWER GRID	1	2	3	4	5	6	7	8	9	10
POWER										
CONSCIENCE										
ALTRUISM										
WISDOM										
COURAGE										
DETERMINATION										
FREE WILL										
VULNERABILITY										

CAPTAIN ULTRA

AFFILIATIONS: Initiative, Defenders, Doc Samson

STATUS: Government agent; identity public

Griffin Gogol claims he was an ordinary plumber until an elderly psychiatrist paid for Gogol's sink-fixing services with hypnotherapy; according to Gogol, the old man turned out to be an alien whose hypnosis unlocked Gogol's superhuman potential. Since then, he's developed super-powers like enhanced physical abilities (especially strength), flight, X-ray vision, intangibility, a sonic scream and more, with new powers emerging over time. In fact, Gogol may literally have more super-powers then he knows what to do with. He's hovered on the fringes of the super-hero community for years, briefly joining the Defenders, pursuing stand-up comedy, and quarreling with fellow heroes like Hellcat, Jack of Hearts and Thor. Ultra seemed to find a niche as leader of Nebraska's Initiative team, though he resented this low-profile posting. When his teammates Gadget & Paragon died, an insecure Ultra hindered the ensuing investigation as much as he helped it, though then-Initiative Director Iron Man's overall assessment of Gogol thereafter was marginally positive. With a bit more training and a lot less attitude, Ultra could be a real asset.

PROS: Wide variety of super-powers, Initiative training, knowledgeable regarding Nebraska.

CONS: Sizable yet fragile ego, quick temper, resents successful peers, formerly suffered from pyrophobia.

POWER GRID	1	2	3	4	5	6	7	8	9	10
POWER										
CONSCIENCE										
ALTRUISM										
WISDOM										
COURAGE										
DETERMINATION										
FREE WILL										
VULNERABILITY										

CHALLENGER

AFFILIATIONS: Freedom Force, Initiative

STATUS: Government agent; identity protected

The Challenger fought alongside many heroes during World War II and fought his share of opponents, including the League of Crime. He began adventuring after his father was murdered for attempting to blow the whistle on government corruption and organized crime. While other heroes used weapons or abilities to fight crime, the Challenger became obsessed with his interpretation of fairness. This meant he would only fight criminals if they were on equal grounds, even arming his opponents in the name of equality. As a result, some of his attempts to capture enemies had fatal consequences. Under circumstances I have not been made privy to yet, he reappeared in New York recently, apparently as young and vital as ever. The Goodman, Lieber, Kurtzberg and Holliway law firm helped him reclaim both his status and former property since he'd been declared legally dead. He joined the Initiative early on, becoming leader of Montana's Freedom Force. Although he fought bravely in the Skrull invasion, Challenger attempted to capture Justice's Avengers Resistance on Norman Osborn's orders, but refused to participate in the siege of Asgard.

PROS: Master of multiple weapons and fighting styles, team player, battlefield experience.

CONS: Competitive attitude, obsessive tendencies, possible unfamiliarity with modern values.

POWER GRID	1	2	3	4	5	6	7	8	9	10
POWER										
CONSCIENCE										
ALTRUISM										
WISDOM										
COURAGE										
DETERMINATION										
FREE WILL										
VULNERABILITY										

AMADEUS CHO

AFFILIATIONS: Hercules, the Olympus Group, Athena, Thor, Hulk

STATUS: Free agent; no dual identity

The 17-year-old CEO of the Olympus Group is a relative unknown and newcomer to the super-hero scene. Cho's life has gone through a series of drastic transformations within the past year: minutes after achieving the highest score on the Excello Soap Company's online "Brain Fight" game, he was approached by an unidentified figure wishing to train him for a higher purpose. Refusing the stranger's offer, Cho's family was killed and he went on the road, eventually developing a devotion to the Hulk following a chance encounter. During the Hulk's attack on New York City, Cho assembled a team of the Hulk's old allies, including the demigod Hercules, in an attempt to help him; but upon the Hulk's surrender, Cho and Hercules were briefly taken into SHIELD custody before escaping. The extent and nature of their travels together is unknown; however, upon Hercules recent demise, Cho has inherited his Golden Mace and been installed as CEO of the Olympus Group, a powerful business organization founded by the Olympian gods on Earth. Though highly intelligent and resourceful, I question whether young Mr. Cho has the maturity and experience to wield his newfound power responsibly.

PROS: Genius-level intellect; access to supernatural artifacts & cutting-edge scientific technology; divine allies.

CONS: Rebellious; overconfident; often exhibits immature, vengeful tendencies.

POWER GRID	1	2	3	4	5	6	7	8	9	10
POWER										
CONSCIENCE										
ALTRUISM										
WISDOM										
COURAGE										
DETERMINATION										
FREE WILL										
VULNERABILITY										

CITIZEN V

AFFILIATIONS: V-Battalion, Thunderbolts

STATUS: Free agent (UK); identity protected

I briefly knew Citizen V's grandfather, the original Citizen V, a British hero who fought behind enemy lines during World War II. Murdered by Heinrich Zemo, he sacrificed everything for freedom, and his lover, the French freedom fighter She-Wolf, carried on his legacy, as did their son years later. Now, the latest generation continues the tradition, ironically thanks to Helmut Zemo, whose possession of Citizen V's body helped bring the hero out of a comatose state. I have not met the current Citizen V, but my contemporaries the Destroyer and Human Torch speak highly of him despite some odd choices on his part. He allowed the original Flag-Smasher to take power in Rumekistan, and although Flag-Smasher has since died and a new government has arisen, I cannot condone the jeopardy he put the people of that nation in. Add to that his connection to the V-Battalion. Though run by many of my wartime allies, reports suggest its involvement in questionable operations dwarfing the Rumekistan incident; more information is needed about their goals and activities.

PROS: Skilled fighter and natural athlete, master negotiator, experienced leader.

CONS: Unpredictable and apparently answers to a clandestine organization.

POWER GRID	1	2	3	4	5	6	7	8	9	10
POWER										
CONSCIENCE										
ALTRUISM										
WISDOM										
COURAGE										
DETERMINATION										
FREE WILL										
VULNERABILITY										

CLOAK

AFFILIATIONS: Dagger, X-Men, Spider-Man

STATUS: Free agent; identity protected

With his partner Dagger, Cloak exhibits a bizarre balance between light and dark. Many victims engulfed within his Darkforce have been extremely traumatized by the experience. Cloak & Dagger have made a strong showing against the New York underworld (particularly the drug trade) and have spent the many years far from the rest of the world's super heroes. Cloak was a valuable ally during the Civil War, but I never got to know him personally. Osborn manipulated this youth into joining his villainous group of X-Men, and Cloak spent a brief time with the true X-Men on Utopia as well, but it has now been confirmed, decidedly, that he is not a mutant, and he and Dagger seem to be back to being vigilantes once again. I wonder if we can't find a place for them to belong.

PROS: Unique skill set with the ability to teleport large groups.

CONS: Cloak is plagued by an overwhelming hunger, perhaps an evil influence from within his darkness. He initially killed criminals, and though that's no longer the case, Cloak often inflicts undue suffering, feeding foes to his hunger.

POWER GRID	1	2	3	4	5	6	7	8	9	10
POWER										
CONSCIENCE										
ALTRUISM										
WISDOM										
COURAGE										
DETERMINATION										
FREE WILL										
VULNERABILITY										

CLOUD 9

AFFILIATIONS: Freedom Force, Initiative, Trauma, Justice

STATUS: Government agent; identity protected

War changes people. Cloud 9 joined the Initiative solely so she could continue using her flight powers, but after seeing a fellow cadet die during a training exercise and killing Hydra troops in battle, she became a hardened, jaded soldier. Her sniping prowess also served to distance her from her fellow cadets, although she forged lasting friendships with a few of them. Whether she wants to return to who she was, and indeed if she can, is a decision only she can make; whichever path she chooses, she'll remain a valued member of the super-hero community. I'm wary of creating future Cloud 9s, however; if someone simply wants to fly, I don't see why they can't just be given the equivalent of a pilot's license; I won't dissuade anyone from joining us, but I don't want to coerce anyone, either. Military service and super-heroics aren't for everyone, and we would be wise to remember that, as much as they seem like second nature to us.

PROS: Highly skilled sniper and aerobat.

CONS: Jaded attitude can unnerve others.

POWER GRID	1	2	3	4	5	6	7	8	9	10
POWER										
CONSCIENCE										
ALTRUISM										
WISDOM										
COURAGE										
DETERMINATION										
FREE WILL										
VULNERABILITY										

COLOSSUS

AFFILIATIONS: X-Men, Excalibur, Defenders, Kitty Pryde, Wolverine, Magik, Acolytes

STATUS: Free agent; identity protected

Colossus is a Russian native, who was recruited by Professor Xavier to join the mutant team known as the X-Men. Colossus is a skilled hand-to-hand combatant with the ability to convert the tissue of his entire body into an organic steel-like substance. The only thing stronger than Colossus' strength is his heart. I still remember how grief stricken he was on Battleworld when the alien healer Zsaji perished to save us all. Beast informs me that Colossus subsequently lost his entire family to the X-Men's

foes, grief leading him to briefly join Magneto's Acolytes. However, he soon regained his senses, and later sacrificed himself to unleash the cure for the Legacy virus which threatened mutants and humans alike. It was a tragic loss, and I was happy to learn of his return. While thankful to see a comrade resurrected, I will still never understand why some heroes get a second chance at life, while others, especially the civilians we protect, do not.

PROS: Loyal, extremely dedicated; gentle demeanor and personality.

CONS: His loyalty can blind him at times.

POWER GRID	1	2	3	4	5	6	7	8	9	10
POWER										
CONSCIENCE										
ALTRUISM										
WISDOM										
COURAGE										
DETERMINATION										
FREE WILL										
VULNERABILITY										

CYCLOPS

AFFILIATIONS: X-Men, X-Factor, X-Force

STATUS: Free agent; identity public

Rarely have I seen such a transformation from a wayward teenager into an accomplished general (Bucky and Nova come to mind), and rarely have I been so concerned. I first met Scott Summers when he was a teenager and part of Charles Xavier's X-Men. I've heard of his struggles with the loss of two wives, both tragically killed, and he has witnessed mass death and intense suffering amongst his fellow mutants. Now that the mutant race has become an endangered species, Cyclops has become a man that I can barely understand, moving

his followers to an isolated island, sanctioning the deaths of their enemies, and seemingly willing to sacrifice even his most trusted allies for a "greater cause." TO
But I can't deny his effectiveness as a leader, and for that, I arranged his awarding of the presidential medal of freedom. I hope to have a close working relationship with him in the future.

PROS: Powerful leader, optic blasts, has spent entire life focused on team dynamics, strategic and tactical genius.

CONS: Willing to condone murder, sacrifice allies, and put the needs of mutants over the rest of the population.

POWER GRID	1	2	3	4	5	6	7	8	9	10
POWER										
CONSCIENCE										
ALTRUISM										
WISDOM										
COURAGE										
DETERMINATION										
FREE WILL										
VULNERABILITY										

DAGGER

AFFILIATIONS: Cloak, X-Men, Spider-Man, New Warriors, Runaways, Daredevil

STATUS: Free agent; identity protected

This young woman's vibrant enthusiasm toward life is only matched by her light-based powers. She possesses enhanced agility, reflexes, and radiates light that she projects into "light daggers," which affect her opponent's metabolism. It is rumored that her powers can cure drug addiction. She has a tendency to surface as a street-level crimefighter every so often and then vanishes, blending in with other teenagers. Dagger is most frequently partnered to Cloak, both unwillingly empowered when the mob used them to test illegal drugs; however, she joined Daredevil's urban crimefighting team alone. Both

Cloak and Dagger were members of the Anti-Registration team during the Superhuman Registration Act debacle. Previously believed to be mutants, current information suggests that they are altered humans, which I am sure has left the two wondering where they belong in the world. Both Dagger and Cloak are great candidates for the Avengers Academy, which I would one day hope that I could get them to join.

PROS: Enthusiastic, moral booster, good at following orders.

CONS: Lacks experience working with team, seems dependent on Cloak.

POWER GRID	1	2	3	4	5	6	7	8	9	10
POWER										
CONSCIENCE										
ALTRUISM										
WISDOM										
COURAGE										
DETERMINATION										
FREE WILL										
VULNERABILITY										

DAMAGE CONTROL

AFFILIATIONS:
Ant-Man,
Hercules,
Wolverine

STATUS:
Free agents;
identity public

A true entrepreneur, Anne Marie Hoag started Damage Control to clean up the mess left by superhuman battles. Based in New York, the company has been active for years, being directly involved in such national crises as one of Galactus' attacks on the Earth, the aptly named "Acts of Vengeance" event, and the Hulk's war on Earth a few months back. Now that I'm working to monitor the country's super heroes, I'm going to need to keep track of the Damage Control super hero division responsible for search and rescue. The new Goliath, Visioneer, and Monstro all appear to be competent and capable operatives, and I have no concerns about them at this time. (Damage Control has also employed Ant-Man and Hercules). I'll also have to keep a close eye on their management; Wolverine claims former CEO Walter Declun dealt power-boosting MGH to Nitro, indirectly leading to the Stamford disaster. Declun has, in some way, been responsible for hiring American criminals in the war against Wakanda and bears close watching.

PROS: Competent organization with good ties to the hero community.

CONS: Entirely profit-focused.

POWER GRID	1	2	3	4	5	6	7	8	9	10
POWER										
CONSCIENCE										
ALTRUISM										
WISDOM										
COURAGE										
DETERMINATION										
FREE WILL										
VULNERABILITY										

DAREDEVIL

AFFILIATIONS: Spider-Man, Luke Cage, Iron Fist, SHIELD, Black Widow, Elektra, White Tiger, Black Tarantula, the Hand

STATUS: Free agent; identity protected

Often referred to as the "Man Without Fear," Daredevil has become the self-proclaimed guardian of Hell's Kitchen, a New York City neighborhood prominent with the city's underworld, especially the mafia crime circles. He can get overprotective of the area at times and can become easily offended another crimefighter shows up there, as he likes to maintain order himself. His fighting style tends to show that he might have been trained by a ninja himself, but has definitely become a rōnin in his own right. Recently, Daredevil's motives have become questionable in gaining order in Hell's Kitchen, including assuming the leadership of the ninja assassin group known as the Hand. The Hand is a group that can corrupt nearly anyone, and his association with them might cause problems for New York. While I trust Daredevil's judgment for the most part, his recent embargo of superhumans in Hell's Kitchen bears monitoring.

PROS: Inspires fear with the criminal elements of New York, dedicated, loyal to friends.

CONS: Association with the Hand, territorial at times.

POWER GRID	1	2	3	4	5	6	7	8	9	10
POWER										
CONSCIENCE										
ALTRUISM										
WISDOM										
COURAGE										
DETERMINATION										
FREE WILL										
VULNERABILITY										

DARKHAWK

AFFILIATIONS:
Loners,
New Warriors, Avengers

STATUS: Free agent; identity protected

According to Nova, young Darkhawk has recently discovered connections between the amulet that grants him his powers and an ancient intergalactic race called the Fraternity of Raptors. How do things like this keep happening on Earth? A young, New York-based teenager named Chris Powell discovers an amulet in an amusement park, and a few years later he is being accused of murdering the Majestrix Lilandra Neramani of the Shi'ar, one of the largest empires in the universe. Darkhawk even served as an Avenger for a brief time, working with the West Coast branch against Dr. Demonicus and with the larger group against Morgan Le Fey. In addition, he had a successful run with the New Warriors, though that doesn't exactly work in his favor at this point, given the public opinion of that team. I don't know him well, and have few ideas of how to help him in his current predicament, but I will encourage Nova to put me into contact with him. As a human, as an Avenger, he deserves our help.

PROS: Vast power source of unmeasured capabilities, including multiple battle armors and types of offensive weaponry.

CONS: Mysterious/ambiguous origins, currently on the run in an alien empire.

POWER GRID	1	2	3	4	5	6	7	8	9	10
POWER										
CONSCIENCE										
ALTRUISM										
WISDOM										
COURAGE										
DETERMINATION										
FREE WILL										
VULNERABILITY										

DAZZLER

AFFILIATIONS: X-Men, Longshot, Excalibur

STATUS: Free agent; identity public

To my knowledge, Alison Blaire has never wanted anything more than a successful career as a performing artist. Despite a difficult family background and a hidden mutant ability to transform sound into light, Alison was well on her way to success, but kept getting pulled into conflicts with heroes and villains, mutants and aliens. After being publicly revealed as a mutant, she joined the X-Men, likely more due to having nowhere else to go. Since then, I understand that she's performed intergalactically with Lila Cheney, fought as a freedom fighter in the Mojoverse, and has even been pregnant with Longshot's child (though I have no information on what happened to the baby). Now, she seems more comfortable than ever among the X-Men on Utopia as she furthers her music career. Recent rumors state her half-sister, Lois London, was involved in the mass murder on Genosha; it is unclear to what extent Dazzler was involved, if any.

PROS: Unique skill set, high regard in media and public.

CONS: Loyal to mutant population, more focused on personal concerns.

POWER GRID	1	2	3	4	5	6	7	8	9	10
POWER										
CONSCIENCE										
ALTRUISM										
WISDOM										
COURAGE										
DETERMINATION										
FREE WILL										
VULNERABILITY										

DEADPOOL

AFFILIATIONS: Deadpool Corps, Code Red, Agency X, Great Lakes Initiative, Six Pack, One World Church, Deadpool Inc., Weapon X, Team Deadpool, Heroes for Hire, Secret Defenders, Frightful Four, Department K

STATUS: Free agent, fugitive; identity protected

How someone like him could ever become a registered Initiative member is beyond me. Deadpool is a despicable assassin who would kill his grandmother if someone paid him for it. He sure is helpful if you want someone killed, but aside from his effectiveness as an assassin there is nothing good about him. Deadpool half-heartedly tried to better himself a few times, but returned to his old ways each time when it didn't work within five days. He is undisciplined, disgusting and not funny. The disturbing thing these days is that he seems to be everywhere, and people I call friends let him get away each and every time they meet him. He has even gathered a team of Deadpools, and according to rumors, they were sent on a mission to save the universe. I honestly hope this narcissist maniac gets sucked into a black hole. Unfortunately his powers make him more resilient than a cockroach. I'm sure he will cause more trouble in the future.

PROS: Healing factor, skilled combatant.

CONS: Insane, mercenary, never shuts up.

POWER GRID	1	2	3	4	5	6	7	8	9	10
POWER										
CONSCIENCE										
ALTRUISM										
WISDOM										
COURAGE										
DETERMINATION										
FREE WILL										
VULNERABILITY										

DEATH'S HEAD

AFFILIATIONS: MI13, Dark Guard

STATUS: Free agent (extra-temporal); no dual identity

Ignore his semantic insistence that he's a "freelance peacekeeping agent"; the cyborg Death's Head is a mercenary, which means he can be an ally one day and a foe the next. To make matters worse, he's also immensely powerful, closer to Thor than Batroc when it comes to the damage he can inflict. Luckily, he has a personal code of honor and won't break a contract; MI13 exploited this by putting him on retainer, so that he can't accept missions conflicting with UK interests. However, Death's Head is also a time-traveler; he's had at least two distinctive looks, and Beast recently encountered the earlier one soon after the later one helped MI13 assault Dracula's castle, so it's entirely possible to run afoul of a Death's Head who predates the one you paid to be your ally. Dr. Strange insists that Death's Head isn't completely immoral, having helped (without pay) in what Stephen calls the "Un-Earth crisis." Still, undertake any encounter with him cautiously, at least until you ascertain what side he is on that day.

PROS: Immense strength, powerful in-built weaponry. Personal code of honor.

CONS: Mercenary, casual killer.

POWER GRID	1	2	3	4	5	6	7	8	9	10
POWER										
CONSCIENCE										
ALTRUISM										
WISDOM										
COURAGE										
DETERMINATION										
FREE WILL										
VULNERABILITY										

DIAMONDBACK

AFFILIATIONS: Initiative, BAD Girls, Inc., SHIELD, Serpent Society

STATUS: Active adventurer; identity protected

Sometimes a so-called "bad girl" just needs someone to bring her back on the right track, and in Diamondback's case, I'm proud to say that it was me. When I first met her, she was part of the Serpent Society, and though she began to trust me and even called me for help, it wasn't easy for me to reciprocate that trust to a criminal like her. When she devoutly chose to go straight everything changed, and we even became involved for awhile. I was very proud when she started the BAD Girls, Inc. with fellow former Society members Black Mamba and Asp. For some time, she even considered ending her Diamondback career, but after Crossbones abducted and brutalized her she continued, and it was the right decision. With each setback she became stronger, and her good influence on the people around her set an example in the Initiative for people who really wanted to change, especially former criminals. When we first met I would never have thought that she would become one of my most trusted friends. I hope she succeeds in her future endeavors.

PROS: Team player, natural leader, skilled hand-to-hand combatant.

CONS: No superhuman powers, criminal brother.

POWER GRID	1	2	3	4	5	6	7	8	9	10
POWER										
CONSCIENCE										
ALTRUISM										
WISDOM										
COURAGE										
DETERMINATION										
FREE WILL										
VULNERABILITY										

DOCTOR STRANGE

AFFILIATIONS: Avengers, Defenders, Hulk, Namor, Jack Russell, Satana, Dr. Voodoo

STATUS: Free agent; identity protected

Doctor Strange is by far one of the most enigmatic beings I've known, most likely due to his knowledge in the mystic arts of magic, which I've never been able to grasp. Once the Earth's Sorcerer Supreme, a title he has turned over to Dr. Voodoo, he rarely involves himself in normal super hero activities, unless it involves magic, in which he is generally on the case well before you. Recently, his powers have seemed to wane, which has become troubling for him to cope with as he acts like he has lost an appendage at times. However, despite this unfortunate act, he is resilient, and I have confidence that he will overcome this obstacle. While he tends to be a loner, even during his sojourn to reacquaint himself with the mystic arts, I'd be honored to have him as an active member of the Avengers.

PROS: Master of mystic arts; team player; loyal.

CONS: Secretive; unnerved by recent power loss; will use dark magic to obtain goals at times.

POWER GRID	1	2	3	4	5	6	7	8	9	10
POWER										
CONSCIENCE										
ALTRUISM										
WISDOM										
COURAGE										
DETERMINATION										
FREE WILL										
VULNERABILITY										

DOCTOR VOODOO

AFFILIATIONS: Dr. Strange; Monica Rambeau; Midnight Sons, the Vodu

STATUS: Free agent (Haitian); identity protected

Dr. Strange informs me that Agamotto the All Seeing was the first Sorcerer Supreme, a line of mages who have protected our reality since the dawn of time. Dr. Voodoo, the Vodu's Lord of the Loa, was recently elevated to that status when the Eye of Agamotto chose his pure heart and clean soul to succeed Stephen Strange, the previous Sorcerer Supreme. Although he possesses considerable mystic knowledge and was briefly trained for his new role by his predecessor, Dr. Voodoo is still growing accustomed to his new powers and responsibilities. Unfortunately, he has inherited a position that doesn't afford much time for a learning curve, as evidenced by the continual incursions into our dimension by mystical despots such as Dormammu, Nightmare, and Shuma-Gorath. Hopefully, Dr. Voodoo realizes his full potential sooner rather than later, as it's a question as to when, not if, we'll need to call on Earth's Sorcerer Supreme for assistance.

PROS: Taps the power of the Loa to perform a wide array of mystical feats; further empowered by a tome of mystic artifacts, including the Book of the Vishanti & the Eye of Agamotto.

CONS: Still learning the powers and responsibilities that come with the position of Sorcerer Supreme.

POWER GRID	1	2	3	4	5	6	7	8	9	10
POWER										
CONSCIENCE										
ALTRUISM										
WISDOM										
COURAGE										
DETERMINATION										
FREE WILL										
VULNERABILITY										

DOG BROTHER #1

AFFILIATIONS: Iron Fist, Fat Cobra

STATUS: Free agent (Chinese?); identity protected

Dog Brother #1 is a legendary figure in Asia, but it's only recently that he's come to our attention. Dog Brother is a champion of the weak and the downtrodden and has attained a mythic status among the underclass, making it difficult to determine which of his exploits are real and which are fictional. There have apparently been a succession of Dog Brothers over the centuries, each accompanied by a pack of orphans and stray dogs; when the Dog Brother appoints a successor, that successor must then execute the current Dog Brother and take his place. Legend has it that the current Dog Brother was a Hong Kong boy, orphaned by the First Opium War in 1841, as impossible as that sounds. He recently joined Iron Fist and the other Immortal Weapons in coming to Earth in search of the lost Eighth Capital City of Heaven and apparently remains here. I don't see much point in seeking him out; if we need him, he'll find us.

PROS: Legendary reputation can intimidate opponents, centuries of experience in battle.

CONS: Answers to no known authority, capabilities and agenda largely unknown.

POWER GRID	1	2	3	4	5	6	7	8	9	10
POWER										
CONSCIENCE										
ALTRUISM										
WISDOM										
COURAGE										
DETERMINATION										
FREE WILL										
VULNERABILITY										

ECHO

AFFILIATIONS: Daredevil, Avengers

STATUS: Free agent; identity protected

With her impressive "photographic reflexes" (she can replicate anything she sees, from piano-playing to advanced martial arts), Echo served as a valuable asset to the Avengers, first as Ronin, seeking to regulate the criminal empire in Japan, and later as Echo. I've had little personal association with her, and I admire how she has not allowed her hearing impairment to hamper her career decisions or super heroics, I have read reports on her tragic background. Raised by a single father who was later killed by Wilson Fisk, Echo was used as an operative against Daredevil, but she ended up falling in love with him and allying with him, and it was on his recommendation that she joined the Avengers. After some violent encounters in the Skrull invasion, Echo has gone missing. I understand from Hawkeye that they had a brief romantic fling (Clint can't seem to keep his romances away from his teammates), and her disappearance may be related to Mockingbird's return. I'd like to find Echo as soon as possible and help her find her true path as a hero.

PROS: Impressive skill set.

CONS: Tortured by her past, relatively isolated even among allies.

POWER GRID	1	2	3	4	5	6	7	8	9	10
POWER										
CONSCIENCE										
ALTRUISM										
WISDOM										
COURAGE										
DETERMINATION										
FREE WILL										
VULNERABILITY										

ELEKTRA

AFFILIATIONS: Daredevil, Wolverine, the Hand, the Chaste

STATUS: Free agent (Greek), fugitive; identity public

Elektra Natchios, from what I know, had very unremarkable beginnings as the daughter of a Greek ambassador, but her father's death drew her into the a career as one of the world's deadliest assassins, working for criminal masterminds like the Kingpin and even leading the Hand, a world-wide network of ninjas and assassins. Elektra has had a lengthy history of tragedy, both with her family and personally. After working for the Kingpin for a time, she was brutally murdered by Bullseye (I can't believe Osborn employed him as Hawkeye!), and later resurrected. Since then, it seems she has battled her very nature of good and evil. Elektra was one of the dozens of Skrull captives who was impersonated, but since her return, she has been right back to her old ways as an assassin. The second she sets foot on American soil, she needs to be arrested and contained; she can't be allowed to roam free, killing people for profit. Though I have had little contact with her over the years, she has close associations with Wolverine and Daredevil, but even they don't trust her completely.

PROS: Disciplined and experienced fighter.

CONS: Assassin-for-hire, has undergone extensive personal tragedy.

POWER GRID	1	2	3	4	5	6	7	8	9	10
POWER										
CONSCIENCE										
ALTRUISM										
WISDOM										
COURAGE										
DETERMINATION										
FREE WILL										
VULNERABILITY										

ETERNALS

AFFILIATIONS: Avengers

STATUS: Foreign race; identities protected

I've met "gods" like Thor and Hercules, but the Eternals are somehow more mysterious. They are said to be an immortal, divergent race of humanity, created by "space gods" called the Celestials. Some of the Eternals choose to live among us, protecting the Earth. I don't know many of them well, but I've served alongside two Eternals, who couldn't be more different, in the Avengers. Though he has been called "the Forgotten One," Gilgamesh was the first recorded superhuman champion, the forerunner of me and all the other "super heroes" of today. I even once time-traveled to ancient Mesopotamia and saw him in action there, a noble and inspiring figure of colossal strength. He's supposedly "died" more than once, but I doubt that an Eternal can ever truly perish. In contrast, at first Sersi seemed more interested in throwing parties than combating evil. But when faced with a serious threat, Sersi becomes a formidable warrior, employing her powers to transform any kind of matter. But in general the Eternals stand apart from humanity, watching over us, but seemingly pursuing their own unknown agendas.

PROS: Extraordinary superhuman powers, access to technology far beyond mainstream humans'.

CONS: Do not consider themselves bound by the laws of the nations of Earth.

POWER GRID	1	2	3	4	5	6	7	8	9	10
POWER										
CONSCIENCE										
ALTRUISM										
WISDOM										
COURAGE										
DETERMINATION										
FREE WILL										
VULNERABILITY										

EXCALIBUR

AFFILIATIONS: MI13, Black Knight

STATUS: UK government agent; identity protected

Excalibur's new to the game, having only gained her powers during the Skrull's attack on Great Britain. Though I haven't met her, what I've heard gives me high hopes that she's going to be a valuable addition to the ranks of the world's heroes. She's the Black Knight's new squire (and girlfriend), and unsurprisingly Dane speaks highly of her, citing exceptional bravery from someone who was thrust unprepared into a dangerous world — she even took down Dracula recently, no mean feat for a novice. Romantically involved or not, I trust Dane's judgment to be unbiased. Besides, even more in her favor than Dane's recommendation is the weapon that provides her code name. Like Thor's hammer, Mjolnir, which only lets the worthy wield it, the sword Excalibur is very particular about who gets to pull it from its stone scabbard; apart from Dane and Captain Britain, the last person I know of that the sword judged a suitable wielder was King Arthur himself.

PROS: Medical expertise combined with restorative powers. Armed with legendary magic weapon.

CONS: Inexperienced, perhaps somewhat naïve. Operates under jurisdiction of foreign government.

POWER GRID	1	2	3	4	5	6	7	8	9	10
POWER										
CONSCIENCE										
ALTRUISM										
WISDOM										
COURAGE										
DETERMINATION										
FREE WILL										
VULNERABILITY										

FALCON

AFFILIATIONS: Captain America, Avengers, SHIELD

STATUS: Free agent; identity public

Hard as it may now be to believe, the Falcon was once a criminal called Sam "Snap" Wilson. But, like Hawkeye and other colleagues of mine, he has succeeded in putting his past behind him and become a true hero. I first met Sam on Exile Island, which had been taken over by the Exiles, Nazis allies of my old nemesis, the Red Skull. I gave Sam a crash course in combat, and he was an amazingly fast learner. I was struck by his bond with his pet falcon, Redwing, which proved to be telepathic, and so we created his own costumed identity, the Falcon. Together we not only overthrew the Exiles but bested the Skull. Returning to America, Sam and I worked for a long time as a team, fighting the Secret Empire, the Royalists and more. Eventually, the Black Panther gave Sam a high-tech harness that enabled him to fly like his namesake. Sam wasn't just my crime-fighting partner, but one of my best friends.

PROS: Excellent in hand-to-hand combat, telepathic ability to communicate with birds.

CONS: Has sometimes resorted to questionable crime-fighting methods.

POWER GRID	1	2	3	4	5	6	7	8	9	10
POWER										
CONSCIENCE										
ALTRUISM										
WISDOM										
COURAGE										
DETERMINATION										
FREE WILL										
VULNERABILITY										

FAT COBRA

AFFILIATIONS:
Iron Fist, Nick Fury, Ulysses Bloodstone

STATUS: Free agent (Peng Lai Island); identity protected

The Immortal Weapons are fairly mysterious, as a group, but there's a wealth of material out there on the deadly Fat Cobra; Ulysses Bloodstone's files, SHIELD mission logs, several dozen paternity suits — I'm pretty sure I even remember seeing him in a couple B-movies in the '30s. After being exiled from his native city of Peng Lai Island to Earth, the Cobra spent decades here before returning and eventually becoming the city's Immortal Weapon; as such, he's quite accustomed to us and our Earthly customs. He's also very outgoing and gregarious, and with Hercules gone, he could serve Herc's old role of a boisterous, brawling morale-booster. If we need one of the Immortal Weapons, Fat Cobra's one of our best bets and will fight by our side with valor — for as long as we can afford to feed him.

PROS: Decades of combat experience and martial arts mastery; capable of unique applications of chi energy.

CONS: Poor impulse control; significant memory loss due to overindulgence; may be called back to Peng Lai Island at any time.

POWER GRID	1	2	3	4	5	6	7	8	9	10
POWER										
CONSCIENCE										
ALTRUISM										
WISDOM										
COURAGE										
DETERMINATION										
FREE WILL										
VULNERABILITY										

FINESSE

AFFILIATIONS: Avengers Academy

STATUS: Free agent; identity protected

What makes a hero — nature or nurture? Raised by distant, materialistic parents with checkered pasts, it's suspected that Finesse is the biological daughter of the notorious mercenary known as the Taskmaster. After all, she possesses all of his trademark abilities — a polymath with eidetic memory and Olympic-level physical aptitude. She is a master of multiple fighting styles (though she has been persuaded to use the less-lethal billy club rather than bladed weapons while training) and possesses advanced degrees in mathematics, engineering, physics, computer science, and psychology — although she tests negative for the mutant gene and exhibits no other known indicator of superhuman power. Finesse graduated from MIT at age 14 and was training for a spot on the U.S. Olympic team when approached by Norman Osborn. But unlike her fellow Avengers Academy trainees, Finesse was not coerced, tortured, or experimented on by Osborn in any way; rather, she jumped at the opportunity to obtain knowledge and talents that she couldn't absorb from text books or video footage. She has the potential to be one of the greatest Avengers ever — or one of our greatest adversaries.

PROS: Polymath; eidetic memory; Olympic-level athlete; high aptitude in most sciences; mastery of multiple fighting styles and a variety of other skills; inquisitive.

CONS: Cold, distant, emotionless; fails to comprehend the nuances of human interaction.

POWER GRID	1	2	3	4	5	6	7	8	9	10
POWER										
CONSCIENCE										
ALTRUISM										
WISDOM										
COURAGE										
DETERMINATION										
FREE WILL										
VULNERABILITY										

FIXER

AFFILIATIONS: Thunderbolts, Baron Helmut Zemo, MACH-IV, Masters of Evil, Hydra, Avengers, Commission on Superhuman Activities, Redeemers

STATUS: Free agent; identity public

While a brilliant tinkerer, Ebersol tends to mask his true scientific knowledge and shows it only when he desires to be praised for his work. The Fixer is a former member of the Masters of Evil that is one of the few successful reformed villains to spawn out of Helmet Zemo's world domination plan involving the Thunderbolts. As a Thunderbolt, Fixer has helped save the world numerous times, which resulted in a presidential pardon of his criminal past. He participated on the pro-registration side of the Superhuman Registration Act and took a job with the Commission on Superhuman Activities shortly after the "Civil War" between heroes had ended and began doing what he loves best for the government. However, with Luke Cage's involvement with the Thunderbolts, Fixer has once again involved himself with that team.

PROS: An intuitive genius.

CONS: Tends to follow his intuitive need to challenge himself, even if it means participating in illegal activities.

POWER GRID	1	2	3	4	5	6	7	8	9	10
POWER										
CONSCIENCE										
ALTRUISM										
WISDOM										
COURAGE										
DETERMINATION										
FREE WILL										
VULNERABILITY										

FORCE

AFFILIATIONS:
Iron Man, White Fang, US Army

STATUS: Free agent; identity protected

Force spiraled into a career as a criminal after he stole a prototype suit of armor and battled the likes of Namor and Iron Man, eventually joining the employ of Justin Hammer. He had a quick change of heart, however, and has been a valuable ally and employee of Iron Man ever since. He's also offered his expertise with combat armor to train US Army operatives. Now a registered hero, Force was recently active against the Hood during Osborn's reign of power and allied with a new hero, White Fang. With his powerful armor and his willingness to fight the good fight, Force may be ready for the front runners as a hero now. He's shown his bravery against powerful men like Hammer and Osborn and has faced the threats of Ultimo and the powerful army of the Hood without flinching. Some assessment into his commitment to the Initiative will need to take place.

PROS: Trained in engineering and physics, close association with Iron Man.

CONS: Non-assertive, slow to accept responsibility.

POWER GRID	1	2	3	4	5	6	7	8	9	10
POWER										
CONSCIENCE										
ALTRUISM										
WISDOM										
COURAGE										
DETERMINATION										
FREE WILL										
VULNERABILITY										

FROG-MAN

AFFILIATIONS:
Action Pack, Spider-Man

STATUS: Free agent; identity protected

Theoretically speaking, Frog-Man should be one of the worst choices for adventurer out there. He's clumsy, has little to no formal training, and inspires little confidence among his peers. Yet time and again, he has proven himself not only a valiant and brave soul, but extremely lucky. He has defeated — singlehandedly or with others — numerous criminals, many of them dangerous enough to give me pause, such as when he aided me against the Yellow Claw. That's the encouraging thing about Frog-Man: Nothing keeps him down, and he will pick himself back up and keep trying to fight the good fight, no matter how out-matched he is. Even after a near-death encounter with Kraven the Hunter and his subsequent abduction by Skrulls, the first thing he did was try to return to his Initiative team, the Action Pack. With some serious training, he could very well be a force to be reckoned with. Until then, he's the type that makes me fear another Stamford.

PROS: Perseverance against greater odds.

CONS: Untrained, success by sheer luck.

POWER GRID	1	2	3	4	5	6	7	8	9	10
POWER										
CONSCIENCE										
ALTRUISM										
WISDOM										
COURAGE										
DETERMINATION										
FREE WILL										
VULNERABILITY										

EMMA FROST

AFFILIATIONS: X-Men, Hellfire Club, Hellions, Generation X, New Mutants, Cyclops

STATUS: Free agent; no dual identity

Emma Frost can be cunning, manipulative, seductive, and territorial when it comes to her students — all the qualities that you want on your side instead of your opponent's. Over the years, she has gone from misguided villainess, to headmistress, to a humble proactive political speaker for mutantkind. As much as she has taught her students over the years, they have taught her just as much, if not more, about humility and what it means to belong to a family. She tends to apply her cutthroat business etiquette to her actions in the field, which makes her an excellent team leader. However, it is this same etiquette that causes you to keep a close eye on her actions. At times they seem personally motivated, while other times it is for a larger cause. While it appears that she has reformed, I would welcome her into the ranks of the Avengers at any given moment so she could dispel any doubt the world, including myself, might have about her.

PROS: Loyal, team leader, excellent teacher.

CONS: While loyal, I'm unsure if it extends to humans as she can be secretive and untrustworthy at times.

POWER GRID	1	2	3	4	5	6	7	8	9	10
POWER										
CONSCIENCE										
ALTRUISM										
WISDOM										
COURAGE										
DETERMINATION										
FREE WILL										
VULNERABILITY										

NICK FURY

AFFILIATIONS: Secret Warriors, SHIELD, US Army (Howling Commandos), CIA

STATUS: Free agent, fugitive; no dual identity

Nick and I both grew up in Manhattan during the Great Depression, but back then we seemed destined for different paths in life: I was a sickly art student, and he was a tough, streetwise kid. But during World War II, we found ourselves allies in combat: me as Captain America, and Nick leading the legendary "Howling Commandos." And thanks to miracles of science, we remain in our physical primes over a half-century later. Soon after I was revived from suspended animation, I teamed with Nick against THEM's androids and the Yellow Claw's soldiers. Nick has become a master combat strategist and an inspiring leader, and remains good enough at hand-to-hand combat to fight me to a draw.

Ironically, Nick, who used to love defying authority, ended up usually aligning himself with the government as director of SHIELD, whereas in recent years I've preferred to follow my own vision of the "American dream," rather than take orders. But nonetheless Nick and I remain staunch friends and allies, two old combat veterans still capable of fighting the good fight.

PROS: Great leadership abilities, master battle strategist, superb hand-to-hand combatant.

CONS: Fury's hot temper and rebellious nature keep him from always being diplomatic with allies. Blind in one eye.

POWER GRID	1	2	3	4	5	6	7	8	9	10
POWER										
CONSCIENCE										
ALTRUISM										
WISDOM										
COURAGE										
DETERMINATION										
FREE WILL										
VULNERABILITY										

GAMBIT

AFFILIATIONS: X-Men, Thieves and Assassins Guilds of New Orleans

STATUS: Free agent, fugitive; identity public

We all know I believe in second chances, but the individual has to want to change. I'll never understand how some individuals can be viewed by the public, or by other heroes, as a hero, and Gambit falls into this category. A professional thief (who seems proud of his thieving ways and has little-to-no desire to change) who has had multiple "confused" relationships with some of the X-Men's most deadly enemies, including Apocalypse, Mr. Sinister, and the Marauders, villains who have been responsible for the deaths of hundreds. Gambit has unquestionably used his power to charge objects with kinetic energy in heroic ways, and Beast tells me that he has been involved in saving the world on multiple occasions, but he has a long way to go before he truly changes, if that is even possible at this point. I can't trust him, and I find myself feeling that way about many of the X-Men's members nowadays.

PROS: Extremely powerful, has a long history with the X-Men.

CONS: Unapologetic criminal.

POWER GRID	1	2	3	4	5	6	7	8	9	10
POWER										
CONSCIENCE										
ALTRUISM										
WISDOM										
COURAGE										
DETERMINATION										
FREE WILL										
VULNERABILITY										

GAUNTLET

AFFILIATIONS: Avengers Resistance, Initiative

STATUS: Free agent; identity public

Although he came to prominence during my recent absence, after reading Sgt. Joseph Green's file, I feel as though he could be a kindred spirit. He is a humble soldier who fought oversees during wartime, thrust into the position of a super hero and symbol, trusted with a unique weapon and stationed stateside at a training camp with the next generation of heroes. Green is armed with an apparently extraterrestrial glove capable of generating an incredibly strong energy hand. On at least one occasion, the alien glove has controlled his actions, although the circumstances that allowed this are still unclear. He would have preferred to operate on the front, but he was recruited to be Camp Hammond's premier drill sergeant training Initiative cadets. Gauntlet remained with the Initiative even when he became aware of serious breaches of public trust, including the MVP debacle, but he joined Justice's Avengers Resistance when the Initiative became more corrupt. She-Hulk informs me that in a possible future, Gauntlet becomes a very prominent hero, inspiring more young heroes.

PROS: Veteran soldier, willing to make tough decisions and follow difficult orders; experienced teacher.

CONS: Can be loyal to a fault; mind and body can be controlled by alien glove.

POWER GRID	1	2	3	4	5	6	7	8	9	10
POWER										
CONSCIENCE										
ALTRUISM										
WISDOM										
COURAGE										
DETERMINATION										
FREE WILL										
VULNERABILITY										

GHOST RIDER

AFFILIATIONS: Defenders, Champions, Dr. Strange, Danny Ketch, Spirits of Vengeance, Midnight Sons

STATUS: Free agent; identity public

Johnny Blaze has become an enigma in his own class over the years. Bonded with what seems to be a demonic symbiote, the former stunt motorcyclist wanders the country searching for a way to escape his family's past. A good man at heart, which is why I assume he has not completely succumbed to the supernatural elements within his life, there are times it seems he has trouble dealing with his demonic side. While I do not completely understand the realm of mystics, Blaze is someone I would recommend as an Avenger specifically for an assault team

on proactive missions. Recently it was rumored that both he and his brother, Daniel Ketch, another Ghost Rider, battled both Heaven and Hell to discover a hidden truth behind his family's involvement in the supernatural. I am not sure if this new revelation has strengthened the man's spirit or the demon within, but one thing is for sure, he is someone that we should keep an eye on as a potential candidate for missions involving the supernatural.

PROS: Loyal, team player; resilient and strong-willed.

CONS: Bonded to a demon and unpredictable at times.

POWER GRID	1	2	3	4	5	6	7	8	9	10
POWER										
CONSCIENCE										
ALTRUISM										
WISDOM										
COURAGE										
DETERMINATION										
FREE WILL										
VULNERABILITY										

GIBBON

AFFILIATIONS: Princess Python, Gorilla Girl

STATUS: Free agent; identity public

Martin Blank was born with an unfortunate mutation, granting him the appearance of an ape. Although he was somewhat recompensed with ape-like agility and strength, without an Xavier-like role model to shape him it's no small wonder that after years of abuse and discrimination that he would vent his frustrations on society, becoming a criminal. After an unlucky era spent working alongside Kraven the Hunter, fighting Spider-Man, joining a so-called "Legion of Losers," marrying Princess Python and nearly losing his life in an attack by the Punisher, the Gibbon seems to have repented his criminal past and seeks to live a normal life. His heart

appears to be in the right place, but he's been repeatedly drawn to an alternate reality where simians are dominant. There's very limited intel on this "ape-verse," but it seems that he's become a hero there, helping overthrow the corrupt heroes of that reality. Who would have expected the Gibbon to save an entire world? As my friend Jarvis has observed, heroism comes in many forms.

PROS: Genuine desire to avoid crime, leading expert on the "ape-verse."

CONS: Criminal history, sensitive about physical appearance.

POWER GRID	1	2	3	4	5	6	7	8	9	10
POWER										
CONSCIENCE										
ALTRUISM										
WISDOM										
COURAGE										
DETERMINATION										
FREE WILL										
VULNERABILITY										

GLORIANA

AFFILIATIONS: MI13, Excalibur

STATUS: UK government agent; identity public

Recently, Gloriana has literally been to hell and back, where, by her own account, she led a revolution against the devil himself. If anyone else told me that, I'd wonder if they were guilty of hyperbole, but dishonesty just isn't in Meggan's nature. Even when she was an empathic metamorph, changing to reflect others' feelings, those reflections were always truthful. Since her diabolic sojourn her appearance, at least, is no longer fluid, and her other ability, to manipulate external energies, has been refined and enhanced, so that now she broadcasts emotions. Meggan and her husband, Captain Britain, are one of the hero community's great love stories; I've rarely known anyone

more right for one another. Now that togetherness has become tactically significant, thanks to the new powers both recently acquired. They were always formidable individually and devastating together, but now Brian's powers are only limited by his confidence, and Meggan is able to boost that confidence almost limitlessly.

PROS: Wide-ranging elemental manipulation, broadcasting empath.

CONS: Operates under jurisdiction of foreign government. Empathy made her (formerly?) susceptible to outside influences.

POWER GRID	1	2	3	4	5	6	7	8	9	10
POWER										
CONSCIENCE										
ALTRUISM										
WISDOM										
COURAGE										
DETERMINATION										
FREE WILL										
VULNERABILITY										

GOLIATH

AFFILIATIONS:
Damage Control

STATUS: Free agent;
identity public

Goliath is new to the super hero game, and to some extent, he represents a dangerous combination of a brilliant mind, unresolved anger, and great physical power. Though he wasn't directly involved, Goliath was in many ways a victim of the super-hero Civil War, as his uncle and predecessor, Bill Foster, was killed during the conflict. Goliath's outrage led him to aggressively pursue revenge against Tony Stark, whom he considered guilty for his uncle's death, going so far as to cheer on the Hulk and his Warbound allies during their assault on New York in hopes they could deliver justice. After finding his uncle's Pym Particles, Goliath quickly realized the folly of vengeance and has since joined Damage Control and dedicated himself to proving worthy of his uncle's legacy. Goliath's intelligence and sense of right gives him great potential to accomplish good if he channels his energies correctly. However, I am concerned by his inexperience and the anger that he may still harbor toward those he holds responsible for his uncle's death. I'll be watching him closely.

PROS: Great intellect; strong sense of justice.

CONS: Inexperience; possible unresolved anger toward the pro-registration heroes.

POWER GRID	1	2	3	4	5	6	7	8	9	10
POWER										
CONSCIENCE										
ALTRUISM										
WISDOM										
COURAGE										
DETERMINATION										
FREE WILL										
VULNERABILITY										

GORILLA GIRL

AFFILIATIONS:
Initiative, Freaks

STATUS: Free agent;
identity protected

I don't believe I ever had the chance to meet the hero known as Gorilla Girl; if so, it was during one crisis or another where pleasantries weren't an option. Our records indicate she was originally a circus performer who was inspired to become a super hero after helping to defeat Hammer and Anvil, which is no easy feat. Chased and beaten by Osborn's ruthless Thunderbolts, she was forced to join the Initiative. Despite not wanting to be there, Gorilla Girl proved herself time and again, showing much more potential than many of her colleagues. Her disappearance from the program is confounding; when questioned, the Gibbon told our agents that she disappeared from existence while saving no less than three realities. If so, how do we still know about her? I'll talk to Director Charles Little Sky at ARMOR to see if we can figure this out. If she's still out there, we need to find her.

PROS: Team player (even under duress), Initiative training.

CONS: Being forced into Initiative may have soured her on heroics; whereabouts unrevealed.

POWER GRID	1	2	3	4	5	6	7	8	9	10
POWER										
CONSCIENCE										
ALTRUISM										
WISDOM										
COURAGE										
DETERMINATION										
FREE WILL										
VULNERABILITY										

GORILLA-MAN

AFFILIATIONS:
Atlas Foundation, SHIELD, X-Men

STATUS: Free agent,
wanted for questioning;
identity protected

Soldier of fortune Ken Hale wanted immortality, but bit off more than he could chew. His prize, obtained by killing the previous Gorilla-Man, came with a curse, transforming him into the next Gorilla-Man. Despite his inauspicious origins, Gorilla-Man quickly turned his life around, working in the 1950s with the G-Men, under FBI agent Jimmy Woo. He retired to Africa for many years, where he helped the young X-Men when their mentor was in trouble, and later he was recruited into SHIELD's "Howling Commandos," comprised of "monsters" and other oddities that didn't fit in normal society. Although many conscripts rebelled against this duty, Gorilla-Man reveled in it, becoming a valued agent, resigning only after learning his friend Woo was in trouble. He subsequently joined Woo's Atlas organization, which like Gorilla-Man had less-than-noble beginnings, but Captain America and Wolverine tell me Gorilla-Man has helped save the Earth from long-hidden enemies. Gorilla-Man could be a hero for years to come, as long as no one seeking immortality kills him.

PROS: Experienced soldier, able to follow orders, natural battlefield commander; immortal.

CONS: Shady past; overly eager to engage in violence.

POWER GRID	1	2	3	4	5	6	7	8	9	10
POWER										
CONSCIENCE										
ALTRUISM										
WISDOM										
COURAGE										
DETERMINATION										
FREE WILL										
VULNERABILITY										

GREAT LAKES INITIATIVE

AFFILIATIONS: Hawkeye, Mockingbird, Deadpool

STATUS: Free agents; identities protected

The current roster of the Great Lakes Initiative (which apparently went through several name changes when I wasn't paying attention, as the Maria Stark Foundation denied them the use of the name "Avengers") includes the undying Mr. Immortal, the massive Big Bertha, the shadowy Doorman, the elongated Flatman, and the unstoppable Squirrel Girl; together, they defend Wisconsin from any and all superhuman menaces. My experience with the GLI is quite limited, although Jim Hammond and I were manipulated into fighting them once, and they valiantly helped the Avengers battle Terminus in St. Louis a while back. While they have potential, most of them have deep roots in the Wisconsin area and would be reluctant to move elsewhere; and anyway, someone needs to protect the Midwest. Ultimately, I think they're best-suited to staying where they are, although we should make sure they're well-stocked with Avengers equipment and transportation if we ever need to call on them. Furthermore, we might be able to look into letting them call themselves Avengers again.

PROS: Excellent team players, diverse power set.

CONS: Lack of experience with powerful foes.

POWER GRID	POW	CON	ALT	WIS	COU	DET	FRW	VUL
BIG BERTHA	7	9	8	7	10	10	9	7
DOORMAN	8	9	8	7	10	10	8	5
FLATMAN	7	9	8	7	10	10	9	7
MR. IMMORTAL	6	10	8	7	10	9	9	0
SQUIRREL GIRL	6	10	10	7	10	10	9	8

NATE GREY

AFFILIATIONS: X-Men, Cable

STATUS: Free agent (extra-temporal), incarcerated; no dual identity

Hailing from an alternate reality ARMOR informs me is designated Earth-295, Nate Grey is a genetic construct engineered with DNA from that reality's Scott Summers and Jean Grey. Grey ended up on our Earth and became a rather public figure in New York years ago when his power to heal others drew masses of followers. Grey disappeared for several months before returning suddenly during Osborn's reign, and he has since been incarcerated. While I am hesitant to trust a young man with such excessive telepathic and telekinetic powers to the X-Men, I must let them handle the mutant situation as so few of them remain. Spider-Man assures me that Grey is a stalwart hero, one who aided him a few years back. To my knowledge, Grey has always struggled a bit with finding a proper path to be on, and Beast informs me that Grey's powers were killing him a few years ago. I hope we can help this young man before his story turns out as tragically as the Sentry's did.

PROS: Vast power source.

CONS: Unstable, struggles to commit to a cause.

POWER GRID	1	2	3	4	5	6	7	8	9	10
POWER										
CONSCIENCE										
ALTRUISM										
WISDOM										
COURAGE										
DETERMINATION										
FREE WILL										
VULNERABILITY										

GUARDIANS OF THE GALAXY

AFFILIATIONS: The Inhumans, Nova

STATUS: Free agents (extraterrestrial); identities public

Space-based adventurers primarily dealing with cosmic-level threats, fighting in other worlds and galaxies, beyond the view of Earth's populace, I'm unfamiliar with most of the Guardians and their specific activities, but Nova reassures me they've saved the world from several threats of which we were never alerted. Despite this, what I do know gives me concerns: NASA's file on Peter Quill, aka Star-Lord, suggests he is unstable, Groot tried to conquer Earth, and Moondragon, while a fellow Avenger, has often fallen prey to darker motivations. My limited experiences with Adam Warlock and Drax were always under extraordinary circumstances, and do little to assuage my concerns. However, I remember Mantis well from her days with the Avengers, and I have full trust in her judgment. The Guardians are a vital defense against extraterrestrial and cosmic threats and will likely continue to operate without oversight from any governing body, on Earth or off it. I would be interested in establishing more regular communication with them, perhaps to develop an advanced warning system of cosmic threats, which they regularly face.

PROS: Experience with cosmic threats, space travel capabilities.

CONS: Not answerable to any Earth government.

POWER GRID	POW	CON	ALT	WIS	COU	DET	FRW	VUL
BUG	6	8	8	8	10	9	9	8
COSMO	7	9	9	9	10	10	8	8
DRAX	9	5	6	9	10	9	9	5
GROOT	8	7	6	10	10	9	9	6
JACK FLAG	5	9	9	7	10	10	9	9
MAJOR VICTORY	8	9	9	9	10	10	9	7
MANTIS	8	9	9	10	10	9	9	6
MOONDRAGON	9	8	8	10	10	10	9	7
ROCKET RACCOON	6	9	9	9	10	10	9	8
STAR LORD	8	8	8	9	10	8	9	8

HARDBALL

AFFILIATIONS: Heavy Hitters, Komodo, Cloud 9

STATUS: Free agent; identity public

Roger Brokeridge, aka Hardball, was one of the inaugural class of the Initiative; his journey to heroism was a little more unorthodox than most, however. He's been a thief, government super-agent, a Hydra leader, a prisoner, and now, it seems, he's going to be a hero. His affiliation with Hydra only came about thanks to the machinations of the Power Broker (apparently not the Broker I've encountered, but a successor); when Roger's brother was injured after receiving the Broker's power-inducing treatments, Roger got powers of his own so he could commit crimes to pay for his brother's care. He became a Hydra double agent in the Initiative and eventually came to lead a branch of the organization, but ultimately came back to the Initiative. I know all too well the damage the Broker can do and of the persuasive powers of Hydra. Given his youth, his desperation, and his subsequent selfless acts of heroism against HAMMER, I can believe that he's rejected Hydra. However, I wonder if his fellow heroes can believe it, too.

PROS: Good teamwork skills; creative with his powers.

CONS: Lingering questions about his loyalty; can be brash and impulsive.

POWER GRID	1	2	3	4	5	6	7	8	9	10
POWER										
CONSCIENCE										
ALTRUISM										
WISDOM										
COURAGE										
DETERMINATION										
FREE WILL										
VULNERABILITY										

HAWKEYE

AFFILIATIONS: Avengers, World Counterterrorism Agency, Thunderbolts, Great Lakes Avengers, Defenders, Mockingbird, Two-Gun Kid, Black Widow

STATUS: Free agent; identity public

Glad as I was to see my friend and comrade Clint Barton after I returned, I'm even gladder to see him back in his old Hawkeye purple and blues. I think getting killed and resurrected twice, then coming back as an outlaw during the problematic-to-nightmarish Stark-to-Osborn transition, had a negative mental effect on Clint. It's like the Ronin identity he adopted during that time was mourning garb — partly for lost comrades, partly for a seemingly lost America, partly because he'd lost touch with himself, lost his way. With the Avengers reunited, order restored and his beloved Mockingbird back, Clint's acting a lot more like his old self — which is good, because we're going to need him. His fighting skills, integrity, courage and teamwork experience are invaluable to the Avengers during this rebuilding period, as is the wisecracking bowman's unique knack for bolstering group morale.

PROS: Perfect aim, expert archer, arsenal of trick arrows, natural acrobat, top unarmed fighter; swordsman, skilled with traditional Japanese weapons nunchaku and shuriken; good pilot and cyclist; experienced leader.

CONS: Can be reckless or overconfident; sometimes abrasive/insensitive, hot-tempered.

POWER GRID	1	2	3	4	5	6	7	8	9	10
POWER										
CONSCIENCE										
ALTRUISM										
WISDOM										
COURAGE										
DETERMINATION										
FREE WILL										
VULNERABILITY										

HAZMAT

AFFILIATIONS: Avengers Academy

STATUS: Free agent; identity protected

Of all the current Avengers Academy trainees, Hazmat was perhaps the most well-adjusted prior to the experiments conducted upon her by Norman Osborn — which also means she lost the most at Osborn's hands. Hazmat was raised in a loving, upper-middle-class Asian-American household in California. Leading a carefree and sheltered life, Hazmat was preparing for college when her toxic-emission powers first manifested, causing her to inadvertently poison and nearly kill her long-term boyfriend. She was quarantined at a local hospital until Osborn orchestrated her abduction and augmented her powers against her will. Now at Avengers Academy, Hazmat is confined to a containment suit while in the vicinity of others — as even her sweat, saliva, and breath are poisonous and can be lethal upon prolonged exposure. Although her parents' employment at Roxxon Energy Corporation has been suggested as a possible cause of her powers, Hazmat clearly blames Osborn for her current state and is consumed by intense feelings of anger, bitterness, and vengeance.

PROS: Body exudes a wide variety of radiation and toxic substances (the limits of which have not yet been tested).

CONS: Prolonged exposure can be fatal to others; anger-management and negativity issues.

POWER GRID	1	2	3	4	5	6	7	8	9	10
POWER										
CONSCIENCE										
ALTRUISM										
WISDOM										
COURAGE										
DETERMINATION										
FREE WILL										
VULNERABILITY										

HELLCAT

AFFILIATIONS: Avengers, Defenders, Initiative, Patsy-Hedy Entertainment, Black Cat, Firestar, Photon, Hellstorm (estranged)

STATUS: Free agent; identity public

One of the few Avengers more celebrated out of costume, Patsy Walker was "America's Sweetheart" as a child star made famous by a line of comic books. As an adult, she divorced her abusive husband, Buzz Baxter (later the villain Mad Dog), and pursued her lifelong dream of becoming a super hero. She talked her friend Beast into letting her apprentice with the Avengers, which led to her finding a physique-enhancing cat suit and joining the group as Hellcat. Unfortunately, she never stayed on full-time, first training with Moondragon, then joining the Defenders, and later retiring to marry demonic Defenders teammate Daimon Hellstrom. Daimon's dark side eventually drove Patsy to madness and suicide, but a mystical resurrection and her unquenchably bright spirit helped her regain her life and her sanity, plus new supernatural powers. Briefly the Initiative's Alaskan-based agent, Patsy's cheerful attitude and unique mix of mystical and physical skills make her an asset wherever she chooses to serve.

PROS: Enhanced strength, gifted acrobat, claws, magic-resistant; can alter appearance; mystically enhanced senses; minor psychic powers; extensive occult knowledge.

CONS: Questionable taste in men; traumatized by time in hell during death (since recovered).

POWER GRID	1	2	3	4	5	6	7	8	9	10
POWER										
CONSCIENCE										
ALTRUISM										
WISDOM										
COURAGE										
DETERMINATION										
FREE WILL										
VULNERABILITY										

MARIA HILL

AFFILIATIONS: SHIELD, Iron Man, Avengers

STATUS: Government agent; no dual identity

Despite a rocky beginning as director of SHIELD, Hill has proved herself to be a proficient and successful military and political commander, able to make difficult calls at a moment's notice. We were at odds during the Civil War, but she later proved herself time and again during the Skrull threats, the implementation of the Fifty State Initiative, and in other national crises. When Osborn took over, Hill went on the run and risked her life and sanity to fight against him, protect state secrets, and save Stark's life. Without powers, she was at the side of the heroes during the war on Asgard. I can, quite literally, think of no one more qualified to manage the new Avengers in the coming months. I am proud to call her an ally and pleased that she has agreed to work with us.

PROS: Trained commander, accustomed to fielding national, international, and extraterrestrial threats.

CONS: Too quick to follow orders, too slow to obey her conscience.

POWER GRID	1	2	3	4	5	6	7	8	9	10
POWER										
CONSCIENCE										
ALTRUISM										
WISDOM										
COURAGE										
DETERMINATION										
FREE WILL										
VULNERABILITY										

HULK

AFFILIATIONS: Avengers, Defenders

STATUS: Free agent; identity public

I've always known the Hulk to be either a tortured soul or a savage monster, or some variation of both. He was impossible to rein in among the Avengers in the early days, and he never quite fit in with the Defenders despite their long association. Bruce Banner has undergone no small amount of personal tragedy in recent years, especially given the deaths of three lady loves, Betty Banner, Jarella, and Caiera. During the time I was "dead," Hulk declared war on Earth and is now involved in some massive conflict involving multiple She-Hulks, a Red Hulk, and the Hulk's son, Skaar, all involved in a plot against some of the Avengers' deadliest villains. This situation has gotten too far out of control, and the Avengers need to investigate. We take care of our own. But it is long past time Bruce Banner was contained.

PROS: Super strength, vast intellect.

CONS: The Hulk has always proved impossible to control or direct. He is a completely emotional creature who cares only about achieving his own self-interest, and that doesn't work well in the field of super heroics.

POWER GRID	1	2	3	4	5	6	7	8	9	10
POWER										
CONSCIENCE										
ALTRUISM										
WISDOM										
COURAGE										
DETERMINATION										
FREE WILL										
VULNERABILITY										

HUMAN ROBOT

AFFILIATIONS:
Atlas Foundation

STATUS: Free agent, wanted for questioning; identity protected

In a world full of gods, mutants, sorcerers and heroes, a walking robot from the 1950s would generally be considered a joke (then again, so would a World War II relic who spent decades frozen in an iceberg), but Wolverine, Bucky, and others assure me that M-11 should be taken very seriously indeed. The Human Robot spent decades in the direct control of Plan Tzu (who I still think of as the Yellow Claw). With a strange electronic network that may or may not be powered by a human consciousness

(and may or may not exist in mainstream time), deadly weaponry, and allies among the Agents of Atlas, the Human Robot is an incredibly deadly force to be reckoned with. Frankly, I find little reason to trust the Atlas Foundation at all (though they did stand against Osborn, indirectly); I need to sit down with Jimmy Woo and find out what he intends for his team. The Agents of Atlas seem to be everywhere lately.

PROS: Obedient, versatile abilities and equipment.

CONS: Mysterious, motivations vague.

POWER GRID	1	2	3	4	5	6	7	8	9	10
POWER										
CONSCIENCE										
ALTRUISM										
WISDOM										
COURAGE										
DETERMINATION										
FREE WILL										
VULNERABILITY										

HUMAN TORCH [JIM HAMMOND]

AFFILIATIONS: NYPD, Invaders, All-Winners Squad, V-Battalion, Heroes for Hire, Avengers, Toro

STATUS: Free agent; identity public

Jim Hammond is one of my oldest and dearest friends. Considered by many to be the first "marvel" of World War II, certainly one of the first media darlings, the original synthozoid Human Torch was an inspiration to many, but more than anything, he is one of the most human people I know. He was active, off-and-on, during the years following my disappearance at the end of the war and maintained a long partnership with Toro and friendly rivalry with the Sub-Mariner. He was revived shortly after the Avengers found me, only to be deactivated again. Johnny Storm continued his legacy, but

Jim returned and joined the Avengers West Coast branch. After a few fluctuations in power, he led such diverse groups as the mercenary-like Heroes for Hire, the cloak-and-dagger V-Battalion and the sometimes subversive New Invaders, with whom he gave his life saving the world. Camp Hammond was named in his honor. Jim was recently revived by the Mad Thinker and is working closely with the revitalized Toro.

PROS: Years of experience; absolute control of fire; honorable personality; trained law enforcement officer.

CONS: Occasionally controlled or manipulated by others due to his artificial nature.

POWER GRID	1	2	3	4	5	6	7	8	9	10
POWER										
CONSCIENCE										
ALTRUISM										
WISDOM										
COURAGE										
DETERMINATION										
FREE WILL										
VULNERABILITY										

HUMAN TORCH [JOHNNY STORM]

AFFILIATIONS:
Fantastic Four, Nova, Black Panther, Inhumans, Namorita, Ant-Man, Lyja, Psionics, Fantastic Force

STATUS: Free agent; identity public

Along with the other members of the Fantastic Four, Johnny Storm gained powers via cosmic radiation, altering his genetics on a cellular level. As with the others, it appears that Storm gained powers based on his demeanor, those of a "hothead." Taking the name the "Human Torch," in tribute to Jim Hammond, the World War II era hero of the same name, Storm used his powers to gain fame as a super hero. This makes me believe that he is playing the motions of a hero for the notoriety that

comes with it, although there have been times that he has proved this theory wrong. Given the proper time and training, I feel that he would make a great leader and good candidate for the Avengers. However, I would rather see him used at the Avengers Academy as an instructor more than a member of the regular roster.

PROS: Loyal, family oriented, team player, and possesses leadership qualities.

CONS: Brash, impulsive, self-serving at times and out for fame.

POWER GRID	1	2	3	4	5	6	7	8	9	10
POWER										
CONSCIENCE										
ALTRUISM										
WISDOM										
COURAGE										
DETERMINATION										
FREE WILL										
VULNERABILITY										

CEMAN

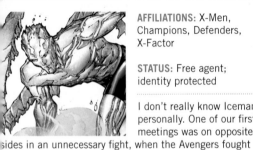

AFFILIATIONS: X-Men, Champions, Defenders, X-Factor

STATUS: Free agent; identity protected

I don't really know Iceman personally. One of our first meetings was on opposite sides in an unnecessary fight, when the Avengers fought the original X-Men, who were tracking down the alien Lucifer. But I feel like I know him thanks to talks with my fellow Avenger, Beast, as he and Iceman were inseparable best friends on Charles Xavier's first X-Men class. Life has changed the other original X-Men, but Iceman remains much like the youth who first joined the team: open, friendly, deeply loyal, and despite occasional moodiness, has a happy, optimistic outlook on life. The Black Widow's

coaching when they were in the Champions means he's not bad in hand-to-hand combat, but his real prowess lies in his mutant power to create intense cold. Only recently has he explored his powers' full potential. Now he can even transform himself into an organic form of ice. Could he come up with the "cold" equivalent of the Human Torch's "nova flame"?

PROS: Team player, mutant ability to induce intense cold, possibly without limits.

CONS: Only fair hand-to-hand combatant; still hasn't mastered his powers' full potential.

POWER GRID	1	2	3	4	5	6	7	8	9	10
POWER										
CONSCIENCE										
ALTRUISM										
WISDOM										
COURAGE										
DETERMINATION										
FREE WILL										
VULNERABILITY										

INHUMANS

AFFILIATIONS: Fantastic Four, Avengers, Kree

STATUS: Foreign race; identities public

A hidden, secret race of super-powered beings, the Inhumans lived on Earth for centuries without detection, removed from society in the Himalayas. In recent years, they have become increasingly involved and well-known to modern society through skirmishes with the Fantastic Four. Young Crystal was even married to Quicksilver and joined the Avengers for a time, and both she and Queen Medusa served on the Fantastic Four and one group of students even attended an American university (that didn't end well). Despite a rocky recent history, with wars

(against Portugal and the US), the multiple movements of their city to the moon and into space, and several superhuman conflicts, they have now, surprisingly, taken over the governance of the entire Kree Empire (this may be the most shocking news I've heard since my resurrection), and Black Bolt has apparently been killed in combat. I am saddened by this news and wish these former allies all the best, but I must focus on Earth.

PROS: Powerful superhuman abilities among hundreds of beings.

CONS: Unavailability, distrusted by many in USA.

POWER GRID	1	2	3	4	5	6	7	8	9	10
POWER										
CONSCIENCE										
ALTRUISM										
WISDOM										
COURAGE										
DETERMINATION										
FREE WILL										
VULNERABILITY										

INVISIBLE WOMAN

AFFILIATIONS: Fantastic Four, Inhumans, Lady Liberators, Avengers

STATUS: Free agent; identity public

Along with the other members of the Fantastic Four, Susan Richards gained powers via cosmic radiation, altering her genetics on a cellular level. As with the others, it appears that Susan gained powers based on her demeanor, that of a woman who would rather stand in the background, or "invisible," until she is pushed to the point that she needs to be active or "seen." Susan can be quite standoffish at times, but make no mistake, just like a lioness protecting her young, if you cross the line and mess with her family, watch out because she will stop at

nothing to protect her family. Previously a member of the Avengers when New York was being assaulted by demons, I'd welcome her to the Avengers any given time. At times I envy Sue's life, and how she has been able to find a balance between family and the life of a super hero. She is an amazing woman and truly an inspiration for mothers all over the world.

PROS: Loyal, family oriented; leadership qualities, strong-willed, outgoing.

CONS: Family life often doesn't blend well with hero life.

POWER GRID	1	2	3	4	5	6	7	8	9	10
POWER										
CONSCIENCE										
ALTRUISM										
WISDOM										
COURAGE										
DETERMINATION										
FREE WILL										
VULNERABILITY										

IRON FIST

AFFILIATIONS: K'un-Lun, Avengers, Heroes for Hire

STATUS: Free agent; identity protected

When my peers initially meet each other, we frequently wind up fighting, as when I mistakenly attacked a green and yellow-garbed intruder in Avengers Mansion - and if I hadn't placed my shield between me and his Iron Fist, I wouldn't be alive to tell the tale. Although Iron Fist became an Avenger, it wasn't under my watch. Still, I'm proud to call him a comrade. Not just a master of unarmed combat; he also carries of wealth of mystical knowledge from his mysterious home, K'un-Lun. He's fiercely devoted to family, friends and the oppressed, but his oft-times aloof personality throws off the uninitiated. During my recent absence, Iron Fist met other "immortal weapons" who have become his fellow adventurers, but he remains close to Luke Cage. Like Cage, Iron Fist took a dim view of super-hero registration. Fortunately, his mystical exploits often take him "off the grid" as it were. Still, he remains available as an irregular Avenger.

PROS: Team player, natural leader, unusual business/magic combat skill set.

CONS: As champion of K'un-Lun, he answers to an authority outside US (or even UN) jurisdiction.

POWER GRID	1	2	3	4	5	6	7	8	9	10
POWER										
CONSCIENCE										
ALTRUISM										
WISDOM										
COURAGE										
DETERMINATION										
FREE WILL										
VULNERABILITY										

IRON MAN

AFFILIATIONS: Avengers, SHIELD, US government

STATUS: Free agent; identity public

I owe my life to Tony Stark, who I first met in his guise as Iron Man. It was Iron Man, along with Thor, Giant-Man and the Wasp, who found me in suspended animation and revived me years ago. They then welcomed me into their new team, the Avengers, as an equal partner. That was the start of my long friendship with Tony, and we stood by each other even in hard times, like when he succumbed to his alcoholism. So it was particularly painful when we found ourselves as the leaders of opposite sides of the super heroes' "Civil War." Thankfully, that experience is now behind us. Iron Man, Thor and I are once again partners in combat, as senior members of the Avengers, and more importantly, friends. And as a child of the Great Depression of the 1930s, I am continually astonished by the 21st century technology that Tony shows me — and in many cases invented. I'm supposed to be a "Super-Soldier," but Iron Man's state-of-the-art battlesuit makes him a virtual one-man army. I'm glad I have Tony back as a friend instead of as my adversary.

PROS: Team player, natural leader; genius in inventing and utilizing advanced technology

CONS: Under severe emotional stress, Tony has succumbed to his alcoholism more than once.

POWER GRID	1	2	3	4	5	6	7	8	9	10
POWER										
CONSCIENCE										
ALTRUISM										
WISDOM										
COURAGE										
DETERMINATION										
FREE WILL										
VULNERABILITY										

JACK FLAG

AFFILIATIONS: Guardians of the Galaxy; Captain America

STATUS: Free agent; identity protected

If Bucky is considered the younger brother I never had, Jack Flag is certainly a first cousin. For better or for worse, Jack's super-hero career has been influenced by my actions as Captain America. While still a teenager, Jack and his brother were inspired by my Stars & Stripes program to become vigilante crimefighters in their hometown of Sandhaven, Arizona. In an altercation with Mr. Hyde, Jack was inadvertently doused with the super villain's strength-augmenting chemical concoction, granting Jack superhuman strength. Jack aided me in defeats of the Serpent Society and Flag-Smasher, and when the Superhuman Registration Act became law, he followed my lead and refused to register. Unfortunately, Jack was crippled for his noncompliance by Norman Osborn's Thunderbolts and locked away in the Negative Zone prison. According to Nova, Jack was freed from the prison during an attack led by the Negative Zone despot Blastaar and has since joined forces with the space-faring Guardians of the Galaxy, who repaired his damaged spine.

PROS: Superhuman strength, stamina & durability; limited regenerative abilities; trained in various forms of combat; strong senses of morality & justice.

CONS: Occasionally acts with his heart rather than with his brain; hearing impaired in his left ear.

POWER GRID	1	2	3	4	5	6	7	8	9	10
POWER										
CONSCIENCE										
ALTRUISM										
WISDOM										
COURAGE										
DETERMINATION										
FREE WILL										
VULNERABILITY										

JACKPOT

X

AFFILIATIONS: Spider-Man, Blue Shield, Fantastic Four

STATUS: Free agent; identity protected

Sometimes, we can't adequately protect our own. Recently, Jackpot, one of New York City's newest vigilantes, had her identity discovered by criminals, resulting in the murder of her husband in front of her and her young daughter. Admirably, she brought the murderers to justice without resorting to lethal force. She's since relocated across the country and adopted a new identity. Whether she returns to active heroics is entirely her prerogative. Curiously, we've received reports of a second woman acting as Jackpot and being killed in action, but the Initiative files only list a single bearer of the identity. Spider-Man fought alongside Jackpot several times, but he's remained curiously tight-lipped about the whole situation, which seems to have been overlooked in the transfer of Initiative command from Stark to Osborn. Normally, I'd investigate further, but for the moment, it seems like the wisest thing to do is to leave Jackpot and her daughter in peace.

PROS: Skilled scientist, largely unknown to underworld.

CONS: Still largely inexperienced, may still be reeling from recent personal tragedy.

POWER GRID	1	2	3	4	5	6	7	8	9	10
POWER										
CONSCIENCE										
ALTRUISM										
WISDOM										
COURAGE										
DETERMINATION										
FREE WILL										
VULNERABILITY										

JEWEL

X

AFFILIATIONS: Luke Cage, Ms. Marvel, Avengers

STATUS: Free agent; identity public

Despite a rocky history within the super-hero community, as well as a life of incredible tragedy, Jessica Jones (who has gone by both Jewel and Knightress) has found a home and a family among the nation's heroes, standing by her husband Luke Cage and his allies during the Civil War and Skrull conflicts. Jessica's primary focus over the past months has been her daughter, Danielle, who was even kidnapped by the Skrull posing as Jarvis. Jessica has suffered many tragedies and setbacks in her life: her biological family was killed when she was a teenager, the Purple Man enslaved her for months, and a misunderstanding he engendered put her in a coma. But she rebuilt her life, becoming a successful private investigator with her own company, Alias Investigations. I look forward to seeing her finally hone her powers and abilities and be accepted as the hero she truly is. I've always seen great potential in Jessica and many of the Avengers concur.

PROS: Savvy, incredibly determined, skills as a private investigator.

CONS: Has been known to be unduly emotional (and definitely foul-mouthed) from time to time.

POWER GRID	1	2	3	4	5	6	7	8	9	10
POWER										
CONSCIENCE										
ALTRUISM										
WISDOM										
COURAGE										
DETERMINATION										
FREE WILL										
VULNERABILITY										

JOCASTA

X

AFFILIATIONS: Wasp (both Henry Pym and Janet Van Dyne), Avengers, the Mavericks

STATUS: Free agent; no dual identity

Despite my years of successful work with the Vision, I'll always have some reservations about any being with direct ties to Ultron, that mass-murdering robot who wiped out the entire country of Slorenia. Jocasta, whose brain patterns are based on those of Janet Van Dyne, was always a background presence in her brief involvements with the Avengers, though she has taken a more active role in Hank's international Avengers team. She registered with the Fifty State Initiative and was active with New Mexico's Mavericks during the Skrull War. Hank Pym now seems to trust her implicitly, with the management of his Infinite Avengers Mansion, despite yet another recent return of Ultron. I have no reason to distrust her, but I'll be keeping a close eye on her. For every Vision and Jocasta, there is an Ultron and an Alkhema. Will we ever find a way to be rid of that mass-murdering monstrosity?

PROS: Vast mechanical resources, virtually indestructible.

CONS: Programming repeatedly comprised by Ultron.

POWER GRID	1	2	3	4	5	6	7	8	9	10
POWER										
CONSCIENCE										
ALTRUISM										
WISDOM										
COURAGE										
DETERMINATION										
FREE WILL										
VULNERABILITY										

JUSTICE

AFFILIATIONS: Avengers Academy, Avengers, Avengers Resistance, Counter-Force, New Warriors, the Thing

STATUS: Free agent; identity public

When Justice first joined the Avengers, he was nervous and uncomfortable working alongside the heroes he had idolized as a boy. It was a pleasure to watch him grow confident in his abilities, and in a short time, I came to value him as a trusted teammate. Justice has engaged in super heroics since his teenage years, and has cemented himself as a leader in the super-powered community. Justice suffered through an abusive childhood, a victim of his father's anti-mutant prejudice, but overcame his past to become a strong force for good. After the super hero Civil War, he became a trainer at Camp Hammond, imparting the benefits of his experience to young heroes. Before long, his unrestrained sense of ethics led him to leave the Initiative and form Counter-Force to act as watchdogs of a sort. This independence makes Justice a trusted moral compass, doing what he thinks is right even if it means acting alone. These principles will make him an able instructor at Avengers Academy, and I'm glad to count him among our ranks.

PROS: Strong commitment to ethics, experienced team player, good leadership skills.

CONS: Received bad press for the accidental murder of his father, extremely passionate about his beliefs, sometimes leading to difficult moral quagmires.

POWER GRID	1	2	3	4	5	6	7	8	9	10
POWER										
CONSCIENCE										
ALTRUISM										
WISDOM										
COURAGE										
DETERMINATION										
FREE WILL										
VULNERABILITY										

KA-ZAR

AFFILIATIONS: Shanna the She-Devil, Black Panther

STATUS: Free agent (UK/Savage Land); identity public

As a boy watching "King Kong," I never imagined that a lost world of prehistoric beasts actually existed. Another boy, Kevin Plunder, traveled with his father to just such a place, the Savage Land, and when his father died, young Kevin was raised by a saber-toothed tiger he named Zabu. Amazingly, Kevin not only survived, but became Ka-Zar, a lord as savage as the land. Returning to England, he relearned civilization's ways and assumed his father's title of Lord Plunder, but he soon went back to the Savage Land, where he lives with his wife, Shanna, and their son. I've always been impressed when I've met Ka-Zar; he has never undergone any form of physical or combat training, but surviving in a prehistoric jungle molded him into a formidable fighter and an extraordinary athlete and acrobat. And he is as dedicated to protecting his adopted home, the Savage Land, as I am to guarding America.

PROS: Extraordinary athletic and acrobatic abilities, formidable hand-to-hand combatant; master at hunting and tracking.

CONS: Self-taught in combat and athletics, Ka-Zar lacks the refined skills that training brings.

POWER GRID	1	2	3	4	5	6	7	8	9	10
POWER										
CONSCIENCE										
ALTRUISM										
WISDOM										
COURAGE										
DETERMINATION										
FREE WILL										
VULNERABILITY										

KOMODO

AFFILIATIONS: Desert Stars, Curt Connors, Hardball

STATUS: Free agent; identity protected

After losing her legs in an accident, Komodo stole Curt Connors' Lizard formula, modified it, and tested it on herself, transforming into a reptilian humanoid with astonishing regenerative abilities, but retaining her human mind and the ability to change back and forth at will. I don't necessarily approve of her actions, although I don't have much room to complain about enhancing one's subpar physique with experimental chemicals. Komodo has proven herself time and again as a hero, battling the Skrulls, enduring a stint in captivity by Hydra, and most recently aiding the Avengers Resistance in a support capacity after her powers were cruelly stripped from her. She also underwent a grueling ordeal when her companion Hardball defected to Hydra, leaving her feeling betrayed; I understand that with Hardball's subsequent reformation, the two have reconciled somewhat. I'm certain she'll continue on as a hero now that her powers have been restored, and I'd like to make use of her scientific skills, now that we've lost Connors to the private sector.

PROS: Gifted scientist, can recover from devastating injuries in moments.

CONS: Can be abrasive and unpleasant, can be mind-controlled by reptilian villains.

POWER GRID	1	2	3	4	5	6	7	8	9	10
POWER										
CONSCIENCE										
ALTRUISM										
WISDOM										
COURAGE										
DETERMINATION										
FREE WILL										
VULNERABILITY										

LONERS

AFFILIATIONS: Runaways, Darkhawk

STATUS: Free agents, retired; identities protected

I cannot fault the reasoning behind the concept of the Loners program. This is a dangerous world and even superhuman powers aren't always enough to give us strength against the constant threats we face. The Loners set out to help adventurers settle back into civilian life — a sort of outreach program for the masked community. Headed by Michiko "Mickey" Musashi, the program hasn't completely found its way away from heroics. Several members have returned to their costumed identities, such as Darkhawk, and even those who remain often find themselves thrust back into their old lives, if only temporarily. With some tweaking, I could see the Loners idea being of great value if done on a larger scale. Programs like it and the similar Vil-Anon are certainly noble and could help reintroduce superhuman adventurers and criminals alike to normal lives. Current reports show that former adventurers Ricochet, Lightspeed and a new Red Ronin are involved in the program.

PROS: Excellent concept, could be taken wider.

CONS: Lack of professionals in counseling roles, large percentage of "relapses."

POWER GRID	POW	CON	ALT	WIS	COU	DET	FRW	VUL
LIGHTSPEED	7	9	8	7	10	7	9	8
RED RONIN	7	6	6	7	10	7	8	6
RICOCHET	7	8	8	7	9	7	9	8
SPIDER-WOMAN	7	8	8	7	10	7	9	8
TURBO	7	8	8	8	9	7	9	8

MACH-5

AFFILIATIONS: CSA, Initiative, Thunderbolts, Burton Canyon Police Department, Hammer Industries, Masters of Evil, Sinister Seven, Maggia, Sinister Syndicate, Lethal Legion

STATUS: Active adventurer; public identity

For someone who worked for years on the other side of the law, this former career criminal and participator in Helmut Zemo's Thunderbolts scheme has gone a long way. Going from one prison sentence to another for years as the Beetle, Jenkins eventually took the opportunity to change, becoming a true hero after the Thunderbolts' criminal alter egos were revealed to the public. Jenkins even went to prison for an earlier crime, showing that he was willing to take responsibility for his past. Hired by the CSA, he became an undercover agent for them against Hammer Industries and after many subsequent missions with the Thunderbolts joined the CSA full-time as a mechanic alongside the inventor Fixer. He recently donned the 5th incarnation of MACH armor to save Songbird and Black Widow from Osborn's black ops Thunderbolts. Though nothing in life is certain, in my opinion Jenkins has shown that there is nothing left of the petty criminal he once was.

PROS: Team player, natural leader, master mechanic, experienced flight combatant.

CONS: Criminal past, mostly inactive.

POWER GRID	1	2	3	4	5	6	7	8	9	10
POWER										
CONSCIENCE										
ALTRUISM										
WISDOM										
COURAGE										
DETERMINATION										
FREE WILL										
VULNERABILITY										

MACHINE MAN

AFFILIATIONS: ARMOR, Nextwave, Avengers

STATUS: Free agent; identity public

I have a lot of respect for Aaron Stack. He has proven his humanity and heroism time and again, but his android nature has often set him apart. Originally created by Dr. Abel Stack as X-51, his body has been upgraded and is highly adaptable, as he seems to have equipment ready for any conceivable situation, but he has long had trouble understanding human duplicity. Although he worked alongside the Avengers periodically, he has gained a pessimistic view of humanity in recent years after becoming infected by mutant-hunting Sentinel programming and later being rejected by cosmic beings known as Celestials. He joined the Nextwave counterterrorism group under Monica Rambeau and during his tenure there expressed constant aggravation with "fleshy" humans. While I do not like this developing character trait, I can understand it. It can be hard to be a man out of place with the world. He maintains a fondness for Jocasta, but her attention is currently divided between Hank Pym and Ultron. Machine Man has continued helping humans, despite claiming to hate them, as a premier agent of ARMOR (Altered-Reality Monitoring and Operational Response), protecting reality from extra-dimensional threats.

PROS: Resourceful, adaptable; skilled in multiple fields.

CONS: Mentally unstable, antisocial; occasionally reprogrammed by others.

POWER GRID	1	2	3	4	5	6	7	8	9	10
POWER										
CONSCIENCE										
ALTRUISM										
WISDOM										
COURAGE										
DETERMINATION										
FREE WILL										
VULNERABILITY										

MAN-THING

AFFILIATIONS: Midnight Sons, Thunderbolts

STATUS: Free agent; identity protected

I am fully aware how fortunate I have been to be a recipient, and a survivor, of Abraham Erskine's super-soldier serum. Erskine was assassinated shortly after I was transformed into Captain America, and the secrets of the formula were lost with him. Over the following decades, multiple government programs have tried to recreate the serum, but all have resulted in multiple casualties and tragedies, such as the insanity of 1950s Cap, Luke Cage's painful transformation, and a scientist's change into the mindless Man-Thing. I hate to think that my own existence has led to the deaths of others. Despite being based in the swamps of Florida, Man-Thing has had a surprising number of conflicts with superhuman beings and has rampaged across New York. There is something strange about that swamp he lives in, but Portal, over at ARMOR, assures me that they have things under control. Man-Thing appeared in federal custody after being savagely apprehended by Ares during Osborn's reign. This has given us a chance to place him on the Thunderbolts; we'll see if Luke can find the man in the monster.

PROS: Virtually indestructible, evidently no malicious behavior.

CONS: Mindless beast of unknown potential; connected to alternate reality conduit, the Nexus of All Realities.

POWER GRID	1	2	3	4	5	6	7	8	9	10
POWER										
CONSCIENCE										
ALTRUISM										
WISDOM										
COURAGE										
DETERMINATION										
FREE WILL										
VULNERABILITY										

MARVEL BOY

AFFILIATIONS: Atlas Foundation

STATUS: Free agent, wanted for questioning; identity protected

In 1934, the infant Marvel Boy was aboard an interplanetary spaceship bound for Uranus. Welcomed by a colony of Uranian Eternals, Marvel Boy was nurtured to his full physical and mental potential by adolescence. The Uranian Eternals hoped that Marvel Boy would return to Earth as their ambassador so that they could escape the native Uranians, who forbade them from leaving the planet. Marvel Boy returned to Earth in the 1950s, where he used Uranian technology as a super hero and assisted the NYPD, United Nations, and Jimmy Woo's FBI-sponsored "G-Men" team. But his attempt to found an embassy for the Uranian Eternals in 1959 prompted the native Uranians to orchestrate the deaths of the colonists. Marvel Boy returned to Uranus and was absorbed into the native Uranian's Membrane collective, his physiology permanently altered to survive in the harsh alien environment. Decades later, he returned to Earth and joined forces with Jimmy Woo's Atlas Foundation, a secret society which regards itself as a continuation of the Mongol Empire. As Atlas seems to be dedicated to bettering the world, I look forward to cooperating with Marvel Boy and his allies in the future.

PROS: Access to advanced Uranian technology; team player; hybrid Terran/Uranian physiology.

CONS: Confined to spacesuit to survive in Earth's atmosphere; feelings of alienation from Earth culture.

POWER GRID	1	2	3	4	5	6	7	8	9	10
POWER										
CONSCIENCE										
ALTRUISM										
WISDOM										
COURAGE										
DETERMINATION										
FREE WILL										
VULNERABILITY										

IAN McNEE

AFFILIATIONS: Oshtur

STATUS: Free agent; identity public

I had to contact Stephen Strange to learn something about this young man, who once challenged Stephen to a contest to become Earth's new Sorcerer Supreme. Stephen humbled him, but McNee intensified his study of the mystic arts and opened up the Cornerstore of Creation in Brooklyn magic and curio shop. From what I could learn about his recent activities, McNee was tricked by the Elder God Chthon, a being I've encountered myself in the past, into gathering the Cornerstones of Creation, supposedly to prevent the destruction of the very structure of magic. McNee's quest ended up involving Chthon's benevolent sister Oshtur, various witches, sorcerers, mystic items, but McNee learned of Chthon's deception early enough to avoid disaster for Earth, and continued his mission to heal the essence of magic. The current Sorcerer Supreme Dr. Voodoo should know about this because Ian might one day succeed him or become a major threat to our world if the dark forces manage to corrupt him like many other dabblers in the mystic arts before him.

PROS: Mystic adept.

CONS: Potential for corruption.

POWER GRID	1	2	3	4	5	6	7	8	9	10
POWER										
CONSCIENCE										
ALTRUISM										
WISDOM										
COURAGE										
DETERMINATION										
FREE WILL										
VULNERABILITY										

METTLE

AFFILIATIONS: Avengers Academy

STATUS: Free agent; identity protected

Raised by progressive parents in the Hawaiian Islands, Mettle was a laid-back, mellow slacker whose most important decisions in life revolved around whether to go surfing or skateboarding on a given day. Unfortunately, it was a surfing accident that led to the manifestation of his superhuman powers. When severe head trauma revealed an invulnerable metal skeleton beneath his flesh, Mettle was taken in by Norman Osborn, who directed his scientists to remove the rest of the flesh from his body and augment his powers. Now existing as an imposing, skeletal behemoth, Mettle's docile and easy-going demeanor remains intact, in sharp contrast to his frightening physical appearance. Mettle possesses superhuman strength and an extremely high degree of superhuman invulnerability, to the point where scientists speculate that he may be able to live forever. However, his newfound immortality comes at a cost, as he no longer needs to breathe and is unable to feel any type of sensation. With such tremendous power at his disposal, it is important that this impressionable young man be exposed to positive role models; as such, he was deemed a prime candidate for Avengers Academy.

PROS: Superhuman strength; phenomenal degree of superhuman invulnerability; theoretical immortality.

CONS: Directionless; often unmotivated; a follower by nature.

POWER GRID	1	2	3	4	5	6	7	8	9	10
POWER										
CONSCIENCE										
ALTRUISM										
WISDOM										
COURAGE										
DETERMINATION										
FREE WILL										
VULNERABILITY										

MISTER FANTASTIC

AFFILIATIONS: Fantastic Four

STATUS: Free agent; identity public

Reed Richards is one of the greatest men I know. Though he and I have never been particularly close, we have worked together on numerous occasions, with the Avengers and Fantastic Four joining up against common threats; in fact, Reed even joined the Avengers during a brief period when the team needed him. Never a stranger to charting his own path, Reed has direct ties to many of the world's hidden secrets, from the Inhumans to the Skrulls to the Negative Zone, and he has saved the world more times than I can recollect. I am concerned, however, over some of his recent decisions, which seem rather short-sighted in retrospect. Sending the Hulk into space, building the prison 42 in the Negative Zone, involving himself in the Illuminati, and other decisions on Reed's part, have led to disastrous consequences for the world. I should sit down with Reed and discuss my concerns fairly soon. Despite these worries, the Fantastic Four remain among the greatest of heroes.

PROS: Valuable scientific intellect, leader of Fantastic Four.

CONS: Reed has struggled with recognizing the long-term results of his choices lately, much like Stark.

POWER GRID	1	2	3	4	5	6	7	8	9	10
POWER										
CONSCIENCE										
ALTRUISM										
WISDOM										
COURAGE										
DETERMINATION										
FREE WILL										
VULNERABILITY										

MOCKINGBIRD

AFFILIATIONS: World Counterterrorism Agency, Avengers, SHIELD, Hawkeye, Nick Fury, Ka-Zar

STATUS: Active adventurer; identity protected

I'd respect Mockingbird even if I'd never met her — partly by virtue of her reputation and partly because two of the best men I know (her mentor Nick Fury and partner Hawkeye) think so highly of her. And having met her, worked with her, I can see why. She's one of the most formidable hand-to-hand fighters I've ever faced and her twin steel battle staves (which snap together and telescope into a staff used for bojutsu fighting or vaulting) enhance her reach considerably in a fight. It's a deceptively simple-looking weapon, but quite dangerous and versatile in skilled hands. She's also one of the best spies SHIELD ever produced, which helped her survive the years she spent trapped on an alien world by the Skrulls. Wrongly believed dead, she recently returned to Earth, rejoining the Avengers and forming her own new spy group, the World Counterterrorism Agency, using intel stolen from the Skrulls to neutralize subversive threats worldwide.

PROS: Extremely skilled unarmed combatant, expert spy, acrobat, armed with battle staves, trained biologist, commands significant intelligence resources via WCA.

CONS: Sometimes overly ruthless, traumatized by Skrull abduction (seems to be recovering).

POWER GRID	1	2	3	4	5	6	7	8	9	10
POWER										
CONSCIENCE										
ALTRUISM										
WISDOM										
COURAGE										
DETERMINATION										
FREE WILL										
VULNERABILITY										

MOON KNIGHT

AFFILIATIONS: Bertrand Crawley, Jack Russell, Punisher, Avengers

STATUS: Free agent; identity protected

The Avengers' relationship with the brutal vigilante known as Moon Knight has been complicated, to say the least. The man was briefly an Avenger, but at last report, he'd burned his membership card and cut all ties with the organization. However, I think it's time to bring him back into the fold; I understand he's tried to rein himself in as of late, and that tells me that maybe he's willing to join us again. We have to understand that nothing we do is going to stop Moon Knight; after all, the man became Moon Knight when he died and refused to stay that way. I honestly believe that you'd have to kill him to make him stop – and the man's died so many times, only to live again, that even that probably wouldn't hinder him. If I can't stop him, I want him in a situation where I can exert some level of control over him, put his talents to good use, and temper his excesses.

PROS: Inspires a great deal of fear among the criminal element; extremely dedicated.

CONS: Not a team player; employs unnecessarily brutal tactics; mentally unstable.

POWER GRID	1	2	3	4	5	6	7	8	9	10
POWER										
CONSCIENCE										
ALTRUISM										
WISDOM										
COURAGE										
DETERMINATION										
FREE WILL										
VULNERABILITY										

MS. MARVEL

AFFILIATIONS: Avengers, X-Men, Starjammers, Operation: Lightning Strike, US Air Force

STATUS: Free agent; identity public

A former spy, NASA security chief Carol Danvers gained powers from the Kree Captain Marvel, and had a brief but commendable super hero career until the mutant Rogue drained her powers and memories. After this Carol spent years struggling with her own identity, and was active for a time in space alongside the Starjammers. Just prior to the Civil War, after Carol won her bout with alcoholism, Ms. Marvel set out to make herself the world's greatest heroine, and she achieved amazing successes against multiple deadly villains. After Osborn took over, Carol was seemingly killed, but she somehow survived (I'm still not clear on the details). Her heroic history, her impressive powers, and her dedication to being the best make her a top choice for one of my new Avengers.

PROS: Flight, super strength, energy blasts and absorption, extensive training as a hero and espionage officer.

CONS: Carol still struggles to connect with many of her most basic emotions and memories, and she has had recent setbacks with her latest death and resurrection (I know how that feels). I'll have to ensure she stays focused on her recovery from alcoholism as well.

POWER GRID	1	2	3	4	5	6	7	8	9	10
POWER										
CONSCIENCE										
ALTRUISM										
WISDOM										
COURAGE										
DETERMINATION										
FREE WILL										
VULNERABILITY										

NAMOR THE SUB-MARINER

AFFILIATIONS: Atlantis, X-Men, Avengers, Defenders, All-Winners Squad, Invaders

STATUS: Atlantean royalty; identity public

As a young man, Prince Namor of Atlantis terrorized humanity with his awesome strength, but I met him facing a greater threat: the Axis Powers. Throughout the war he proved an unswerving ally. Despite claims against all surface-dwellers, the Sub-Mariner has long championed justice and freedom. In the modern era he has worked alongside villains and heroes, and has even led Atlantean forces against the surface world, but some of that erratic behavior is not his fault; Reed Richards discovered that Namor's hybrid nature makes him irrational if he spends too long in only one environment, either air or water. Namor professes to only care about Atlanteans, but he has served with many heroic teams, and even joined Norman Osborn's ersatz X-Men secretly planning to undermine them before reconnecting with Cyclops' group. The recent Atlantean diaspora has weakened his army, but I suspect he has troops ready in every sea. I only hope they remain on our side.

PROS: Natural leader with a strict code of honor, willing to take on any challenge.

CONS: As ruler of Atlantis, he is responsible for citizens outside US jurisdiction; bouts of mental instability.

POWER GRID	1	2	3	4	5	6	7	8	9	10
POWER										
CONSCIENCE										
ALTRUISM										
WISDOM										
COURAGE										
DETERMINATION										
FREE WILL										
VULNERABILITY										

NAMORA

AFFILIATIONS: Atlas Foundation, Sub-Mariner, Hercules

STATUS: Atlantean royalty, wanted for questioning; no dual identity

Though Namor is an exceptional individual, a blend between Atlantean and human genetics, his "cousin" Namora shares his vast powers, including immense strength and winged ankles, due to her similarly hybrid nature. Another hero who was active during the War and believed dead for decades, the Agents of Atlas recently discovered Namora in suspended animation. Since awakening to learn of the loss of her cloned daughter, Namorita, to Nitro, she has not been at all shy to show her feelings and back her words with action. She allied (indirectly) with the Hulk during his attack on Earth, actively stood against Osborn and the Skrulls, and has worked tirelessly to fight for the life of sea creatures, Atlanteans, and other innocents. Namora has been romantically linked to Namor and Hercules in recent months. Namora has a lot to offer the Initiative, and we should try to convince her that supporting us is in her best interests.

PROS: Vast power, ties to Atlantis and the mysterious Atlas Foundation.

CONS: Princess of a foreign power; her relationship with the Agents of Atlas is vague, and I don't know how far I can trust her.

POWER GRID	1	2	3	4	5	6	7	8	9	10
POWER										
CONSCIENCE										
ALTRUISM										
WISDOM										
COURAGE										
DETERMINATION										
FREE WILL										
VULNERABILITY										

NEW MUTANTS

AFFILIATIONS: X-Men, Cyclops, Professor X, Magneto, Cable

STATUS: Free agents; identities protected

I had limited involvement with the original New Mutants group, formed by Professor Xavier as the next generation of mutant heroes when his X-Men were believed dead. These youths have now grown into capable adults, accomplished in the use of their powers, and they have rejoined for special missions now that the X-Men have relocated onto Utopia. Talented and powerful operatives like Cannonball, Sunspot, Magma, Karma, and Moonstar (despite the absence of her powers) alongside returns Magik (who sets off all kinds of mystical warnings), Cypher (who was believed deceased for years) and Warlock (back from space, apparently). The New Mutants have had recent battles against the Savage Land Mutates and the Right. As much as I would love to utilize this talented group, they report directly to Cyclops and focus primarily on mutant rights. I can't help but wonder why Cyclops sanctions these individual team activities when the entire mutant population seems melded into one military unit of late.

PROS: A diverse power set and a capable group of young mutants; highly trained.

CONS: This group is isolated among the rest of the mutants on Utopia.

POWER GRID	POW	CON	ALT	WIS	COU	DET	FRW	VUL
CANNONBALL	8	9	10	9	10	10	9	7
CYPHER	7	9	9	10	10	9	9	8
KARMA	8	9	10	9	10	9	9	9
MAGIK	8	5	6	9	10	10	9	8
MAGMA	8	9	10	9	10	9	9	8
MOONSTAR	6	9	10	9	10	10	9	7
SUNSPOT	8	9	9	9	10	9	9	7
WARLOCK	9	10	10	10	10	10	9	6

NIGHT NURSE

AFFILIATIONS: Dr. Strange, Daredevil

STATUS: Free agent; identity protected

Though I cannot condone acting outside the laws of our country, I recognize that most of our nation's super heroes have acted of their own accord and at tremendous personal sacrifice, with very few public or private benefits. The mysteriously named Night Nurse, though not possessing super-powers, has provided free medical services for heroes like Daredevil, Spider-Man, and Luke Cage when they would not have received services otherwise, and also at great personal sacrifice. Heroes come in all forms, and the Night Nurse is definitely a hero. She has recently been romantically linked to Dr. Strange (who was a medical doctor in his former life), and aided him in a mystical battle, though I am unsure of the current status of their relationship. She would be an excellent resource to the Avengers on a regular basis. I'm not sure where the name "Night Nurse" came from; perhaps a code word among the heroes who privately sought her for services.

PROS: Expert medical training; cool head in the face of extreme pressure.

CONS: Is accustomed to operating outside the law and providing services "off-the-books."

POWER GRID	1	2	3	4	5	6	7	8	9	10
POWER										
CONSCIENCE										
ALTRUISM										
WISDOM										
COURAGE										
DETERMINATION										
FREE WILL										
VULNERABILITY										

NIGHT THRASHER

AFFILIATIONS: New Warriors, Counter-Force, Avengers Resistance

STATUS: Active vigilante; identity protected

Night Thrasher is a troubled young former mutant with bioelectrical powers similar to an electric eel, who is hell-bent on proving himself equal to or better than his deceased brother, the previous Night Thrasher. Previously going by the code name "Bandit," he took up the mantle of Night Thrasher and when his brother was killed in the Stamford incident. I see a lot of Tony Stark's qualities in him, like his desire to lead and take control of situations due to lack of trust in others. It is because of these qualities that we need to keep an eye on him until he can prove himself. He is a perfect candidate for the Avengers Academy as a student, but I can't see him agreeing to join the school to be trained. He is good in the tactical department, but someone you'd want to keep away from secret data and computers.

PROS: Leadership potential.

CONS: Lives in his brother's shadow too much, causing him to be unreliable at times; driven to prove himself at all times.

POWER GRID	1	2	3	4	5	6	7	8	9	10
POWER										
CONSCIENCE										
ALTRUISM										
WISDOM										
COURAGE										
DETERMINATION										
FREE WILL										
VULNERABILITY										

NIGHTHAWK

AFFILIATIONS: Defenders, SHIELD

STATUS: Free agent; identity protected

Nighthawk is a former SHIELD agent, who joined the group to make up for his father's involvement with the Sons of the Serpent. He was caught leading a team to destroy the Serpent's Mad Bomb weapon, but countered the device's maddening effects with SHIELD-tech until his predecessor as Nighthawk, Kyle Richmond, and She-Hulk aided him in finishing the mission. Richmond started training the SHIELD agent after Tony Stark stripped Richmond of his heroic persona in a dispute over unauthorized missions. Showing his prowess with a new Nighthawk suit, the SHIELD agent soon joined the Richmond-sponsored Defenders, a team that was unfortunately shut down by Norman Osborn. With all the training the new Nighthawk received, it wouldn't surprise me if his destiny continues despite the Defenders' ending. I need more material on this new Nighthawk to determine how good he really is. I know too little about him, and despite the trust his SHIELD superiors had in him, I fear his inexperience in the field as Nighthawk could be a problem.

PROS: Team player, SHIELD training.

CONS: Inexperienced as Nighthawk.

POWER GRID	1	2	3	4	5	6	7	8	9	10
POWER										
CONSCIENCE										
ALTRUISM										
WISDOM										
COURAGE										
DETERMINATION										
FREE WILL										
VULNERABILITY										

NORTHSTAR

AFFILIATIONS: X-Men, Alpha Flight

STATUS: Free agent (Canadian); identity public

One of the few surviving members of the original Alpha Flight, who were tragically killed in the battle with the Collective, Jean-Paul Beaubier seems actively involved with the X-Men, which actually surprises me. During my brief associations with Northstar, I have noticed him to be intensely fast-moving, quick-tempered, and impetuous, frequently struggling with his past as a misguided terrorist and his relationship to his twin sister, the confused and often mentally impaired Aurora. Northstar has been a very public hero, especially in Canada, with his Olympic-level skiing and his public media outing as a homosexual. To further complicate matters, Northstar was killed and resurrected a few years ago, but Wolverine assures me that Northstar has been more focused and successful than ever as a hero in recent months. Under the right circumstances, Northstar could make a very talented Avenger, and I believe he could benefit from the associations with the team, as we would benefit from having him.

PROS: Trained super hero with a long history of teamwork.

CONS: High amounts of media controversy; focuses on mutant causes primarily.

POWER GRID	1	2	3	4	5	6	7	8	9	10
POWER										
CONSCIENCE										
ALTRUISM										
WISDOM										
COURAGE										
DETERMINATION										
FREE WILL										
VULNERABILITY										

NOVA

AFFILIATIONS: New Warriors, Nova Corps, Secret Avengers

STATUS: Free agent; identity protected

I remember all too well those early days, when I went through such intense training and learned the rigors and pains of war. I watched hundreds of men die in World War II, sacrificing themselves for the greater good of their country. However, it was these same experiences that transformed me into a man capable of commanding the Avengers, and helped me to be able to call the hard shots. It seems that Nova has undergone a similar growth process. From a wayward hero on Earth to a space-traversing war general, Nova has a long history as a hero now and has single-handedly saved millions of lives across the universe. He has agreed to take part in my Secret Avengers project, despite his ongoing duties as an intergalactic protector and the leader of the Nova Corps trainees (which apparently contain a few humans). His access to the extraterrestrial database the Worldmind grants him vast knowledge of the universe, a resource we would do well to approach.

PROS: Extremely powerful, with intergalactic connections and capabilities.

CONS: I worry that Nova has lost some of his connection to his home planet, but he assures me that Earth will always be home to him.

POWER GRID	1	2	3	4	5	6	7	8	9	10
POWER										
CONSCIENCE										
ALTRUISM										
WISDOM										
COURAGE										
DETERMINATION										
FREE WILL										
VULNERABILITY										

PALADIN

AFFILIATIONS: Thunderbolts, Defenders, Initiative, SHIELD, Heroes for Hire, Intruders, Outlaws, Silver Sable, Wasp

STATUS: Free agent; identity protected

Never been sure what to make of this guy, and it seems I'm not alone. Even with my new job's intelligence resources, I can't find much about his background or real identity. With or without his mask, the only name he ever uses is Paladin. He's an elite mercenary, one of the highest-paid and most skillful men in his field. He's worked with many heroes, including the Avengers and myself, and I can vouch for his abilities and courage — he seems to be a good man at his core; but depending on what job he's doing and who's hiring him, he can be dangerously amoral and ruthless. He's betrayed allies like me and Daredevil, for instance, when the price was right. His cold professionalism has its limits, though; while he worked with Norman Osborn's corrupt black ops Thunderbolts, reports indicate he repeatedly subverted the group's more sinister activities and eventually played a key role in their defeat by the Avengers.

PROS: Slightly superhuman physical abilities, skilled unarmed combatant, veteran covert operative, expert marksman, carries stun gun and other weapons.

CONS: Shifting loyalties and values, greedy, womanizer, sometimes ruthless.

POWER GRID	1	2	3	4	5	6	7	8	9	10
POWER										
CONSCIENCE										
ALTRUISM										
WISDOM										
COURAGE										
DETERMINATION										
FREE WILL										
VULNERABILITY										

PEOPLE'S DEFENSE FORCE

AFFILIATIONS: USAgent, Quicksilver

STATUS: Chinese government agents; identities protected

The People's Defense Force is China's newest team of super heroes, replacing Radioactive Man's Force. It includes at least a dozen individuals; intelligence on the team is sketchy, but among its members are the Collective Man, Radioactive Man, Princess of Clouds, Scientific Beast, Most Perfect Hero, Lady of Ten Suns, and the Ninth Immortal (names loosely translated). We have large files on Collective Man and Radioactive Man, of course, as both men have had extensive dealings with the West, but the other members have, to the best of our knowledge, never operated outside China and are largely mysterious to us. The West recently got its first full glimpse of them when they teamed with Hank Pym's Avengers to defend China from the exiled Inhuman king the Unspoken. They did eventually unite to defeat the threat, but relations between the teams were fraught with tension; in hindsight, maybe USAgent and Quicksilver weren't the best Avengers to send to make first contact with the team. I sincerely hope our next meeting with them will be friendlier.

PROS: Diverse power sets; good teamwork skills.

CONS: Primary loyalty is to China; full capabilities largely unknown.

POWER GRID	POW	CON	ALT	WIS	COU	DET	FRW	VUL
COLLECTIVE MAN	8	9	10	9	10	10	8	7
LADY OF TEN SUNS	8	9	9	9	10	10	8	8
MOST PERFECT HERO	9	9	9	9	10	10	8	6
NINTH IMMORTAL	9	9	9	9	10	10	8	6
PRINCESS OF CLOUDS	8	9	9	9	10	10	8	7
RADIOACTIVE MAN	9	8	10	10	10	10	8	7
SCIENTIFIC BEAST	9	9	9	10	10	10	8	6

PHOTON

AFFILIATIONS: Avengers, Nextwave Squad

STATUS: Free agent; identity public

A New Orleans native, Monica Rambeau was always dedicated to helping others. Her initial career choice with the New Orleans Harbor Patrol was a natural choice. After being exposed to other-dimensional energies, Monica gained the extraordinary ability to transform herself into any kind of energy in the electromagnetic spectrum. Monica was still new to the super-hero game when she joined the Avengers as a member-in-training, but quickly grew confident in her abilities, becoming one of the teams' most dependable members. When the Wasp resigned as Avengers chairman, I nominated Monica for the role, and she proudly led the team through a number of travails for a time. Even after her full-time service ended, Monica always stayed committed to the Avengers, aiding them from time to time in various missions. She is also a strong family woman and maintains a close relationship with her parents, who constantly fear for their daughter's safety. Monica's experience, power, and sense of right make her a valued ally, and I am confident she will continue serving honorably.

PROS: Strong leadership skills; experienced team player; space travel capability.

CONS: Her family has pushed her in the past to give up super heroics.

POWER GRID	1	2	3	4	5	6	7	8	9	10
POWER										
CONSCIENCE										
ALTRUISM										
WISDOM										
COURAGE										
DETERMINATION										
FREE WILL										
VULNERABILITY										

PORTAL

AFFILIATIONS: ARMOR, Darkhawk

STATUS: Government agent; identity protected

Portal has certainly come a long way in a relatively short time. Born and raised in Hartsdale, New Mexico, it was only a few years ago that he fled his Kisani tribal community upon the manifestation of his mutant ability to create and/or access dimensional warps to transport himself and others. Now, he serves as director of the Alternate Reality Monitoring and Operational Response Agency (ARMOR), a top-secret United Nations–established international organization. Under Portal's leadership, ARMOR acts as a first responder to all incidents of trans-reality conflict, guarding our own Earth-616 against contamination by extradimensional agents and disruptions to the timestream. Based in the Hollow, a self-sufficient bunker sunk many miles underground that is accessible only via teleportation, ARMOR forecasters track the "Planetstorms" caused by converging alternate realities. But Portal does not merely serve a supervisory function as director of ARMOR — he also uses a directional mechanism built into his body armor (believed to be extraterrestrial in origin) to focus his innate warp powers and transport ARMOR agents to extradimensional missions.

PROS: Mutant ability to generate dimensional warps; access to sizeable assets and resources as director of ARMOR.

CONS: Portal is sometimes impeded by the inefficiency that plagues every massive bureaucracy.

POWER GRID	1	2	3	4	5	6	7	8	9	10
POWER										
CONSCIENCE										
ALTRUISM										
WISDOM										
COURAGE										
DETERMINATION										
FREE WILL										
VULNERABILITY										

PRINCE OF ORPHANS

AFFILIATIONS: Iron Fist, Fat Cobra, Lei-Kung the Thunderer

STATUS: Free agent; identity protected

The Prince of Orphans' origins are mysterious, although he apparently originates on Earth, unlike most of the Immortal Weapons. In addition to his martial arts prowess and apparent immortality, he can also transform into a green mist. We know he was an Immortal Weapon by the '30s, when he began pursuing then-Iron Fist Orson Randall over some arcane rule violation. Randall eventually won him over to his side, and he began training an army of female warriors in K'un-Lun with Lei-Kung, the Thunderer. Decades later, he unleashed this army on a Hydra force determined to destroy K'un-Lun, and they were victorious. After aiding Iron Fist and the Weapons against several foes, he continues to train the Weapons and was recently spotted battling a ghostly army in Kunming, China. I'd be interested in seeing if the Prince would be willing to help train our agents, as he did for the Thunderer.

PROS: Decades of experience; capable of raising and training an army.

CONS: Answers to unknown authority; capabilities and agenda largely unknown.

POWER GRID	1	2	3	4	5	6	7	8	9	10
POWER										
CONSCIENCE										
ALTRUISM										
WISDOM										
COURAGE										
DETERMINATION										
FREE WILL										
VULNERABILITY										

PRODIGY

AFFILIATIONS: Heavy Hitters, Slingers

STATUS: Free agent; identity protected

After Spider-Man adopted four alternative identities (one of many questionable decisions he has made over the years), those identities were later adopted by four young fledgling heroes who made up the group the Slingers. One of them, Prodigy, struggled with defining his heroic role, especially when he learned of the group's manipulation by my old ally the Black Marvel. During the Civil War, Prodigy got drunk and publicly protested the Initiative but was soon defeated by Iron Man and incarcerated. Ironically, he later registered and was manipulated by Osborn into pursuing criminal activities among the Nevada-based Heavy Hitters, but Prodigy made the right choice and tried exposing Osborn for the criminal he was. This young man has had a difficult career as a hero thus far, but he could be a powerful addition to the Avengers with the right amount of training and supervision.

PROS: Willing to take public stands and risks to do the right thing.

CONS: Has frequently struggled with poor decision-making; has had struggles with public drunkenness and incarceration; is bitter about recent involvement with the government.

POWER GRID	1	2	3	4	5	6	7	8	9	10
POWER										
CONSCIENCE										
ALTRUISM										
WISDOM										
COURAGE										
DETERMINATION										
FREE WILL										
VULNERABILITY										

PROFESSOR X

AFFILIATIONS: X-Men, Shi'ar, Illuminati

STATUS: Free agent; no dual identity

I understand how dire the mutant situation is, I really do, but I would not respond to the threats of extinction they face in the same way that they have. For years, Charles Xavier has purported that his ultimate goal is a peaceful coexistence between humans and mutants, but this is consistently done according to his own definition of success. There are multiple examples of him using his telepathic abilities to erase or alter the minds of others, for reasons justified solely by him. He has lied to governments and his own allies on multiple occasions. In addition, his struggles with sanity (resulting in the Onslaught incident) and his connections to the Shi'ar, his propensity for healing and then paralyzing his legs, dying and coming back, and losing and regaining his powers are among the many reasons that I lack faith in this man. Beast seems to share many of my concerns. Professor X is one to watch closely.

PROS: World-renowned expert on mutation; widely seen as a humanitarian.

CONS: Has used powers for his own benefit, often at the expense of other humans and mutants.

POWER GRID	1	2	3	4	5	6	7	8	9	10
POWER										
CONSCIENCE										
ALTRUISM										
WISDOM										
COURAGE										
DETERMINATION										
FREE WILL										
VULNERABILITY										

PROTECTOR

AFFILIATIONS: Kree Empire, "Avengers," 18th Kree Diplomatic Gestalt

STATUS: Free agent (extraterrestrial); identity protected

Protector, a formerly Captain Marvel of Osborn's Avengers, comes from an alternate reality. He is a genetically engineered Kree/cockroach hybrid, whose ship was shot down by the Midas Foundation. As the lone survivor of his ship's crew, he understandably had less than peaceful plans for Earth and planned to conquer the planet and force his world view on humanity. SHIELD caught and incarcerated him at the Cube prison after a few altercations. Aided by the Young Avengers and the Runaways, he later took over the prison. Acting on humanity's behalf during the Skrulls' invasion of Earth, he was asked to join Osborn's version of the Avengers, but left them when he realized they were actually madmen and criminals. Fleeing from them, he changed under unrevealed circumstances into the Protector, bearer of a new set of Nega-Bands. There is a lot of potential in him, and though he only wore the name Captain Marvel in a very dark era of our country, I see him becoming a hero like the late Mar-Vell.

PROS: Superhuman strength & speed, Nega-Bands.

CONS: Unknown power source; Kree world view.

POWER GRID	1	2	3	4	5	6	7	8	9	10
POWER										
CONSCIENCE										
ALTRUISM										
WISDOM										
COURAGE										
DETERMINATION										
FREE WILL										
VULNERABILITY										

KITTY PRYDE

AFFILIATIONS: X-Men, Excalibur, SHIELD

STATUS: Free agent; no dual identity

I thought that Bucky Barnes was young when he became my teammate at 15. But Kitty Pryde discovered her mutant abilities and joined the X-Men when she was only 13-and-a-half! She was seemingly an ordinary girl living in a Chicago suburb when she learned she could become intangible and "phase" through walls. She soon found herself embroiled in a struggle between the X-Men and Hellfire Club, but showed herself brave and capable in this trial by fire and started studying at Xavier's school soon afterward. Kitty is still quite young, but has proved to be mature beyond her years. She not only holds her own among her older fellow X-Men, but has even briefly served as SHIELD's youngest agent. She turned out to be brilliant in computer science, speaks many languages, and can pilot aircraft. Wolverine has even trained her in samurai martial arts. But her spirit hasn't been hardened by all the battles she's gone through. Whenever she and I occasionally cross paths, she remains a fresh-faced, enthusiastic young girl.

PROS: Team player; virtually invulnerable when intangible; possible genius in computer science, moderate skills in Japanese martial arts.

CONS: Mutant "phasing" power is primarily used for defense, not offense.

POWER GRID	1	2	3	4	5	6	7	8	9	10
POWER										
CONSCIENCE										
ALTRUISM										
WISDOM										
COURAGE										
DETERMINATION										
FREE WILL										
VULNERABILITY										

PSYLOCKE

AFFILIATIONS: Captain Britain, X-Men, Exiles

STATUS: Free agent (UK); identity protected

Psylocke, twin sister of Captain Britain, who has proved a trusted ally on multiple occasions, has had a difficult and complex history as a hero. A former S.T.R.I.K.E. agent, she then joined the X-Men, soon finding herself against immensely dangerous villains like Sabretooth and Mojo, and in time, as part of a villainous plot, her mind and powers were transplanted into the body of an Asian assassin named Kwannon. (I've asked Beast for more clarification on this, but he says it's better not to ask). After deaths, resurrections, and inter-dimensional heroics, she is back with the X-Men, using her psychic sword in defense of the mutant cause. I'm concerned to no small degree about Psylocke's recent activities in Japan, but Beast and Wolverine assure me that she is a trustworthy member of the X-Men who has proved herself time and again. However, I don't see any way to utilize her as long as she remains so closely connected to the X-Men, though we have had success with Wolverine.

PROS: Martial artist and telepath of no small renown.

CONS: Multiple deaths and resurrections have caused identity crises and shifts in her power sets.

POWER GRID	1	2	3	4	5	6	7	8	9	10
POWER										
CONSCIENCE										
ALTRUISM										
WISDOM										
COURAGE										
DETERMINATION										
FREE WILL										
VULNERABILITY										

PUNISHER

AFFILIATIONS: Morbius

STATUS: Free agent, fugitive; identity public

I remember what it was like to be in the war. Lethal force, though always a last resort, was sometimes necessary to accomplish the tasks facing the Allied forces. In this day and age, it sometimes feels like we are always at war, but killing should always be the last option. Though many of my current allies, including Wolverine, Bucky, and Moon Knight, have slain many evildoers, they seem to be working toward the greater good, toward saving the world and acting as heroes. The Punisher remains the exception. When Frank Castle's family was killed, he dedicated his life to violently eradicating criminals, and he has killed hundreds of men on the streets of New York and around the world. Lethal force is the Punisher's preference; I made a mistake when I allied with him during the "Civil War." Castle himself was murdered at the hands of Osborn's Wolverine, but there are rumors that he is now beneath the streets as a Frankenstein being, with Morbius watching over him.

PROS: Tireless efforts spent curbing international criminal activity.

CONS: Frank Castle is a savage murderer.

POWER GRID	1	2	3	4	5	6	7	8	9	10
POWER										
CONSCIENCE										
ALTRUISM										
WISDOM										
COURAGE										
DETERMINATION										
FREE WILL										
VULNERABILITY										

QUASAR

AFFILIATIONS: Avengers, Guardians of the Galaxy, Star Masters, Project: PEGASUS

STATUS: Free agent; identity protected

Quasar considered himself quite an everyman and was once denied a field agent position in SHIELD due to lack of a "killer instinct." Needless to say, he was surprised when the cosmic entity Eon chose him as Protector of the Universe. During Quasar's tenure as an Avenger, he gained a reputation for holding himself and his colleagues to the highest ethical standards. He also has an immense threshold for self-sacrifice, once exiling himself from Earth after he absorbed the essence of Ego, the Living Planet. In short, Quasar's commitment to doing the right thing, even at personal expense, knows no bounds. He wields the Quantum Bands, which among many other things, give him the ability to create solid energy constructs, an ability he employs with considerable innovation. Nowadays, the majority of Quasar's adventures take him off Earth, addressing cosmic-scale threats alongside other space-faring adventurers. Wherever he is, I am confident he will remain as dedicated a protector as I remember him to be.

PROS: Space travel ability, familiarity with extraterrestrials; strong moral compass.

CONS: Rarely on Earth for long.

POWER GRID	1	2	3	4	5	6	7	8	9	10
POWER										
CONSCIENCE										
ALTRUISM										
WISDOM										
COURAGE										
DETERMINATION										
FREE WILL										
VULNERABILITY										

QUICKSILVER

AFFILIATIONS: Avengers Academy, Avengers, Knights of Wundagore, X-Factor, Inhumans

STATUS: Free agent; identity public

Pietro Maximoff is one of the first Avengers I ever trained. The odds were against him as the son of infamous mutant terrorist Magneto, and yet Pietro's largely risen above that legacy. Granted, he started out in Magneto's Brotherhood of Evil Mutants, and Pietro's instability has pulled him back onto the wrong side of the law on occasion, but his long-term instincts are always to do and be good. Quicksilver's later rogue periods were due to either mental manipulation by Maximus or alien imposters, so his truly criminal days seem long past. He has recently become an instructor at our new Avengers Academy. As someone who's played both hero and villain, he offers our students a unique opportunity to learn from both his achievements and his mistakes. Sadly, Pietro's greatest vulnerability might be his family: an evil father, a beloved but criminally insane sister (poor Wanda), a failed marriage (to Crystal of the Inhumans) and an estranged daughter (Luna) make Pietro one of our more melancholy Avengers, albeit a dedicated one given his lack of a personal life.

PROS: Superhuman speed, fast learner, combat veteran, tactical skills, leadership experience.

CONS: Mentally unstable, arrogant, mutant chauvinist, troubled family ties.

POWER GRID	1	2	3	4	5	6	7	8	9	10
POWER										
CONSCIENCE										
ALTRUISM										
WISDOM										
COURAGE										
DETERMINATION										
FREE WILL										
VULNERABILITY										

RAGE

AFFILIATIONS: Avengers Resistance, New Warriors, Counter Force, Initiative, Avengers, Psionex

STATUS: Free agent; identity protected

This young man tricked his way into the Avengers' ranks, and though he has done a lot of good while working with the New Warriors and other teams, will in my eyes always stay a huge liability. Looking at his track record working for the Initiative, he once again showed that he has problems with authority figures, and he still tends to act extremely impulsively. Despite all the things he had gone through over the last couple of years, he still doesn't seem to know how to take responsibility for his actions. I trained him, and I think I know how the kid ticks; and maybe I should be more forgiving, but the way he acts is dangerous and could lead to people dying in a dire situation because they don't have bulletproof skin like him or Luke Cage. The loss of his grandmother and foster father obviously didn't help him when it comes to controlling his rage. Despite my respect for the good work he did alongside others, he is still a teenager, who has a lot of growing up to do.

PROS: Team player; superhuman strength & durability.

CONS: Acts irresponsibly.

POWER GRID	1	2	3	4	5	6	7	8	9	10
POWER										
CONSCIENCE										
ALTRUISM										
WISDOM										
COURAGE										
DETERMINATION										
FREE WILL										
VULNERABILITY										

AFFILIATIONS: Initiative, Avengers, Spider-Man, Hulk, Rick Jones

STATUS: Government agents; identities protected

It's a weird quirk of fate how a distress call from Rick Jones and a crisis involving the Hulk first brought the Rangers together, just as Hulk and Rick helped bring together the Avengers years earlier. Of course, the Rangers haven't been quite as successful since their members are scattered across several different states, making the group's activities sporadic for years. They hit their stride as the Initiative's state team in Texas, which gave them steady funding, oversight and direction. How they'll fare post-Initiative remains to be seen. Firebird and Living Lightning both have Avengers experience, not to mention Miguel's electrical powers, Firebird's flame powers and her apparent immortality; serenely wise beyond her years, Bonita may be the glue that holds the group together. Tornado-generating ex-SHIELD agent Texas Twister, his pistol-packing girlfriend Shooting Star, ghostly cowboy Phantom Rider and Cheyenne warrior Red Wolf round out the team formidably. Armor-hided powerhouse Antonio Rodriguez - Armadillo - also joined for a while, but soon returned to crime — a pity, since I've long believed Rodriguez has the potential to reform.

PROS: All experienced, trained and capable; foremost protectors of Southwestern USA.

CONS: Slade and Daniels sometimes unstable, Star and Daniels prone to mercenary outlook.

POWER GRID	POW	CON	ALT	WIS	COU	DET	FRW	VUL
FIREBIRD	8	10	10	9	10	10	8	8
LIVING LIGHTNING	8	9	10	9	10	9	8	8
PHANTOM RIDER	8	9	9	9	10	10	7	8
RED WOLF	7	10	10	9	10	10	7	9
SHOOTING STAR	6	9	9	9	10	10	8	9
TEXAS TWISTER	7	9	9	9	10	10	8	8

AFFILIATIONS: Avengers Academy, Ka-Zar, Tigra, Moon-Boy

STATUS: Free agent; identity protected

Reptil, a young boy with the ability to take on the attributes of dinosaurs, illustrates the failings of the Initiative under the control of both SHIELD and HAMMER. Under SHIELD, Reptil sacrificed a promising future as an Initiative hero to save Moon-Boy from captivity; even worse, once Osborn took control of the Initiative, Reptil was imprisoned and subjected to several torturous experimental procedures. He's a good kid; optimistic, brave, and selfless, and he'll make a fine Avenger some day. Unfortunately, I fear that his traumatic experiences with Osborn, combined with the loss of his parents, may have left him with lasting psychological scars, and if he falls under the wrong influences, the results could be catastrophic both for himself and the world. Luckily, we have just the place for him, and others like him; I recommend that he be enrolled in Avengers Academy immediately. He's already had some Initiative training, and his experiences have been less traumatic than those of the other students, so I hope he can exert some influence on them.

PROS: Good attitude; prior Initiative training.

CONS: Psychological potential for self-destructive actions; empathic abilities only useful on dinosaurs.

POWER GRID	1	2	3	4	5	6	7	8	9	10
POWER										
CONSCIENCE										
ALTRUISM										
WISDOM										
COURAGE										
DETERMINATION										
FREE WILL										
VULNERABILITY										

AFFILIATIONS: X-Men, Wolverine, Ms. Marvel, Mystique, Nightcrawler

STATUS: Free agent; identity protected

A self-described Southern belle, Rogue has had a troubled life dealing with her mutant absorption powers via direct contact as both an adolescent and adult. Seeking help to control her powers, she joined the mutant group the X-Men and has proven herself time and time again to be worthy of being a member of that team. Unfortunately due to her powers, her psyche often becomes unstable, and she has been known to take on aspects of a villain's personality, causing her to turn on her team. I believe with proper meditation training it is possible that she could effectively learn to control her powers. She would be a great asset to any team as its leader or second-in-command and would benefit a young team like the Runaways or the group of adolescents calling themselves the Young Masters. One of the most notable villains to successfully reform through hard work and dedication, she would be a perfect candidate to lead the Thunderbolts if Luke Cage were to decide to step down from that position.

PROS: Loyal; leadership qualities; team player.

CONS: Unstable at times due to powers.

POWER GRID	1	2	3	4	5	6	7	8	9	10
POWER										
CONSCIENCE										
ALTRUISM										
WISDOM										
COURAGE										
DETERMINATION										
FREE WILL										
VULNERABILITY										

RUNAWAYS

AFFILIATIONS: Cloak, Dagger, Young Avengers

STATUS: Free agents; no dual identities

Virtually no team out there frustrates me the way the Runaways do. Repeatedly living up to their name, this group of young superhumans seems to get themselves in constant danger, while simultaneously eschewing our attempts to help them. Since my first encounter with them after they defeated their criminal parents the Pride, their subsequent encounters with the Avengers, X-Men and SHIELD have proven fruitless in helping them. Led by spellcaster Nico Minoru, the others include super-strong preteen Molly Hayes, alien Karolina Dean, semi-android Victor Mancha and plant-controlling Klara Prast. Unlike the many other youthful teams that have sprung up, the Runaways have little interest in proper training, preferring to keep to themselves and always distrusting us; not that they haven't been given proper reason due to several misunderstandings. They've tragically lost several members already, and one was hospitalized at last report. I only hope we can convince them to stop running sooner than later, before they lose more.

PROS: Tight family unit; vast resources left behind by the Pride.

CONS: Untrusting and inexperienced; possible ties to the Kingpin.

POWER GRID	POW	CON	ALT	WIS	COU	DET	FRW	VUL
MOLLY HAYES	8	10	8	5	10	8	9	7
KAROLINA DEAN	5	8	8	7	9	8	10	8
VICTOR MANCHA	8	8	8	10	9	8	10	6
KLARA PLAST	5	10	7	5	7	7	9	8
NICO MINORU	8	8	8	7	10	8	10	8

SABRA

AFFILIATIONS: Mossod, X-Corporation

STATUS: Israeli government agent; identity protected

Sabra is the graduate of an Israeli super-soldier program, and once modeled her costume after her nation's flag. A patriotic hero, I can certainly relate to her experience. A capable soldier, she is thoroughly trained in espionage and various forms of combat and has gone toe-to-toe with the Hulk. Her ability to work effectively behind the scenes and familiarity with military style hierarchy makes her a valuable agent. However, she is an operative of the Israeli government and loyal first and foremost to her native land. Sabra is a mutant, who, with her government's permission, worked closely with Charles Xavier's X-Corporation, and has a long history of association with heroes from the United States. Her strong, proud personality may irk those who have little experience with her, but her motivation and work ethic are undeniable. Sabra is a valuable ally in the Middle East, and maintaining a good working relationship with her will bring great benefits should our missions bring us to that region.

PROS: Extensive training in covert operations, combat, and intelligence gathering.

CONS: Operates under the jurisdiction of a foreign government.

POWER GRID	1	2	3	4	5	6	7	8	9	10
POWER										
CONSCIENCE										
ALTRUISM										
WISDOM										
COURAGE										
DETERMINATION										
FREE WILL										
VULNERABILITY										

SASQUATCH

AFFILIATIONS: Alpha Flight, Hulk

STATUS: Canadian government agent; identity protected

Although a Canadian by birth, Sasquatch has considerable ties with the US. While studying physics at Pennsylvania State University on a football scholarship, he met Bruce Banner and became interested in gamma ray research. Upon graduation, Sasquatch played professional football for the Green Bay Packers for 3 years, but retired when Banner's transformations into the Hulk due to gamma ray exposure became public knowledge. Sasquatch enrolled at the Massachusetts Institute of Technology and earned his Ph.D. in physics before returning to Canada and joining the staff of Department H. Upon experimenting with gamma rays north of the Arctic Circle, he unwittingly pierced a mystic barrier that melded his body with the monstrous Great Beast Tanaraq. Since then, Sasquatch has been a stalwart member of Canada's Alpha Flight team and most recently worked with Omega Flight, a joint Canadian-US operation designed to protect Canada from superhuman refugees fleeing jurisdiction of the US Superhuman Registration Act. Given these extensive ties to the US, we will be reaching out to Sasquatch as a potential ally north of the border.

PROS: Enhanced senses; superhuman strength & durability; regenerative abilities; expertise in physics and radiation.

CONS: Occasionally succumbs to the influence of the Great Beast Tanaraq.

POWER GRID	1	2	3	4	5	6	7	8	9	10
POWER										
CONSCIENCE										
ALTRUISM										
WISDOM										
COURAGE										
DETERMINATION										
FREE WILL										
VULNERABILITY										

SCARLET SPIDER

AFFILIATIONS: Justice, Ultragirl, Rage, Night Thrasher

STATUS: Free agent; identity public

More than anyone else, the Scarlet Spider is a creation of the Initiative; he is one of a trio of clones grown from the cells of Michael Van Patrick, a fallen Initiative cadet, and garbed in Spider-Man's technologically advanced "Iron Spider" costume. His fellow clones, who were essentially his brothers, were slain in battle with the renegade Initiative creations KIA and Ragnarok; the Spider is somewhat adrift without them, although his teammates in the anti-Initiative teams Counter-Force and later the Avengers Resistance provided some much-needed moral support. He even maintained the strength to resist the offer by his malign creator, Baron von Blitzschlag, to resurrect his brothers. I understand that he and I share some common ground; Abraham Erskine, the creator of the super-soldier serum, was Van Patrick's grandfather and devised the exercise plan and organic diet that shaped the boy's development. I never met the original Scarlet Spider, but I'm told that Spider-Man speaks well of him; whatever his origins, the current Scarlet Spider has done the name proud.

PROS: Excellent stealth capabilities; good teamwork skills.

CONS: Still off-balance after the deaths of his brothers.

POWER GRID	1	2	3	4	5	6	7	8	9	10
POWER										
CONSCIENCE										
ALTRUISM										
WISDOM										
COURAGE										
DETERMINATION										
FREE WILL										
VULNERABILITY										

SCORPION

AFFILIATIONS: Hardball, X-23, SHIELD

STATUS: Free agent, fugitive; identity protected

The Scorpion is the daughter of AIM's current Scientist Supreme, Monica Rappaccini, and an unidentified father. Placed with a family of sleeper agents, she developed a toxic biochemistry and accidentally killed a boy; she subsequently became a vagrant until SHIELD recruited her. She eventually left SHIELD's service, only to join Hydra, but subsequently betrayed them, too. A recent encounter with Spider-Man indicates that she's gained the ability to temporarily neutralize superhuman powers and is apparently working as a mercenary. We don't know who her current employers are, or why she chose them over both Hydra and SHIELD, but I want her brought in. With her SHIELD training and new abilities, she's too dangerous to be left to fall into the wrong hands, especially her mother's. I wonder if maybe she shouldn't have been given a chance at a normal life, but for the daughter of AIM's Scientist Supreme, was a normal life ever possible?

PROS: Power-neutralizing abilities could allow us to take down major threats with ease.

CONS: Uncertain loyalties; power-neutralizing abilities have a short-lived effect.

POWER GRID	1	2	3	4	5	6	7	8	9	10
POWER										
CONSCIENCE										
ALTRUISM										
WISDOM										
COURAGE										
DETERMINATION										
FREE WILL										
VULNERABILITY										

SECRET WARRIORS

AFFILIATIONS: Howling Commandos, Avengers

STATUS: Free agents; identities protected

The Secret Warriors are Nick Fury's personal strike team of secret operatives, assembled from the sons and daughters of superhumans — "caterpillars", as Nick calls them. They include fear-inducing Phobos, speedster Slingshot, metamorphing Stonewall, pyrokinetic Hellfire, teleporting Eden Fesi, and tremor-inducing Quake; the team initially included the mystic Druid, but Fury has apparently dismissed him. The door's open to them coming into the fold, but Nick's apparently discovered some troubling information about SHIELD and Hydra and wants them kept off the grid. I've also received some intel that indicates Fury may have at least two other caterpillar teams in action that we know nothing about; Nick's always kept his cards close to his chest, but it's my job to know what he's up to and this obsessive level of secrecy is troubling. His Secret Warriors have scored some impressive wins against the Skrulls, Hydra, and HAMMER; I saw them in battle against Osborn's forces in Asgard, and they're an impressive group, but they're very green. For their sakes, I hope Nick knows what he's doing.

PROS: Strong leadership from Fury.

CONS: Most of the team is young and largely inexperienced

POWER GRID	POW	CON	ALT	WIS	COU	DET	FRW	UUL
EDEN FESI	7	9	8	8	9	8	8	8
HELLFIRE	7	5	5	8	9	8	8	8
PHOBOS	8	8	8	10	10	10	7	6
QUAKE	8	8	8	9	10	9	9	8
SLINGSHOT	7	9	8	7	9	9	8	9
STONEWALL	8	9	8	7	10	9	8	7

SEPULCRE

AFFILIATIONS: Roxxon Blackridge, Secret Defenders, Shock Troop

STATUS: Free agent; identity protected

She is a victim of the late Dr. Druid's schemes. Bonded to a mystical artifact after being killed by a demon, Sepulcre, originally known as Shadowoman, ended up believing Druid's lies about her empowerment and worked with him against several mystic threats to our planet joining him and others in the Shock Troop and later the Secret Defenders. She was nearly killed when Druid attempted to summon the powerful, malevolent being Slorioth to Earth, but was saved by the Cognoscenti. Since then Sepulcre helped save Spider-Woman and Arachne from the extradimensional Void-Eater. After retiring she came into conflict with Osborn's Thunderbolts after she failed to register when the SHRA was passed. She escaped the government's jurisdiction by accepting a job offer in the Middle East by Roxxon Blackridge. Though I'm not happy seeing someone like her working for a corrupt corporation like Roxxon, I can't deny that at the time she took the job she had no other choice. I don't see her returning to the United States any time soon after the ill-mannered treatment our people inflicted on the costumed community.

PROS: Darkforce energy manipulation, occult knowledge, low-level psychic abilities.

CONS: Dangerous power source, works for Roxxon.

POWER GRID	1	2	3	4	5	6	7	8	9	10
POWER										
CONSCIENCE										
ALTRUISM										
WISDOM										
COURAGE										
DETERMINATION										
FREE WILL										
VULNERABILITY										

SHANG-CHI

AFFILIATIONS: MI6, Freelance Restorations, Heroes for Hire

STATUS: Free agent (Chinese); no dual identity

Shang-Chi is the son of China's most dangerous man, a sinister genius who had Shang-Chi trained to become a living weapon, the greatest master of kung fu. Sent on a mission of assassination, Shang-Chi met his father's nemesis, Sir Denis Nayland Smith, who opened his eyes to his father's evil. Since then, Shang-Chi has turned his great talents to battling both his father and other criminals. I admit to being astounded whenever I have witnessed Shang-Chi in action. He has no super-powers, and yet his unmatched prowess in every Asian martial art makes him seem nearly superhuman in combat. I would have to fight at the peak of my ability to best him in a hand-to-hand battle. To Shang-Chi, the martial arts are indeed an art form that he has perfected. Yet Shang-Chi disdains what he calls the "games of deceit and death" on which he combats evil. There is a side of him that would prefer to live apart from the world of combat, in obscurity and peace.

PROS: Absolute master of all known Asian martial arts. Highly adept with traditional Asian weaponry such as swords and shuriken.

CONS: Ambivalence toward the morality of using violence to combat evil.

POWER GRID	1	2	3	4	5	6	7	8	9	10
POWER										
CONSCIENCE										
ALTRUISM										
WISDOM										
COURAGE										
DETERMINATION										
FREE WILL										
VULNERABILITY										

SHANNA THE SHE-DEVIL

AFFILIATIONS: Ka-Zar, Daredevil

STATUS: Free agent; identity public

Despite being an American citizen, Shanna O'Hara Plunder has spent the bulk of her heroic career overseas in Africa, India, and the Savage Land, and she is now married to Kevin, Lord Plunder (Ka-Zar), a British citizen. With their son, Adam, the two have made their home in the Savage Land, and they have consistently proved themselves willing allies of any heroes who end up in the Savage Land on a mission (including the Avengers' own recent investigation of Sauron after the Raft breakout); they have had their fair share of adventures over the years, against several deadly foes, including demons, gods, and pirates. Shanna has been active on American soil from time to time, against such threats as the Mandrill, Nekra, and one of the Thanosi, a battle that left her with temporary godlike powers. I trust she and Ka-Zar will continue to prove powerful allies when needed, and I will make the Avengers available to them as needed in return.

PROS: Powerful athlete, trained veterinarian.

CONS: Is primarily loyal to animals and the environment; has spent extended amounts of time away from the United States.

POWER GRID	1	2	3	4	5	6	7	8	9	10
POWER										
CONSCIENCE										
ALTRUISM										
WISDOM										
COURAGE										
DETERMINATION										
FREE WILL										
VULNERABILITY										

SHE-HULK

AFFILIATIONS:
Avengers, Fantastic Four,
Heroes for Hire, the Hulk

STATUS: Free agent;
identity public

Many heroes periodically
experience moral dilemmas
when they tread the fine line between enforcing and
violating the law. For She-Hulk, this experience must
be profoundly stranger than for the rest of us, as she is
publicly known both as a super hero and a lawyer. She
takes her name from her more famous cousin, but her
transformations and mental clarity have been infinitely
more stable than his, though she has had episodes in
which she lost control. She-Hulk has a good deal of
experience working in teams and has served as a proud
member of the Avengers and Fantastic Four. Her good

nature brought levity to the constant danger in which we
found ourselves and her sense of law and fairness made
her an especially responsible hero. She-Hulk genuinely
enjoys her life as an adventurer, and despite occasional
bad press that her rather high-profile life sometimes
attracts, her dedication to her colleagues and to the law
make me glad to have her on our side.

PROS: Familiarity with law; experienced team player.

CONS: A number of high-profile relationships may bring
her bad press; has occasionally lost control of her
transformations.

POWER GRID	1	2	3	4	5	6	7	8	9	10
POWER										
CONSCIENCE										
ALTRUISM										
WISDOM										
COURAGE										
DETERMINATION										
FREE WILL										
VULNERABILITY										

SHROUD

AFFILIATIONS: Arachne,
Moon Knight, Avengers

STATUS: Free agent, fugitive;
identity protected

From the tragic deaths of his parents,
the Shroud became disciplined in both
mind and body, sacrificing his eyesight
to obtain mystical senses that make him one of the most
dangerous men alive. He spent years posing as a criminal
mastermind to infiltrate gangs from within, during which
time he led the Night Shift, supernatural criminals he hoped
to redeem from their ill-spent careers. I was one of many
heroes who cooperated with this masquerade, but while its
time has elapsed, he retains an impressive knowledge of
the underworld. His skills at evading the law came into play
during the "Civil War" conflict when he fought at my side.
He's also been romantically involved with Arachne, hopefully

to some good end. From our first meeting in a pitched fight
with the Red Skull, I have never regretted placing my trust
in the Shroud. Although the Registration Act has fallen, the
Shroud remains in the shadows; it's where he works best. If
(Heaven forfend) Moon Knight doesn't work out, the Shroud
would be a capable operative.

PROS: Expert criminologist, natural leader, excellent
martial artist.

CONS: Darkforce powers have occasionally held undue
influence; masquerade as criminal has forced compliance
in several crimes.

POWER GRID	1	2	3	4	5	6	7	8	9	10
POWER										
CONSCIENCE										
ALTRUISM										
WISDOM										
COURAGE										
DETERMINATION										
FREE WILL										
VULNERABILITY										

SILHOUETTE

AFFILIATIONS:
New Warriors,
Night Thrasher

STATUS: Free agent;
identity protected

Silhouette Chord and her
twin brother, the criminal
Midnight's Fire, received
their powers due to a mystic connection to a Cambodian
energy well, though they grew up on the streets of New
York. Silhouette had a long-standing alliance with the
Night Thrasher who was killed in the Stamford disaster,
and the new Night Thrasher, who has been operating
outside the law with a New Warriors team of former
mutants and more recently with the Avengers Resistance
against Osborn. Silhouette joined my side during the
Civil War, but then chose to register and has remained

active in the Initiative since, though she has not received
much media attention. As with any Darkforce wielders,
I grow concerned about the source of her powers, but
I admire her ability to fight crime and use her powers
despite her handicap (a permanent injury related to
being shot years ago).

PROS: Powerful fighter with a unique skill set, including
teleportation of herself and others, phasing, and
manipulation of Darkforce energy.

CONS: Silhouette has a history of changing allies, and her
Darkforce powers are a concern to me.

POWER GRID	1	2	3	4	5	6	7	8	9	10
POWER										
CONSCIENCE										
ALTRUISM										
WISDOM										
COURAGE										
DETERMINATION										
FREE WILL										
VULNERABILITY										

SILVER SABLE

AFFILIATIONS:
Spider-Man,
Paladin, Domino

STATUS: Free agent
(Symkarian);
identity public

Symkarian mercenary Silver Sablinova, aka Silver Sable, is a tough woman to get close to. I've encountered her a few times; she's essentially a good person, but she hides it well underneath a business-like shell of icy disdain. Her methods are a little too brutal for my liking, but I can't dispute her results; there's a very good reason why she can charge the outrageous rates she does. She's also rather indiscriminate about who she works for, although she'll refuse a mission if it's totally beyond the pale. Located in Symkaria, she's an excellent source of information in the European theater and can provide us with a great deal of intelligence in the area. She also has a good relationship with Dr. Doom and could be a go-between in our dealings with him. I understand she's recently had a falling-out with the Wild Pack, but I suspect she'll be back on her feet in no time. If we need her, we'll need to bring a checkbook.

PROS: Highly professional; excellent networking skills; extremely disciplined.

CONS: Questionable choice in associates; can be difficult to work with.

POWER GRID	1	2	3	4	5	6	7	8	9	10
POWER										
CONSCIENCE										
ALTRUISM										
WISDOM										
COURAGE										
DETERMINATION										
FREE WILL										
VULNERABILITY										

SILVER SURFER

AFFILIATIONS: Galactus,
Defenders, Fantastic Four

STATUS: Free agent
(extraterrestrial);
identity protected

As with many of these cosmic types, I haven't often adventured alongside the Silver Surfer. However, from the many stories I've heard from Reed Richards, I know him to be an honorable man. Still, I sometimes find his nobility irreconcilable with the fact that he delivered countless worlds to Galactus' hunger, no matter how noble his reasons for taking the job in the first place. After Silver Surfer left Galactus' service, he was stranded on Earth for several years, and though he consistently felt deprived of the stars, he came to consider Earth a second home. Since Galactus lifted his imprisonment, the Surfer has returned to Earth many times, but made his home among the stars. A wanderer by nature, I can only imagine the adventures he's had in faraway galaxies. I've heard that he has become Galactus' herald once again. Although I trust he won't bring his master to a planet he holds dear, this causes me a great deal of concern. The Surfer I remember would never sacrifice his liberty; perhaps he has changed in more ways than we realize. I remain cautiously optimistic that no confrontation will be necessary.

PROS: Space travel capabilities; knowledge of alien worlds; extremely powerful.

CONS: Current herald of Galactus.

POWER GRID	1	2	3	4	5	6	7	8	9	10
POWER										
CONSCIENCE										
ALTRUISM										
WISDOM										
COURAGE										
DETERMINATION										
FREE WILL										
VULNERABILITY										

SKAAR

AFFILIATIONS:
Hulk, Wolverine

STATUS: Free agent;
no dual identity

I have forever been uneasy about the Hulk, from my earliest associations with the Avengers, even during times when Bruce Banner (at times with the help of Leonard Samson) had the Hulk under control. Now the Hulk has a son! Skaar, to my understanding, was born in the explosions of the world Sakaar (which directly preceded the Hulk War on Earth), and was raised without his parents. Now, a savagely strong being intent on destroying his father, Skaar has made his home on Earth and has somehow been convinced to fight several deadly combats across the globe. He has had massive battles with the Juggernaut and this newly revealed group of super-criminals called the Intel, and even aided Wolverine in his war against Romulus. This is a being that bears close watching. I can't trust Bruce to handle it on his own. There have been a lot of Hulk-level threats running around lately, in green and red forms, and I'm not entirely sure what the best response to these threats is outside of containment.

PROS: Vast super strength, tectonic manipulation powers.

CONS: No loyalties to anyone, and pursuing his own agenda only.

POWER GRID	1	2	3	4	5	6	7	8	9	10
POWER										
CONSCIENCE										
ALTRUISM										
WISDOM										
COURAGE										
DETERMINATION										
FREE WILL										
VULNERABILITY										

SLAPSTICK

AFFILIATIONS: Avengers Resistance, Counter-Force, New Warriors

STATUS: Free agent; identity protected

Slapstick is a strange case in more ways than one. Sometimes it's easy to forget that beneath his animated exterior, Slapstick is still just a normal teenager. After a confrontation with clown-like aliens from Dimension X, he gained the ability to transform into a living cartoon, able to recover from any injury and pull items out of subspace, often for comedic effect. At first he used his powers for good as a solo adventurer, but he joined up with the New Warriors, working with them on multiple occasions. Following the New Warriors' disaster in Stamford, Connecticut, Slapstick joined the Initiative. I understand he and his former teammates felt somewhat persecuted at Camp Hammond. Although the hard feelings were apparently

dealt with, Slapstick left with Justice's Counter-Force, which became the Avengers Resistance to oppose Norman Osborn' administration. Despite the seriousness of the situation, however, Slapstick continued his flippant behavior. Based or his track record, Slapstick seems like the ideal young hero, but I have some reservations about his mental state.

PROS: Optimistic outlook; indestructibility; access to seemingly unlimited subspace cache.

CONS: Erratic behavior; emotionally distant from other humans, possible disconnect from reality.

POWER GRID	1	2	3	4	5	6	7	8	9	10
POWER										
CONSCIENCE										
ALTRUISM										
WISDOM										
COURAGE										
DETERMINATION										
FREE WILL										
VULNERABILITY										

SNOWBIRD

AFFILIATIONS: Alpha Flight, Hercules

STATUS: Free agent (Canadian); identity protected

According to Thor, Snowbird is a demigoddess conceived by a mortal archeologist and Nelvanna — Goddess of the Northern Lights — when the Northern Gods worshipped by the Inuit people sought to sire an Earthbound champion to prevent the return of the extradimensional Great Beasts. She fulfilled that purpose, having defended the Earth from the Great Beasts on multiple occasions as a member of Canada's Alpha Flight team. However, recent tragedies have left Snowbird alone and questioning her purpose in the mortal realm. First, many of her friends and allies in Alpha Flight were killed by the sentient amalgam of mutant energy known as the Collective, the stress of which caused her marriage to self-proclaimed demigod Yukon Jack to fall apart.

Most recently, she faced another hardship upon the seemin; death of her occasional paramour Hercules. Hopefully, she will find the purpose that she's looking for as a partner in ou mission of maintaining global peace and security.

PROS: Transmorph capable of assuming the form of any animal native to Canada; limited post-cognitive abilities; superhuman strength & durability; extensive RCMP training team player.

CONS: Her never-ending mission to slay any Great Beast tha enters the Earth realm takes priority over all other objective: considerable trauma related to deaths of loved ones.

POWER GRID	1	2	3	4	5	6	7	8	9	10
POWER										
CONSCIENCE										
ALTRUISM										
WISDOM										
COURAGE										
DETERMINATION										
FREE WILL										
VULNERABILITY										

SONGBIRD

AFFILIATIONS: Thunderbolts, Hawkeye, MACH-V, Radioactive Man, Masters of Evil, Grapplers

STATUS: Free agent; identity public

I may never have a real family of my own — this business doesn't lend itself to settling down — but I often feel vaguely grandfatherly seeing Songbird in action. She and I don't know each other well yet, but there's still something satisfying about knowing that a hero I mentored, Hawkeye, went on to train such an impressive young fighter like Melissa Gold. Seeing the Songbird of today is also a bit surreal, having met her a time or two as minor super-criminal Screaming Mimi years ago, before she joined the Thunderbolts and reformed. The difference is night and day — from ludicrous small-time thug to capable, commanding

heroine. She's the best proof so far of the Thunderbolts' potential in terms of rehabilitating ex-villains. We even offere her Avengers membership a while back, though she turned u down. Remarkable young woman. Now if I could only forget that she ever dated Baron Zemo!

PROS: Solid-sound construct generation, flight, debilitatin sonic scream, natural combat tactician, skilled wrestler.

CONS: Self-esteem issues due to criminal past, troubled family background and checkered romantic history; prone to risky, even self-destructive choices in pursuit of the greater good.

POWER GRID	1	2	3	4	5	6	7	8	9	10
POWER										
CONSCIENCE										
ALTRUISM										
WISDOM										
COURAGE										
DETERMINATION										
FREE WILL										
VULNERABILITY										

SPEEDBALL

AFFILIATIONS: Avengers Academy, New Warriors

STATUS: Free agent; identity public

Speedball was once the epitome of the carefree super hero. With a body that generated an energy field that absorbed, amplified and redirected kinetic energy, he battled crime in his hometown of Springdale, Connecticut, and became a founding member of the New Warriors while still a teenager. However, his life was forever changed while filming a reality television show in Stamford, Connecticut. A confrontation with a team of super villains triggered an explosion that left several of Speedball's New Warriors teammates and over 600 civilians dead. Speedball became the scapegoat for the Stamford Disaster, and he chose to become a superhuman federal marshal in Norman Osborn's Thunderbolts program rather than face a trial. Unfortunately, rechristened as the self-mutilating

"Penance," Speedball was drugged and brainwashed by Osborn and his cronies. Today, Speedball serves as an instructor at Avengers Academy, where he will hopefully be able to teach the trainees how to replicate his successes and avoid his mistakes. Although he still seems haunted by his time as Penance, his fellow New Warriors teammate Justice assures me that he has moved past his problems.

PROS: Valuable experience as a teenaged super hero that can be imparted to the teenaged superhumans of today.

CONS: Often seems grim and haunted by his time as Penance.

POWER GRID	1	2	3	4	5	6	7	8	9	10
POWER										
CONSCIENCE										
ALTRUISM										
WISDOM										
COURAGE										
DETERMINATION										
FREE WILL										
VULNERABILITY										

SPIDER-MAN

AFFILIATIONS: Avengers, Human Torch, Daredevil, Wolverine

STATUS: Free agent; identity protected

Spider-Man's always been an odd duck. At the beginning of his career, I've tried to recruit him into the Avengers, but he balked at joining. Unlike almost every vigilante of his stature, he continually declined to join any super-team for any length of time, although he accepted reserve Avengers membership a few years back (admittedly, he may have done so solely so he wouldn't be attacked by the Mansion's security systems every time he needed to visit). Only recently has he accepted to be a full-time Avengers member, and we're glad to have him. He's one of the most

responsible young men I know, and his years of experience battling everything from would-be world conquerors to two-bit hoods in animal costumes have made him an ideal Avenger. I understand Spider-Man's going through a rough patch right now, in both his personal and professional lives. The man needs a home, and I'm glad that he's finally found one in the Avengers.

PROS: Often underestimated by foes; years of intense combat experience; frequently-overlooked scientific skills.

CONS: Vast number of enemies; unaccustomed to group action.

POWER GRID	1	2	3	4	5	6	7	8	9	10
POWER										
CONSCIENCE										
ALTRUISM										
WISDOM										
COURAGE										
DETERMINATION										
FREE WILL										
VULNERABILITY										

SPIDER-WOMAN

AFFILIATIONS: Avengers, SWORD., SHIELD

STATUS: Free agent; identity protected

Despite spending the bulk of her life in suspended animation after she was experimented on by her father and the High Evolutionary, Spider-Woman has a long career as a super hero, first based in California and later as a private investigator and spy. Despite confusing ties to Hydra and SHIELD, frequently waning powers, a strong sense of unworthiness, and high levels of mistrust regarding Spider-Woman around the world (and hero community), I handpicked her to be on the Avengers. No one is savvier, and few heroes deserve a shot at redemption more. When the Skrulls invaded Earth, the Skrull queen chose Spider-Woman as her template,

and our Spider-Woman underwent no small amount of torture at their hands. She has reentered the world, seeking to belong more than ever, and I want to give her that opportunity.

PROS: History as a hero and private investigator; pheromone powers that influence others; venom blasts.

CONS: Has a lot of barriers in front of her if she's going to make it as a hero, primarily as a result of her Skrull captivity and life as a spy; pheromone powers cause women to dislike her.

POWER GRID	1	2	3	4	5	6	7	8	9	10
POWER										
CONSCIENCE										
ALTRUISM										
WISDOM										
COURAGE										
DETERMINATION										
FREE WILL										
VULNERABILITY										

SPITFIRE

AFFILIATIONS: MI13, Invaders

STATUS: UK government agent; identity public

What defines Jac to me, far more than being able to outrun bullets, is her indomitable spirit. She comes from a heroic heritage, and even before gaining her powers from a bite from Baron Blood (her Uncle John) and a transfusion from the Torch (Hammond, not Storm), she risked her life operating undercover behind enemy lines and helping the injured during the London Blitz. For nearly four years during the war, I fought alongside Jac and her brother, Brian, and I never once had cause to question their courage or integrity. During the decades I unwillingly slumbered after the war, Jac aged gracefully, but returned to full vitality following another transfusion. These days she's with MI13, and apparently something recently triggered the vampirism that had been latent within her all those years; though that last gives me some cause for concern, as does her somewhat troubling and perplexing romantic involvement with the vampire slayer Blade, if there's one person who can cope with fangs without giving way to the attendant bloodlust, it's Jac.

PROS: Military and espionage training, decades of experience, superhuman speed combined with vampire strength and durability.

CONS: Operates under jurisdiction of foreign government, potential to lose control to vampiric bloodlust.

POWER GRID	1	2	3	4	5	6	7	8	9	10
POWER										
CONSCIENCE										
ALTRUISM										
WISDOM										
COURAGE										
DETERMINATION										
FREE WILL										
VULNERABILITY										

STARFOX

AFFILIATIONS: Eternals of Titan, Avengers

STATUS: Free agent (extraterrestrial); identity public

Starfox is an Eternal of Titan with the unique ability to stimulate the pleasure centers of the brain, an ability very much in line with his lively personality. Starfox has a well-known appreciation for the finer things in life and has sought romance and adventure across multiple star systems. It was Starfox's sense of adventure that led him to seek membership in the Avengers, and he learned a great deal about teamwork and responsibility during his short tenure. Despite Starfox's fun-loving ways, he also has a strong sense of loyalty; he was a close confidant of the late Captain Mar-Vell and also formed a strong bond with the former Galactus herald Firelord. Starfox served admirably during his time as an Avenger, and his access to advanced Titanian technology and spacecrafts were an invaluable resource. His adventurous spirit usually keeps him from settling in one place for very long, but chances are it won't be long until his wanderings bring him to Earth once again.

PROS: Familiarity with many extraterrestrial races; access to advanced technology.

CONS: Overly fond of earthly pleasures; wanderlust; primary allegiance to Titan rather than Earth.

POWER GRID	1	2	3	4	5	6	7	8	9	10
POWER										
CONSCIENCE										
ALTRUISM										
WISDOM										
COURAGE										
DETERMINATION										
FREE WILL										
VULNERABILITY										

STEEL SPIDER

AFFILIATIONS: Spider-Man, Frog-Man, American Eagle

STATUS: Incarcerated; identity public

The Steel Spider is, unfortunately, one of the most high-profile examples of Norman Osborn's excesses. Inspired by Spider-Man, Osnick became a vigilante while still a teenager, dubbing himself "Spider-Kid." As he aged, he became the Steel Spider, and his methods began to verge on excessive brutality. A more responsible organization might have simply brought Osnick in and had a talk with him, but Osborn, then merely the director of the Thunderbolts, instead sent in his team of hero-hunters, turning the streets of Phoenix into a war zone. When Osnick resisted arrest, the Thunderbolt Venom went berserk and bit Osnick's left arm off, eating it. Amazingly, despite this flagrant abuse of power, Osborn was allowed to carry on as he pleased. It seems like a terrible waste to let a man of Osnick's talents languish in jail, and I'm surprised there aren't any pending lawsuits against the government yet. That said, given his proclivity for overkill, it might be more prudent to put him in a behind-the-scenes role.

PROS: Technologically adept; experienced brawler.

CONS: Immature; frequently uses excessive force.

POWER GRID	1	2	3	4	5	6	7	8	9	10
POWER										
CONSCIENCE										
ALTRUISM										
WISDOM										
COURAGE										
DETERMINATION										
FREE WILL										
VULNERABILITY										

STORM

AFFILIATIONS: Wakanda, X-Men, Fantastic Four, X-Treme Sanctions Executive, X-Treme X-Men

STATUS: Wakandan royalty; identity public

When I attended the wedding of my old friend T'Challa, the Black Panther, and Ororo, Storm of the X-Men, I was struck by how well matched they were. Each has a commanding, regal presence and seems a born leader. Long before she became Wakanda's queen, Ororo was worshiped as a weather goddess in Africa. When she first joined the X-Men, she seemed naïve and unworldly, but quickly adjusted to her new life and rose to become one of the X-Men's leaders. She doesn't rely on just her mutant powers and is surprisingly effective in hand-to-hand combat. Like my old friend and colleague Thor, Storm has the power to control the weather. Who knows what might happen if she and Thor jointly used their powers over the weather ⊠ or if they turned their weather powers against one another. Although she is now queen of Wakanda, Storm has chosen to continue working with the X-Men in America, but I wonder if her two roles will ever come in conflict.

PROS: Team player; formidable leader; mutant power to control the weather; capable hand-to-hand combatant.

CONS: If she loses control of her emotions, it can have devastating effects on the weather around her.

POWER GRID	1	2	3	4	5	6	7	8	9	10
POWER										
CONSCIENCE										
ALTRUISM										
WISDOM										
COURAGE										
DETERMINATION										
FREE WILL										
VULNERABILITY										

STRIKER

AFFILIATIONS: Avengers Academy

STATUS: Free agent; identity protected

A majority of the young superhumans currently trained at Avengers Academy were selected because they sustained the most damage (either physically, psychologically, or both) as a result of the experiments conducted upon them at the behest of Norman Osborn. However, the Academy's training staff has determined that it's in the students' best interests to not immediately divulge this information for fear that they would internalize the negative labels placed upon them and become self-fulfilling prophecies, re: the Pygmalion effect. This fear is perhaps greatest with the Avengers Academy trainee code-named Striker. Raised by his wealthy, socialite, divorcee mother in southern Florida, Striker's ability to manipulate electromagnetic energy is overshadowed by his overconfidence, self-centeredness, and disregard for authority. Striker's psychological profile suggests that he will rebel and act out to an even greater degree if confronted with the truth about the reasons for his presence at Avengers Academy.

PROS: Can manipulate electromagnetic energy for a variety of effects, including electrical bolt projection and interference with electrical devices; alpha male with inherent leadership qualities.

CONS: Overconfident; self-centered; rebellious; egotistical.

POWER GRID	1	2	3	4	5	6	7	8	9	10
POWER										
CONSCIENCE										
ALTRUISM										
WISDOM										
COURAGE										
DETERMINATION										
FREE WILL										
VULNERABILITY										

TALISMAN

AFFILIATIONS: Alpha Flight, Omega Flight

STATUS: Free agent (Canadian); identity protected

Descended from 40 generations of Sarcee mystics, Talisman followed in the footsteps of her father, Shaman, and joined Canada's Alpha Flight. Using her Circlet of Enchantment to tap into the mystical forces and command the spirits of the natural world, she assisted Alpha Flight against numerous threats, supernatural or otherwise. However, since the death of her father and several of their Alpha Flight teammates at the hands of the sentient amalgam of mutant energy known as the Collective and the subsequent superhuman "Civil War" in the United States, Talisman has developed anti-American sentiments. Blaming the US for Canada's pollution and gun crime as well as the influx of superhuman refugees caused by passage of the Superhuman Registration Act, Talisman nonetheless rose to the occasion and assisted the joint Canadian/US Omega Flight task force in fending off an extradimensional attack from the Great Beasts. Although she'll need to be approached tactfully, I believe Talisman will be a willing partner in our mission to maintain global peace and security.

PROS: Able to tap into mystical forces & command the spirits of the natural world; intimate knowledge of Canada's First Nations (particularly the Tsuu T'ina Nation).

CONS: Recent exacerbation of anti-US sentiment; bitterness over recent death of father and friends.

POWER GRID	1	2	3	4	5	6	7	8	9	10
POWER										
CONSCIENCE										
ALTRUISM										
WISDOM										
COURAGE										
DETERMINATION										
FREE WILL										
VULNERABILITY										

TARANTULA

AFFILIATIONS: Heroes for Hire

STATUS: Free agent; identity protected

Those who examine Tarantula's case file often conclude that she's self-contradictory. Although she was one of the most fervent supporters of the Superhuman Registration Act (SHRA) and advocated for increased superhuman accountability, she is all too eager to resort to excessive (and often lethal) force when battling opponents. Her outspoken support for the SHRA is easy to understand: raised in an affluent Latino household in Connecticut, her younger sister was killed in the Stamford Disaster. She put her college studies on hold and registered with the government to prevent other superhumans from repeating the mistakes that led to Stamford tragedy — but her methods and tactics were brutal and violent, as if she experienced a perverse exhilaration through these acts. She was hired by the Manhattan-based Heroes for Hire, Inc., which was contracted by the federal government to arrest unregistered superhumans. The team eventually disbanded, but not before running afoul of crimeboss Celia Riccadonna, who sent a team of ninjas to assassinate Tarantula, though they killed only her father. Having lost two family members and a team, Tarantula remains a true wild card.

PROS: Skilled in mixed martial arts/Brazilian jiujitsu, proficient in bladed weaponry, biophysics & engineering.

CONS: Propensity for violence & lethal tactics, anger management issues, rebellious, poor team player.

POWER GRID	1	2	3	4	5	6	7	8	9	10
POWER										
CONSCIENCE										
ALTRUISM										
WISDOM										
COURAGE										
DETERMINATION										
FREE WILL										
VULNERABILITY										

THING

AFFILIATIONS: Fantastic Four, Avengers, Project: PEGASUS, Aquarian, Justice, Quasar, Thunderiders, Unlimited Class Wrestling Federation

STATUS: Free agent; identity public

It's funny how one of the most likeable members of our unique profession looks like he just shambled out of an old-time monster movie. Transformed into a rock-skinned powerhouse by the same cosmic accident that empowered his fellow Fantastic Four founders, Ben Grimm may have stopped looking human, but he's never stopped being human — one of the warmest, funniest, kindest men I know and one of the toughest, bravest fighters I've ever met. In addition to his FF exploits, Ben has also served with the Avengers on occasion, and we were delighted to welcome him back to the group recently. He brings tremendous raw power and battle savvy to any roster, plus an interesting knack for forging friendships with his peers. He even helped found the floating poker games so popular among New York's super heroes. Things aren't always easy for Ben given his unique condition, but he's always made the most of the cards life dealt him.

PROS: Superhuman strength and durability; expert pilot; astronaut training; teamwork veteran; never-say-die fighting spirit; social connections throughout super-hero community

CONS: Violent temper; occasional bouts of depression or self-pity due to monstrous form.

POWER GRID	1	2	3	4	5	6	7	8	9	10
POWER										
CONSCIENCE										
ALTRUISM										
WISDOM										
COURAGE										
DETERMINATION										
FREE WILL										
VULNERABILITY										

THOR

AFFILIATIONS: Asgardians, Avengers

STATUS: Asgardian royalty; identity protected

After the Avengers retrieved me from the ice, one of the first things I heard was Thor's voice. He became one of my most trusted colleagues and a valued friend. Over the years, I've had the pleasure of serving on a number of Avengers rosters with Thor, and even though his adventures regularly take him to other worlds and dimensions, his dedication to the mortal world has never wavered. A prince of the Asgardian gods, Thor wields the powerful mystic hammer Mjolnir, but his greatest power is in his warrior's mind and unbreakable will. Although his pride and quick temper can be intimidating, Thor has proved himself to be a valuable team player. At times, Thor's responsibilities to Asgard have pulled him away from the Avengers, but recently, the Asgardians have come to reside on Earth. It remains to be seen how Thor will continue to balance his princely duties with his heroic activities.

PROS: Experienced leader; extremely powerful; intense loyalty to friends and colleagues; familiarity with Earth's many pantheons.

CONS: As a prince of Asgard, Thor's duties to his home sometimes conflict with his heroic activities on Earth.

POWER GRID	1	2	3	4	5	6	7	8	9	10
POWER										
CONSCIENCE										
ALTRUISM										
WISDOM										
COURAGE										
DETERMINATION										
FREE WILL										
VULNERABILITY										

THOR GIRL

AFFILIATIONS: Thor, Asgard

STATUS: Free agent; identity protected

Despite her name and appearance, Thor Girl isn't a native Asgardian. She was born on the Nucleus of Hope as the Designate, a being destined to evolve into a powerful form capable of uniting the universe. She forsook this destiny after Thor saved her life, choosing instead to assume an Asgardian form and aid her newfound idol on Earth. However, her time with Thor was short, as the Asgardians succumbed to Ragnarok while Thor Girl was on Earth. Thor Girl registered as a licensed superhuman pursuant to the Superhuman Registration Act, but was soon captured by the Skrulls and replaced with a doppelganger as part of their secret invasion of Earth. Upon the Skrull's defeat, Thor Girl underwent psychiatric treatment for post-abduction readjustment at Camp Hammond. However, Thor Girl felt no post-abduction trauma — only shame for allowing the Skrulls to defeat her and deceive her allies. When a cybernetic clone based on Thor's DNA attacked the camp, Thor Girl was instrumental in its defeat. Now that the Asgardians have been reborn, she has returned to serve at their side once more.

PROS: Superhuman strength & durability, skilled combatant, swordsman, and horseman; possesses enchanted Asgardian hammer.

CONS: Extremely high levels of devotion and intensity of feeling for Thor may distract her from realizing her own true potential.

POWER GRID	1	2	3	4	5	6	7	8	9	10
POWER										
CONSCIENCE										
ALTRUISM										
WISDOM										
COURAGE										
DETERMINATION										
FREE WILL										
VULNERABILITY										

3-D MAN

AFFILIATIONS: Atlas Foundation, Avengers, Initiative, Skrull Kill Krew

STATUS: Free agent; identity public

Initially an accomplished track & field athlete, Delroy Garrett was stripped of his honors and livelihood after testing positive for performance-enhancing drugs. Through the Triune Understanding he became Triathlon and later joined the Initiative, where he was eventually promoted to leader of Hawaii's federally-sanctioned team, the Point Men. Adopting the name and equipment of the 3-D Man of the 1950s, he gained the ability to detect extraterrestrial Skrulls via Tri-Force energy and was a key player in foiling their invasion of Earth. He voluntarily left the Initiative after killing Initiative trainee Crusader; although Crusader was revealed as a Skrull, and 3-D Man was cleared of all wrongdoing, several Initiative members felt that Crusader was a legitimate Skrull defector. 3-D Man joined the Skrull Kill Krew, an anti-Skrull militia composed of humans whose physiology had been altered by unwitting consumption of Skrull flesh, but was frozen out of the group, evidently to his dismay. On his own once again, 3-D Man has recently been sighted trailing Jimmy Woo's Atlas Foundation.

PROS: Physical abilities enhanced to three times peak human potential; able to channel Tri-Force energy to detect Skrulls; Initiative-trained hero; leadership experience.

CONS: Involved in controversial killing of Initiative trainee Crusader; possibly dealing with issues of rejection/loneliness.

POWER GRID	1	2	3	4	5	6	7	8	9	10
POWER										
CONSCIENCE										
ALTRUISM										
WISDOM										
COURAGE										
DETERMINATION										
FREE WILL										
VULNERABILITY										

TIGER'S BEAUTIFUL DAUGHTER

AFFILIATIONS: Iron Fist, Dog Brother #1, Prince of Orphans

STATUS: Free agent (non-USA); identity protected

Like the other Immortal Weapons, Tiger's Beautiful Daughter is evidently from a mystical city; her people are protected by a fierce cadre of warrior women, of which she is the leader and the most powerful. In fact, she apparently founded the current all-female army there, after the previous generation of women was forcibly demilitarized by an invading army. Although badly injured by Davos, the Steel Serpent, during a tournament, she joined Iron Fist in finding and infiltrating the Eighth Capital City of Heaven and was instrumental in the Weapons' escape from that hellish place. To the best of our knowledge, her experience on Earth is limited, and she came here for the first time with Iron Fist. She has apparently remained on Earth and continues to train with the other Weapons under the tutelage of the Prince of Orphans. She seems to be among the more approachable of the Weapons, should we need their assistance.

PROS: Skilled fighter and war leader.

CONS: Allegiances lay with unknown mystical city.

POWER GRID	1	2	3	4	5	6	7	8	9	10
POWER										
CONSCIENCE										
ALTRUISM										
WISDOM										
COURAGE										
DETERMINATION										
FREE WILL										
VULNERABILITY										

TIGRA

AFFILIATIONS: Avengers Academy, Avengers, Lady Liberators

STATUS: Free agent; identity public

A veteran of the Avengers (both East and West Coast incarnations) as well as the Initiative and the New York Police Department, Tigra serves as a head instructor at the Avengers Academy, where she teaches all facets of law enforcement. Tigra has overcome much adversity in recent months. First, when the supernatural crime boss the Hood sought to make an example of an established hero to demonstrate his power to prospective gang members, he targeted Tigra. The Hood ambushed Tigra in her home, videotaping her as he brutally beat and shot her. Shortly afterward, the recovering Tigra discovered that the "Hank Pym" she was dating was actually a shape-shifting Skrull imposter involved in a clandestine attack on Earth and that she was pregnant with the Skrull's child. Deciding that she could not bring herself to terminate the pregnancy, Tigra quit the Initiative when Norman Osborn appointed the Hood as an Initiative executive and threatened that he would seize her half-alien child for scientific study. After a brief stint as a fugitive outlaw, at which time she participated in a guerrilla-style campaign against Osborn's Initiative, Tigra was pardoned following Osborn's arrest.

PROS: Superhuman physical attributes; limited psychic ability; extensive law-enforcement training.

CONS: Recent hardships may distract her from performing at her full potential.

POWER GRID	1	2	3	4	5	6	7	8	9	10
POWER										
CONSCIENCE										
ALTRUISM										
WISDOM										
COURAGE										
DETERMINATION										
FREE WILL										
VULNERABILITY										

TORO

AFFILIATIONS: All-Winners Squad, Kid Commandos, Invaders, Young Allies, Human Torch, Aarkus the Vision

STATUS: Free agent; identity protected

Toro was always a hard-luck case. He was orphaned at a young age and taken in by circus folk, only to be discovered by the Human Torch and adopted as his protégé, as his powers seemingly mimicked Jim's. Apparently, Toro's parents worked closely with Jim's creator, and some of the Horton Cells used to give life to Jim somehow affected Toro. He fought bravely alongside myself and other heroes in World War II, but after Jim disappeared in the late 1940s, Toro became a brainwashed Soviet pawn. He was eventually rescued by Jim, and the two adventured again until Jim's deactivation in 1955. Toro retired to civilian life, eventually marrying, but he died after an incident involving the Mad Thinker. After a recent time-travel adventure involving the current Captain America and a Cosmic Cube, Toro was revived. I do not believe Toro has contacted his estranged wife, but he has made contact with other heroes and is helping the original Human Torch regain his humanity.

PROS: Team player; years of experience; willing to dedicate himself to an important cause.

CONS: Can become overly dedicated to personal causes; susceptible to mind control.

POWER GRID	1	2	3	4	5	6	7	8	9	10
POWER										
CONSCIENCE										
ALTRUISM										
WISDOM										
COURAGE										
DETERMINATION										
FREE WILL										
VULNERABILITY										

TRAUMA

AFFILIATIONS: Danielle Moonstar, Cloud 9, Physique, Initiative

STATUS: Free agent; identity protected

Some people just aren't cut out for combat, and I'm always happy to see those who aren't put their abilities to good use elsewhere. Trauma, the son of a human woman and the dream demon Nightmare, can sense an individual's greatest fear and shape-shift into it. While former Avengers liaison Henry Gyrich tried to turn him into a weapon, Trauma was no soldier. Danielle Moonstar trained him to control his powers, and he used them to counsel the staff and cadets at Camp Hammond until his father took possession of him. Luckily, he overcame it, but he left the Initiative to wander the Earth; reports have him popping up all over the globe. I don't know where he is right now, but I hope he'll come back someday. I don't recommend that we actively seek him out; when he wants us to find him, he'll come to us.

PROS: Excellent counselor and therapist; can neutralize opponents with fear without engaging them in combat.

CONS: May still be susceptible to Nightmare's influence; not much of a combatant.

POWER GRID	1	2	3	4	5	6	7	8	9	10
POWER										
CONSCIENCE										
ALTRUISM										
WISDOM										
COURAGE										
DETERMINATION										
FREE WILL										
VULNERABILITY										

TRUE BELIEVERS

AFFILIATIONS: Tenuous ties to SHIELD, Fantastic Four and Iron Man

STATUS: Free agents; identities protected

Somewhere between a watchdog group, paparazzi and terrorists, the True Believers maintain a Web site that exposes the ugly underbelly of society, even taking aim at those in the superhuman community. Is believed the group consists of a Symbiote-wearer called Payback, an empath called Headtrip, the armored Battalus and Red Zone, who possesses apparent extraterrestrial technology. Their efforts have exposed government corruption and halted a Hydra terrorism plot, but they also published false accusations about the Fantastic Four's Reed Richards and kidnapped former SHIELD Director Maria Hill. In both cases, the group made amends and parted ways on amicable

terms, but jumping to conclusions in such a public way can be dangerous, both in terms of safety and public perception. That said, I feel operatives with their capabilities could be useful in certain operations. I understand SHIELD data analyst Mavis Trent has the most experience investigating this group. She should be consulted.

PROS: Able to collect hidden information, cover their own tracks and overcome powerful opponents; willingness to correct mistakes.

CONS: No apparent loyalties; unpredictable behavior, unchecked operations, willingness to commit illegal acts.

POWER GRID	POW	CON	ALT	WIS	COU	DET	FAW	UUL
BATTALUS	8	9	8	10	9	8	9	9
HEADTRIP	7	9	8	9	8	10	9	9
PAYBACK	8	9	8	9	10	10	10	7
RED ZONE	7	9	8	9	9	9	9	9

TWO-GUN KID

AFFILIATIONS: Desert Stars, Avengers, Initiative, Hawkeye, She-Hulk

STATUS: Government agent; identity public

Two-Gun joined the Avengers years ago (signing onto the reserves while partnered with Hawkeye), but he and I have never served together for any length of time. That's too bad, since I feel we'd have a lot in common as a couple of time-displaced "living legends" — in his case, a famous masked cowboy hero of the Old West trapped in the modern era. I remember reading about Matt Hawk in old dime novels and comics as a boy...just think of the stories he could tell. He's lived in our time period twice now, once by choice and more recently after a TVA time travel decree relocated him here permanently.

He often found the future overwhelming during his first time trip, but Hawk is adjusting much better the second time around, adopting modern technology and adapting to modern customs. He has served the Initiative well as leader of Arizona's state team, the Desert Stars, and I hope that group has a post-Initiative future.

PROS: Phenomenally swift and accurate sharpshooter; strong unarmed combat and equestrian skills; natural leader; flying robot horse; high-tech specialty firearms.

CONS: Occasional gaps in his knowledge of modern times.

POWER GRID	1	2	3	4	5	6	7	8	9	10
POWER										
CONSCIENCE										
ALTRUISM										
WISDOM										
COURAGE										
DETERMINATION										
FREE WILL										
VULNERABILITY										

ULTRAGIRL

AFFILIATIONS: New Warriors, Avengers Resistance, Cavalry, Initiative, Justice, Ms. Marvel

STATUS: Active adventurer; identity public

Suzy Sherman is one of the most impressive young heroines to emerge in recent years. Very powerful, but also very idealistic and enthusiastic, eager to make a difference. She's been a highly public figure from the start, no secret identity, which along with her good looks, sunny disposition and California-bred knack for public relations makes her a particularly media-friendly heroine. Very principled, she served in my outlaw "Secret Avengers" opposing the SHRA law. We lost that fight, but she made the best of it and served with the Initiative despite that organization's hostility to ex-New Warriors like herself. When most of the Initiative's other ex-Warriors left the organization

in protest of ethical breaches, Suzy stayed on, trying to improve the Initiative from the inside, leading both the Junior Guardsmen youth group and Georgia's state team the Cavalry, but she eventually quit to rejoin the Warriors after the clearly corrupt Norman Osborn took over the Initiative. She, her fellow Warriors and others ultimately formed the "Avengers Resistance" movement that helped bring Osborn down.

PROS: Superhuman strength and durability; flight; enhanced vision; adaptable powers; strong moral character; leadership skills.

CONS: Emotion sometimes clouds judgment.

POWER GRID	1	2	3	4	5	6	7	8	9	10
POWER										
CONSCIENCE										
ALTRUISM										
WISDOM										
COURAGE										
DETERMINATION										
FREE WILL										
VULNERABILITY										

UNION JACK

AFFILIATIONS: MI5, Invaders, Knights of Pendragon

STATUS: UK government agent; identity protected

Union Jack is, in a way, Captain America's father, brother and son. As a boy, I grew up enthralled by the stories of the Great War hero Union Jack, and when I finally met him soon after coming to England with the Invaders, he didn't disappoint. The next Jack honored the legacy he inherited fighting against the Axis, and was, in so many ways, my British counterpart, right down to imbibing a super-soldier serum. Decades later it was my turn to be the childhood idol, as the current Jack told me that during his youth his uncle had regaled him with tales of my exploits. Three generations of exceptional bravery, and all men I'm proud to call friend. Unlike his predecessors, the current Jack had little preparation before donning the costume, but he took the responsibility of upholding the legacy very seriously, and in a few short years he's gone from being a kid who knew a few fighting moves to one of MI5's top operatives.

PROS: Wide-range of weapons expertise, unwavering determination to do the right thing.

CONS: Operates under jurisdiction of foreign government.

POWER GRID	1	2	3	4	5	6	7	8	9	10
POWER										
CONSCIENCE										
ALTRUISM										
WISDOM										
COURAGE										
DETERMINATION										
FREE WILL										
VULNERABILITY										

USAGENT

AFFILIATIONS: Avengers, GRAMPA, Omega Flight, Invaders, STARS, Jury, Force Works, CSA, Watchdogs, US Army

STATUS: Free agent; identity protected

Sometimes your worst enemy can become a friend, but with John Walker it was more complicated than that. He pretended to be a hero as Super-Patriot and served as a reminder of what was wrong with our country at the time when the CSA bestowed the Captain America identity upon him, eventually leading him to bloody showdowns with his foes. I didn't know how much he suffered during his tenure as Captain America or that the CSA brainwashed him to become USAgent after faking his death or how they kept on lying to him. It impresses me that after all that happened to him he keeps on fighting for our country. Although he made some unfortunate decisions over the years he always ended up on the right side to make up for his mistakes. I have to admit that despite our checkered past USAgent and I have grown to respect each other, drawn from a mutual love for our nation. Demanding to return to service as soon as possible after being severely injured by the Thunderbolts' Nuke he became the Raft's new warden.

PROS: Team player, superhuman strength, skilled unarmed combatant.

CONS: Temper issues, maybe out of action indefinitely.

POWER GRID	1	2	3	4	5	6	7	8	9	10
POWER										
CONSCIENCE										
ALTRUISM										
WISDOM										
COURAGE										
DETERMINATION										
FREE WILL										
VULNERABILITY										

VALKYRIE

AFFILIATIONS: Thor, Balder, Asgard, Avengers, Lady Liberators, Defenders

STATUS: Free agent (Asgardian); identity protected

Brunnhilde the Valkyrie was certainly not the first name that came to mind when recruiting a team of super-powered espionage agents, but her unique background and power set (although unconventional in the world of traditional cloak-and-dagger warfare) provides the team with a versatility that it wouldn't otherwise possess. Ages ago, Brunnhilde was handpicked by Odin, late father of Thor and former monarch of the Asgardian gods, to lead the Valkyrior, an assemblage of warrior goddesses who appeared over the battlefields of the Asgardians' mortal worshippers and selected the fallen combatants worthy of Valhalla, Land of the Honored Dead. An extensively trained combatant, swordsman, and horseman, she also possesses the phenomenal strength and durability inherent to her race. Although we're still working on her stealth combat skills and ability to maintain cover (which is usually blown as soon as her feminist sensibilities are offended), Valkyrie is progressing quite nicely as both a strike force member and an Avengers Academy armed combat instructor.

PROS: Superhuman strength & durability; skilled combatant, swordsman, and horseman; possesses enchanted Asgardian weaponry.

CONS: Unaccustomed to espionage tactics.

POWER GRID	1	2	3	4	5	6	7	8	9	10
POWER										
CONSCIENCE										
ALTRUISM										
WISDOM										
COURAGE										
DETERMINATION										
FREE WILL										
VULNERABILITY										

VEIL

AFFILIATIONS: Avengers Academy

STATUS: Free agent; identity protected

Whether you're a tall, lanky boy growing up in Manhattan's Lower East Side during the Great Depression or an insecure, socially-awkward young woman living in a lower-class trailer park in the modern-day suburbs of Minneapolis, one truism remains constant: adolescence is a difficult phase for just about everyone. For Veil, however, these years of personal growth and transition have been especially adverse. In addition to dealing with feelings of insecurity and betrayal, Veil was identified by Norman Osborn as a potential superhuman recruit when her powers of self-sublimation were inadvertently triggered at school. Osborn and his underlings subjected Veil to inhumane experiments and forced her body to repeatedly undergo significant physical transformations before it was ready. The process severely damaged Veil's molecular structure, and Hank Pym believes that her body will eventually discorporate into nothingness unless a method of reversing the damage is found. In the meantime, she'll hopefully be able to obtain the sense of belonging that she craves and the self-confidence that she needs at Avengers Academy.

PROS: Able to sublimate her body into a variety of different gases (her range is expected to increase as she learns more about the chemical composition of gases); empathic.

CONS: Low confidence and self-esteem; desperate desire for acceptance from others; naïve.

POWER GRID	1	2	3	4	5	6	7	8	9	10
POWER										
CONSCIENCE										
ALTRUISM										
WISDOM										
COURAGE										
DETERMINATION										
FREE WILL										
VULNERABILITY										

VENUS

AFFILIATIONS: Olympian gods, Atlas Foundation

STATUS: Free agent (Olympian), wanted for questioning; no dual identity

Even the most senior intelligence operatives and most prominent mythologists on my payroll can't agree on the details of this one. The being known as Venus is the proverbial enigma wrapped in a riddle shrouded in mystery. Sources indicate she began existence as one of the sirens of legend, using her otherworldly voice to lure sailors to their watery deaths in the Tyrrhenian Sea. At some point in the late 19th century, she became aware and repentant of her behavior and fled to a convent. By the mid-20th century, she resurfaced in the US where she usurped the name and appearance of the Olympian love goddess, apparently without said love goddess' permission, attempting to make amends for her past sins by bringing peace and love to humanity. By all accounts, the vengeful love goddess finally caught up with Venus recently, but realized that she had been negligent in her godly duties and passed her title and magical Cestus to Venus so that she would be recognized as the new Olympian goddess of love. Her powers make her a formidable instrument in the Agents of Atlas.

PROS: Virtual immortality; ability to influence the emotions of others with her voice; thousands of years of life experience.

CONS: Prone to succumbing to emotion.

POWER GRID	1	2	3	4	5	6	7	8	9	10
POWER										
CONSCIENCE										
ALTRUISM										
WISDOM										
COURAGE										
DETERMINATION										
FREE WILL										
VULNERABILITY										

WAR MACHINE

AFFILIATIONS: Iron Man, Avengers

STATUS: Free agent; identity protected

War Machine is a hero with whom I can truly relate. A fellow military man, he served his country as a Marine for several tours of duty in the war-torn jungles of Sin Cong and other southeast Asian locales. Following his separation from service, he used his expert piloting skills to land a job at Stark International, where he became the personal pilot for CEO Tony Stark and gained access to the War Machine armor that became his namesake. Although their technologies are similar, War Machine and Iron Man have two vastly different philosophies when it comes to taking action. War Machine is much less hesitant to use force in order to take down the international despots who commit unspeakable atrocities around the globe. He understands and embraces the need for stealth tactics and preemptive intervention. Given his technological skill set, strong moral code, and dedication to country, War Machine would be one of my top recruits for any superhuman strike force.

PROS: Expert pilot, trained extensively in aviation engineering and military combat; years of combat experience.

CONS: Occasionally disobeys orders in order to accomplish what he believes to be the just course of action; sometimes described as "obstinate."

POWER GRID	1	2	3	4	5	6	7	8	9	10
POWER										
CONSCIENCE										
ALTRUISM										
WISDOM										
COURAGE										
DETERMINATION										
FREE WILL										
VULNERABILITY										

WARBOUND

AFFILIATIONS: The Hulk, Skaar

STATUS: Free agents (extraterrestrial); identities public

A group of warriors that became active on Earth during my recent absence, the Warbound are a powerful group of extraterrestrials. They were slaves to the tyrannical Red King of the planet Sakaar, forced to fight as gladiators for his entertainment. When several of Earth's heroes exiled the Hulk to Sakaar, he formed a strong bond with these gladiators and brought them back to Earth after their world's devastation. Though they aided the Hulk in capturing a number of the Earth's heroes whom he mistakenly held responsible for Sakaar's destruction, the Warbound showed mercy even in the midst of battle, taking no lives. Recently, the Warbound have taken SHIELD agent Katherine Waynesboro as one of their own. If the Warbound's power and discipline are correctly channeled, they have immense potential for good. But they are also stranded on a world not their own, possibly distrusting of Earth's population. Furthermore, some of Earth's heroes may find it hard to work alongside aliens who first arrived with a declaration of war. Still, Earth has counted many aliens among its defenders in the past; I hope the Warbound can be brought into the fold.

PROS: Skilled warriors, strict adherence to a warrior's code.

CONS: Do not consider themselves answerable to any Earth government.

POWER GRID	POW	CON	ALT	WIS	COU	DET	FRW	VUL
ELLOE KAIFI	6	7	9	8	10	9	10	8
KORG	8	9	9	8	10	10	10	7
NO-NAME	7	6	6	8	10	10	10	8
KATE WAYNESBORO	9	9	9	10	8	9	10	6

WASP

AFFILIATIONS: Avengers Academy, Avengers, Defenders, Jocasta

STATUS: Free agent; identity public

Sometimes Hank Pym inspires me and sometimes he worries me. A brilliant inventor and a brave, experienced fighter, he's also an Avengers founder, not to mention the man who freed me from the ice all those years ago — without Hank Pym, there'd be no Avengers, no Steve Rogers. He's empowered or equipped many heroes and saved the world many times over. But he's also had multiple mental breakdowns, betraying his team and abusing his wife and partner, the original Wasp, during the worst of them. Hank has long since recovered and redeemed himself, becoming a respected hero again, but recent times have not been kind. The Skrulls abducted and impersonated him, his ex-wife, Janet, and his best friends Scott Lang and Bill Foster, all died, and his robotic girlfriend Jocasta left him — that's a lot of pressure for a man who's snapped before. He seems to be coping, though, and is serving capably at Avengers Academy, where his many career highs and lows help him advise the students from a unique perspective.

PROS: Multidisciplinary scientific genius; size-changing powers; flight; insect control; stun gun; miniaturized high-tech arsenal; leadership skills.

CONS: Mental instability; self esteem issues; obsessive; depressive.

POWER GRID	1	2	3	4	5	6	7	8	9	10
POWER										
CONSCIENCE										
ALTRUISM										
WISDOM										
COURAGE										
DETERMINATION										
FREE WILL										
VULNERABILITY										

WHITE TIGER

AFFILIATIONS: Hand, FBI

STATUS: Free agent, fugitive; identity protected

How a woman like White Tiger could end up with an organization like the Hand baffles me. To my knowledge she is a former FBI agent empowered by the legendary Tiger Amulets with strong connections to the late Hector Ayala, her predecessor as White Tiger. She fought against the Yakuza and other criminal organizations alongside people I'm proud to call my friends and overall protected the people of New York City. Killed, resurrected and reprogrammed by the ninja cult known as the Hand she has become a ruthless assassin, turning against everything she once stood for. I'm aware how the Hand's influence can corrupt people, but she has a lot to make up for after what she did for the Hand. When Daredevil took leadership of the Hand, White Tiger quickly rose in their ranks, becoming one of their leading figures representing the USA. I still hope Daredevil knows what he is doing and that White Tiger works with him, but with every passing day I loose more confidence in whatever they are up to.

PROS: Skilled martial artist.

CONS: Associated with the Hand, no qualms about killing, mystic power source.

POWER GRID	1	2	3	4	5	6	7	8	9	10
POWER										
CONSCIENCE										
ALTRUISM										
WISDOM										
COURAGE										
DETERMINATION										
FREE WILL										
VULNERABILITY										

WINTER GUARD

AFFILIATIONS: Russia, Lady Liberators

STATUS: Russian government agents; identities protected

Succeeding the Soviet Super Soldiers and People's Protectorate, the Winter Guard has become a loyal instrument for the Russian government under the supervision of the Russian Executive Security Committee, who appointed Dmitri Bukharin, the former Crimson Dynamo and Airstrike, as the team's strategic liaison. She-Hulk and War Machine told me they are willing to oppose direct orders for the greater good showing that they are more than mere soldiers and actually care about the people they are meant to protect. I'm glad to see a veteran like Ursa Major among them, but at the same time am worried about the Russian's obvious cover up of replacing fallen members with new agents with questionable experience. The current Red Guardian is as much of an unknown to me as the current Darkstar and the woman wearing the Crimson Dynamo armor. It would be interesting to know how they transferred the late Darkstar's power set on her successor and it wouldn't startle me if the original Darkstar's brother Vanguard and her father Presence had something to say against it.

PROS: Trained government agents, differing power sets.

CONS: Answer to Russian government, constant lineup changes.

POWER GRID	POW	CON	ALT	WIS	COU	DET	FRW	VUL
CRIMSON DYNAMO	8	8	9	9	10	9	8	7
DARKSTAR	8	9	9	8	9	9	8	8
RED GUARDIAN	7	8	9	9	10	10	8	7
URSA MAJOR	8	8	9	8	10	9	8	8

PETE WISDOM

AFFILIATIONS: MI13, the Department, X-Force, Excalibur, Black Air, MI6

STATUS: UK government agent; no dual identity

Pete Wisdom and I have similar jobs, running agencies handling supra-normal threats using the super-powered resources available to us, albeit his domain as head of Britain's MI13 is only a single nation. Captain Britain speaks well of him; my old ally Lance Hunter, former STRIKE commander and now Britain's Joint Intelligence chairman and Wisdom's superior, respects him. Yet I can't help but feel wary. In the past, Wisdom was reputedly the most dangerous black-ops agent Britain ever produced and his handling of Dracula's declaration of war against Britain paints him as unashamedly manipulative. As British intelligence operatives go, he's far more Francis Walsingham, Queen Elizabeth the First's remorseless spymaster, than the romantic notions Hollywood blockbusters perpetuate. A mutant, he can generate energy blades as hot as the sun, but his cunning and willingness to do whatever it takes to win, no matter how distasteful, are what makes him truly dangerous.

PROS: Generates energy blades, tactical thinker, experienced espionage operative.

CONS: Operates under jurisdiction of foreign government; ruthless.

POWER GRID	1	2	3	4	5	6	7	8	9	10
POWER										
CONSCIENCE										
ALTRUISM										
WISDOM										
COURAGE										
DETERMINATION										
FREE WILL										
VULNERABILITY										

WOLVERINE

AFFILIATIONS: X-Men, X-Force, CIA, Department H, Team X, Avengers

STATUS: Free agent (Canadian); identity protected

My friend Hawkeye likes to call me "Methuselah," but when I first met Wolverine early in World War II, I was still new in my role as Captain America, and he was already a battle-hardened veteran of World War I. Wolverine and I are both products of "super-soldier" programs, but I'm fortunate that "Operation: Rebirth" did not inflict the horrors on me that the Weapon X program did on him. His mutant healing factor has kept him alive and young for over a century, and the Adamantium Weapon X infused into his claws and skeleton makes them nearly as indestructible as my shield. I am well aware of Wolverine's tendencies toward berserker madness in battle, and I admire his long struggles to master his inner demons. But, as a soldier who has done his best to avoid killing whenever possible, I am troubled by Wolverine's willingness to use lethal force. I trust him, and I'm pleased he joined the Avengers, but his ways are not my ways.

PROS: Virtually unkillable, extraordinary hand-to-hand combatant, a century of combat experience.

CONS: Potentially suffers from berserker rages in which he becomes uncontrollably violent.

POWER GRID	1	2	3	4	5	6	7	8	9	10
POWER										
CONSCIENCE										
ALTRUISM										
WISDOM										
COURAGE										
DETERMINATION										
FREE WILL										
VULNERABILITY										

WONDER MAN

AFFILIATIONS: Avengers, Vision, Beast, Scarlet Witch

STATUS: Free agent; identity public

In the earliest days of the Avengers, we lost Simon Williams in battle with the Masters of Evil, only to learn years later that his ionic powers allowed him to survive indefinitely as Wonder Man. Despite dying time and again, Wonder Man has proven a mainstay to the Avengers legacy in multiple incarnations of the team, including the West Coast branch and as part of the Mighty Avengers post-registration. But something happened to Simon during Osborn's reign; he allied himself with the Lethal Legion, broke multiple laws, and ended up in prison. I could overlook this, but Simon has chosen to distance himself from the Avengers, and he adamantly refused to involve himself with any of the current incarnations of the team. I don't know how to break through to my old friend, and I can only hope that he will come around and choose to fight for the right again.

PROS: Ionic powers, including super strength, flight, and seeming immortality.

CONS: Simon seems to have chosen a different life path at this time, despite the world needing heroes more than ever before.

POWER GRID	1	2	3	4	5	6	7	8	9	10
POWER										
CONSCIENCE										
ALTRUISM										
WISDOM										
COURAGE										
DETERMINATION										
FREE WILL										
VULNERABILITY										

JIMMY WOO

AFFILIATIONS: Atlas Foundation, FBI, SHIELD

STATUS: Free agent, wanted for questioning; identity public

During the 1950s, a young Asian-American FBI agent named Jimmy Woo repeatedly thwarted the criminal mastermind then known in America as the Yellow Claw – though I'm told that "Golden Claw" is a more accurate translation of his title – both as a solo agent and as leader of the G-Men. Years later I fought the Claw alongside Woo, and was impressed with his courage and determination. Woo became a member of SHIELD and was close to retiring with honor. But while I was out of action recently, Woo's life took strange turns. He was somehow rejuvenated and became the Atlas Foundation's CEO, apparently inheriting this title from the Claw. Now, Woo leads the reassembled G-Men, now calling themselves the Agents of Atlas. They sided with Norman Osborn and have fought different Avengers teams. Did Woo make some sort of Faustian bargain with his old enemy? I can't believe I've misjudged his character. I like to think that he has turned the Claw's organization to covertly pursuing the cause of justice. But as yet I cannot be certain whether or not my theory is correct.

PROS: Long experience in investigating and combating criminal organizations, skilled in leadership.

CONS: Woo's current agenda and loyalties are unknown.

POWER GRID	1	2	3	4	5	6	7	8	9	10
POWER										
CONSCIENCE										
ALTRUISM										
WISDOM										
COURAGE										
DETERMINATION										
FREE WILL										
VULNERABILITY										

X-FACTOR

AFFILIATIONS: X-Men, O*N*E

STATUS: Free agents; identities protected

Although several members of the Manhattan-based X-Factor Investigations detective agency were once members of the federally-sanctioned team of mutants known as X-Factor, the current incarnation of the team is a different beast altogether. Funded by Jamie Madrox (also known as the Multiple Man), with money he won on a television game show, X-Factor Investigations clearly operates according to its own agenda. For instance, its members registered pursuant to the Superhuman Registration Act, only to denounce the legislation shortly after. However, they have also cooperated with federal authorities since their reorganization into a private detective agency, such as when their former government supervisor Valerie Cooper persuaded them to confront X-Cell, a terrorist group comprised of former mutants who blamed the government for depowering them on M-Day. However, Madrox has made it very clear that he and his allies are not interested in becoming full-fledged government agents again; however, Valerie Cooper promised to allow the agency to maintain its autonomy if they agreed to handle select government cases.

PROS: Unique combination of mutants & genetically-engineered humanoids native to the Mojoverse; private investigation skill sets.

CONS: Evidence of internal conflict between team members; resistance to working too closely with the federal government.

POWER GRID	POW	CON	ALT	WIS	COU	DET	FRW	VUL
DARWIN	8	9	8	8	9	8	9	5
LONGSHOT	7	10	10	7	10	9	9	7
M	8	8	8	10	10	9	9	7
LAYLA MILLER	8	8	7	10	9	10	8	7
MULTIPLE MAN	8	8	8	9	9	8	8	8
RICTOR	5	8	8	8	9	9	9	9
SHATTERSTAR	7	8	8	7	10	10	9	8
SIRYN	8	8	8	8	9	9	9	8
STRONG GUY	8	8	8	8	10	10	9	7

AFFILIATIONS: X-Men

STATUS: Free agents; identities protected

Few things have horrified me more than the knowledge of this new X-Force. Wolverine, Warpath, Domino, Elixir, Wolfsbane, Vanisher, X-23, and Archangel. Hand-selected and assigned by Cyclops to wipe out the X-Men's deadliest threats with extreme prejudice. Not capturing or involving the authorities, but intentionally murdering them in bloody, savage fights. I have heard of massacres across the globe against the Purifiers, the Right, the Sapiens League, the Facility, Selene, and more. I can't believe the X-Men would condone something like this! When I confronted Wolverine about this, I was told, in no small terms, that it is a mutant matter and not an

Avengers matter. I try to trust Wolverine, but his team may be my limit. I'm shocked and appalled that an international terrorist like the Vanisher and a genetic weapon like X-23 have been placed on a team with such dark purposes. And why would youths like Elixir and Wolfsbane choose to be involved? I've got to find a way to address this. There has to be another way.

PROS: Novice and experienced fighters; proactive attacks on anti-mutant criminals.

CONS: If knowledge of this group becomes public, the results for mutants could be catastrophic.

POWER GRID	POW	CON	ALT	WIS	COU	DET	FRW	VUL
ANGEL	7	8	10	8	10	8	9	7
DOMINO	7	5	7	9	10	10	9	8
ELIXIR	8	5	5	7	7	7	9	6
VANISHER	6	1	1	8	5	5	8	8
WARPATH	8	8	9	8	10	9	9	7
WOLVERINE	7	5	9	10	10	10	9	6
X-23	7	5	6	8	10	10	9	6

AFFILIATIONS: New Warriors, Young Avengers, Great Lakes Avengers, Black Widow, Ms. Marvel

STATUS: Free agents; identities protected

While I cannot recall everything that happened after the Avengers and I encountered the Onslaught entity, I apparently worked with a girl called Bucky, who impressed me when we met again in an incident involving Counter-Earth. Nomad reminds me of her and also claims to have been trained by me. She has formed a team, named for my original partner's World War II group. Nomad is joined by the experienced former New Warrior Firestar, who is recovering from a bout with cancer. Unlike many other young heroes, member Araña has family support and the benefit of Ms. Marvel's training in the Initiative. Fellow Initiative-alum

Gravity, recently of the Great Lake Initiative (or whatever they are called now), has earned respect in his brief career, having served as Protector of the Universe and fought alongside the Fantastic Four against Galactus and his heralds. There is also a newcomer named Toro, apparently a bull-like individual similar to one I met from Counter-Earth. I look forward to seeing what these novice adventurers can do.

PROS: A dedicated team of eager young heroes with a range of experience and ideas.

CONS: Possible problems with authority, too eager to prove themselves.

POWER GRID	POW	CON	ALT	WIS	COU	DET	FRW	VUL
ARAÑA	7	9	9	7	10	10	9	8
FIRESTAR	8	9	9	8	10	9	9	8
GRAVITY	8	9	9	8	10	10	9	8
NOMAD	7	9	9	7	10	10	9	9
TORO	8	7	7	7	9	9	9	8

AFFILIATIONS: Avengers, Runaways

STATUS: Free agents; identities protected

Believe it or not, this team of super-powered adolescents was formed when Kang the Conqueror, one of our greatest foes, traveled back in time while still an idealistic teenager and recruited youths identified as possible Avengers replacements to defeat his megalomaniacal future-self. The kids created costumes and code names based on popular Avengers, and the 24-hour news networks had a field day with covering their exploits. At first, I felt personally responsible for any potential harm that these inexperienced young heroes inflicted upon themselves or others, as I believed they were nothing more than reckless thrill-seekers trying to follow my example.

However, they have proven themselves to be capable, responsible heroes time and time again – whether during superhuman civil wars, shape-shifting alien invasions, or, most recently, by my side as key allies in defense of Asgard during Norman Osborn's siege. I've come to accept the Young Avengers as trusted partners in crimefighting and have high expectations for their future performance.

PROS: Proven heroes with a genuine enthusiasm for crimefighting that is often absent in older superhumans.

CONS: Despite their good intentions and enthusiasm, there's no substitute for experience.

POWER GRID	POW	CON	ALT	WIS	COU	DET	FRW	VUL
HAWKEYE	6	9	9	8	10	10	9	9
HULKLING	8	9	9	7	10	9	9	7
PATRIOT	8	9	9	8	10	10	9	8
SPEED	8	8	7	7	9	8	9	8
STATURE	8	10	9	7	9	9	9	7
VISION	8	10	9	9	10	10	9	6
WICCAN	8	9	9	8	10	10	9	8

"Villain."

It's hardly a politically correct term, but I know villains exist. I've lived long enough to see Nazi leader Adolf Hitler worshiped and criminal businessman Wilson Fisk exonerated. Both men had their apologists; both men also allied themselves with the Red Skull; both men inflicted misery on scores of others.

The one good to come of villains is that they inspire good men to awaken their inner heroism. I joined the armed service to oppose Hitler, which eventually transformed me into a super-soldier. I donned my country's colors in response to the activities of the swastika-garbed Red Skull, a little propagandistic counteraction, if you will. But I wasn't the first costumed hero, I arrived during a spate of increased heroism, not only from the men who joined the armed services or fought the Axis in local resistance, but every man who donned a cape or mask to overturn crime, injustice and oppression, from my friends Bucky and Nick to Citizen V and the Angel.

Of late, I've given a lot of thought to how I can better treat villainy. Costumed criminals keep emerging regardless of how the environment changes, no matter how often we confiscate their equipment, dampen their powers or lock them up. Justin Hammer was one of the most notorious outfitters and organizers of super villains, but his death had almost no impact on the ranks of villainy. The Tinkerer has been busted by authorities repeatedly, but always returns to design new arsenals for criminals. Hydra has outposts spanning the globe, with an unsettling amount stationed in my homeland. The racist regime on the island nation Genosha was overthrown, only to lead to internal strife, suffering and finally near-extinction of its populace. When I consider that Genosha saw the deaths of almost as many people killed as in the Holocaust, it can be difficult to remain idealistic.

Villains reveal themselves through their deeds, but advancing beyond merely reacting to their schemes to proactively curbing criminal behavior is far more challenging. I face villainy every day; on a good day, I stop a liquor store hold-up; on an average day, hundreds of lives are in jeopardy; on a very bad day, the universe is in peril. From a gun-waving first-time offender to a novice wearing tights to an interstellar warlord seeking ultimate power, all villains seek to undermine the freedoms of others, often the freedom of life itself.

With such varying levels of power, resources and motivation, there is no obvious single treatment for all villains. At my most optimistic, I believe in reformation. So many people on the wrong path (costumed or otherwise) have skills that could be put to better use. From Hawkeye to Diamondback, I've seen the power of redemption; it's the very reason for Luke Cage's Thunderbolts program. I would like to see more effort devoted to rehabilitating

young super criminals; I admire Hank for using the Avengers Academy to address criminal behavior before it emerges.

Some people we consider villains are simply misguided; simple acts of arbitration can be made to peacefully end hostilities. For instance, the Avengers have repeatedly held back invasions by Arkon of Polemachus by repairing his world's source of energy; a fair exchange, given that Arkon's initially proposed solution was to destroy our planet! I also find that extraterrestrials are frequently misunderstood, such as the Fantastic Four's encounter with the "Infant Terrible" who proved to be a lost child.

Still, redemption isn't possible for everyone. Some villains suffer mental problems, ranging from delusional megalomaniacs to sociopaths. Unfortunately, many criminals lack the psychiatric care they deserve due to the landmark case Ra the Avenger v. State of New York, which blurred the line between costumed criminal and mental illness.

Incarceration poses additional problems, chiefly being that so many of the villains I face cannot be held through conventional means. Attempts to create "super-villain holding facilities" such as the Vault, the Raft and Prison 42 have each invariably led to a disastrous breakout, as well as incarcerating costumed heroes alongside their enemies. Even if the perfect prison existed, it would do little to correct the content of its inmates' souls, to rehabilitate them into productive members of society.

Execution cannot be regarded as a permanent solution in many cases, given the propensity of criminals to defy death itself. Whether through the unorthodox cloning procedures of Arnim Zola or the mystic rites of the Hand, many criminals I thought were gone have resumed their activities. Even where death does succeed, we invariably find new crooks assuming the guise of a fallen miscreant, be it Kraven the Hunter or the Ringer. I have taken lives in my mission, but only ever as the last option.

I know all too well how well-meaning interference from the super-hero community can have horrible consequences, thanks to the example played out on the Squadron Supreme's world, where efforts to stamp out crime created the framework for fascism. The perfect solution to villainy may not be found in my lifetime, but I will continue the fight each day with my heart and soul.

ABSORBING MAN

AFFILIATIONS: Titania, Loki, Masters of Evil, Lethal Legion

ENEMIES: Thor, Hulk, Avengers, Captain America, Spider-Man, She-Hulk

A brutal, small-time boxer who turned to crime, Carl "Crusher" Creel was serving a prison term when the Asgardian god Loki chose him as his pawn. Loki magically endowed not only Creel but also his prison ball and chain to absorb the physical properties of any matter or energy he touches. Once an obscure failure, Creel found himself one of the most powerful beings on Earth, battling Thor and even aiding Loki in an attempt to dethrone Odin and take over Asgard. Nonetheless, Thor and other heroes repeatedly bested Creel. Moreover, when he once turned into water and merged with the ocean, the experience drove him temporarily insane. Meeting his fellow super-criminal Titania during the first "Secret War" was a turning point in Creel's life. His love for her seems to have awakened the better side of his personality. Perhaps tiring of his many defeats, Creel scaled down his criminal activities for a time and married Titania. Once Creel even absorbed the properties of my shield to protect New York City from an explosion. Though Creel remains a criminal, I believe he is capable of reform.

TREATMENT: Recommend Creel remain incarcerated, but enter a special rehabilitation program for super-criminals.

CLASSIFICATION	MUTATE
GOALS	WEALTH & FAME
SCOPE	NATIONAL
MEANS	ROBBERY

AIM

AFFILIATIONS: MODOK, Hydra, Super-Adaptoid

ENEMIES: Nick Fury, SHIELD, Captain America, Iron Man, Hulk, Ms. Marvel

Advanced Idea Mechanics (AIM) might best be described as the dark counterpart of Microsoft or Stark Industries or Apple: a criminal cabal of innovative scientists and inventors out to amass political and economic power. Founded as the subversive organization Hydra's scientific research and development arm, AIM went independent, developing threats to the world including the Cosmic Cube, able to alter reality on a global scale at the wielder's whim - subsequent misusers of this device include my archfoe, the Red Skull; the Super-Adaptoid, which can duplicate anyone's powers and appearance and which once took over AIM in the guise of Alessandro Brannex; and the grotesque "living computer" MODOK (Mobile Organism Designed Only for Killing), mutated AIM underling George Tarleton, who has controlled AIM for much of its subsequent history. As "Brannex" the Adaptoid sought to turn AIM into a manufacturer and dealer in advanced high-tech weaponry to super-criminals and other clients. But with MODOK in charge again, I fear AIM remains a direct threat to the security of governments throughout the world.

TREATMENT: AIM recruit the best and brightest. Monitor universities and recruit AIM's next generation first. Starve them of new blood, the ones AIM has yet to corrupt.

CLASSIFICATION	GROUP
GOALS	CONQUEST
SCOPE	INTERNATIONAL
MEANS	TERRORISM

ANSWER

AFFILIATIONS: Hood, Kingpin, Ruby Thursday

ENEMIES: Spider-Man, Avengers, Toxin, Punisher

Given his ability to ferret out solutions to almost any problem, even adapting specific powers, abilities, and skill sets to his own body as needed, Aaron Nicholson's dedication to crime bosses and criminal activity in general baffles me. He was a top hit man for the Kingpin before voluntarily subjecting himself to experiments that left him with his bizarre powers, which have ranged from flight to super-strength to surviving death. Despite extended jail sentences, the Answer returns to crime every time he finds a way out; he seems to need someone to call the shots for him. Nicholson appears to have developed feelings for the bizarre Ruby Thursday, and he has lately been partnered with the aptly named Sidekick. If the Answer is ever to be an asset to the heroic community, he would have to first complete extensive self-discovery. I would need to understand if his motivations are more than profit through crime, before I could ever trust the answers he provides. Nicholson could use work on personal morals as well; death and crime are not viable solutions to righting wrongs.

TREATMENT: Recommend long-term incarceration with extensive therapy. The Answer could be a potential candidate for Luke's Thunderbolts program.

CLASSIFICATION	MUTATE
GOALS	WEALTH & FAME
SCOPE	LOCAL
MEANS	MERCENARY

ARMADILLO

AFFILIATIONS: Puma, Nightshade, Rangers, Dr. Karl Malus

ENEMIES: Captain America, New Warriors, Punisher

Antonio Rodriguez is a good man with extremely poor judgment. Transformed into the behemoth he is now by Dr. Malus in hopes Malus would cure his ailing wife, Armadillo has been, at most, a nuisance to our community. Too often, he's simply manipulated into conflict by smarter people, or he goes along with whatever is happening at the time, as witnessed in his various half-hearted prison breakouts. He's tried going straight numerous times, often working as a professional fighter, and even briefly joined the Initiative as a member of the Rangers before being led back into a criminal element — most notably as part of a mercenary team put together by MODOK — though I should note he refused to join the Hood's army when given the chance. It's a shame he keeps making bad choices, as he has remarkable strength and endurance and with proper guidance could be doing something worthwhile with his life. Perhaps his recent run-in with Hydra will help convince him he's a better man than he thinks he is.

TREATMENT: Recommend proper guidance counseling and subsequent monitoring.

CLASSIFICATION	MUTATE
GOALS	CURE
SCOPE	LOCAL
MEANS	ROBBERY

ATTUMA

AFFILIATIONS: Denizens of Skarka, Byrrah, Krang, Ghaur, Llyra, U-Man

ENEMIES: Namor, Fantastic Four, Avengers, Captain America, Andromeda, Defenders, Phoenix, Dr. Doom

While my old ally Namor is prince of the legendary civilization of Atlantis, his enemy Attuma is the chieftain of the barbarians of the undersea realm of Skarka. Attuma is a cruel and brutal warlord, determined to conquer the people of Atlantis and the surface world or wipe them out. When, alongside the Avengers, I first encountered Attuma, he was attempting to raise the oceans' tides to flood the surface world. I am astounded that after his repeated attacks on their nation, the people of Atlantis once allowed this tyrant and would-be mass murderer to become their ruler. Attuma soon led the Atlantean forces in an unsuccessful invasion of New York City. I was relieved to see the captured Attuma put on trial by the United Nations. If only he hadn't regained his freedom! Attuma then aided Kang in his conquest of Earth, and more recently invaded New York yet again. The Atlanteans have come to their senses and turned against him. The world is fortunate that Attuma's intelligence does not equal his ambition or passion for wreaking destruction, even genocide.

TREATMENT: Should Attuma ever be recaptured, he should be imprisoned for life. I see no sign he would ever give up his ambition of enslaving or exterminating humanity.

CLASSIFICATION	SUB-SPECIES
GOALS	CONQUEST
SCOPE	INTERNATIONAL
MEANS	WARFARE

BADD AXE

AFFILIATIONS: Vampiro, Firearms, Norman Osborn, the Hood, Taskmaster

ENEMIES: Spider-Man, Nova

Though details of his early life are sketchy at best, unverified sources in HAMMER conjecture Badd Axe was once a mere a motorcycle gang road captain in Hollister, California, before somehow stumbling into possession of his powerful labrys axe. Though unconfirmed, Thor suspects the weapon may be have actually been forged by the divine weaponeer Hephaestus in Olympus eons ago before eventually finding its way to Earth. Regardless, Badd Axe formed a superhuman gang of his own alongside fellow criminals Vampiro and Firearms. The trio joined Norman Osborn's Initiative training program; however, Osborn's representative the Hood almost immediately killed Vampiro as an example to the others, while Firearms was slain during Osborn's attempt to retake Negative Zone Prison 42 from the warlord Blastaar. The last surviving member of his clique, Badd Axe dutifully served in Osborn's Initiative until Osborn's fall from grace. Like many of Osborn's criminal foot soldiers, Badd Axe is currently incarcerated at the Raft.

TREATMENT: Although little more than a brawler with a powerful melee weapon, Badd Axe shows promise for rehabilitation. He saw his closest allies needlessly lose their lives during the Osborn administration. Our criminal psychologists believe they can channel Badd Axe's survivor's guilt and anger into a constructive force and render him eligible for future Thunderbolts squad incarnations.

CLASSIFICATION	HUMAN
GOALS	WEALTH & FAME
SCOPE	LOCAL
MEANS	MERCENARY

BADOON

AFFILIATIONS: Kree, Thanos

ENEMIES: Skrulls, Silver Surfer, Namor

Although they are native to our galaxy (originating on the planet Lotiara in the Capella star system, to be exact), we know more about the distant Skrulls than the reptilian Badoon. They are believed to be older than either the Kree or Skrull races, although a genetic aversion to the opposite gender kept them in a state of perpetual conflict with little technological progress for millennia, finally achieving progress after instituting strict gender segregation directives. When the Kree and Skrulls went to war, the Badoon allied with the Kree in an attempt to alter the borders of the Badoon/Skrull Neutral Zone in their favor. The Badoon continued attempts to slowly expand

their empire in the borderlands between the Milky Way and Andromeda galaxies, but were kept in check by more powerful factions. With the Skrulls, Kree and Shi'ar in a state of decline, the Badoon Hegemony has seized the opportunity to aggressively expand into Spartoi territory in the outlying systems of the Greater Magellanic Cloud.

TREATMENT: With a power vacuum left in the universe following recent events, the once insignificant Badoon Hegemony is aggressively expanding at an alarming rate. If left unchecked, they could pose a serious threat to Earth in the not-too-distant future.

CLASSIFICATION	EXTRATERRESTRIALS
GOALS	CONQUEST
SCOPE	INTERPLANETARY
MEANS	WARFARE

BARON VON BLITZSCHLAG

AFFILIATIONS: Fifty State Initiative

ENEMIES: Isaiah Bradley, Whizzer, Miss America, Thin Man

Scientist Baron Wernher von Blitzschlag served in Hitler's Schutzstaffel during World War II, employing his mastery of genetics to imbue himself with the ability to generate and absorb electrostatic energy. Although I never faced Blitzschlag directly during the war, I battled a number of his genetically-altered superhumans, such as Master Man and Warrior Woman. Blitzschlag also faced my fellow super-soldier, Isaiah Bradley, and my allies, Whizzer and Miss America, before hiding in a bunker for years following the demise of the Third Reich. More recently, when Tony started the Fifty State Initiative, Blitzschlag was recruited as a federal Initiative scientist at Camp Hammond in

Stamford, Connecticut. Although Blitzschlag remained a willing participant in the Initiative following Norman Osborn's takeover of the program, he has been spared a prison sentence under my administration due to his continuing cooperation with the authorities investigating the illegal acts committed under Osborn's reign.

TREATMENT: Blitzschlag is a cunning strategist who appears to be dedicated to nothing more than his own self-preservation; he should remain under house arrest while investigations are pending into his possible involvement in the rehabilitation/release of the Asgardian Ragnarok clone/cyborg and the inhumane experimentation on the Avengers Academy cadets.

CLASSIFICATION	MUTATE
GOALS	CHALLENGES
SCOPE	LOCAL
MEANS	SCIENCE

BARON ZEMO

AFFILIATIONS: Arnim Zola, Avengers, Baron Strucker, Batroc's Brigade, Commission on Superhuman Activities, Fixer, Iron Man, Masters of Evil, Primus, Red Skull, Secret Empire, Sin, Thunderbolts

ENEMIES: Avengers, Baron Strucker, Captain America, Citizen V, Grandmaster, Graviton, Hercules, Nomad/Scourge, Purple Man, Squadron Sinister, Thunderbolts

The son of Heinrich Zemo fits the old cliché of "like father, like son," but unlike his villainous father, he has also done some good. Admittedly his motives can be puzzling to the point I can't tell whose side he is on other than his own. Even though he is a master strategist and manipulator,

he tends to overlook the most obvious attributes in those he aligns himself with, including the humanitarian within himself, which lucky for everyone, tends to be his downfall. I've thought long and hard about which area he should be filed, be it heroic or villainous, but ultimately his misdeeds and personal agendas outweigh the overall good he has done for the world.

TREATMENT: He's apparently dealing with deep-rooted psychological issues stemming from trying to outdo his father's accomplishments. I'd recommend incarceration with intense psychiatric counselling.

CLASSIFICATION	HUMAN
GOALS	CONQUEST
SCOPE	INTERNATIONAL
MEANS	LEADERSHIP

BASTARDS OF EVIL

MEMBERSHIP: Aftershock, Ember, Mortar, Singularity, Superior, Warhead

ENEMIES: Young Allies

Electro – U.S. national Maxwell Dillon. Graviton – Canadian national Franklin Hall. Pyro – Australian national St. John Allerdyce. Grey Gargoyle – French national Paul Pierre Duval. Radioactive Man – Chinese national Chen Lu. Their crimes, while often heinous, were motivated by greed, nationalism, and/or mutant rights. As such, this generation of super-criminals could often be reasoned with and their behavior could be predicted. However, the Bastards of Evil, a team of young superhumans alleging to be the illegitimate progeny of the aforementioned super villains, are an entirely different beast altogether. The Bastards, claiming to have gained their powers via their fathers' metahuman and mutant physiologies, seem to engage in acts of mayhem simply for mayhem's sake. Although genetic testing has revealed that the Bastards are not, in fact, the children of super villains (and that they only gained their powers 6 months ago when their bodies were bombarded with radiation), this fact does not make them any less dangerous. Possibly brainwashed into forgetting their real names and families, these violent young superhumans are perhaps one of the greatest immediate threats to our national security.

TREATMENT: Reversing the effects of the apparent brainwashing inflicted upon Aftershock, Ember, Mortar, and Singularity should be out first priority. If successful, I recommend eventual enrollment in Avengers Academy.

CLASSIFICATION	GROUP
GOALS	NIHILISM
SCOPE	NATIONAL
MEANS	TERRORISM

BEHEMOTH

AFFILIATIONS: Seetorak

ENEMIES: She-Hulk, Lady Liberators, Iron Man

Manfred Ellsworth Haller was once a promising hydraulic engineer and generous philanthropist. As the founder of Haller Hydraulics, he designed and developed a suit of exoskeleton armor to enable explorers to survive hostile environments and allow rescue personnel to traverse hazardous terrain. He used the suit to battle and nearly defeat the fugitive She-Hulk in hopes of gaining publicity and endorsements, but ended the fight when she was found innocent. Unfortunately, after the Superhuman Registration Act became law, Tony Stark discovered Ellsworth was clandestinely supplying unregistered, tech-based heroes with parts and services. Haller Hydraulics was closed and Haller's assets were frozen. Haller fled to Timbuktu, Mali, in search of enlightenment, but instead found an elderly devotee of the Hindu god Ganesha who foresaw his arrival and bestowed upon him the vastly powerful Seetorak gem, which warped Haller's mind and transformed him into the pachyderm-like Behemoth. He returned to the US to seek vengeance upon She-Hulk, but was defeated by her allies the Lady Liberators.

TREATMENT: Haller is a brilliant scientific mind with the potential to make significant breakthroughs in law-enforcement and emergency-rescue technology. However, the first step to his rehabilitaion is to separate him from his power source – the Seetorak gem.

CLASSIFICATION	MUTATE
GOALS	REVENGE
SCOPE	LOCAL
MEANS	MERCENARY

BISON

AFFILIATIONS: Condor, Luke Cage, Justine Hammer, Arthur Nagan

ENEMIES: Guardians of the Galaxy, Initiative, SHIELD, Thunderbolts

When a basketball injury crushed Billy Kitson's dreams of college scholarship, he turned to the death god Seth to fix his leg. Like all deals with devils, Billy got more — and less — than he asked for. Transformed into the monstrous Bison, Billy was forced to become Seth's agent, pitting him against SHIELD when Seth sought the Inferno 42 WMD. Bison's girlfriend Shamari Asbery turned to Luke Cage for help, and Bison finally turned against Seth when Seth's agents Quicksand and Mongoose threatened Shamari's life. Billy left Seth's employ, but was trapped in his unwanted monstrous body. Since then, Bison followed more ill-considered plots to regain his humanity, such as joining Justine Hammer's Masters of Evil. While incarcerated in Prison 42, Bison was conscripted into Blastaar's army to combat the Initiative but was returned to cell when the Initiative recaptured the facility.

TREATMENT: No man as young as Billy Kitson deserves a lifetime of punishment over one poor decision. Confer with Luke re: potential for Thunderbolts program. Run SHIELD medical files past Beast; he may see the way to reverse Seth's genetic engineering.

CLASSIFICATION	MUTATE
GOALS	CURE
SCOPE	LOCAL
MEANS	MERCENARY

BLACK TALON

AFFILIATIONS: Hood, Grim Reaper, Lethal Legion

ENEMIES: Avengers, Midnight Sons, She-Hulk

Samuel David Barone is one of three men known to have taken up the mantle of voodoo sorcerer Black Talon and stands, by far, to be the most dangerous. While the others — Desmond Drew and Thibodaux Boudreaux — enjoyed relatively short stints, Barone has been a persistent thorn in the Avengers' side as well as many others. Many would probably not take him seriously at first, given what, to those outside his faith, appears to be a somewhat comical attire, but he is underestimated at their peril, as he is one of the world's most powerful known voodoo practitioners. His ability to create and command zombies makes him a exceptionally dangerous; in the past he even dabbled in raising dead mutants to gain super-powered zombie slaves. Worse, he has removed himself from the typical costumed battles of late, preferring to build a criminal empire on the island Taino, maintaining a large drug trade from there. As this narcotic empire grows, Black Talon becomes more powerful with each passing day.

TREATMENT: Recommend long-term incarceration; containment of mystic items also recommended.

CLASSIFICATION	MAGICAL BEING
GOALS	WEALTH & POWER
SCOPE	INTERNATIONAL
MEANS	MAGIC

BLACKOUT

AFFILIATIONS: Hood, Deathwatch, Lilith, Lilin

ENEMIES: Ghost Riders, Avengers, Midnight Sons

Blackout originally styled himself after vampires because of his light-dampening powers and albino complexion. He later learned he truly was a demonic descendant of the ancient sorceress Lilith. In either role, he has reveled as an assassin, going so far as to murder a woman on television during a live news broadcast. He's done a thorough job of hiding his activities prior to first clashing with Ghost Rider, and has proved an especially persistent foe, constantly returning after seeming death, and even murdering the vigilante's sister. Though he reportedly forsook his demonic heritage after Lilith's failed invasion of Earth, he remains vicious and deadly. Most recently taking part in the Hood's army and their attacks on the Avengers before striking out against both current Ghost Riders, he is not to be confused with the other Blackout (Marcus Daniels), who was recruited into the Hood's group as well.

TREATMENT: Recommend long-term incarceration, until and unless psychiatric aid can break his vicious habits. He is light-sensitive, and this weakness should be utilized for incarceration.

CLASSIFICATION	MAGICAL BEING
GOALS	NIHILISM
SCOPE	LOCAL
MEANS	MERCENARY

BLANK

AFFILIATIONS: Graviton

ENEMIES: Avengers, FBI, Spider-Man

The Blank is little more than a man with a gun, but it would be a mistake to underestimate him. Possessing an experimental force field generator (now fused to his body), the Blank's personal force field custom-fits his body, rendering his features an indistinct haze and making him immune to most harm. The Blank has used his powers for little more than conventional robberies, but he proved a challenge for the Avengers' west coast branch when he served as a front man for Graviton. However, the Blank's alliance with Graviton was short-lived, and he hasn't made other allies in the super-criminal underground. Most recently the Blank has sought money to have his force field removed, but to a weary public upset with their financial institutions, his string of bank robberies made him a veritable Jesse James-like folk hero. That notoriety put him on Spider-Man's radar, who quickly bested the Blank and turned him over to the FBI.

TREATMENT: Consult experimental surgeons to have his force field removed and impounded; determine origin of the force field (Blank is not clever enough to have built it, nor well-connected enough to be in with the Tinkerer); deprived of his technology, any prison can hold the Blank.

CLASSIFICATION	MUTATE
GOALS	WEALTH & FAME
SCOPE	LOCAL
MEANS	ROBBERY

BLINDSIDE

AFFILIATIONS: Commanda, Walter Declun

ENEMIES: Spider-Man, Jackpot, Daredevil

Some people just want to be super villains; I don't understand why, but the lifestyle must have some attractive qualities given how many people choose to pursue it. Scientist Nick Chernin probably could have parlayed his blindness-inducing Oedipus neurotoxin into a nice Christmas bonus, but instead he stole it from his employer, Declun International, made himself a costume and used the toxin to start robbing banks as Blindside. Although Chernin was the lead suspect in Oedipus' theft, Declun didn't seem to pursue the case with much enthusiasm; given Declun's extremely shady past activities, his connections to Blindside and other villains bears investigation. Chernin

has since integrated fully into the super-villain community, patronizing the Bar With No Name and dating French techno-thief Commanda. He's a pretty low-level threat, although one of his victims died when the toxin reacted negatively with other drugs in her system. So far, his gimmick is fairly one-note, but Chernin is a skilled chemist, so I wouldn't be surprised if he adds to his arsenal soon.

TREATMENT: Recommend incarceration; in the event of escape, make sure to have the antidote for his serum on-hand. Ensure any staff apprehending Chernin have no exotic substances in their system to avoid dangerous drug interactions.

CLASSIFICATION	HUMAN
GOALS	WEALTH & FAME
SCOPE	LOCAL
MEANS	ROBBERY

BLOODSHED

AFFILIATIONS: Hood

ENEMIES: Phillipe Bazin, Spider-Man, Heroes for Hire

By all accounts, Manhattan native Wyndell Dichinson is an accomplished hand-to-hand combatant with a good head on his shoulders. The only thing keeping him from renouncing his past and redeeming himself is his own stubbornness and issues with authority figures. As an adolescent, Dichinson convinced his younger brother to serve as his accomplice in an automobile theft. The duo was stopped by Spider-Man, but while the younger Dichinson brother cooperated with authorities, Wyndell fled to Asia prior to his trial where he trained to become the costumed mercenary Bloodshed. He retuned to the US guarding narcotic shipments for crimelord Phillipe Bazin, but had a falling out with Bazin after losing the cargo. Dichinson's brother convinced him to join the witness

relocation program and testify against Bazin's empire, but Dichinson escaped custody when his prison transport was attacked by Bazin's men, and dedicated himself to single-handedly dismantling Bazin's empire. However, Bazin was finally toppled by Darkhawk; Bloodshed only recently reemerged as one of the Hood's underlings.

TREATMENT: With superhuman strength, durability, and advanced training in several martial arts as well as self-taught street fighting skills, Dichinson would be an ideal candidate for the Thunderbolts program. He must learn he needs to operate within the confines of the law if he wishes to fight crime.

CLASSIFICATION	MUTATE
GOALS	WEALTH & FAME
SCOPE	LOCAL
MEANS	MERCENARY

BULLSEYE

AFFILIATIONS: AIM, Deadpool, Domino, Juggernaut, Kingpin, Mysterio, Norman Osborn, Osborn's Avengers, Sabretooth, Silver Sable, Thunderbolts, Vulture

ENEMIES: American Eagle, Black Widow, Captain America, Crossbones, Daredevil, Deadpool, Elektra, Hawkeye, Moon Knight, Morgan Le Fay, Punisher, Songbird

A former agent of the National Security Agency who became a sadistic psychotic assassin, Bullseye can use any object, even a paper clip or playing card, as a lethal projectile. Bullseye tends to stay within a comfort zone of fighting those who rely on skill rather than super-powers to give him an advantage. He dislikes Daredevil, even going as far as attacking and killing Daredevil's friends Karen Page

and Elektra. Daredevil once beat him into a pulp, only for Bullseye to receive Adamantium implants to strengthen his bones. In the past, he has worked for the Kingpin, Mysterio, and most recently Norman Osborn, desecrating the identity of my friend Hawkeye. He also crippled my former sidekick, Jack Flag. Rumors have surfaced alleging Bullseye attacked Daredevil at Shadowland, Daredevil's ninja base in Hell's Kitchen, where Daredevil murdered Bullseye by running a sai through his heart, much like how Bullseye killed Elektra years ago.

TREATMENT: Recommend lifetime incarceration with no chance of parole.

CLASSIFICATION	HUMAN
GOALS	NIHILISM
SCOPE	NATIONAL
MEANS	MERCENARY

BUSHMAN

AFFILIATIONS: Scarecrow, the Hood

ENEMIES: Moon Knight

Raoul Bushman, who most would consider to be the archnemesis of Moon Knight, was a foreign mercenary for years, committing murders-for-hire and political assassinations. At one time, years ago, as I understand it, he employed the future Moon Knight. Committing terrible crimes against humanity, including rampant destruction of desert villages, mass murder, and rape, Bushman took perverse pleasure in striking fear into the hearts of those he came across, including tattooing a frightening death mask on his face. Bushman brought his drug trade to America where he has embarked upon multiple revenge schemes against Moon Knight, who eventually savagely killed him. I have yet to address this with Moon Knight, who is participating in my Secret Avengers; he seems to have gone quite insane for a time, during which he left a trail of bodies and blood in his wake; I'm still keeping a close eye on him. Ironically, Bushman was recently resurrected by the Hood, though he now sits in a psychiatric institution for the criminally insane. I understand Moon Knight chose not to kill Bushman a second time, which gives me hope for Moon Knight.

TREATMENT: If and when he regains his sanity, I recommend he be given lifetime incarceration under maximum security. However, his homeland Burunda – where he was once president – has made requests for extradition.

CLASSIFICATION	HUMAN
GOALS	WEALTH & FAME
SCOPE	INTERNATIONAL
MEANS	MERCENARY

CANCERVERSE

AFFILIATIONS: Lord Mar-Vell, Revengers, Defenders of the Realm, Ex-Men

ENEMIES: Adam Warlock, Death, Guardians of the Galaxy, Imperial Guard, Nova, Vision (Cancerverse), Quasar

Information is scarce about the Cancerverse and its inhabitants, but based on the reports of both Quasar and Nova, after a Terrigen bomb detonated between Kree and Shi'ar space, it created the Fault, a wound in time/space creating a gateway to other universes. Apparently the entity Death was destroyed, causing everyone and thing in that universe to no longer experience death. The universe became a gigantic, twisted, organic mass that has been consumed by the Many-Angled Ones, a race of demon gods, who are trying to metastasize into our universe. The corruption of the universe caused by the Many-Angled Ones has turned its inhabitants into slaves with the sole purpose of maintaining their survival.

TREATMENT: Restore Death to the universe and free its inhabitants from the clutches of the Many Angled-Ones influence. First priority is to seal the universe to stop the influence from spreading.

CLASSIFICATION	ALIEN DIMENSION
GOALS	CONQUEST
SCOPE	INTERDIMENTIONAL
MEANS	WARFARE

CAPTAIN AMERICA [BURNSIDE]

AFFILIATIONS: National Force, Red Skull, Watchdogs, Dr. Faustus

ENEMIES: Avengers, Daredevil, Dr. Faustus, Captain America, Falcon, Nomad, Albert Malik, Arnim Zola

An avid fan of Captain America, William Burnside discovered both my secret identity and formula for the super-soldier serum while researching Project: Rebirth. Burnside tried to use the information to become the next Captain America, even undergoing plastic surgery to look and sound like me. When the communist Red Skull Albert Malik surfaced, Burnside used the formula on himself and Jack Monroe to become Captain America and Bucky to keep alive the spirit and symbolism Captain America inspired in America during wartime. Due to a lack of vita-ray treatment, which stabilizes the formula and subject's state of mind, Burnside and Monroe succumbed to paranoia and hysteria and were later held in suspended animation until a cure could be found. The duo was released and manipulated by the original Red Skull and Dr. Faustus. Burnside attempted suicide due to Faustus' psychological manipulation, but later resurfaced, once more as Faustus and the Skull's pawn. For a time he became affiliated with the fundamentalist Watchdogs. Burnside is believed to have been killed during a battle with Captain America (Barnes).

TREATMENT: Recommend vita-ray treatment with psychiatric counseling.

CLASSIFICATION	HUMAN
GOALS	CHALLENGES
SCOPE	NATIONAL
MEANS	LEADERSHIP

CAPTAIN FATE

AFFILIATIONS: Dracula, Lilith, Thog

ENEMIES: Man-Thing, Black Knight, Captain Britain, MI13, Chris Claremont, Maura Spinner, Khordes

An immortal, apparently spectral, 19th century pirate, Captain Jebediah Fate spent over 200 years plundering, pillaging and abducting people. While other long-lived individuals mature over the years, or those who find themselves in a new time period, like me, learn to adjust, Fate doesn't seem to have changed. What's worse, the people he kidnapped were eventually brainwashed into joining his crew, apparently due to the same magic that powers his Magus Sword and his flying ship, the Serpent's Crown. Although his reign of terror was dealt a setback after an encounter with the Man-

Thing, Fate forged alliances with the demon Thog and the vampire lord Dracula, increasing his power each time. The latter partnership led to a war with the United Kingdom, thankfully thwarted by Captain Britain and his allies. The Black Knight tells me he defeated Fate by separating him from the Magus Sword that maintains his curse, but the sword and Serpent's Crown were lost in the Atlantic.

TREATMENT: The Magus Sword should be found and destroyed if possible, if not, it should be magically locked away. The Serpent's Crown should be investigated for any possible connection to the Elder God Set's Serpent Crown.

CLASSIFICATION	MAGICAL BEING
GOALS	WEALTH & FAME
SCOPE	INTERNATIONAL
MEANS	MAGIC

CARRION

AFFILIATIONS: Hive

ENEMIES: Nightcrawler, Spider-Man

Carrion is one of those cases where it is hard to tell if the man behind the creature is responsible for his actions. The virus that caused Carrion's mutation was created years ago by the Jackal (Miles Warren), who mixed it with his own DNA to seemingly transfer his mind into different hosts. Dr. William Allen was infected and mutated by it while studying an infected corpse. Gaining Jackal's memories and a variety of powers, including an organic matter decaying touch, regenerative abilities, levitation and low-level telepathy, Allen seemingly kept control over his body and willingly became as Carrion a major threat to civilians in New York City until Spider-

Man stopped him. Though Carrion was put in stasis in a SHIELD facility he escaped at some point and fell under the demon Hive's control in a plot against the mutant Nightcrawler. Caught again Carrion was transferred to Negative Zone Prison 42, which was soon overrun by Blastaar's forces. Though Allen was deemed incurable unlike his predecessor I'm sure someone out there knows how to cure him and prevent Carrion from harming innocents in the future.

TREATMENT: Recommend genetic therapy to reverse mutation and psychiatric aid to help him become a valuable asset to SHIELD again.

CLASSIFICATION	MUTATE
GOALS	NIHILISM
SCOPE	LOCAL
MEANS	MERCENARY

CHAMELEON

AFFILIATIONS: Sasha Kravinoff, Kraven the Hunter, Hammerhead, Hydra, the Leader, Sinister Twelve, Exterminators

ENEMIES: Spider-Man, Captain America, Hulk, Iron Man, Daredevil, Kingpin

The Chameleon is a master of disguise, capable of impersonating virtually anyone. It is ironic, therefore, he suffers from an identity crisis. Born in Russia and reportedly named Dmitri Smerdyakov, the Chameleon was the illegitimate half-brother of Sergei Kravinoff, the original Kraven the Hunter. Sergei and their father forced Smerdyakov to work as their servant, making him feel as if he were a nonentity, worthy of contempt. As a result, Smerdyakov impersonated other people and worked as a spy for the Russian government. Later, he became a freelance criminal, working for clients like Hydra and the Leader, or operating independently.

Once he even impersonated me and convinced Iron Man that I was the Chameleon, resulting in my having to fight my friend! Spider-Man has been the Chameleon's leading adversary, and he tells me Chameleon has grown increasingly insane over the years. Although he allegedly feigned a suicide attempt, reliable reports claim he considers himself a hero, murdering his victims and impersonating them in order to "correct" their lives. Such deluded, self-righteous vigilantes are especially dangerous.

TREATMENT: Recommend long-term incarceration in a prison hospital for the criminally insane, under heavy security, to make sure he does not impersonate a guard and escape.

CLASSIFICATION	HUMAN
GOALS	WEALTH & CHALLENGES
SCOPE	INTERNATIONAL
MEANS	MERCENARY

CHAOS KING

AFFILIATIONS: None

ENEMIES: Amatsu-kami, Olympians

According to Shinto legend, in the beginning, the universe was an expanse of chaos and nothingness. The Shinto gave a name to this formless void: Amatsu-Mikaboshi – "the August Star of Heaven." The Shinto gods Izanagi and Izanami populated the nothingness with life – acts of creation which enraged Mikaboshi by disrupting his static, controlling power. After Mikaboshi's attempts to destroy the Shinto gods were foiled, he was imprisoned in the nether realm of Yomi for millennia. In modern times, Mikaboshi escaped his prison and wrought havoc upon the Shinto pantheon before destroying Olympus, home of the Greek gods. Fortunately, it was reported Mikaboshi met his end while battling the Skrull goddess Sl'gur't during the Skrull invasion of Earth. However, Thor reports whispers among the community of gods that an "ancient darkness" is slowly descending upon the planet. Could it be reports of the Chaos King's demise were premature?

TREATMENT: Can the embodiment of primordial chaos and nothingness ever be treated or physically restrained? I often wish those types of metaphysical quandaries were beyond my pay grade. Unfortunately, they need to be addressed. Since the Amatsu-kami previously managed successful long-term containment of the Chaos King, should he indeed reemerge, perhaps an arrangement can be made to return the Chaos King to the custody of the Shinto gods.

CLASSIFICATION	MAGICAL BEING
GOALS	CONQUEST
SCOPE	UNIVERSAL
MEANS	WARFARE

CHTHON

AFFILIATIONS: Darkholders, Modred the Mystic

ENEMIES: Dr. Strange, Darkhold Redeemers, Avengers, Demogorge, Merlin, Morgan Le Fey, St. Brendan, Magnus, Knights of Wundagore

Though no supernatural authority, I have an interest in Chthon because of the effect he has had on my friends Wanda and Pietro Maximoff, the Scarlet Witch and Quicksilver. According to Strange, Chthon was one of the "Elder Gods" who originated in primeval times and degenerated into a demon. Anticipating the Elder Gods fall, Chthon inscribed his knowledge of evil magic onto the indestructible parchments that became the Darkhold. Strange says it is the most powerful book of "black magic" in existence, and one forfeits his soul merely by reading it. Chthon escaped into another dimension, intending someday to return. In the time of King Arthur, Morgan Le Fey summoned Chthon to Earth but then buried his essence beneath Wundagore Mountain in Transia. When Wanda was born on Wundagore Mountain, Chthon bonded with her. Decades later he took mental possession of her, but the Avengers freed her from his control. Recently, Chthon tried again, taking control of her brother, Pietro, but the Avengers saved Pietro and bested Chthon.

TREATMENT: Inapplicable. Even if Chthon could somehow be captured, he is essentially pure evil. Perhaps Dr. Strange could appeal to one of his patron deities and arrange some form of permanent confinement.

CLASSIFICATION	MAGICAL BEING
GOALS	CONQUEST
SCOPE	EXTRADIMENSIONAL
MEANS	MAGIC

CLOWN

AFFILIATIONS: Zodiac, Death Reaper, Manslaughter Marsdale, Trapster

ENEMIES: Fantastic Four, Human Torch

The man currently calling himself the Clown is the half-brother of Eliot Franklin, the Clown who was part of the Circus of Crime and is now — in mutated form — part of the Gamma Corps as the Griffin. Like Franklin, this Clown has displayed psychopathic and sociopathic traits in the little time he has been on the radar. After Franklin stopped wearing the Clown costume, this Clown took it up, using the reputation built by his sibling for his benefit. Details are sketchy, but it appears he has been recruited by the enigmatic anarchist Zodiac as part of a group bent on bringing chaos to other superhumans, heroic or not. If this is the case, he's at least partly responsible for the destruction of a hospital housing the injured Human Torch (Johnny Storm), an act which took numerous lives. A bank robbery around the same time attributed to him left numerous dead as well. Armed only with a gun, this Clown has proved to be no laughing matter.

TREATMENT: Recommend long-term incarceration; no special requirements for confinement, other than keeping him beyond the reach of his allies.

CLASSIFICATION	HUMAN
GOALS	WEALTH & FAME
SCOPE	LOCAL
MEANS	TERRORISM

CONDOR

AFFILIATIONS: Terrible Trio, Blastaar, Arthur Nagan, Skeleton Ki, Bison

ENEMIES: Nova, Sphinx, Fantastic Four, Avians, Guardians of the Galaxy

A rogue native of the Bird People of Sky Island, Condor has been using his wings, fighting skills, and technology for years to gain a criminal reputation in the States. When Nova described his early confrontations with Condor, he laughed as he recounted how the Sphinx ended the fight by transforming Condor into an actual bird, a state he remained in for years. Still, Condor's use of memory-altering technology and willingness to kill make him a force to be reckoned with. Condor has been in and out of jail for years, but always seems to find trouble when he's free. While in Prison 42 in the Negative Zone, Condor joined Blastaar when the prison was overtaken, but that ended in disaster for all involved; many criminals were killed, and Osborn's efforts to quell the attacks with his hand-selected cannon fodder in the Shadow Initiative led to even more deaths. Though Condor has most often battled Nova, he has fought several other super heroes as well. Red Raven and the Avians launched themselves on New York a few years back in an effort to reclaim Condor, and it makes sense to give him back to the Bird People for long-term incarceration.

TREATMENT: Deport back to Sky-Island for incarceration.

CLASSIFICATION	SUB-SPECIES
GOALS	CHALLENGES
SCOPE	LOCAL
MEANS	SCIENCE

CONSTRICTOR

AFFILIATIONS: Diamondback, Thing, Taskmaster, Corporation, SHIELD

ENEMIES: Hulk, Captain America, Daredevil, Deadpool, SHIELD

Frank Payne, aka Frank Schlichting, is a complicated man. A SHIELD agent who became too involved in an undercover assignment, eventually he became the thing SHIELD was designed to combat: a super-powered threat. As a mercenary with cybernetic Vibranium-enhanced arms and extendable snake-like tendrils, the Constrictor has worked with a number of shady individuals and organizations, from the Masters of Evil to the Frightful Four. He has tried to turn over a new leaf, first as a member of GW Bridge's Six Pack, then teaming with the Thing and Nighthawk against the murderous Arcade. It troubles me that Constrictor took assignments with Henry Gyrich's Shadow Initiative knowing several missions worked against the Initiative's mandate, and that Norman Osborn and the Taskmaster saw the Constrictor as their subversive poster boy for Camp HAMMER. Diamondback, whose opinion I value highly, claims he genuinely wants to reform. If so, I think Constrictor deserves to be given another chance. As a side note, it is unknown how the Constrictor may have been affected by the recent Vibranium crisis.

TREATMENT: Suggest a rehabilitation program, preferably in a team environment where he can be monitored and guided.

CLASSIFICATION	CYBORG
GOALS	WEALTH & FAME
SCOPE	INTERNATIONAL
MEANS	MERCENARY

CONTROLLER

AFFILIATIONS: Thanos, Red Skull, Master of the World, the Hood

ENEMIES: Iron Man, Captain America, Sub-Mariner, Avengers, Captain Mar-Vell

Crippled, horribly scarred and bedridden by an explosion accidentally caused by his brother, Vincent, research scientist Basil Sandhurst became obsessed with using his mind to gain control not just over his body and fate but over the world. He invented a device called an "absorbatron" and "slave discs" that he could fasten to other people. Through the "slave discs," Sandhurst could not only control his victims' minds but also drain their mental energies into a powerful exoskeleton he wore, amplifying his physical strength to superhuman levels. It was Iron Man who first opposed him and who remains his primary adversary. Sometimes Sandhurst operates alone, but other times he works for greater menaces, such as Thanos. The Red Skull once hired him to send a controlled Sub-Mariner to destroy me; I survived and found and defeated the Controller instead. Without his exoskeleton, Basil Sandhurst needs life support equipment to survive. I suspect he needs psychiatric care as well, driven as he is by his fear of reverting to physical helplessness without the energies he absorbs into his Controller battlesuit.

TREATMENT: Recommend imprisonment in a prison hospital and any psychiatric help that may be needed.

CLASSIFICATION	HUMAN
GOALS	CONQUEST
SCOPE	NATIONAL
MEANS	LEADERSHIP

CORTEX

AFFILIATIONS: Anthony Falcone, Damian Tryp

ENEMIES: X-Factor, Jamie Madrox

Cortex's background is convoluted and headache inducing, but it will help if you've seen *The Terminator*. The short version is that he is a cyborg sent back from the future to kill the ancestors of future resistance members. The longer version is that he was originally a duplicate of present day mutant Jamie Madrox, aka the Multiple Man, who was sent into the future to investigate how the recent mass mutant depowering might be reversed. Apparently when he tried to return home he got trapped between the timelines, from where he was retrieved and bionically modified to become an assassin for an anti-mutant regime some 80 years in our future, before then being sent back to our time to carry out his mission. Able to control others' minds, he eliminated several targets before he was stopped by X-Factor; Madrox informs me that Cortex was returned to the future and slain, but since Cortex reportedly also possessed exceptional regenerative abilities, we can't rule him as out for good. Besides, time travel means we might run into a younger version of him at a later date. As I said: Headache inducing.

TREATMENT: Should he reappear, we'll need to figure out how to block his time travel and mind-control capabilities if we want to incarcerate him.

CLASSIFICATION	CYBORG
GOALS	TEMPORAL MODIFICATION
SCOPE	NATIONAL
MEANS	ASSASSINATION

COTTONMOUTH

AFFILIATIONS: Serpent Society, Erik Killmonger, Headlok, Nightshade

ENEMIES: Captain America, Black Panther, Hawkeye, American Eagle, Luke Cage

I first encountered Burchell Clemens in the middle of his Serpent Society team's murder of MODOK, and to this day he remains one of the most vicious and brutal assassins I have come across. As Cottonmouth, he stayed out of the public eye for years while operating in Southern states. Once recruited into the Society, he has become one of their top agents. With his steel teeth, cybernetic jaw and neck muscles, which allow him to extend his mouth greatly, he takes pleasure in his murderous ways. He often uses his teammate Bushmaster's real name, Quincy McIver, as an alias.

I have fought him numerous times, and each time his ruthlessness seems to grow. Due to this, I tend to target him first; once he's down, I feel a lot more comfortable. I wonder if Roxxon was responsible for his bionic implants, as they were so many of his Society teammates.

TREATMENT: Recommend long-term incarceration, explore options to have his bionic implants surgically removed.

CLASSIFICATION	CYBORG
GOALS	WEALTH & FAME
SCOPE	NATIONAL
MEANS	ROBBERY

CROSSBONES

AFFILIATIONS: Thunderbolts, Sin, Red Skull, Skeleton Crew

ENEMIES: Captain America

Given our tumultuous history, I'll be the first to admit I can't render an impartial assessment of Brock Rumlow. Oddly enough, we both spent our formative years in Manhattan's Lower East Side (albeit separated by a number of decades); but while I focused on the study of arts and humanities, Rumlow assembled his street gang the Savage Crims, engaging in a laundry list of crimes ranging from armed burglary, to sexual assault, to murder. Rumlow trained under Taskmaster and eventually caught the attention of the Red Skull, who dubbed him "Crossbones" and made him his chief henchman. Since then, whenever Red Skull or his daughter Sin have reared their heads, Crossbones is usually not far behind. He was even instrumental in my recent "assassination," wounding me with a sniper rifle from long range in order to distract authorities from the Skull's master plan. As someone who's reveled in murder and mayhem since childhood, it's hard to see any hope of redemption for Brock Rumlow.

TREATMENT: Rumlow has been incarcerated in the Raft ever since being captured by Captain America. Although I can't say I agree with their logic, our criminal psychologists at the Raft recommended Rumlow for inclusion in the Thunderbolts program, believing Rumlow is so heinous and repulsive his fellow inmates will gravitate toward Luke's leadership. I pray they're right.

CLASSIFICATION	HUMAN
GOALS	NIHILISM
SCOPE	NATIONAL
MEANS	TERRORISM

CROSSFIRE

AFFILIATIONS: Hood, Mandrill, Corruptor, Controller, Mr. Fear

ENEMIES: Hawkeye, Mockingbird, U-Foes

CIA interrogation and brainwashing specialist William Cross worked with CIA scientists developing an extremely effective method of brainwashing via ultrasonics; however, he soon faked his death and stole the technology, using his skill and resourcefulness for criminal operations. After losing his left ear and left eye in an explosion orchestrated by his rivals, Cross replaced them with cybernetic implants and became Crossfire, a high-tech freelance subversive seeking to foment disorder for profit. When secretly constructing components for his projects at his cousin's research and development firm Cross Technological Enterprises, Cross came into conflict with Hawkeye and Mockingbird and has since maintained a vendetta against the couple. During Norman Osborn's reign as commander of the government's superhuman infrastructure, Crossfire joined a group of super-criminals led by the Hood, who was closely affiliated with Osborn. Following the defeat and incarceration of Osborn and the Hood, Crossfire has avoided capture while consolidating weapons and mercenaries in New York City for a criminal army of his own.

TREATMENT: Recommend long-term incarceration; his technological prowess makes consideration for Thunderbolts program too risky, as he may be able to override the nanite system used to control the inmates.

CLASSIFICATION	HUMAN
GOALS	WEALTH & FAME
SCOPE	NATIONAL
MEANS	MERCENARY

CUTTHROAT

AFFILIATIONS: Hood, Red Skull, Skeleton Crew, Savage Crims

ENEMIES: Avengers, Captain America, Spider-Man

It is hard for me to stay unbiased in Cutthroat's case due to my respect for his sister. Despite not having any superhuman abilities, Cutthroat has trained to become a deadly hand-to-hand combatant, sniper and knife-thrower, skills he honed for the sole purpose to become a well-paid assassin and henchman for some of the most despicable men I know, including the Red Skull and the Hood. It also baffles me that Cutthroat did not learn anything from the time Crossbones, an ally of his, nearly killed him. Incarcerated at the Raft for some time, Cutthroat was among the escapees during a mass breakout orchestrated by Electro. Cutthroat has since joined the Hood's army and continued his life of crime without batting an eyelash. Despite his sister's feelings for him, the long-lost brother routine does not cut it for me, and I hope she realizes a brother who leaves his family in dire times will always choose the easy way out. I honestly see no future for him and I doubt he will walk a similar way as his sister did. He is too much of a coward in my opinion.

TREATMENT: Recommend long-term incarceration and regular visits from his sister, who hopefully can talk some sense into him.

CLASSIFICATION	HUMAN
GOALS	WEALTH & FAME
SCOPE	LOCAL
MEANS	MERCENARY

DAKEN

AFFILIATIONS: Norman Osborn, Romulus

ENEMIES: Wolverine, X-Men, Fantastic Four, Punisher

Despite being more than half a century old, Daken seems very immature, desperate to torture and manipulate others for his own pleasures; Wolverine does not share this assessment. I am amazed by all the things Wolverine has done in his life (ranging from soldier to samurai), but even that life experience didn't prepare him when he recently learned he was a father. Wolverine tells me he sees a lot of himself in Daken, who was savagely harvested from the womb of his mother, Itsu, as she lay dying. Trained as a bloodthirsty warrior by Romulus, Daken (Japanese for mongrel) only recently crossed paths with his father, and they have been at odds ever since. On his own and as part of Norman Osborn's Avengers, Daken has made multiple plays for power, manipulating the Fantastic Four and slicing up the Punisher along the way. Wolverine blames Romulus for Daken's challenges, but I don't know how redeemable Daken is, no matter how much I believe in second chances. Wolverine assures me Daken has recently learned some difficult lessons. I hope that will stop the bodies from falling around him.

TREATMENT: Recommend long-term incarceration with extensive therapy. It is important to involve Wolverine in any recovery processes as this is a very personal matter to him.

CLASSIFICATION	MUTANT
GOALS	NIHILISM
SCOPE	NATIONAL
MEANS	MERCENARY

DANSEN MACABRE

AFFILIATIONS: Night Shift, Satannish, Hood, Cult of Shiva

ENEMIES: Avengers, Midnight Sons, Shroud, Spider-Man

Beautiful and graceful, Dansen Macabre is proof of the time-old saying you can't judge a book by its cover. All we know of her past is that she was an exotic dancer for a time before falling into a cult worshiping Shiva. Eventually, she turned up as a member of the Shroud's Night Shift, criminals he recruited for a vigilante crusade without telling them his true intentions. Though she was revealed and cast aside, the Night Shift continued and have proved a consistent thorn in our sides, with Dansen often acting as their field leader. She was among Night Shift members working for the Hood in his attempt to gain access to an extradimensional zombie-creating virus.

TREATMENT: Her hypnotic dance can cause most any person to follow her every wish, and it is imperative that anyone who confronts her is equipped for this. It is also important to remember she almost never travels alone. When we find her, there's bound to be more Night Shift members lurking about in the shadows.

CLASSIFICATION	MAGICAL BEING
GOALS	WEALTH & FAME
SCOPE	LOCAL
MEANS	ROBBERY

DEACON

AFFILIATIONS: Zadkiel, Ghost Rider Assassination League

ENEMIES: Ghost Rider, Danny Ketch, Caretaker

After deceiving himself into thinking he is a servant of God, the massive, tattoo-covered Deacon has "rebuked" those he considers to be "sinners", by slaughtering them, reciting religious rhetoric along the way. We'd had him safely locked away in a maximum security prison's solitary confinement, but a rogue guard released him. With enhanced strength and mystically-enhanced golden daggers, allegedly given to him by a rogue angel named Zadkiel who tried to overthrow Heaven, the Deacon slaughtered a group of prisoners and a convent full of nuns. He later turned his attention to defeating the two Ghost Riders. As Zadkiel was finally being defeated, I understand that the Deacon was left paralyzed and incarcerated after a battle with the sword-wielding Caretaker.

TREATMENT: As much as I try to understand the mystical parts of our world, I can never quite grasp it; luckily men like Dr. Strange and Dr. Voodoo are around to assist me. I do know that there are mystic forces that tend to manifest themselves through those on Earth (powering operatives such as Red Wolf, Thunderstrike, the Wrecking Crew, the Absorbing Man, etc). We need an effective way of limiting power-sets being supplied to villains.

CLASSIFICATION	MAGICAL BEING
GOALS	NIHILISM
SCOPE	LOCAL
MEANS	MERCENARY

DEADLY DOZEN

AFFILIATIONS: Hood, Microchip

ENEMIES: Punisher, GW Bridge

It never ceases to amaze me that in my line of work almost no one stays dead, hero or villain. I witnessed the autopsies of several of the Deadly Dozen members — all victims of the Scourge of the Underworld vigilante organization. The Hood resurrected 18 such criminals in his quest to get rid of the Punisher, but Castle, in disgustingly typical Castle fashion, quickly took that number down to just 12. The survivors apparently are still out there somewhere, even without the Hood empowering them, and most likely still targeting the Punisher. Each of them more vicious and evil than when they first died, it is imperative we contain them before they kill anyone else, as they did the wife of former SHIELD agent GW Bridge, as well as a hospital room full of war veterans. Dr. Strange and Dr. Voodoo may be able to help us given the nature of their resurrections. Of the Dozen, Death Adder and Basilisk are top priority for capture.

TREATMENT: Recommend separation and long-term incarceration. Cross-reference individual files.

CLASSIFICATION	GROUP
GOALS	WEALTH & FAME
SCOPE	NATIONAL
MEANS	MERCENARIES

DEADPOOL

AFFILIATIONS: Deadpool Corps, Code Red, Agency X, Great Lakes Initiative, Six Pack, One World Church, Deadpool Inc., Weapon X, Team Deadpool, Heroes for Hire, Secret Defenders, Frightful Four, Department K

ENEMIES: Captain America, Spider-Man, Wolverine, X-Men

It's telling that the best thing I can say about Deadpool is that when I was possessed by the alien Messiah, he incapacitated me with a low blow to save the universe. He is a mentally disturbed lunatic, who hears voices in his head. Looking at all the things he did over the years, I have to question if the things that actually could be considered good are enough to redeem him for all the cruel and

twisted crimes he committed. The answer is clearly no in my opinion, but he can nonetheless be helpful in certain situations. His healing factor alone could save millions of lives if he went out of his way and started a career as a crash test dummy, but the problem is Deadpool is more interested in maiming people. I honestly don't know what to do with him. Putting him in prison endangers the other inmates, and letting him get away with everything endangers countless civilians. The biggest surprise to me is that people actually hire him because in many cases his clients end up dead as he doesn't know the meaning of loyalty.

TREATMENT: Recommend long-term incarceration in a mental hospital and psychiatric aid, though I don't think the latter will work.

CLASSIFICATION	GROUP
GOALS	WEALTH & FAME
SCOPE	INTERPLANETARY
MEANS	MERCENARY

DEATH REAPER

AFFILIATIONS: Zodiac, Clown, Manslaughter Marsdale, Trapster

ENEMIES: Norman Osborn

Despite her ominous choice for a codename, thus far Death Reaper has been less a super villain, and more an ardent fan of them, a "groupie" if you will. Though she claims to be the daughter of psychotic mutant priestess Nekra, we've been able to turn up little real background information on her prior to her hooking up with a group led by the new, anarchist Zodiac. Even her abilities are vague, but she appears to be a Darkforce wielder. She's apparently Zodiac's lover, but outside that there's no reports of her taking an active role in his terror spree. Still, she's

certainly an accomplice to his numerous crimes, and should not be taken lightly by any means. Our first order of business after detaining her is verifying her heritage; she's one of a disturbingly growing number of criminals claiming to be the children of our old foes. We need to start finding these young people before they follow in their parents' footsteps, not cleaning up the messes they're causing afterward.

TREATMENT: Recommend long-term incarceration, likely requires psychiatric observation.

CLASSIFICATION	MUTATE
GOALS	WEALTH & FAME
SCOPE	LOCAL
MEANS	TERRORISM

DEATH THROWS

AFFILIATIONS: Crossfire

ENEMIES: Nick Fury, Hawkeye, Mockingbird, SHIELD Super Agents

The original Death Throws were a group of criminal jugglers, who used a variety of objects and tossed them with deadly precision. The new Death THROWS are fully automated smart soldiers originally known as Magnum Zs. THROWS stands for Techno Hybrid Remotely Operated Weapons Systems. They are designed to withstand a multitude of variable assaults making them virtually indestructible. The Magnum Zs were created for the United States, but the US Senate stopped their funding when they realized that the Magnum Zs' abilities were in conflict with the Geneva Convention. Crossfire acquired some of

them after they were deemed illegal and first used them in a mad plot to conquer the Isle of El Guapo. At the time, the Magnum Zs' only weakness was their external power source, which was deactivated by Nick Fury. Crossfire later deployed them in a plot against Hawkeye and Mockingbird. They respond to threatening gestures and are armed with sonic blasters. It is unfortunate that government sanctioned creations fell into criminal hands, but dealing with these things is definitely a lot easier than human criminals.

TREATMENT: Recommend deactivation and dismantling. I doubt there is anything noteworthy to salvage from Magnum Z technology. They were clearly a step back and in the wrong direction.

CLASSIFICATION	ROBOTS
GOALS	SERVANTHOOD
SCOPE	LOCAL
MEANS	FOLLOWERS

DEATHLOKS

AFFILIATIONS: Roxxon (in the future)

ENEMIES: Wolverine, Captain America, Steve Rogers, Avengers, Slag

I hate time travel. I always have, but especially after my months spent lost in time during my recent "death." Recently, a group of Deathlok soldiers began assassinating targets all over the country, including women, children and one fledgling super hero named Slag. The details are sketchy and come from my brief association with Miranda Bayer (who possessed telepathic visions of the future), but as I understand it, in a possible future Roxxon has killed nearly all super heroes with these deadly cyborgs. Based on the late David Heimerdinger's work, which was authorized by Osborn (what was he thinking?), these cyborgs are created from deadly criminals' corpses. This batch of Deathloks sought to kill heroes that would cause them problems in the future. The Avengers and I stopped them after a particularly violent fight, but not before the Deathloks left a high body count. We'll need to explore if these Deathloks have any connections to the other Deathloks active in recent years; if nothing else, the future soldiers were patterned after these.

TREATMENT: Containment in their own future timeline. ARMOR has been informed about what happened and tasked with finding a way to contain this.

CLASSIFICATION	CYBORGS
GOALS	SERVANTHOOD
SCOPE	NATIONAL
MEANS	FOLLOWERS

WALTER DECLUN

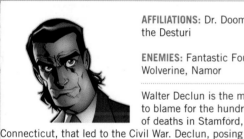

AFFILIATIONS: Dr. Doom, the Desturi

ENEMIES: Fantastic Four, Wolverine, Namor

Walter Declun is the man to blame for the hundreds of deaths in Stamford, Connecticut, that led to the Civil War. Declun, posing as the CEO of Damage Control, supplied Mutant Growth Hormone to Nitro, who blew up in Stamford. While more recently working as the Broker, Declun formed an alliance with Dr. Doom during his attack on Wakanda. Declun used MGH, alien technology, and power upgrades to enhance American criminals like Porcupine, Hydro-Man, and Lady Octopus in a savage battle against the Fantastic Four and Namor (who he had tried framing for the war on Wakanda). With the end of that plot, Declun and his assistant Mrs. Tickle faded into the background again. Declun's experimentation on his own DNA allows him to teleport, and giving him other, as-yet-unknown powers. Regular users of MGH have ended up dead; I should have Reed or Hank look into the long-term effects of MGH on the human genome. Who knows what kind of damage Declun is doing to himself?

TREATMENT: Declun must be purged of his MGH-derived abilities before incarceration; he may require special protection because even the prison population would want the head of the man behind-the-scenes of the Stamford explosion.

CLASSIFICATION	MUTATE
GOALS	WEALTH & FAME
SCOPE	INTERNATIONAL
MEANS	BUSINESS

DELPHYNE GORGON

AFFILIATIONS: Hephaestus, Hera, Amazons, Amadeus Cho

ENEMIES: Athena, Poseidon, Amadeus Cho

Apparently a descendent of the original Gorgons who were cursed by Athena, Amazon warrior Delphyne Gorgon recently saved Hercules, her sometime-lover Amadeus Cho and the world by defeating the previous Amazon queen and taking her place. Unfortunately, she continued her predecessor's misdeeds by allying herself with the goddess Hera, who was attempting to remake the world in her image, apparently out of an ancestral hatred of Athena. Although Delphyne initially did not have the ability to petrify people with her gaze like some Gorgons, she unlocked that ability with the aid of the smith-god Hephaestus and turned Athena to stone in the middle of a battle between the Avengers and Hera's forces. Removing the goddess of wisdom at this key point may have contributed to the deaths of Hercules, Zeus and Hera. Upon recovery, Athena punished Delphyne by placing her in New Tartarus — a sort of mythical prison for the Olympians. Delphyne apparently aided Athena during an attack by Vali Halfling's Pantheon, so there may be hope for her yet. Cho seems to think she could be reformed, and his insights have proven invaluable on several occasions.

TREATMENT: Her rehabilitation is being handled by Olympian authorities.

CLASSIFICATION	MAGICAL BEING
GOALS	REVENGE
SCOPE	INTERNATIONAL
MEANS	WARFARE

DEVOS

AFFILIATIONS: None

ENEMIES: Avengers, Fantastic Four, Inhumans, Kree, Skrulls

Devos the Devastator is an extraterrestrial with a laudable goal: that men might make war no more. However, Devos pursues this end by murdering anyone capable of waging war. Since every human (and presumably every alien) is susceptible to conflict, in Devos' eyes we are all potential targets. Hardly one for allies, Devos only trusts his robot drones to stand at his side. Devos is primarily concerned with races other than humans (particularly with all the in-fighting amongst Kree, Shi'ar and Skrulls), but Ben Grimm assures me that he's already placed Earth on his "to do list." It's truly regrettable that Devos' noble desire has somehow become so twisted that he's overseen the destruction of entire worlds. In another life, he could have been a hero.

TREATMENT: Devos has rebuilt his armaments after each defeat — the supply of his weaponry must be found and cut off. The Avengers recently placed him into Kree custody, but for all we know that's exactly where he wants to be. Check with Inhumans to ensure he hasn't transmitted his location to his autopiloted Death Cruiser, as he once did while visiting the Skrull homeworld.

CLASSIFICATION	EXTRATERRESTRIAL
GOALS	NIHILISM
SCOPE	INTERPLANETARY
MEANS	WARFARE

DIRE WRAITHS

AFFILIATIONS: Eugene Stivak, Quasimodo

ENEMIES: Forge, Rom, Galador's Spaceknights, Project Watchwraith, Winter Guard

Dire Wraiths are an offshoot of the shape-shifting Skrulls who recently invaded Earth; however, where the Skrulls are militaristic, the Wraiths are malevolent. Immured in black magic, they slay those whose forms they take, absorbing the victim's knowledge and literally consuming their soul. Having lost an invasion of a distant galaxy two centuries ago, the Wraiths fled that galaxy's defenders, the Galadorian Spaceknights, and infiltrated many worlds, our own included. Arriving shortly after WWII, they spent decades covertly working to conquer us until the Spaceknight Rom arrived, revealed their presence and rallied Earth's defenders, narrowly preventing them from merging our planet with their dark homeworld. Though Rom banished the defeated invaders to an interdimensional Limbo, reports from Russia indicate some recently escape and battled the Winter Guard. If the outbreak is not contained there, we need to mobilize quickly; the Wraith threat cannot be underestimated.

TREATMENT: In 200 years encountering thousands of Wraiths, Rom reported meeting two who rejected their species' evil. Sadly, that tiny percentage leads me to conclude if the Wraiths ever threaten Earth again, and we can't trust Limbo to hold them, then our only option will be to kill or be killed.

CLASSIFICATION	EXTRATERRESTRIALS
GOALS	CONQUEST
SCOPE	INTERPLANETARY
MEANS	WARFARE

DOC TRAMMA

AFFILIATIONS: Mr. Negative, Hammerhead, Rhino

ENEMIES: Spider-Man, Black Cat

With Jonas Harrow dead at the hands of the Hood, Doc Tramma appears to have become the New York underworld's favorite surgeon. Spider-Man tells us that Tramma was a North Korean scientist/spy who defected to Japan, and eventually opened up a clinic to make people "more artificial" with radical surgical procedures. She's only recently relocated to America, but already she's had several prominent clients; Chinatown crimelord Mr. Negative allegedly hired her to outfit the dying gangster Hammerhead with a new mechanical skeleton, which he's since used to become Negative's chief enforcer and right-hand man; his enhancements make him a physical match for superhumans like Spider-Man. She also provided an armored suit to a man who wished to replace then-retired Alexsei Sytsevich as the Rhino; although Sytsevich eventual killed the imposter, our analysis of the suit indicates this is woman of keen skill. Spider-Man and the Black Cat recently captured her; she's probably too amoral to be of any use to us in a scientific capacity, but hopefully she's mercenary enough to sell out as many of her clients as possible to earn leniency. I'm particularly interested in how she acquired several of Abe Jenkins' old Beetle armors for her henchmen.

TREATMENT: Recommend long-term incarceration; investigate deporting her to Japan.

CLASSIFICATION	HUMAN
GOALS	CHALLENGES
SCOPE	LOCAL
MEANS	SCIENCE

DOCTOR DOOM

AFFILIATIONS: Norman Osborn, Loki, the Cabal

ENEMIES: Fantastic Four, Avengers, Silver Surfer, Spider-Man, Daredevil, Black Panther, X-Men

Victor von Doom is unquestionably the most dangerous person on Earth. His tiny Eastern European kingdom of Latveria possesses weaponry that equals or surpasses even a superpower like the United States; no nation dares attack Doom's country for fear of retaliation. Instead, my colleagues and I must watch for his next attempt to take over the world and stand ready to oppose him. Yet I cannot think of Doom the way I do of many criminals in these files. Doom is a quandary. He can be ruthless and sadistic, as when he murdered his boyhood love, Valeria. Yet he can also demonstrate genuine courage and a strange sense of honor. He may rule Latveria with an iron hand, but I recognize his love for his nation. Doom intends to conquer the planet, but he has also proved willing to risk his life to defend it. Should Dr. Doom ever succeed in ruling Earth, he would destroy all of humanity's freedoms. He is therefore my enemy, and yet he has a greatness I must respect.

TREATMENT: Doom will never be swayed from his goal of world domination. He has escaped imprisonment and apparent death so many times I wonder if he can ever be permanently defeated.

CLASSIFICATION	MAGICAL BEING
GOALS	CONQUEST
SCOPE	INTERNATIONAL
MEANS	SCIENCE

DOCTOR FAUSTUS

AFFILIATIONS: Red Skull, Arnim Zola, Moonstone, Grand Director, National Force, Everyman

ENEMIES: Steve Rogers, Captain America, Mr. Fantastic, Spider-Man

It's often revealing to consider a criminal's choice of alias. Viennese Dr. Johann Fennhoff dubbed himself "Dr. Faustus" after the medieval scholar who infamously sold his soul to the devil, before turning his considerable knowledge of psychiatry to criminal ends, sadistically manipulating his opponents' psyches. When we first clashed, Faustus subjected me to hallucinations to try to drive me insane. He has tried to manipulate both Reed Richards and me into committing suicide. His attempts against us failed, but he succeeded in brainwashing the Captain America of the 1950s, who was already mentally unstable, into becoming the "Grand Director" of his neo-fascist "National Force." But to my mind, his greatest crime was hypnotizing SHIELD agent Sharon Carter to shoot me repeatedly following the end of the super heroes' "Civil War." Strangely enough, what he did to me does not bother me as much as what he did to Sharon, a woman who has meant so much to me. After all, I survived the assassination attempt, but he violated her mind, an act I find totally despicable.

TREATMENT: Recommend imprisonment for as long as the courts may determine. I see little hope for his reform.

CLASSIFICATION	HUMAN
GOALS	CHALLENGES
SCOPE	INTERNATIONAL
MEANS	SCIENCE

DOCTOR OCTOPUS

AFFILIATIONS: Lady Octopus, Stunner, Stewart Ward

ENEMIES: Spider-Man, Fantastic Four, Punisher, Owl, Hammerhead

Otto Octavius' genius intellect makes him one of the most dangerous men alive. We've been lucky he's used his intelligence for years only to menace Spider-Man; had he turned it on the world at large, he'd have become a threat to the Avengers a long time ago. Unfortunately, it now looks like that time has come. Octavius is dying, and before he does, he wants to leave his mark on the world. He recently tried to seize control of New York City with an army of miniature Octobots, and although he failed, we know he won't go gently into that good night. Octavius is at large, and we need to find him; he doesn't want money or even revenge anymore, he wants power. He wants a legacy. It's tempting to just wait Octavius out and let him succumb to his illness, but I've fought my way through a lot of deathtraps set by dead lunatics; I don't want to need a dead man to defuse a bomb.

TREATMENT: Recommend long-term incarceration, as well as immediate surgical removal and destruction of his mechanical arms.

CLASSIFICATION	MUTATE
GOALS	SURVIVAL
SCOPE	NATIONAL
MEANS	SCIENCE

DOCTOR SAX

AFFILIATIONS: Johnny Guitar, the Initiative

ENEMIES: Dazzler

Growing up in the small town of Clack, Mississippi, Jack Dulouz played in a high school rock band with Jonathan "Johnny" Logan, both dreaming of becoming famous recording artists; but when they got their girlfriends pregnant, they were forced to go on the road to earn money to support their families. Trying to supplement their income through crime, they were stopped by their band mates and turned over to authorities. Dulouz was permanently blinded during the altercation. After their release Dulouz and Logan purchased weaponized instruments from the Techmaster and set out to become the super-criminals "Dr. Sax and Johnny Guitar," but were never taken seriously by the super-villain community. When they heard Norman Osborn was seeking criminal recruits for the Initiative, they didn't hesitate to register. But when Logan realized they were being sent on a suicide mission to the Negative Zone, Logan injured Dulouz, forcing them to send Dulouz home to his family; Logan was later killed in action.

TREATMENT: Dr. Sax is living with his wife and three children, with no outstanding warrants against him. Should he again run afoul of the law, he should be considered a prime candidate for the Thunderbolts program. His misguided crimes have always been motivated by financial need rather than malice. Perhaps he can make something more of himself with the proper inspiration and guidance.

CLASSIFICATION	HUMAN
GOALS	WEALTH & FAME
SCOPE	LOCAL
MEANS	ROBBERY

DRAGON MAN

AFFILIATIONS: Diablo, Erich Paine, Enforcers, Future Foundation, X-Men, Power Pack

ENEMIES: Avengers, Sub-Mariner, Hulk, Captain America, Spider-Man, Nova Corps

Despite his name, Dragon Man is neither reptile nor human, but an android created by Professor Gregson Gilbert of Reed Richards' alma mater, State University. However, it was the alchemist Diablo who brought Dragon Man to life and first sent him to attack the Fantastic Four. Superhumanly strong, able to fly and shoot flame from his jaws, and ferocious when enraged, Dragon Man can be a formidable threat to the most powerful heroes. But he is hardly a criminal. In intelligence and even in personality, Dragon Man is like a dog and will loyally serve a master. Unfortunately, too often criminals have taken command of Dragon Man, as when Machinesmith turned him against me. But Dragon Man has also acted like a friendly pet with Power Pack and the original X-Men. For a time Gregson and Dragon Man even worked at a theme park, entertaining children. Dragon Man has proved especially devoted to such women as Susan Richards, Jean Grey and Komodo. Recently, Reed Richards finally found a good home for him as a member of his Future Foundation.

TREATMENT: Recommend Dragon Man remain in Reed and Susan Richards' custody. As long as he receives loving care from masters like the Richards, Dragon Man should remain tame.

CLASSIFICATION	ROBOT
GOALS	FRIENDSHIP
SCOPE	LOCAL
MEANS	FOLLOWER

EAGLESTAR INTERNATIONAL

AFFILIATIONS: Phillip Prometheus, Roxxon

ENEMIES: "Team War Machine"

Eaglestar is a private security organization with billion dollar no-bid contracts. Under former CEO Davis Harmon, Eaglestar illegally acquired an experimental virus based on Ultimo-tech from Dr. Prometheus and tested it on innocents during a mission in Aqiria; the nation was endangered when Ares released the infected victims. War Machine contained the outbreak and deactivated the virus strain while Glenda Sandoval, one of Eaglestar's test subjects, killed Harmon. As a private military contractor, Eaglestar contractors received a special status and couldn't be prosecuted in any court, allowing them to get away with murder. With connections to Roxxon and Human Engineering Life Laboratories, Eaglestar not only tested dangerous technologies but also provided tech they found under unrevealed circumstances to their allies. There are no signs anything changed within Eaglestar after Harmon's death, as they seemingly continued business as usual after the Aqiria incident. Norman Osborn was well-aware of Eaglestar's illegal activities but never took action against them due to legal and political reasons, which just means he saw some use in their activities.

TREATMENT: I recommend reversing their legal immunity and incarcerating Eaglestar employees for their illegal activities.

CLASSIFICATION	GROUP
GOALS	WEALTH & FAME
SCOPE	INTERNATIONAL
MEANS	BUSINESS

ECHO PEOPLE

AFFILIATIONS: Yellow Claw, Mr. Lao

ENEMIES: 3-D Man, Jimmy Woo, Gorilla-Man, Venus, Namora, M-11, Uranian

In 1958, while I was still on ice, Jimmy Woo's group of operatives was active in the country. In one of their more bizarre cases, the Agents fought a group of living dead in a cemetery in Maine until they shut down the machine that powered them. In recent weeks, 3-D Man was framed for the murder of Chuck Chandler (what a terrible loss) and the attack on his brother, Hal. 3-D Man reports he has been attacked by men at a club in Hollywood and later by his girlfriend Sheri Dennon, all who later had no memory of committing the attacks; Sheri later jumped to her death. Now there is word that the Echo People have struck at the heart of the Atlas Foundation itself in an effort to get at the 3-D Man, who, it appears, they cannot use their powers on. I wonder if this somehow ties into the Trion aliens who were behind the Triune Understanding a few years ago. The Echo People seem capable of possessing human host bodies, emitting a red energy when entering or leaving the body, and manifesting as a third eye during the possession.

TREATMENT: Assessment pending; further intelligence required.

CLASSIFICATION	EXTRATERRESTRIALS
GOALS	CONQUEST
SCOPE	INTERNATIONAL
MEANS	WARFARE

EGO THE LIVING PLANET

AFFILIATIONS: Elders of the Universe

ENEMIES: Thor, Galactus, Fantastic Four, Silver Surfer, Quasar, Nova, Nova Corps

Over millions of years in the distant Black Galaxy, Ego the Living Planet evolved, growing to planetary size and gaining consciousness. The only one of its kind, isolated in the vast vacuum of outer space, it is no wonder Ego had no empathy for other beings. It became a threat to the alien Colonizers of Rigel, but Thor drew upon his powers as thunder god to conjure planetwide storms to defeat Ego. Subsequent events caused Ego to go insane, becoming even more dangerous. At one point the alien Ruul somehow managed to reduce Ego's immense mass into a spore that it sent to Earth, where Ego began to grow again, threatening to consume our planet. Reed Richards enabled my fellow Avenger Quasar to contain Ego within his body. But Ego has subsequently freed itself and regained its size. Ego now exists in the vast reaches of space, and I pray it never returns to Earth.

TREATMENT: Capturing Ego and curing it of its madness are feats beyond the capabilities of Earth science. Stephen Strange claims there are sentient stars: perhaps it would take a living star to tame a living planet.

CLASSIFICATION	EXTRATERRESTRIAL
GOALS	SURVIVAL
SCOPE	INTERPLANETARY
MEANS	CONSUMPTION

ELECTRO

AFFILIATIONS: Sinister Six, Sinister Seven, Sinister Twelve, Emissaries of Evil, Frightful Four, Exterminators, Hammerhead, the Hood, the Rose

ENEMIES: Spider-Man, Daredevil, Fantastic Four, Avengers

With his power to generate and control electricity, Max Dillon, alias Electro, is potentially one of the most powerful and dangerous criminals. It's a blessing Dillon has never lived up to that potential. Dillon originally wanted to become an electrical engineer, but his mother convinced him he was not smart enough. So Dillon became an electrical lineman and was repairing a power line when he was hit by lightning, endowing him with his electrical powers, and he became the costumed criminal Electro, hoping for fame and fortune. But J. Jonah Jameson claimed in the Daily Bugle that Electro was Spider-Man in disguise! Spider-Man has since repeatedly bested Electro, once even on television, a particularly humiliating defeat. Electro has tried forming his own criminal team, more often worked with other criminals, and tried to seize control of New York City's power supply, but is continually thwarted by Spider-Man and other heroes. He has tried retiring from crime and even once attempted suicide. But Electro always returns to crime, hoping for a spectacular success that still eludes him.

TREATMENT: Dillon has retired from crime in the past and might well be responsive to rehabilitation when he is next sent to prison. Perhaps he could become an electrical engineer.

CLASSIFICATION	MUTATE
GOALS	WEALTH & FAME
SCOPE	LOCAL
MEANS	MERCENARY

ENFORCER

AFFILIATIONS: Charles Delazny Jr

ENEMIES: The Hood, the Wrecking Crew

The original Enforcer, Charles Delazny, proved a successful criminal in the western United States, most frequently coming into conflict with foes Ghost Rider and Werewolf by Night. Delazny considered himself to be some sort of expert on mystical foes and used a powerful disintegrator ring and hired operatives such as Gladiator (Melvin Potter) and Water Wizard (now Aqueduct) for power and profit. Later, the Enforcer became a professional hitman, during which time he fought Spider-Man and Spider-Woman, but he was eventually killed by the Scourge organization. Before his death, Delazny apparently trained his relative Mike Nero to take his place. Nero, after incurring major debts to the mob has used his mystic prowess and weapons as an assassin, taking on supernatural threats like zombies, werewolves, and vampires. When the Hood tried recruiting him, Nero refused and fought his way free. He is under the radar now, and his motivations and capabilities remain somewhat vague.

TREATMENT: A man of Nero's skills could prove valuable to keeping track of the world's mystical threats, but I would need a clear understanding of what he is seeking to achieve before I could utilize him. In addition, Nero's methods of murdering his opponents, if one can call killing the undead murder, would need to be put into check.

CLASSIFICATION	HUMAN
GOALS	REVENGE
SCOPE	LOCAL
MEANS	VIGILANTE

EXTREMIST

AFFILIATIONS: Doc Tramma

ENEMIES: Spider-Man, J. Jonah Jameson

According to Professor Charles Xavier's files, Tyler Smithson's mother, convinced her son was a mutant, applied several times for his admittance to Xavier's school; Xavier determined the boy was not a mutant and rejected him. Years later, he resurfaced, calling himself the Extremist, exhibiting all the powers his mother claimed he had (thanks to the science of Doc Tramma), and waged a war on opponents of super heroes, murdering a pundit and attacking a blogger and New York City Mayor J. Jonah Jameson. He views the world in terms of absolute good and absolute evil and believes anyone who criticizes the superhuman community is an enemy to be targeted with lethal force. Not only is he a living black mark on everything we stand for, but his twisted logic has led him to target even heroes like Spider-Man. Thankfully, we have him in custody now; with his disregard for human life, he could easily elicit a Stamford-level reaction from the public, undoing all the work we've done. His intentions are ultimately noble, but he's so mentally unstable he may not even be qualified for the Thunderbolts.

TREATMENT: Recommend psychiatric assessment. Likely a danger to other inmates; keep isolated.

CLASSIFICATION	MUTATE
GOALS	REVENGE
SCOPE	LOCAL
MEANS	VIGILANTE

FORCE OF NATURE

AFFILIATIONS: Norman Osborn, Project: Earth

ENEMIES: Heavy Hitters, New Warriors, Thor

With a schtick based on the classic elements, Force of Nature's water, sky and earth lineup has been stable, respectively represented by mutate Aqueduct, the Inhuman Skybreaker and the independent Plantman simuloid Terraformer. For various reasons the fire representative has repeatedly changed; most recently the spot was filled by Initiative trainee Sunstreak, who is the sole member I see with a bright future due to her young age. In the past, Force of Nature got involved in international conflicts and, due to their mercenary status, I'm pretty sure Osborn paid them as well. Aqueduct is a pure criminal. I'd like to send Skybreaker back to his people, but I'm not even sure they want him back. Terraformer was grown evil and is worse than the man he was based on. Sunstreak, on the other hand, could join Butterball's team in North Carolina. I heard there was some connection between them, and maybe he can make her realize how wrong it was to join Osborn's cause.

TREATMENT: Recommend long-term incarceration for Aqueduct, Skybreaker and Terraformer. I hope I'm not wrong about her, but Sunstreak should be given another chance.

CLASSIFICATION	GROUP
GOALS	REVENGE
SCOPE	INTERNATIONAL
MEANS	TERRORISM

FRATERNITY OF RAPTORS

AFFILIATIONS: Shi'ar, Blastaar, Annihilus

ENEMIES: Darkhawk, Nova

Though never a mainstay, Darkhawk served with the Avengers from time to time and had fair success as a hero on Earth. Now, according to Nova, he is a refugee in space, accused of killing Lilandra of the Shi'ar! As Nova explains it, Darkhawk's amulet is a conduit to "the data song of the null source," where an ancient group of intergalactic spies, the Fraternity of Raptors, waits to be awakened to act as "architects of the universal fate." When the Inhumans used their echo-weapons in their war against the Skrulls and the Shi'ar, they weakened dimensional barriers in space, freeing some of the Raptors to take control of alien forms; Talon replaced a Skrull while Kyte and Strel replaced Plutonia and Mentor of the Imperial Guard. The Fraternity, who slightly predate humanity, seems set on altering destiny and has been exposed in manipulations of the Shi'ar in their recent wars. With deadly black sorcery behind them and the ability to call upon various powerful armors, it remains to be seen how the Fraternity will affect Earth.

TREATMENT: I trust the Shi'ar and Kree to handle their own affairs, for now, though the Avengers are prepared to step in as needed.

CLASSIFICATION	EXTRATERRESTRIALS
GOALS	CONQUEST
SCOPE	INTERPLANETARY
MEANS	WARFARE

GALACTUS

AFFILIATIONS: Silver Surfer, Firelord, Nova, Stardust, Terrax

ENEMIES: Fantastic Four, Silver Surfer, Ego, Tyrant

It's miraculous that so far the Fantastic Four and other champions have prevented Galactus from destroying our planet. According to Reed Richards, Galactus is not simply an alien invader, but a force of nature. Even all of Earth's nuclear arsenals could not defeat Galactus. Thor has told me Galactus was once Galan, a mortal humanoid from a universe that existed before our own. The "Big Bang" that created our universe also recreated Galan, who became Galactus, a being of inconceivable power, who had to renew his energies by feeding on planets, usually destroying them in the process. Over the ages, Galactus has suppressed Galan's empathy for other mortal beings. He has convinced himself that he is a superior life-form, that beings like us are no more than ants in comparison to his greatness, and he perpetrates his planetwide genocides only because he must sustain his own life. However, if Galactus goes long enough without feeding, he becomes vulnerable. Richards once saved Galactus' life when he was starving, and Galactus gratefully pledged not to prey upon the Earth. Let us hope he never violates that promise.

TREATMENT: Earth does not have the capability to capture and imprison Galactus. Our best hope is to rely on people such as Reed Richards to persuade Galactus it is in his interest to spare Earth.

CLASSIFICATION	EXTRATERRESTRIAL
GOALS	SURVIVAL
SCOPE	UNIVERSAL
MEANS	CONSUMPTION

GAMMA CORPS

AFFILIATIONS: Hulk, Norman Osborn

ENEMIES: General John Ryker

Few things get my goat as much as men that profess to emulate and uphold the American dream, yet use that as a cover and justification for their crimes and immoral activities. Gen. Ryker has used the American flag to excuse his ties to political torture, chemical warfare, and presidential assassination, and I am disgusted. After a Gamma-treatment failed to cure Ryker's wife, Lucy, of cancer, he sought revenge on the Hulk, and he used government clearance to mutate and train citizens into the superhumans Grey, Mess, Mr. Gideon, Prodigy, and Griffin (formerly the Clown of the Circus of Crime), all of who have personal and tragic ties to the Hulk. The Gamma Corps killed another Gamma being, Flux, before attacking the Hulk during the Hulk's war on Earth, but when the Hulk exposed Ryker as the true manipulator of their tragedies they turned to hunting down other superhumans at Norman Osborn's behest. These five are unknown quantities to me, and I need to have them assessed before I can decide what to do with them. Osborn pardoned them for their crimes, but that doesn't make them reliable. They need a leader they can trust.

TREATMENT: Incarceration and evaluation to determine fitness for duty.

CLASSIFICATION	GROUP
GOALS	REVENGE
SCOPE	INTERNATIONAL
MEANS	MERCENARIES

GHOST

AFFILIATIONS: Thunderbolts

ENEMIES: Iron Man

Although highly intelligent and insightful, Ghost is a deeply conflicted and disturbed loner. One of the world's most notorious industrial saboteurs, he has taken pains to hide his identity and most of his past, but claims to have been an executive at a Fortune 500 corporation, but this is unconfirmed. What we do know is Ghost exhibits classic paranoid schizophrenia, harboring a strong distrust for the government and an intense hatred for private corporations. Although he presented himself as a mercenary to employers who sought to ruin their competitors, Ghost was known to forgo payment simply for the thrill of committing acts of corporate sabotage. Although he briefly aided the Avengers against his fellow Thunderbolts during the siege of Asgard, Ghost has admitted to a recent attempt on Tony Stark's life, although he vehemently denies assaulting Initiative drill instructor Gauntlet on the grounds of Camp Hammond, an incident that is still under investigation.

TREATMENT: Since his incarceration at the Raft following Norman Osborn's failed assault on Asgard, Ghost has exhibited relatively good behavior (although the same can't be said for his social skills and personal hygiene). He is a willing participant in the Thunderbolts program, although he is not to be left alone for extended periods of time, as he may use his formidable hacking skills to disable his nanites.

CLASSIFICATION	HUMAN
GOALS	REVENGE
SCOPE	INTERNATIONAL
MEANS	MERCENARY

GREAT WALL

AFFILIATIONS: Atlas Foundation

ENEMIES: Atlas Foundation

Most of what I've gleaned about the Society of the Great Wall comes from rumors and hearsay. Apparently the criminal organization splintered off the Yellow Claw's Atlas Foundation, taking over much of the East Asian underworld and making occasional wars with Atlas. The society's leader, Jade Claw, is apparently Yellow Claw's grandniece Suwan, the former lover of Jimmy Woo, a once-respected government agent and an old friend. If true, I feel some personal remorse, as I was present when the Yellow Claw cursed Suwan with the corrupt soul of the Egyptian warrior princess Fan-le-tamen, giving her treacherous desires and tactical cunning. She became so ruthless, she betrayed her uncle before he seemingly killed her. Woo is now in charge of the Atlas Foundation, and I understand he has forged an alliance with the Great Wall, placing his associate Temujin at Suwan's side as part of the agreement. I believe Woo plans to reform the clandestine group, but if the Jade Claw is his old flame Suwan, I worry she is still the same power-mad dictator I saw created by the Yellow Claw.

TREATMENT: Not to be trusted. The group should be located, monitored, and broken up if possible. Jade Claw might benefit from a cleansing by a powerful mystic.

CLASSIFICATION	GROUP
GOALS	CONQUEST
SCOPE	INTERNATIONAL
MEANS	WARFARE

GRIFFIN

AFFILIATIONS: Hood, Namor, Headlok, Secret Empire

ENEMIES: Beast, Avengers, Spider-Man, Champions

Johnny Horton is little more than a street thug in a monster's body. The Secret Empire transformed Horton into a creature resembling the mythical Griffin, and Horton has little direction, often hiring himself out to anyone with money and an agenda. He hates his form and is desperate to be human again, which is an aspect I believe we can use in trying to contain him. For a while, he continued to mutate, becoming mindless and more lion-like. At some point after this incarnation, he befriended Namor and was left to roam the Savage Land; he regained his mental faculties and returned to a life of crime. Incredibly resilient, he has returned from seeming death numerous times. A recent run-in with Spider-Man has left him incarcerated again, so this may be our chance to cure him. Apparently, Secret Warriors member Slingshot is his daughter, though details on how she inherited any powers from him is unexplained. He should not be confused with Eliot Franklin, formerly the Clown, who has taken the Griffin name as part of the Gamma Corps.

TREATMENT: Recommend long-term incarceration and research the possibility of returning him to human form.

CLASSIFICATION	MUTATE
GOALS	CURE
SCOPE	LOCAL
MEANS	ROBBERY

GRIZZLY

AFFILIATIONS: Thunderbolts, HAMMER, Gibbon, the Hood, ATF

ENEMIES: Avengers, J. Jonah Jameson, Punisher, Spider-Man

Banned from professional wrestling for excessive violence thanks to editorials from reporter J. Jonah Jameson, Maxwell Markham purchased an exoskeleton and, as the Grizzly, sought revenge against Jameson but was stopped by Spider-Man. After regaining a measure of self-respect when Spider-Man threw the match, Grizzly tried to be a crimefighter for a while, partnering with the Gibbon, but his low self-esteem soon saw him backslide into becoming a thug for hire, upgrading his powers with implants, working for the Owl and repeatedly clashing with the Punisher, encounters that always ended to Markham's detriment. One of the numerous crooks from the Hood's crime syndicate who joined Osborn's Initiative, Grizzly was assigned first to the ATF and then the Thunderbolts, alongside whom he attacked Asgard before being captured by the Avengers.

TREATMENT: Though his time with the Hood and the Thunderbolts suggest Markham has fallen exceptionally far from the hero he once aspired to be, Spider-Man's estimation of the Grizzly leads me to think it isn't too late to turn him away from crime. He's a prime candidate to join the revamped Thunderbolts' scheme.

CLASSIFICATION	CYBORG
GOALS	WEALTH & FAME
SCOPE	INTERNATIONAL
MEANS	MERCENARY

GROTESK

AFFILIATIONS: Mole Man, Tyrannus, Lava Men

ENEMIES: Thor, Avengers, Ms. Marvel, X-Men, Lava Men

Underground atomic tests accidentally annihilated an ancient subterranean civilization and apparently left only one survivor – the grief-stricken and mutated Prince Gor-Tok, now insane and calling himself Grotesk. I'm reminded of my wartime ally Rockman. He told me his people were lost in a similar tragedy, and while it crushed him emotionally, he continued to fight for justice. Grotesk, on the other hand, has repeatedly attacked innocent surface dwellers and fought several heroes over the years. Notably, he convinced the Avengers to work with him during the Subterranean War, but we put a stop to his plans when his duplicity was revealed. Even in death, Grotesk has continued his war against the surface world. He died a few years ago fighting Thor, but his magically-inclined followers, the Lava Men, somehow preserved his spirit in a suit of armor. His shell was apparently destroyed in a battle with the X-Men in San Francisco, freeing his spirit, but time will tell if he remains dead.

TREATMENT: If the armor is indeed haunted, it should be cleansed or destroyed by mystics; however, if there is a possibility of rehabilitating Prince Gor-Tok, he might benefit from psychological counseling.

CLASSIFICATION	SUB-SPECIES
GOALS	CONQUEST
SCOPE	INTERNATIONAL
MEANS	LEADERSHIP

JUSTINE HAMMER

AFFILIATIONS: Sasha Hammer, Detroit Steel, Spymaster, Masters of Evil

ENEMIES: Iron Man, Thunderbolts, Silver Sable

Justine Hammer, the somewhat-estranged daughter of Justin Hammer, a longtime corporate foe of Tony Stark, inherited her father's company and money. Justine, as Hawkeye tells me, was behind many of the weather catastrophes that plagued the country in her effort to form an organized, criminal organization called the Masters of Evil; she was later defeated by the Thunderbolts (many of who were former Masters of Evil). After another defeat by the Thunderbolts (this one involving a bio-weapon her dad developed), Justine was relatively absent for a time from the criminal scene until she and her daughter, Sasha, recently returned in a scheme to manipulate the American military and foreign terrorist cells into investing in their new project Detroit Steel. Hammer International was at the recent incident in Japan, but Tony assures me that he has things under control; I hope this isn't the beginning of him refusing to ask for help yet again. There have been rumors that Hammer is connected with Spymaster, who has had it out for Stark for years. At the first sign of illegal dealings, we'll need to be prepared to take her down.

TREATMENT: Still gathering evidence on wrongdoing; hope to arrange arrest before she goes too far.

CLASSIFICATION	HUMAN
GOALS	WEALTH & FAME
SCOPE	INTERNATIONAL
MEANS	BUSINESS

SASHA HAMMER

AFFILIATIONS: Ezekiel Stane, Justine Hammer, Detroit Steel, Spymaster

ENEMIES: Iron Man, the Triumph Division

Sasha used her command of technology to upgrade Ezekiel Stane's biological system to contain massive technological capabilities during Stane's war against Tony Stark (in large part over the death of Stane's father, Obadiah). Sasha was complicit in terrorist acts in multiple nations, including the one that killed the entire Triumph Division in the Philippines, and I understand she herself was converted into one of Ezekiel's biological weapons. Despite these atrocities, Tony was barely aware of Sasha's behind-the-scenes actions, even after he publicly defeated Stane; he remained unaware until Sasha and her mother

(the former Crimson Cowl of the Masters of Evil) recently took over Hammer International and began marketing Detroit Steel to the American military (and, rumors say, to foreign terrorist cells). Sasha seems to be incorporating the tech she used on Stane into her new company, and they've been buying Osborn's HAMMER tech to complete their mission. It remains to be seen how, legally, we will be able to expose and thwart the Hammers. Tony assures me he can handle Sasha himself, but I don't know if he can.

TREATMENT: Ready to proceed with arrest at a moment's notice; waiting for response from Iron Man.

CLASSIFICATION	HUMAN
GOALS	WEALTH & FAME
SCOPE	INTERNATIONAL
MEANS	BUSINESS

HAMMERHEAD

AFFILIATIONS: Maggia, Dr. Jonas Harrow, Mr. Negative, Chameleon, Taskmaster, Tinkerer, Sinister Twelve

ENEMIES: Spider-Man, Dr. Octopus, Don Fortunato, Hydra, Kingpin, Silver Sable, Tombstone

Since I spent so many years in suspended animation, Hawkeye likes to joke that I'm mentally stuck in the 1940s. But the gangster known as Hammerhead really was psychologically frozen in the past. Reportedly, he was born in Russia but grew up in Italy, where he joined the Maggia and came to the United States, working as a hitman. Someone — no one knows who or why — beat him up, smashing his skull and leaving him for dead in a New York City alley. Delirious, the dying gangster fixated

on the sight of a nearby poster for a movie called "The Al Capone Mob." He was found by the criminal surgeon Dr. Jonas Harrow, who not only saved his life but experimented on him, replacing his skull with a steel alloy. Reviving, the gangster had amnesia, but he started dressing, talking, and behaving like a 1920s mobster like Capone and calling himself Hammerhead. You might think he became a laughingstock, but instead he rose to the top of one of the New York Maggia "families." Ruthless and formidable, Hammerhead recently became even more dangerous when his new ally Mr. Negative had his skull and upper skeleton replaced with unbreakable Adamantium.

TREATMENT: Recommend capture and imprisonment along with psychological examination.

CLASSIFICATION	HUMAN
GOALS	WEALTH & FAME
SCOPE	NATIONAL
MEANS	FOLLOWER

THE HAND

AFFILIATIONS: Daredevil, Black Tarantula, White Tiger

ENEMIES: Spider-Man, Wolverine, the Avengers

An ancient sect consisting of thousands of half-dead ninjas, which seem to evaporate in a puff of smoke when killed, the Hand has become increasingly active on American soil in recent years. Various factions of the Hand seem to have opposing goals; the Dawn of the White Light tried taking over the country with an army of resurrected villains; the Snakeroot tried utilizing the deadly virus About Face; a squad of female assassins tried assassinating the Punisher; and Scimitar funded terrorist activities. The Hand is united once again, however, under the leadership of Daredevil, who is utilizing

them in a bizarre bid for order. They have constructed a massive prison, Shadowland, in the middle of Hell's Kitchen! Several heroes that I trust, including Luke Cage, Iron Fist, Spider-Man, Moon Knight, and the Daughters of the Dragon, have been investigating and are trying to talk sense into Daredevil (who I have never been close to), but the Avengers may need to step in soon. The Hand is imprisoning cops and criminals without due cause, and traditionally they worship demons. We can't have this kind of influence free on the streets, not so soon after Osborn's takedown.

TREATMENT: This organization needs to be dismantled once and for all.

CLASSIFICATION	GROUP
GOALS	CONQUEST
SCOPE	INTERNATIONAL
MEANS	ASSASSINATIONS

HEAVY METTLE

AFFILIATIONS: Blackwing, Fifty State Initiative

ENEMIES: New Warriors, Blastaar, Asgardians

The son of Maggia crimelord Silvio "Silvermane" Manfredi, Joseph Manfredi was always more of a follower than a leader, whether in his father's syndicate, a performer in the Circus of Crime, or member of Red Skull's elite Skeleton Crew. Heavy Mettle was his first attempt at a major leadership role, handing down his Blackwing identity to a subordinate and founding the team to steal the nuclear-powered battlesuit of New Warriors member Turbo. The plan failed, and Heavy Mettle was incarcerated, with team leader Firestrike betraying Manfredi and testifying against him. After Norman Osborn's rise to power, the remaining members of Heavy Mettle enrolled in the Initiative training program at Camp HAMMER, New Mexico. They were used as cannon fodder by Osborn's lieutenants and sent into battle against gods during the siege of Asgard. Although underwater specialist Barracuda and strength-augmented Stronghold survived, archery specialist Warbow, sonic-boom-producing Riot and aerial specialist Blackwing were casualties of war.

TREATMENT: Every member of Heavy Mettle is human — their unique powers are derived exclusively from their high-tech battlesuits. As such, they don't need to be held in a maximum security environment once separated from their technology. Individual psychological assessments recommended.

CLASSIFICATION	GROUP
GOALS	WEALTH & FAME
SCOPE	LOCAL
MEANS	ROBBERY

HELA

AFFILIATIONS: Loki, Moonstar

ENEMIES: Thor, the Asgardians

Hela is the Asgardian goddess of death. Although he may be biased, Thor assures me Hela (who is his step-niece) is more honorable than other death gods. Although Hela has often sought to capture the souls of Thor and his father, Odin, as well as forcibly annex portions of Asgard, she has also acted with compassion and justness when moved by feats of bravery or expressions of true love. However, when Thor resurrected the Asgardians following the latest Ragnarok, Hela lost large portions of her underworld realms of Hel and Niffleheim. Forced to spend most of her time in a Las Vegas hotel penthouse, she struck a bargain with the Hell-lord Mephisto wherein he granted her the Land of the Perfidious Diaspora within his nether realm to act as a temporary Norse afterlife. However, Mephisto soon permitted the Disir, cursed Valkyrior whom he obtained in the bargain, to attack Hela's newly-granted realm, prompting Thor to come to her aid.

TREATMENT: Any punishment rendered upon Hela should be administered by the Asgardians. I'm not sure that even the Raft's Ultra Block would be equipped to handle a goddess of her power.

CLASSIFICATION	MAGICAL BEING
GOALS	CONQUEST
SCOPE	INTERDIMENSIONAL
MEANS	MAGIC

HELLSGAARD

AFFILIATIONS: Ulysses Bloodstone, Monster Hunters

ENEMIES: Manphibian, Morbius, Dracula, Punisher

Though I have heard rumors of the monster hunter Robert Hellsgaard, famous in Germany, Japan, and elsewhere in recent years, I have never crossed paths with him. Over the past few decades, Hellsgaard has led a group of armored and armed men in slaughtering the monsters of the world, from werewolves to vampires to alien and extradimensional beings. Though I don't agree with their methods, they have not, as far as I know, come onto US soil until recently. Hellsgaard, a disfigured man in a powerful suit of armor that has extended his life, was convicted in the 1890s of slaughtering nearly 80 people in his small German town, though he later claimed he was trying to stop them from becoming werewolves (this according to SHIELD Howling Commandos' files). After hunting monsters with Ulysses Bloodstone, Hellsgaard was trapped in Limbo for decades and has apparently returned there after an extended battle over a bloodstone shard with the Punisher and the world's remaining monsters, which are now living under New York. In my opinion, Hellsgaard and the Punisher are more similar than different; both slaughter men in a vain revenge scheme and both need to be incarcerated.

TREATMENT: Work with the Legion of Monsters to secure apprehension and ensure they don't exact vigilante justice.

CLASSIFICATION	HUMAN
GOALS	REVENGE
SCOPE	INTERNATIONAL
MEANS	VIGILANTE

HIGH EVOLUTIONARY

AFFILIATIONS: Knights of Wundagore, Kree Empire, Adam Warlock

ENEMIES: Thor, Avengers, Fantastic Four, X-Men, Ultron

While some individuals are easy to define as good or evil, others, like Herbert Wyndham, defy classification. For nearly a century, the High Evolutionary has pushed the boundaries of science and ignored the boundaries of human decency. He altered humans and other animals against their will and created entire worlds. The High Evolutionary sees himself as a god, and for all he has done, it's a hard claim to challenge. Nova tells me the High Evolutionary was instrumental in several of the catastrophic events that ravaged nearby galaxies recently, but true to form, it's hard to define whose side he was on. Given his experience with mutations, he would seem the ideal individual to assist the X-Men in their struggles after "M-Day," when so many mutants lost their abilities, but the High Evolutionary isn't known for helping people out of altruism.

TREATMENT: Seemingly impossible to destroy and difficult to confine, the High Evolutionary should be located and monitored at all times. He responds well to challenges, so something should be found to put his skills to good use.

CLASSIFICATION	MUTATE
GOALS	CHALLENGES
SCOPE	INTERPLANETARY
MEANS	SCIENCE

HIT-MONKEY

AFFILIATIONS: None

ENEMIES: Deadpool, Bullseye

Spider-Man tells me Hit-Monkey is exactly what he seems to be: a Japanese macaque with uncanny fighting skills and proficiency with a variety of firearms. How such a creature came to be, I can only guess, but he apparently utilizes his abilities as an assassin, primarily targeting other assassins. Rumors describe him as a feared figure in the underworld; the murderous Bullseye is even said to have a vendetta against him. Despite the seemingly noble goal of stopping other hired killers, I cannot condone murder for any reason. He has killed assassins, grocers and cops, all with apparent ties to the criminal underworld, but most were killed with no pretense of self-defense or even out of some animalistic rage, as investigators have found no indications anyone angered the creature before being targeted — with the notable exception of Deadpool. The mercenary who claims he's a hero worked with Spider-Man to save himself from Hit-Monkey's attacks, ultimately faking Spider-Man's death in an elaborate ruse to publicly expose and anger Hit-Monkey. The incident resulted in Deadpool's all-too-temporary incarceration and Hit-Monkey's disappearance.

TREATMENT: Animal behaviorists should be consulted in dealing with Hit-Monkey, but if he is a normal macaque, he should be captured and placed in a well-guarded wildlife preserve.

CLASSIFICATION	MONKEY
GOALS	REVENGE
SCOPE	LOCAL
MEANS	MERCENARY

HOOD

AFFILIATIONS: Dormammu, Loki, Norman Osborn, Madame Masque

ENEMIES: Avengers, Punisher, Tigra, Stranger

I was not around for Parker Robbins' rise to power but I was there to watch him fall. Stealing a mystic cloak (and boots, which we have yet to recover), Robbins discovered it gave him superhuman powers. A petty thief, records left by the Wasp indicate Robbins toyed briefly with heroics while stranded on a recreated Battleworld, though I suspect it was more out of self-preservation. Gathering one of the largest groups of costumed criminals ever, the Hood attacked the underground Avengers numerous times and found a way into the graces of Norman Osborn, helping turn the well-intentioned Initiative program into an abomination. Though stripped of his powers and defeated, we've opted to keep him under absolute maximum security imprisonment given the circumstances. Not just because we still consider him a major potential threat, but also because I imagine every former ally of his besides his lover Madam Masque wants his hide as well.

TREATMENT: Maintain current lockdown; given his connections to mystical forces, investigate means to barricade his cell from any would-be allies... or foes.

CLASSIFICATION	MAGICAL BEING
GOALS	WEALTH & FAME
SCOPE	NATIONAL
MEANS	ROBBERY

HYDRA

AFFILIATIONS: Baron (Wolfgang) von Strucker, Kingpin, Red Skull, Viper, AIM, Secret Empire

ENEMIES: Nick Fury, Secret Warriors, Leviathan, SHIELD, the governments of the United Nations

Named after the many-headed monster that my fellow Avenger Hercules once battled, Hydra is the most dangerous subversive organization on earth. During World War II, the Red Skull sent his fellow Nazi Wolfgang von Strucker to Japan, where he took over a secret society and remodeled it into a neo-fascist organization bent on world domination. In short, it was a new version of Nazism, with Baron Strucker as its "fuhrer," the Supreme Hydra. Hydra became such a serious worldwide threat that SHIELD was founded specifically to combat them. When Strucker has been absent, Hydra tends to fragment and decline. But when Strucker is in command, Hydra has proved a menace to world security, threatening nuclear disaster with the Overkill Horn or biological warfare with the Death Spore. Nowadays, Hydra deals in sophisticated terrorist attacks on the United States and other nations. Though I have fought against Hydra, it is Nick Fury and agents loyal to him who have proved best-suited to thwarting Hydra's attacks against freedom.

TREATMENT: My old friend Nick Fury is the best man not only to direct operations against Hydra, but also to rid US government agencies of any Hydra double agents.

CLASSIFICATION	GROUP
GOALS	CONQUEST
SCOPE	INTERNATIONAL
MEANS	TERRORISM

HYDRO-MAN

AFFILIATIONS: Frightful Four, Sinister Six, Justin Hammer, Shocker

ENEMIES: Spider-Man, Avengers, Black Panther, Gambit, Fantastic Four

Morris Bench is a career criminal with little imagination and a steady lack of motivation (outside basic personal rewards like criminal profits and immediate gratifications). Unfortunately, it is intensely difficult to keep a man composed primarily of water incarcerated. I've rarely crossed paths with Bench, though he was part of Electro's mass Raft breakout when the Avengers reformed. He has worked in several solo criminal ventures and has joined a few teams, including (like so many criminals) the Masters of Evil and the Sinister Syndicate. Bench has acted as a thief, an assassin, a soldier, and, most recently, a terrorist. Hydro-Man, using new focusing cannons, participated in Dr. Doom and the Desturi's war upon Wakanda. Given proper motivation and an opportunity at therapy and redemption, it is my hope Bench could stabilize and use his powers for good, though we would have to address the murders he has committed first. Bench is not an educated man, but I suspect his frequent transformations have affected his cognitive abilities somewhat; he seems very easily directed by criminal heads like the Broker, the Wizard, and the Crimson Cowl.

TREATMENT: Recommend long-term incarceration with extensive therapy. Hydro-Man could be a potential candidate for Luke's Thunderbolts program.

CLASSIFICATION	MUTATE
GOALS	WEALTH & FAME
SCOPE	INTERNATIONAL
MEANS	ROBBERY

INTELLIGENCIA

AFFILIATIONS: AIM, Doc Samson, Red Hulk, Red She-Hulk

ENEMIES: A-Bomb, Avengers, Black Panther, Fantastic Four, Hulk

The Intelligencia ("Intel"), comprising Dr. Doom, Egghead, the Leader, Mad Thinker, MODOK, Red Ghost and Wizard, were a deadly combination of brains and cruelty. To my amazement, they were bound together for years without anyone — even SHIELD — catching on. Their mutual alliance eroded when Doom betrayed the others, but the remaining members realigned recently in schemes that led to the creation of the Red Hulk and Red She-Hulk, the transformation of my friend Rick Jones into A-Bomb and, most disturbingly, corrupted the heroic Doc Samson into their collaborator. It was only through the genius of Bruce Banner and the life-giving sacrifice of a repentant Samson that the Intel's goal of controlling an army of Hulks was finally averted. Although MODOK and Leader were stripped of their powers, most of the Intel remains at large.

TREATMENT: A villainous alliance usually collapses on its own, but while Doom has left the Intel's ranks, the rest seem devoted to the partnership. Interrogators are advised to carefully plant suspicions in their minds to form wedges in their ranks. If the Intel believe their fellows would betray them as callously as Doom did, the flow of information will terminate.

CLASSIFICATION	GROUP
GOALS	CONQUEST
SCOPE	INTERNATIONAL
MEANS	CONSPIRACY

IRON MAIDEN

AFFILIATIONS: Remont Six, Superia, Femizons

ENEMIES: Winter Guard, Black Widow, Captain America, Jimmy Woo

Born in the mining/commercial town of Serov in Russia's Sverdlovsk Oblast, Melina Vostokovna was trained by the Sluzhba Vneshney Razvedki (Russia's Foreign Intelligence Service) to be an elite espionage agent. Developing an intense jealousy and hatred for her more accomplished fellow Russian agent Black Widow, Vostokovna became a freelance operative and was hired to kill the Widow, although she failed. She later joined forces with the super-powered misandrist Superia and her Femizons attempting to sterilize a majority of the world's women. It was at this time I initially encountered Vostokovna's combat and swordsmanship skills firsthand, as she was instrumental in my defeat when

I attempted to infiltrate Superia's base. Since Superia's apparent demise, however, Vostokovna has returned to Russia and affiliated herself with the Soviet revolutionary group Remont Six. According to Russian intelligence reports after Remont Six raided an Advanced Idea Mechanics (AIM) facility outside the Forbidden Zone near Kyshtym, Russia, they were engaged by Russia's official super-team the Winter Guard, defeated, and placed in Russian custody.

TREATMENT: Currently in the Mantlov Facility; pending a psychiatric evaluation, has potential as an effective espionage agent again (if not partnered with Black Widow) should she ever return to the US.

CLASSIFICATION	HUMAN
GOALS	WEALTH & FAME
SCOPE	INTERNATIONAL
MEANS	MERCENARY

JACK O'LANTERN

AFFILIATIONS: Norman Osborn, Satan

ENEMIES: NYPD

Jack O'Lantern is a name several people have used over the years, including Steve Levins, the current Jack's brother, who I faced off with when he was part of Red Skull's Skeleton Crew. Forced to serve with the Thunderbolts during the conflicts over the Superhuman Registration Act, the Punisher killed him, but he later turned up in Sleepy Hollow. Reports from Ghost Rider indicate Jack was actually possessed by Lucifer at this point. This all sounds surreal, but it really happened, and now the previous Jack's brother, according to police reports, sacrificed a young girl to Satan to receive supernatural powers and avenge his brother's death.

Despite confessing to the murder, Norman Osborn made a deal to set him free. Surprisingly, Osborn hasn't used him since then, and one has to wonder if Jack O'Lantern reneged on his deal with Osborn and instead of working for him went AWOL to start his crusade on those responsible for his brother's death. With the lack of info I possess on the current Jack O'Lantern's powers, I'd like some supernatural aid to deal with him.

TREATMENT: Recommend long-term incarceration with mystic restraints. Maybe an exorcism if that works on him. I'm pretty sure the likes of Strange, Voodoo, Hellstorm or even Ghost Rider could deal with him in a far better way than me.

CLASSIFICATION	MAGICAL BEING
GOALS	REVENGE
SCOPE	LOCAL
MEANS	MAGIC

JUGGERNAUT

AFFILIATIONS: Thunderbolts, Cyttorak, Excalibur, Brotherhood of Mutants, Black Tom Cassidy

ENEMIES: X-Men, Exemplars, Hulk

Our criminal psychologists claim it's difficult to get a handle on Cain Marko's personality. The stepbrother of mutant rights activist Professor Charles Xavier, Marko matured into an antiauthoritarian bully under his father's abusive hands. During his Army service he found the mystic Ruby of Cyttorak that transformed him into the unstoppable Juggernaut, the earthly avatar of the evil extradimensional entity Cyttorak. Since then, we believe Marko's aberrant behavior and mood swings may be a result of Cyttorak's vile influence. However, I can speak from personal experience

for the potential for good that exists within Marko: when his fellow Exemplars sought to enslave mankind in the name of their masters in the Octessence, Marko rebelled and joined forces with the Avengers and me to stop them. Most recently, however, Marko was briefly possessed by the Enigma Force, which seems to have interfered with the power he drew from Cyttorak. As such, he is significantly weaker than before, again requiring oxygen to survive and unable to immediately initiate his "unstoppable" kinetic charge.

TREATMENT: In his weakened state, Juggernaut was incarcerated in the Ultra Block, reserved for the Raft's most powerful prisoners. Although he applied as a joke, Marko accepted an offer to join the Thunderbolts but shows little interest in redemption.

CLASSIFICATION	MAGICAL BEING
GOALS	WEALTH & FAME
SCOPE	NATIONAL
MEANS	ROBBERY

KAINE

AFFILIATIONS: Spider-Man

ENEMIES: Raptor, Jackal, Kraven, Spidercide

We know very little about Kaine. Even after several incarcerations, we don't have so much as a birth certificate for him, much less an explanation of where he got his super-powers or his disfiguring scars; he's even altered his fingerprints. He simply popped into existence several years ago and began working for a variety of low-level crime bosses as a hitman. He's inexplicably obsessed with photojournalist Peter Parker, going so far as to frame him for murder a few years back. After confessing to the murders, clearing Parker, and later participating in the gladiatorial Great Game, Kaine dropped off the radar for some time, only to resurface recently, allied with the delusional geneticist Raptor. Spider-Man tells me Kaine recently apparently died heroically, sacrificing himself to the deranged Kraven family to save Spider-Man; Kaine has died before, however, only to come back. I sense Spider-Man knows more about Kaine than he's letting on, but pressing him for information has never gotten us very far. Let's hope, for his sake, Kaine rests in peace this time.

TREATMENT: Recommend keeping Kaine file open, contacting key witnesses in Parker case if Kaine resurfaces — Jacob Raven, Janine Godbe, etc.

CLASSIFICATION	MUTATE
GOALS	REVENGE
SCOPE	INTERNATIONAL
MEANS	VIGILANTE

KANG

AFFILIATIONS: Anachronauts, Dr. Doom, Scarlet Centurion, Terminatrix

ENEMIES: Avengers, Fantastic Four, Thor, Spider-Man, Hulk, Rama-Tut, Immortus, Alioth, Time Keepers, Zarrko the Tomorrow Man

One of the Avengers' greatest enemies, Kang the Conqueror is one of the few men to have conquered the Earth. Born in the 30th century AD, he discovered a time machine and traveled to ancient Egypt, ruling there as Pharaoh Rama-Tut, before journeying to the 40th century AD, where he became the warlord Kang. Mastering the incredibly advanced science of the future, Kang not only conquered Earth but forged an interstellar empire. But not even this could sate his ambition. Kang has repeatedly invaded our time, obsessed with pitting himself in combat against the Avengers and other heroes of the "Age of Marvels." Ultimately in the "Kang War," commanding armies and war machines from the future, he destroyed Washington, DC, massacring millions of people. To our shame, the Avengers and the world's nations surrendered. But the Avengers fought back, and I had the privilege of defeating this bloodthirsty tyrant in combat. We finally imprisoned him, until his son, Marcus, freed him. And so I fear the world will surely again face the threat of Kang.

TREATMENT: I find it hard to believe the Kang who devastated my nation's capital could ever be reformed. Should we ever recapture this mass murderer, he should be imprisoned for life.

CLASSIFICATION	HUMAN
GOALS	CONQUEST
SCOPE	MULTIVERSAL
MEANS	WARFARE

KINGPIN

AFFILIATIONS: Bullseye, Elektra, Typhoid Mary, Nuke, the Owl, Lady Bullseye

ENEMIES: Daredevil, Spider-Man, Hydra, the Maggia, Echo, the Hand, Red Skull, FBI, Richard Fisk

For years, Wilson Fisk persuaded the public he was a respectable businessman in the spice trade. But my colleagues and the authorities knew the truth: Fisk was the Kingpin of Crime, a cunning, ruthless man who seized control of New York City's organized crime from the Maggia and other gangs. Built like a sumo wrestler, and astonishingly agile for a man of his bulk, Fisk has proved strong enough to hold his own in combat even with Spider-Man. But it is Daredevil who has become Fisk's greatest nemesis, and Fisk has viciously tried over the years to destroy Daredevil's career, life, and even his sanity. It is a testament to my colleague's strength of character that he has survived. I cannot forgive the Kingpin for unleashing the insane "super-soldier" Nuke, who slaughtered people in Manhattan's "Hell's Kitchen," as part of Fisk's obsessive feud with Daredevil. Fisk has been publicly exposed and imprisoned, but no matter how many times he falls, Fisk always seems to return to power.

TREATMENT: Fisk has never stayed in prison for long, thanks to his skill in legally covering his tracks. But I am confident a clever lawyer like Matt Murdock will find a way to keep Fisk behind bars for good.

CLASSIFICATION	HUMAN
GOALS	CONQUEST
SCOPE	INTERNATIONAL
MEANS	LEADERSHIP

KRANG

AFFILIATIONS: Atlanteans, Attuma, Byrrah, Orka, Serpent Squad

ENEMIES: Namor, U-Man, Dr. Doom, Atlas Foundation, Winter Guard

Born into an aristocratic Atlantean family, Krang has struggled his entire life to reconcile his place in society with his delusions of grandeur. As a royal Atlantean officer, he was celebrated for his commanding the Great Thakorrian Militia and leading entire armies through the treacherous Laurentian Abyss; but shortly after Namor was crowned king of Atlantis, the over-ambitious Krang staged a coup and seized the throne. He was eventually deposed by Namor, but continued his sinister machinations, as when he seized the Serpent Crown and attempted to raise the sunken continent of Lemuria. But Krang underwent a profound change following the destruction of the Atlantean capital New Pangea, believing it was his duty as a worshiper of Poseidon to defend the Earth's oceans by any means necessary. Unfortunately, Krang was recently infected by a psychosis-inducing contagion causing him to abduct Namora and attempt to mate with her in the Zolotoy Rog Bay near Vladivostok, Russia. Namora was rescued by the Atlas Foundation and Winter Guard, while Krang and his followers were pulled into an interdimensional aperture; having since returned to Earth, Krang has rededicated himself to Namor.

TREATMENT: Require coordination with Namor to see that Krang has been completely cured of his contagion. Nighthawk, in particular, has expressed an interest in seeing Krang is rehabilitated.

CLASSIFICATION	SUB-SPECIES
GOALS	CONQUEST
SCOPE	INTERNATIONAL
MEANS	WARFARE

ANA KRAVEN

AFFILIATIONS: Kraven the Hunter, Chameleon, Electro, Mysterio

ENEMIES: Spider-Man, Arachne, Spider-Girl, Madame Web

I recently had a talk with Spider-Man about a lengthy plot against him. Years ago, one of his greatest foes, Kraven the Hunter, buried him alive before committing suicide. Kraven had several children and a wife that Spider-Man did not know about then, and these children have come back to fight him one by one over the years. Recently, Ana, Kraven's daughter, and her mother, Sasha, have been gunning for Spider-Man, utilizing a number of his old foes to wear him down. Spider-Man suffered personal tragedies in his battles with Electro, Mysterio, the Rhino, the Chameleon, and others, and only recently learned the Kravinoffs were behind it. They resurrected Kraven, but Mattie Franklin and Kaine were killed, while Arachne was transformed into a new version of Madame Web. No one seems to know where Kraven and his children, including Ana, are now. They are intensely dangerous and are not to be underestimated. The tragedy they inflicted on New York is astounding, and the trail of bodies truly tragic. Ana Kraven is a tortured soul who needs to pay for her crimes.

TREATMENT: Recommend long-term incarceration with extensive therapy. She's still young enough to find another path in her life.

CLASSIFICATION	HUMAN
GOALS	CHALLENGES
SCOPE	INTERNATIONAL
MEANS	MURDERS

KREE

AFFILIATIONS: The Inhumans, the Shi'ar, Blastaar

ENEMIES: The Cancer-Verse, the Skrulls, the Phalanx

I am frustrated by how frequently the Kree have attacked, manipulated, and experimented upon the people of Earth. The Avengers have faced the Kree Sentries, the Supreme Intelligence, the Ruul, Ronan the Accuser, the Lunatic Legion, and Starforce. The Kree have made Earth a war zone in their battles with the Skrulls and the Shi'ar (both conflicts pulled in the Avengers), and they have experimented on humans, creating the Inhuman race, and first awakening the Destiny Force in my former protégé Rick Jones, eventually leading to the Destiny War. They even made Earth an intergalactic penal colony for a time! Though they pride themselves on their advanced culture, command of technology, and military capabilities, they are a race entrenched in warfare, racism, and ethnocentrism. In recent months, the Supreme Intelligence has been killed, the Shi'ar, Annihilus' army, and the Phalanx have wiped out vast amounts of the Kree, and the Inhumans have taken over governing the race. Now, the Kree apparently have jurisdiction over the Shi'ar and their hundreds of worlds. We need to keep a very close eye on this race and keep them far from Earth.

TREATMENT: I need to discuss containment and avoidance strategies with Abigail Brand of SWORD.

CLASSIFICATION	EXTRATERRESTRIALS
GOALS	CONQUEST
SCOPE	UNIVERSAL
MEANS	WARFARE

LADY BULLSEYE

AFFILIATIONS: The Kingpin

ENEMIES: The Hand, Daredevil, Black Tarantula, Iron Fist

Most of what I've been able to learn about Lady Bullseye has come from Iron Fist, who has little good to say about the woman. She was kidnapped and put into some sort of human trafficking holding cell when she witnessed Bullseye slaughter the criminals who had taken her. (I can't believe Osborn made Bullseye an Avenger!) Styling herself after him, the woman adopted the name Lady Bullseye and trained under Master Izo of the Hand, and in recent years she entered a bid to take leadership of the Hand. In a bizarre plot, she worked with the Hand's leadership to recruit Daredevil while she tried destroying

his life. She also posed as a lawyer, trying to separate Matt Murdock from his insane wife, Milla Donovan. When Daredevil proved difficult, she pulled the Kingpin out of exile and eventually ended up working for him. Lady Bullseye, despite having no super-powers, is a skilled combatant who has left a long trail of bodies in her wake. All this business with rogue ninjas across the city has got to stop; Lady Bullseye, and all the rest of them, need to be apprehended and sent home to their own countries for imprisonment.

TREATMENT: Recommend deportation and long-term incarceration.

CLASSIFICATION	HUMAN
GOALS	REVENGE
SCOPE	INTERNATIONAL
MEANS	MERCENARY

LADY DEATHSTRIKE

AFFILIATIONS: Sisterhood of Evil Mutants, Reavers

ENEMIES: Wolverine, X-Men, Daredevil, Alpha Flight

When I battled the savage and bloodthirsty Lady Deathstrike, a cyborg possessing lengthening claws and deadly fighting prowess and skills, I found her a formidable opponent. Wolverine tells me that Yuriko Oyama has been a savage opponent of his and the X-Men for years, still dealing with her father issues (Lord Dark Wind initially designed Adamantium, which she claims was stolen from him). With the Reavers, Oyama targeted the X-Men for death in Australia, where she crucified Wolverine on an X-shaped cross. Her crimes include assassination, sabotage, international terrorism and destruction. My fear for Lady Deathstrike, who

Wolverine describes as a fairly noble soul, is that she has lost so much of her humanity she is now just a series of emotional responses, constantly seeking revenge for herself, or for her father's death, and that she is subject to the whims of her latest leader, deadly criminals like Donald Pierce, William Stryker, and the Red Queen. I'm afraid she'd need to be separated from her cyborg body if we ever hope to see her humanity return to the surface.

TREATMENT: Recommend surgical reconstruction to remove cybernetics, then extensive incarceration.

CLASSIFICATION	CYBORG
GOALS	CONQUEST
SCOPE	INTERNATIONAL
MEANS	MERCENARY

LADY STILT-MAN

AFFILIATIONS: None

ENEMIES: Spider-Man, Deadpool

I understand why some iconic costumed identities are passed down like honored legacies when the original bearer is killed or incapacitated. When the world believed I was dead following my "assassination," Bucky Barnes continued on as Captain America. But, for the life of me, I can't comprehend why so many would-be super villains have longed to inherit the name and equipment of Wilbur Day, the original Stilt-Man. The second person to don Day's battlesuit and hydraulic stilts since his death at the hands of the Punisher, "Lady Stilt-Man" purportedly adopted the moniker as an homage to Day.

However, her fledgling criminal career has gotten off to a rocky start, as she has been defeated by Spider-Man on two occasions in a relatively short span.

TREATMENT: Currently incarcerated, Lady Stilt-Man seems like the type of inmate who'd respond well to rehabilitation/redemption efforts. However, I question her competency. Not everyone is cut out for the Thunderbolts program. Perhaps once she serves her sentence she'd feel more at home with Mr. Immortal and his band of Great Lakes heroes?

CLASSIFICATION	HUMAN
GOALS	WEALTH & FAME
SCOPE	LOCAL
MEANS	ROBBERY

LAVA MEN

AFFILIATIONS: Grotesk, Kala, Cha'sa'dra

ENEMIES: Avengers, Agents of Atlas, Thor, X-Force

When I first awakened from the iceberg I was disoriented, and the Avengers helped me acclimate after decades in suspended animation. I suppose being beset by a number of foes helped me keep my mind off things for a time. The Lava Men were among the first enemies I faced with the Avengers at my side, and their giant rock monster definitely kept me distracted. The Lava Men are generally peaceful, living in small tribes underneath the Earth's surface. Though their conflicts with other tribes, such as the Moloids or the Tyrranoids, have boiled over to the surface, they usually keep to themselves unless provoked. Certain factions of the Lava Men have been known to worship demons, while others have been easily manipulated into attacking the surface, but these conflicts are almost always short-lived. Thor and Beast both tell me they have found nobility among individual members of the Lava Men, though we have never entered a formal peace agreement with them.

TREATMENT: I am willing to let the Lava Men live in peace, so long as they don't keep attacking the surface world. Any conflicts with them should be ended quickly and decisively, and peace re-established.

CLASSIFICATION	SUB-SPECIES
GOALS	CONQUEST
SCOPE	INTERNATIONAL
MEANS	WARFARE

LETHAL LEGION

AFFILIATIONS: Satannish

ENEMIES: Norman Osborn, Ares, Bullseye, Daken, Marvel Boy, Moonstone, Venom

After Wonder Man was seemingly killed during an early Avengers' mission, his brother, the Grim Reaper, attempted revenge on us repeatedly, often as part of his loosely formed Lethal Legion. The group reformed a few times, once under Satannish and the Hangman, but the Grim Reaper has always been its driving force. When Osborn rose to power, many criminals felt slighted and sought revenge, and they unified behind Reaper to get it. What shocks me most of all is Wonder Man joined the group! After publicly speaking against Osborn, Simon sought to do some good and thought he could convert these career criminals like I did with my Kooky Quartet, or Hawkeye with the Thunderbolts, but monsters like Hyde can't ever be free. Needless to say, when they fought Osborn's Avengers, the Lethal Legion was swiftly defeated and incarcerated. Wonder Man is out of jail now, but he has refused to participate with the new Avengers, and the Grim Reaper is apparently dead. Somehow, I can't help but think Osborn had his hand in this group's formation.

TREATMENT: Each of the Lethal Legion's members are career-hardened criminals; if they persist in working together it will only make it that much easier to round them up.

CLASSIFICATION	GROUP
GOALS	WEALTH & FAME
SCOPE	NATIONAL
MEANS	ROBBERY

LEVIATHAN

AFFILIATIONS: Magadan, Orion, Contessa Valentina Allegro de la Fontaine

ENEMIES: Baron Strucker, Silver Samurai, Gorgon, Madame Hydra, Kraken

I've read about Leviathan, of course. They were a secret branch of the USSR's intelligence agency, or at least they were until every member of Leviathan disappeared. I assumed that they'd been eliminated in some Soviet purge. Their attack on Hydra in Kyoto proved that I was wrong – that we were all wrong. It also proved that they're just as ruthless as Hydra, and just as dangerous. I don't know where they've been, but they're back now. We know they've infiltrated the US government, and they've also infiltrated Nick Fury's inner circle – and Nick is not a man who lends his trust easily. If Contessa Valentina de la Fontaine is a double agent for Leviathan, they know damn near everything about us. We've got to deal with them fast, but our intelligence on them is extremely limited. Before we do anything, I need to know everything we can possibly find out about them, and that means going to Fury. There's word that he has a team of operatives solely devoted to investigating them, and they're bound to have information that I need.

TREATMENT: Recommend sharing intelligence with Nick Fury, locating Leviathan double agents in national intelligence infrastructure.

CLASSIFICATION	GROUP
GOALS	CONQUEST
SCOPE	INTERNATIONAL
MEANS	TERRORISM

LILITH

AFFILIATIONS: The Lilin, the Annunaki, Dracula, Zarathos

ENEMIES: The Midnight Sons, Ghost Rider, Dr. Strange, Topaz, Jennifer Kale, Satanna

The Mothers of Demons. The Vampire Goddess. Lilitu. The Archmother of Witchcraft. By any name, the enigmatic Lilith is evil incarnate. She is so ancient and shrouded in mystery that even Thor and Valkyrie, my usual experts on divinities, are uncertain as to her true nature and origin. The Vatican believes she was originally a member of the Heavenly Hosts who stood alongside Satan during his rebellion against heaven. Archaeological evidence suggests she once associated with the Annunaki, the gods worshipped in Babylon and Mesopotamia, and later resided in Atlantis prior to the Great Cataclysm at the time of the creation of the first vampire. In modern times, she continued her ages-old quest to conceive a legion of powerful children, the Lilin, who she hoped would overrun the world in her name. Whether she's a goddess, a vampire, or something in between, it's a safe bet Lilith will try to take advantage of the turmoil within the world's vampire sects following Dracula's assassination.

TREATMENT: I'm afraid even our most advanced technology at the Raft would be woefully inadequate to restrain Lilith. In the past, she has been sealed in extradimensional realms via powerful incantations; failing that, I fear Lilith's destruction may be our only other option.

CLASSIFICATION	MAGICAL BEING
GOALS	CONQUEST
SCOPE	INTERDIMENSIONAL
MEANS	MAGIC

LIVING LASER

AFFILIATIONS: Hood, Mandarin, Lethal Legion, MODOK

ENEMIES: Avengers, Iron Man

One of the Avengers' earliest and most recurring foes, Arthur Parks turned a brilliant weapons design, an advanced knowledge of physics, and an unrequited crush on Janet Van Dyne into a megalomaniacal desire for power and revenge. Years ago, Parks was transformed from a technology-wielding villain using laser equipment to an actual living laser inhabited by his consciousness. Parks' sanity seems to be in question as his motivations vacillate between massive revenge schemes (generally against Iron Man) to world domination (he once took over Costa Verde) to subservience and dedication to criminal organizations, such as those led by the Hood or MODOK. I have faced Parks in both his human and energy forms, most recently after my resurrection (alongside Bucky), and it is frightening how little of his humanity remains now that he no longer has a body. Parks has been contained and incarcerated in the past, and that needs to happen again. Tony has faced the Living Laser repeatedly and has struggled to find any long-term solutions regarding containment; firing him off into space will not work.

TREATMENT: Recommend long-term incarceration and scientific exploration into how to get Arthur Parks' body back.

CLASSIFICATION	MUTATE
GOALS	CURE
SCOPE	INTERNATIONAL
MEANS	MERCENARY

LIZARD

AFFILIATIONS: None

ENEMIES: Spider-Man, Stegron, Iguana

For years, scientist Curt Connors and his family lived with a curse; due to one of Connors' failed experiments, he periodically transformed into the Lizard, a savage reptilian creature with designs on destroying mankind. It now appears Connors' battle against his savage alter ego is over — and the Lizard has won, killing Connors' son, Billy, and destroying Curt's psyche. Gone are the days when the Lizard's rampages could be halted by the antidote to his serum, or through the love of his now-dead family; the Lizard is all that remains, and he's on the loose. Even worse, he's now able to telepathically unlock the primal instincts in humans, making him more dangerous than ever and one of our priority targets. Even if Connors is truly gone, it may be possible to revert the Lizard to a more containable form once he's apprehended; I recommend we consult with Komodo, who has modified Connors' formula in the past.

TREATMENT: We have samples of the formula Connors used to repress his transformations; Spider-Man used it on himself to resist the Lizard's mind-altering abilities, so make it available to all personnel involved in capturing and containing him. Recommend long-term incarceration; keep isolated from other inmates.

CLASSIFICATION	MUTATE
GOALS	SURVIVAL
SCOPE	LOCAL
MEANS	LEADERSHIP

MAD DOG

AFFILIATIONS: Secret Empire, Professor Power, Mutant Force

ENEMIES: Hellcat, Avengers, Nomad, Araña

Robert "Buzz" Baxter was a proud Air Force member married to Patsy Walker, who was world-famous from the comic books her mother produced about her. Patsy tells me Baxter considered her a trophy wife, and he eventually grew rather mean. Their marriage fell apart while Baxter was working at the Brand Corporation (during a brief association with the Beast, after he turned furry). In time, Patsy joined the Avengers and the Defenders as Hellcat, and Baxter, submitting himself to genetic experiments, became Mad Dog. Thus began a lengthy criminal career ranging from petty revenge schemes against Patsy to espionage (Mad Dog led a group of criminals in taking over the SHIELD Helicarrier) and even world domination. Mad Dog worked closely with Professor Power, the Secret Empire, and the Mutant Force (who I faced as the Brotherhood of Evil Mutants) for a time, and that association has been renewed for unrevealed purposes. Despite a new marriage, Baxter has been further mutated and has recently fought Nomad and Araña. Araña tells me Mad Dog is less human than ever before, and it saddens me to know how far Buzz Baxter has fallen.

TREATMENT: Recommend long-term incarceration with extensive therapy. Mad Dog could be a candidate for Luke's Thunderbolts program.

CLASSIFICATION	MUTATE
GOALS	WEALTH & FAME
SCOPE	NATIONAL
MEANS	FOLLOWER

MAGGIA

AFFILIATIONS: Count Luchino Nefaria, Hammerhead, Silvermane, Caesar Cicero, Man-Mountain Marko, Madame Masque, Don Fortunato

ENEMIES: Spider-Man, Daredevil, Avengers, Fantastic Four, Kingpin

The crime syndicate Maggia seems like a mix of the past and the future. Originating in southern Italy, this secret criminal society had spread to the United States by the 1890s. Over the decades, the Maggia moved into conventional areas of crime, such as gambling, narcotics and loan sharking. Rather than having a central authority, the Maggia is divided into separate "families." But despite their devotion to tradition, in recent years several notorious Maggia "family" leaders have made use of futuristic technology. The Maggia's most powerful leader, Count Luchino Nefaria, once held all of Washington, DC, hostage, attempted to take over the missile base at Valhalla Mountain, and ultimately acquired vast super-powers. The legendary Maggia leader Silvio "Silvermane" Manfredi has extended his long life by being converted into a cyborg. Another "family" head, Hammerhead, acts like a throwback to the 1920s, but even he now had a skeleton partly made of unbreakable Adamantium. Costumed crimefighters such as Spider-Man have dealt major setbacks to various Maggioso, but the Maggia may have more to fear from their criminal rivals, such as the Kingpin.

TREATMENT: Spider-Man and other costumed heroes can effectively combat Maggia members. But ultimately the FBI and police are best suited to stopping the Maggia's more conventional criminal operations.

CLASSIFICATION	GROUP
GOALS	CONQUEST
SCOPE	INTERNATIONAL
MEANS	LEADERSHIP

MOSES MAGNUM

AFFILIATIONS: Emmy Doolin, the Inquisitor, Cutthroat

ENEMIES: Avengers, Punisher, Spider-Man, Black Panther, Daken, X-Men

Originally from Ethiopia, Moses Magnum has become an international arms dealer, terrorist, and drug runner, and he has fought heroes all over the world. Years ago, he was experimented upon by Apocalypse and granted the ability to create seismic waves, powers he has used to threaten Japan, the United States, and other countries. Despite his incredible powers and technological resources, Magnum has suffered multiple defeats. After he fought the Avengers on his ship, the Evangeline, he seemed to disappear, and just months ago he was stabbed by the Punisher and narrowly saved by Spider-Man. Most recently, however, in a complicated plot by Norman Osborn, Magnum escaped from jail with the help of fellow criminals, including Emmy Doolin, killing several citizens in the process. After a complex battle with Daken, some of these criminals turned up dead. Magnum is a dangerous opponent with no regard for human life. He tends to be unpredictable, power hungry, and unstable, all terrible attributes for someone with his abilities. The second he shows himself, the Avengers need to be there to take him down and see him go to jail once and for all.

TREATMENT: Recommend long-term maximum security incarceration. Extradition back to Africa may prove necessary.

CLASSIFICATION	MUTATE
GOALS	CONQUEST
SCOPE	INTERNATIONAL
MEANS	LEADERSHIP

X

MALEKITH

AFFILIATIONS: Dark Elves, Grendell, Surtur, Loki

ENEMIES: Thor, Asgardians, Kurse, Hercules

Malekith the Accursed was once ruler of the Dark Elves (or "Svartalfar," as Thor sometimes calls them), natives of Svartalfheim, the darkest of the Nine Worlds of Asgardian cosmology. Notorious for their greedy and troublesome nature, the Dark Elves were often blamed by the ancient Scandinavians for many of the hardships befalling humanity. In modern times, Malekith renewed his allegiance to the fire demon Surtur of Muspelheim and rededicated himself to conquering all Nine Worlds of Asgard. But Thor and his fellow Asgardians thwarted Malekith's schemes each and every time. The Dark Elves subsequently fell under the leadership of Queen

Alflyse of the Eastern Spires, who continued to plot against the other Nine Worlds but was much less malevolent than Malekith. When Malekith recently resurfaced with the Dark Elf Grendell and attempted to overthrow Alflyse, he was soundly defeated by the Olympian Skyfather Zeus.

TREATMENT: While Alflyse is not an ideal choice for ruler of the Dark Elves, Thor assures me her regime is much less bloodthirsty than Malekith's. As such, Malekith should be prevented from regaining political power at all costs. Should he be captured, I recommend incarceration in a specially-designed iron prison, as he is vulnerable to the metal.

CLASSIFICATION	MAGICAL BEING
GOALS	CONQUEST
SCOPE	INTERDIMENSIONAL
MEANS	MAGIC

X

MAN-KILLER

AFFILIATIONS: Masters of Evil, Ultimate Brawling League, Thunderbolts

ENEMIES: Tigra, Spider-Man, She-Hulk, Black Widow, Daredevil

Every time Katrina Luisa van Horn is on the verge of reformation, she falters due to her insecurities. Once a star skier on the German Olympic team, she challenged male chauvinist skier Karl Lubbings to a race; but Lubbings caused a collision that disfigured and crippled van Horn. Transformed into a fanatical misogynist by the tragedy, she underwent physical rehabilitation to regain her mobility and was outfitted with an exoskeleton by a militant feminist group, becoming their agent "Man-Killer." She was later employed by criminal organizations such as Advanced Idea Mechanics (AIM) and Hydra, and even softened her radical misogynistic views so she could accept contracts from male

employers (the thought of working for men had once caused mental breakdowns). Hawkeye tells me it was during van Horn's stint with the Masters of Evil when she defected to the Thunderbolts and demonstrated great courage and valor on several missions before abandoning the team. Since then, she briefly participated in a superhuman professional fighting league before returning to mercenary work.

TREATMENT: Although currently at large, van Horn would be an ideal candidate for the Thunderbolts program. She has entertained thoughts of reformation in the past, and with the proper support and encouragement, I believe she can overcome her insecurities and become a true hero.

CLASSIFICATION	MUTATE
GOALS	WEALTH & FAME
SCOPE	LOCAL
MEANS	MERCENARY

X

MANSLAUGHTER MARSDALE

AFFILIATIONS: Clown, Death Reaper, Trapster, Zodiac

ENEMIES: HAMMER, Spider-Man

Unable to feel pain, Marsdale once ran a boxing gym in New York City with Madame Fang. When Marsdale, on Fang's orders, tried to coerce boxer Bobby Chance, the gym's finest student, into renewing his contract with them, threatening to hurt or even cripple him, he ran afoul of Spider-Man. Though he worked on the fringe of legality in the past, he later escalated his criminality when he joined up with the lunatic new Zodiac; it seems Zodiac revived a comatose Marsdale after unidentified attackers hospitalized him. It wouldn't surprise me if Marsdale's recruitment into Zodiac's crew was more than just a coincidence because

according to the Human Torch, Zodiac seemed to share Marsdale's inability to feel no pain. Having helped Zodiac's crew bomb a hospital, Marsdale took advantage of the general chaos during a Zodiac-orchestrated attack by the robot Red Ronin on New York City to track down Chance to a bar, then beat him and several other patrons to death.

TREATMENT: In the past Marsdale was nothing more than a common henchmen according to Spider-Man. At that point in his career some time in prison could've worked wonders, but since than everything has changed. Marsdale has become a terrorist, who shows no regard for human life and lowers himself to murder for petty revenge. His most recent activities make it clear there is no way to redeem him; recommend long-term incarceration.

CLASSIFICATION	HUMAN
GOALS	WEALTH & FAME
SCOPE	LOCAL
MEANS	TERRORISM

MIMIC

AFFILIATIONS: Norman Osborn's X-Men, Brotherhood of Mutants

ENEMIES: X-Men, Hulk

Calvin Rankin is a tortured soul. With his ability to mimic the powers of others and a serious bipolar condition (which can be treated with medication), Rankin has always struggled to find his place in the world, seeking lengthy isolations, at times due to his malfunctioning powers, and other times affiliating himself with those with dark purposes. Rankin was one of the earliest X-Men, though his stint with them, even briefly as team leader, did not last long, and his short list of enemies included the Puppet Master and the Super Adaptoid. He has maintained the five power sets of the earliest X-Men, however, including Angel's wings and Cyclops' optic blasts. Wolverine tells me Rankin briefly impersonated him, though it was involuntary. Recently, Rankin was one of Osborn's choices for his version of the X-Men. Teamed with mass murderers such as Dark Beast, Daken, and Mystique, Rankin could not have lasted long on this team, and he now seems to have returned to isolation. Rankin needs someone to guide him and show him what it means to be a hero, then he can finally have the opportunity to choose his own path.

TREATMENT: Extensive therapy and medication monitoring.

CLASSIFICATION	MUTATE
GOALS	GUIDANCE
SCOPE	LOCAL
MEANS	FOLLOWER

MISTER HYDE

AFFILIATIONS: Cobra, Jester, Masters of Evil, Purple Man, Scorpion, Batroc, the Hood, Lethal Legion

ENEMIES: Thor, Daredevil, Captain America, Cobra, Spider-Man, Ghost Rider, Hulk, Iron Man, Avengers, Norman Osborn

In Robert Louis Stevenson's story, Dr. Jekyll intends to separate the good and evil in his soul into separate personalities. It is after Jekyll's other self that the monstrous criminal I know as Mr. Hyde took his name. He has acquired superhuman strength so vast he has been able to wage hand-to-hand combat with Thor. In prison, Hyde is notorious for attacking, even murdering, fellow inmates. Hyde once attempted to blow up a Roxxon Oil ship to destroy Manhattan out of his sheer hatred of humanity. But my most vivid memory of Hyde is when he was a member of Helmut Zemo's Masters of Evil and helped them capture Avengers Mansion. While I watched, bound and helpless, Hyde first crushed memorabilia from my past and then beat our loyal butler Edwin Jarvis nearly to death — just to see my reaction. If there once was any good in the soul of this Mr. Hyde, it must long ago have been obliterated.

TREATMENT: If Hyde is recaptured, the authorities must find the means to restrain him despite his colossal strength. He requires psychiatric care, but more importantly, a way must be found to permanently undo his transformation.

CLASSIFICATION	MUTATE
GOALS	WEALTH & FAME
SCOPE	NATIONAL
MEANS	ROBBERY

MISTER NEGATIVE

AFFILIATIONS: Hammerhead, Inner Demons, Doc Tramma

ENEMIES: Hood, Maggia, Spider-Man

A mysterious gangster operating from Manhattan's Chinatown, Mr. Negative has a particular grudge against the Maggia crime families, something that goes beyond a mere turf war. Disturbingly, he has the power to transform people with his touch, making them a "negative" version of themselves, exposing the worst side of their personalities. Spider-Man was briefly transformed this way and described it as "the most frighteningly clear-headed [he's] ever been." Mr. Negative's army of "Inner Demons" are seemingly invulnerable henchmen; coupled with Hammerhead as his chief enforcer, he could become the most dangerous mobster since Wilson Fisk. The pitched resistance from other crime bosses to keep Negative out of their territory is the only thing holding him back just now, but the last thing we want is to encourage a full-out gang war. I fear with the tumult Daredevil has raised in Hell's Kitchen, Negative will continue to profit from in-fighting amongst his peers.

TREATMENT: Research means to apprehend and incarcerate while avoiding physical contact; possibly an android/robot task force or multiple telekinesis wielders. It's been suggested he's tied to the Darkforce dimension; consult Shroud on possible sting operation, analyze the specifics of his powers.

CLASSIFICATION	MUTATE
GOALS	CONQUEST
SCOPE	INTERNATIONAL
MEANS	LEADERSHIP

MISTER X

AFFILIATIONS: Thunderbolts

ENEMIES: Agents of Atlas, Avengers, Black Widow, Songbird, Wolverine

Mr. X is a wealthy sociopath, who kills people for the sole purpose of telepathically experiencing their deaths through a psychic bond. Killing is a sport for this man and has been for years, though he always evaded arrest due to US government connections. Through his low-level telepathy, he can anticipate an opponent's every move, making every confrontation with him an uneven fight. He was a regular participant in Madripoor's annual Bloodsport tournament and therefore well-respected there. When Osborn took control over the Initiative, he turned the Thunderbolts into his personal assassin squad and offered Mr. X membership after staging X's death in Madripoor. X took the job and participated in several missions, including one during the siege of Asgard in which he killed an Asgardian. Rarely defeated in a fight, Mr. X was no match for Wolverine, who defeated him twice by succumbing to his berserker rage, and recently the speedster Quicksilver, whose attacks were too fast for Mr. X to counter.

TREATMENT: Recommend long-term incarceration. Psychic barriers to block his addiction to killing could at least calm him down enough to protect fellow inmates from his savagery.

CLASSIFICATION	MUTANT
GOALS	CHALLENGES
SCOPE	INTERNATIONAL
MEANS	MERCENARY

MOJO

AFFILIATIONS: Spiral, Major Domo, Warwolves

ENEMIES: Longshot, X-Men, New Mutants, X-Babies, Dr. Strange, Mojo II, Exiles

I prefer dealing with adversaries whose schemes make sense, so I am relieved I have not had to contend with the X-Men's foe Mojo, who revels in his irrationality. Mojo rules an otherdimensional planet he not so modestly named Mojoworld. He is also a member of a race of grotesquely massive creatures called the Spineless Ones and relies on a mechanical platform for mobility. The Spineless Ones dominate a genetically engineered slave race of humanoids, one of whom, Longshot, has led rebellions against Mojo's tyranny. Mojo also controls his world's television industry and regards himself as a showman. (Wonder Man, who has Hollywood experience, claims Mojo is not all that different from real studio executives). He has become obsessed with televising the adventures of the X-Men, whom he regards as his biggest stars, and even created his own versions of the X-Men as toddlers, the "X-Babies." Despite his bulk, Mojo is a formidable combatant. Mojo does not yet seem to be a threat to Earth, though he has been a dangerous nuisance to the X-Men. But who knows what mad idea might next occur to him to boost his ratings?

TREATMENT: Should Mojo be captured, he obviously needs psychiatric care, but I suspect his sort of insanity is beyond curing.

CLASSIFICATION	EXTRATERRESTRIAL
GOALS	WEALTH & FAME
SCOPE	INTERDIMENSIONAL
MEANS	BUSINESS

MOONSTONE

AFFILIATIONS: Norman Osborn's Avengers, Corporation, Dr. Faustus, Masters of Evil, Leonard Samson, Thunderbolts, Baron (Helmut) Zemo

ENEMIES: Avengers, Blackout, Blue Streak, Dazzler, Caprice, Captain America, Justine Hammer, Graviton, Hulk, Inhumans, ISAAC, Jack Flag, Mentor, Mind-Wave, Mirage, Ms. Marvel, Nefarius, Nova, Norman Osborn, Penance, Phantom Eagle, Photon, Quasar, Secret Empire, Volcana

After receiving a Ph.D. in psychology, Karla Sofen became a psychiatrist in Chicago, Illinois, and later sought tutelage from the criminal mastermind Dr. Faustus. Learning of Lloyd Bloch, Moonstone, she became his psychiatrist and manipulated him into rejecting his Moongem in order to give herself its power. The Moongem has seemed to affect her both physically and mentally, causing her to be unpredictable and mentally unstable at times. Each time it seems she is actually trying to reform, her mental state changes as quick as the tides of the ocean created by the gravity of the moon. This makes me wonder if she will ever be able to completely reform while in possession of the Moongem. After her participation in Norman Osborn's Avengers facade, we've placed her with Luke Cage's Thunderbolts; I'd like to be optimistic about her chances for reform, but we've thrown her a rope before.

TREATMENT: Recommend removal of the Moongem and incarceration with possible parole upon good behavior.

CLASSIFICATION	MUTATE
GOALS	WEALTH & FAME
SCOPE	NATIONAL
MEANS	LEADERSHIP

MORLUN

AFFILIATIONS: The Ancients

ENEMIES: Spider-Man, Black Panther, Man-Ape

Though I have never crossed paths with Morlun, both Spider-Man and the Black Panther say he is one of the deadliest foes they have ever faced. Morlun is apparently an immortal who has spent the centuries feeding on the "totemitstic forces" of Earth, those humans who have received powers from animal-based gods (this is likely a loose interpretation of Morlun's origins and abilities). A few years back, Spider-Man was forced to face up to the animal nature of his powers and abilities, which he originally derived from a spider bite. He managed to stop Morlun, but was somehow killed and reborn in the process. More recently, Morlun was reawakened by an African tribe who sought to exploit and invade Wakanda when T'Challa was in a coma. Morlun drained the life of the tribe that reawakened him and later killed our long-time foe Man-Ape before attacking Wakanda. A new Black Panther narrowly defeated Morlun by somehow trapping him in one of the realms of hell. I don't know that I condone this type of victory, but Morlun has claimed far too many lives so far.

TREATMENT: Recommend long-term incarceration, within a mystical prison of some sort. I should consult with Dr. Strange.

CLASSIFICATION	MUTATE
GOALS	SURVIVAL
SCOPE	INTERNATIONAL
MEANS	CONSUMPTION

MYSTERIO

AFFILIATIONS: Chameleon, Sasha Kraven, Mad Jack

ENEMIES: Spider-Man, Daredevil

In hindsight, it was probably a mistake to assume Quentin Beck was dead. Beck made his career fooling people into believing the impossible – first as a Hollywood special effects genius, and then as the criminal illusionist Mysterio. A while back, allegedly dying of cancer, he shot himself in the head after a long campaign of psychological torment against Daredevil. Of course, now we've discovered that he's spent years helping fake deaths for the Maggia, so it should come as no surprise that he's faked his own – assuming this *is* Beck. Replacement Mysterio Danny Berkhart claimed he was Beck, too, and we have yet to bring this Mysterio in, so he could be Berkhart, Francis Klum, or even Beck's cousin Maguire "Mad Jack" Beck. But whoever this Mysterio is, he should be a high-priority target; helping mobsters fake their own deaths is problematic enough, but if he starts seeking out a supervillainous clientèle, we could be in serious trouble. We have enough trouble telling which of our enemies are dead or not as-is without a professional stepping in.

TREATMENT: Recommend long-term incarceration. If Mysterio is captured dead or alive, verify that he is not a clone, robot, or impersonator.

CLASSIFICATION	HUMAN
GOALS	WEALTH & FAME
SCOPE	LOCAL
MEANS	MERCENARY

N'ASTIRH

AFFILIATIONS: S'ym, Goblin Queen, Hobgoblin

ENEMIES: Magik, New Mutants, X-Men

According to accounts we've gathered through various X-Men, N'astirh is the extradimensional demon responsible for the "Inferno" event some time back, in which New York City was briefly transformed into a twisted, demonic place. During this time, I re-formed the Avengers to combat the goings-on, but it was the X-Men and their young trainees the New Mutants that ultimately defeated N'astirh before he could sacrifice thirteen babies and open a portal to his home dimension Otherplace (aka limbo). Though he was willingly infected with an alien techno-organic virus during the event — and subsequently seemingly destroyed by the X-Man Storm — he has reportedly resurfaced in Otherplace, returned to his original form and seeking to conquer that realm. A master manipulator, he has seduced heroes and villains alike with increased powers. It is only a matter of time before this would-be ruler makes another attempt at our world. Consultation with not only the X-Men but Dr. Voodoo would be recommended.

TREATMENT: Permanent banishment to his home realm.

CLASSIFICATION	MAGICAL BEING
GOALS	CONQUEST
SCOPE	INTERDIMENSIONAL
MEANS	MAGIC

NEGATIVE ZONE

AFFILIATIONS: Annihilus, Blastaar, Ravenous, Centurions, Threska

ENEMIES: Fantastic Four, Avengers, Skrulls

Years ago, Reed Richards opened a portal between our universe and the Negative Zone, a universe with antimatter properties. While I don't know the science behind it, I understand any transport between the universes is dangerous and could result in cataclysm. Since Reed's discovery, multiple threats from the Negative Zone have attacked our universe, including the bombastic Blastaar (who I once faced in the N-Zone) and the deadly Annihilus, who led massive attacks, killing billions across space. Though I mourn the loss of those lives, we are blessed Earth was not directly involved in that attack. As I understand it, there are now settlements of Negative Zone natives living in the Kree Empire as part of a peace treaty. Tony and Reed also sanctioned Prison 42 and the use of the Negative Zone for teleportation of the Initiative teams across the country to respond to crises. Both of these ideas led to more deaths as the prisons were overrun, and the gates were nearly used as weapons of mass destruction by the Skrulls.

TREATMENT: We need to close off the gates to the Negative Zone once and for all. The threats that exist by keeping them open are far in excess of the benefits of having them.

CLASSIFICATION	ALIEN DIMENSION
GOALS	CONQUEST
SCOPE	UNIVERSAL
MEANS	WARFARE

NIGHTMARE

AFFILIATIONS: Doggerel, Dreamqueen, Nyx

ENEMIES: Black Panther, Captain America, Doc Samson, Dr. Strange, Dr. Voodoo, Hercules, Hulk, Spider-Man, Realm of Madness

Nightmare is one of the most active demonic beings of our time. He has tried to conquer the waking world so many times that most mystics have specialized defenses against him, but Nightmare learns from each failure and has consistently managed to get around these wards. For the public, it is impossible to defend against his attacks, and there were a few times he managed to trap people, including me, in his realm while using their corporal forms as agents in the real world. Other times he merged reality and unreality. There are also instances when he haunted the dreams of a single being to get revenge for past defeats or to cause anguish. Nightmare is inconsistent with what he wants, but he is a major threat; however, we have to realize for as many problems as he causes, he is needed, unless we want to fall victim to madness.

TREATMENT: Recommend mystic barriers against his malevolent influence in case he attempts to conquer Earth again. Maybe we can find something even he is afraid of and keep him in check with it. Strange once told me about Nightmare's greatest enemy the Gulgol. Maybe this Gulgol could help us against Nightmare.

CLASSIFICATION	MAGICAL BEING
GOALS	CONQUEST
SCOPE	INTERPLANETARY
MEANS	WARFARE

OHYAKU

AFFILIATIONS: Dr. Doom, Walter Declun, the Desturi

ENEMIES: Black Panther (Shuri)

Recently, Dr. Doom pulled together a deadly group to overthrow Wakanda, including the Desturi (Swahili for custom or tradition), a group of African traditionalists seeking to return Wakanda to its ancient roots, and Walter Declun, who has utilized a group of super-powered criminals. One of his agents was Ohyaku, a tech-enhanced warrior woman with electrified whips, a brutal fighter with vast technological and monetary backing and a savage nature. Ohyaku led multiple attacks on the new Black Panther on United States soil, giving the new Black Panther a serious work out until Shuri finally defeated her. Ohyaku and her soldiers attacked Washington, DC, Newark, New Jersey, and Brooklyn, New York. Ohyaku led the Black Panther into believing Namor was complicit in their attacks, resulting in a savage battle between the two heroes. In her battles with Shuri, Ohyaku was generally flanked by a group of armored, artillery-wielding men. Criminals of this nature seem a dime a dozen nowadays, but her connections and resources make Ohyaku dangerous. Ohyaku's origins and whereabouts remain a mystery.

TREATMENT: Recommend long-term incarceration with therapy.

CLASSIFICATION	HUMAN
GOALS	WEALTH & FAME
SCOPE	INTERNATIONAL
MEANS	MERCENARY

ORB

AFFILIATIONS: Orblings, Ghost Rider Assassination League

ENEMIES: Ghost Riders, Spider-Man

The all-new Orb is a mentally ill mutate with a genuine eye in place of his head. I don't know who equipped him with a repulsor ray gun or how he ended up working as a mercenary, but when the malevolent angel Zadkiel hired him he became a serious threat to the likes of Ghost Rider. He worked with some of my more mentally disturbed rogues like Madcap and Scarecrow, which shows how much of a nutcase Orb is. Recent reports from Spider-Man about Orb employing his own crew called the Orblings cemented this opinion even further, but there lies the problem; it seems like nobody takes him seriously enough to put him into an actual cell. I can understand the tendency to underestimate him. At first glance people think that if they take away his gun then he is just a deformed man with mental problems, but he is also a remorseless murderer. I'm not sure how much his condition plays a part in his mental problems because I'm not a doctor or psychiatrist, but I once heard an irritated or injured eye can drive people crazy.

TREATMENT: Recommend long-term incarceration in a mental hospital and give him special protection for his eyeball like a globe filled with artificial tear fluid.

CLASSIFICATION	MUTATE
GOALS	WEALTH & FAME
SCOPE	LOCAL
MEANS	MERCENARY

NORMAN OSBORN

AFFILIATIONS: Cabal, "Dark Avengers," HAMMER, Initiative, Kraven the Hunter, Sinister Twelve, Thunderbolts

ENEMIES: Spider-Man, Steve Rogers, Nick Fury, Tony Stark, Thor

How could the America I know let Norman Osborn rise so high in our government? At the time of my "death," he was already publicly exposed as the costumed madman Green Goblin. I am horrified when my colleague Spider-Man tells me about the Goblin's past crimes. Yet certain people in the government thought they could control Osborn, and put him in charge of the Thunderbolts. The public was so horrified by the alien Skrulls' invasion they embraced Osborn as a hero when he publicly killed the Skrull queen. Cunning, charismatic, and ruthless, Osborn took advantage of his new popularity, becoming head of SHIELD and even organizing his own team of Avengers, with himself as the "Iron Patriot." While posing as America's protector, Osborn formed a cabal with the likes of Dr. Doom, and finally overreached himself by destroying Asgard. I was out of action for much of Osborn's dark reign, but I am grateful I returned in time to capture him and see him sent to prison. I vow I will prevent any psychopath from gaining such power in our country ever again.

TREATMENT: Recommend continued incarceration under heavy security and intensive psychiatric treatment, in the hope of finding a way to permanently eliminate his "Green Goblin" personality

CLASSIFICATION	MUTATE
GOALS	NIHILISM
SCOPE	INTERNATIONAL
MEANS	LEADERSHIP

OWL

AFFILIATIONS: Man-Bull, the Maggia, Owl Gang, Gang of Four

ENEMIES: Daredevil, Spider-Man, Black Widow, Kingpin, the Hood, Dr. Octopus

Starting out as an eccentric crime boss, Leland Owlsley began ingesting a serum that allowed him to glide short distances and has made him more avian over the years. The serum has altered the Owl's intelligence and genetic structure repeatedly, even putting him temporarily in a wheelchair. The Owl has led multiple gangs across the country in several criminal ventures, including extortion, theft, and the drug trade. Owl has, at times, been a savage murderer, but is generally a greedy criminal who thinks himself a mastermind. A man with few allies, the Owl is frequently at odds with other criminals, and he has battled many heroes, though most frequently he fights Daredevil. Spider-Man describes the Owl as an unpredictable and annoying foe who is often easily underestimated. The Owl is currently free and leading a gang in the city.

TREATMENT: I don't understand why the Owl keeps returning to crime over and over, given that he has been shot, stabbed, and paralyzed repeatedly, and his defeats generally end in either imprisonment or a near-death experience. A long steady period of incarceration and rehabilitative mental health services would do him well.

CLASSIFICATION	MUTATE
GOALS	WEALTH & FAME
SCOPE	NATIONAL
MEANS	LEADERSHIP

PHANTOM RIDER

AFFILIATIONS: Crossfire, Death-THROWS

ENEMIES: Hawkeye, Mockingbird, World Counterterrorism Agency

Most consider the Ghost Rider (later Phantom Rider) of the Wild West to be a hero, but Mockingbird has a different story. When she was trapped in the past during an Avengers' mission, the Lincoln Slade Phantom Rider drugged and raped her, and she later did nothing to stop him from dying. This eventually led to Hawkeye and Mockingbird's break-up (while I could never condone the purposeful death of another, many of the current Avengers do not share this sympathy). A new, female Phantom Rider has now surfaced, and seems to be possessed by the Lincoln Slade Rider, who describes himself as the Bringer of Vengeance. Hawkeye said this Rider says she is both "the spirit and the heir", some sort of combination of the old and new. This new Rider has teamed with Crossfire, now an arms dealer. They have targeted Hawkeye and Mockingbird, and they've already shot Susan Morse, an innocent connected to the heroes, and inflicted vast amounts of property damage on the city. This new Phantom Rider has bullets that can phase through anything, incapacitating light bullets, and some sort of psychic link to Mockingbird.

TREATMENT: Confer with the Hamilton Slade Phantom Rider of Texas' Rangers for advice on disrupting her power source to enable capture.

CLASSIFICATION	MAGICAL BEING
GOALS	REVENGE
SCOPE	LOCAL
MEANS	MAGIC

PLOKTA

AFFILIATIONS: Mindless Ones

ENEMIES: Dormammu, MI13

Remembering how I had to square my religious convictions with Thor and Hercules' claims to be ancient gods, I know many will struggle to accept the entity Plokta's claims to be a "Duke of Hell." However, whether his story is literally true isn't important; just accept he is an immensely powerful and malevolent extradimensional entity. Like other "Hell-lords," he delights in tricking mortals into detrimental deals, in his case offering to grant an individual's greatest desire. Anyone foolish enough to accept gets only illusions, albeit very convincing ones, and is slowly drained of energy, becoming a battery to power the creation of brutish engines of destruction known as Mindless Ones. Dr. Strange informs me Plokta has previously unleashed Mindless Ones in various demonic rivals' realms, tying up their resources, so ironically we can thank him for reducing the threat those rivals posed to Earth, but he didn't do it for our benefit. MI13 captured Plokta when he attacked Britain recently, but released him in return for his help against Dracula's subsequent invasion.

TREATMENT: If Plokta turns his attention back to Earth, we need to have our magical "big guns" ready. Capturing him will be hard — we need to borrow or reproduce the tech MI13 used to imprison Plokta.

CLASSIFICATION	MAGICAL BEING
GOALS	CONQUEST
SCOPE	INTERDIMENSIONAL
MEANS	MAGIC

PLUTO

AFFILIATIONS: Persephone, Olympians, Lords of the Splinter Realms

ENEMIES: Hercules, Thor, Zeus

Of all the Olympian gods, Pluto is one of the most morally repugnant. Unlike Hela, his Asgardian counterpart, Pluto is never moved by demonstrations of valor or love; rather, he seems motivated exclusively by greed and the acquisition of wealth and power. Pluto is the elder brother of the gods Poseidon and Zeus, but was placed in charge of the underworld of Hades while his younger brothers ruled over the seas and the heavens, respectively. Pluto grew increasingly rebellious under Zeus' rule, and challenged the Olympians on a number of occasions before shifting interest to his lucrative holdings in the mortal world. Following the recent deaths of several prominent Olympians (including Zeus, Hera, Ares, and Hercules), Pluto made a bid to rule the pantheon. Fortunately, the goddess of wisdom Athena prevailed.

TREATMENT: Given Pluto's vast powers and resources as the Olympian god of the dead, imprisoning him in any mortal prison would be risky, to say the least. Unfortunately, he frequently conducts his business in the Earth realm (especially since the destruction of Olympus), so it's likely he'll run afoul of our laws sooner or later. In that event, we'll have to consult the Asgardians or surviving Olympians to discuss the best method of dealing with him.

CLASSIFICATION	MAGICAL BEING
GOALS	CONQUEST
SCOPE	INTERDIMENSIONAL
MEANS	MAGIC

THE PRESENCE

AFFILIATIONS: Fantasma, Dire Wraiths, Igor Drenkov, Starlight

ENEMIES: Winter Guard, Protectorate, Pieter Phobos, Defenders, Quasar, Avengers

I have known the Presence as both an enemy and an ally. Russian nuclear physicist Sergei Krylov attempted to cure himself of radiation poisoning by setting off a cobalt bomb that transformed him and Russian dissident Tania Belinsky (later Starlight) into radioactive superhumans, both able to manipulate matter and energy at an atomic level. When the radiation began to spread, Krylov and Belinsky absorbed it and left Earth to dispose of it. Upon his return, Krylov was unhappy to see how his country had declined. Although the Avengers and Russia's Winter Guard defeated him during his attempt to improve Russia by controlling its populace via telepathy, Krylov later aided us when the time-traveling Kang briefly conquered the planet. While incarcerated at Russia's Citadel, Krylov helped trigger the rebirth of the extraterrestrial Dire Wraiths. He was defeated by the Protectorate and the Winter Guard and is presumed dead, though given his tremendous power, I doubt we have seen the last of him.

TREATMENT: Krylov is so powerful no Russian prison is capable of restraining him. If he should return, he will need to be incarcerated in a maximum security holding cell — such as those in Negative Zone Prison 42.

CLASSIFICATION	MUTATE
GOALS	CONQUEST
SCOPE	INTERNATIONAL
MEANS	LEADERSHIP

THE PROFILE

AFFILIATIONS: Hood, Norman Osborn, Bushman, Scarecrow

ENEMIES: Moon Knight

The Profile is a relative newcomer to the criminal scene in New York. With his mysterious (perhaps mutant) ability to see a person's deepest secrets, wants, and desires, the Profile uses this knowledge to exploit, manipulate, and blackmail his targets. Various criminal factions, including, notably, Norman Osborn and the Hood, have used the Profile to seek out weak points in rival heroes or criminal organizations. The Profile most frequently clashed with Moon Knight, but aided him in the defeat of Midnight and psycho-analyzed Spector's various personalities. The Profile also convinced the Hood to resurrect Bushman, who subsequently formed an army of the criminally insane, including the Scarecrow, to rampage across the city; the army was defeated and the villains incarcerated again. The Profile recently had some sort of religious epiphany and was allegedly recruited by the Egyptian god of revenge, Khonshu, the same deity said to patronize Moon Knight. Through some sort of dealing with Daredevil, the Profile has helped recruit the new and deadly Shadow Knight, who has left a bloody trail across the city. Though not a physical threat, the Profile is a master manipulator and is intensely dangerous.

TREATMENT: Recommend long-term incarceration with extensive therapy; anyone who approaches him should be warned of his knack for head games.

CLASSIFICATION	MUTATE
GOALS	WEALTH & FAME
SCOPE	LOCAL
MEANS	MERCENARY

PHILLIP PROMETHEUS

AFFILIATIONS: Computrex, Eaglestar, Ultimo

ENEMIES: War Machine, Ray Coffin, Enigma Force

Nearly killed by cosmic rays while visiting NASA's orbiting Starlab, astronaut and scientist Phillip Prometheus survived by becoming a cyborg, something he hid upon his return to Earth. NASA later appointed him director of Human Engineering Life Laboratories (HELL); while there he learned of the subatomic Microverse and became obsessed with using that realm's technology to transcend his remaining humanity and become a god. Fellow ex-astronaut Ray Coffin and Microverse rebels Enigma Force, exposed his plans, and Prometheus was put in an asylum. Wrongly judged harmless and released, Prometheus, calling himself the Toymaster, created a remote-controlled miniature army using Microverse technology, but again ran foul of Enigma Force. This second clash saw his human side die when he fell down an elevator shaft, but the malevolent AI Computrex reactivated Phillip's robotic remains and drew him back to HELL for another battle with the Microns, which ended with Prometheus buried after HELL exploded. He recently resurfaced, his mind his own once more, to provide Eaglestar with a virus based on Ultimo's technology.

TREATMENT: Sad to see a once great man fall so far, but the world doesn't need another criminal scientist. We need to find hard proof of his crimes and lock him up.

CLASSIFICATION	CYBORG
GOALS	CHALLENGES
SCOPE	LOCAL
MEANS	SCIENCE

PSIONEX

AFFILIATIONS: The Initiative, Norman Osborn

ENEMIES: New Warriors, Terrax the Tamer

When Norman Osborn took over the Fifty State Initiative, he placed teams of villains into positions of trust throughout the country, among them the U-Foes, the Force of Nature, and Psionex, who took over defense of Maryland. Despite their limited involvement in the siege of Asgard, I don't believe the members of Psionex are truly evil, but they need guidance. The members of Psionex, as I understand it from Nova and Justice, have always been a group of misfits; the five original members received their powers in genetic experiments by the company Genetech, though the experiments also deteriorated their mental health. Despite a rocky history as

Genetech operatives and popular crime-fighting vigilantes, the members of Psionex have been able to do the right thing in the end every time; after fighting the New Warriors, they joined them against Terrax, and after their alliance with Henrique Gallante resulted in the death of a child they were immediately repentant. Psionex expressed immediate interest in enrolling with the Initiative, and I have faith that Coronary, Impulse, Mathemanic, Pretty Persuasions, and the new Asylum can be effective heroes, so long as Osborn didn't influence them overmuch.

TREATMENT: Monitor their status as rising heroes, but be quick to provide sound guidance to correct their old habits.

CLASSIFICATION	GROUP
GOALS	WEALTH & FAME
SCOPE	LOCAL
MEANS	VIGILANTES

PUPPET MASTER

AFFILIATIONS: Mad Thinker, Doctor Doom, Egghead, Wizard

ENEMIES: Fantastic Four, Spider-Man, Sub-Mariner, X-Men

Born in the Eastern European country of Transia, Philip Masters was a brilliant but deeply lonely child, who regarded the puppets he played with as his only friends. He succeeded in marrying but when his wife died, he went temporarily insane. Though he recovered, Masters has since felt rage towards the rest of humanity. He discovered a strange form of radioactive clay in his native Transia. Masters found he could mentally control a person by using the clay to model a puppet in his or her image. Intoxicated with his new power, Masters, as the Puppet Master, even plotted to take over the world. Masters has clashed repeatedly with the Fantastic Four and other heroes, and

teamed with criminals such as Doctor Doom and, most often, the Mad Thinker. But I do not believe Masters to be irredeemably evil. He genuinely loves his stepdaughter, the blind sculptress Alicia Masters, and he has made attempts at retiring from crime, even working with SHIELD. Recently, though, he and the Thinker meddled in the super heroes' "Civil War" and he took a turn selling mind controlled superhuman slaves in South America.

TREATMENT: Masters could be rehabilitated if he receives emotional support and is given a beneficial outlet for his talents, as SHIELD once provided. Perhaps Alicia Masters could help.

CLASSIFICATION	MUTATE
GOALS	REVENGE
SCOPE	LOCAL
MEANS	MAGIC

PURPLE MAN

AFFILIATIONS: Baron Zemo, Hood, Kingpin

ENEMIES: Jewel, Luke Cage, Thunderbolts, Dr. Doom, Daredevil

While several people listed here have made bad choices or might be redeemable someday, few are as unashamedly evil as Zebediah Killgrave, the Purple Man. He has used his power to control minds to commit a multitude of crimes, including theft, treason, murder and rape. He apparently has no remorse, repenting only when threatened with death. He has manipulated several heroes for months at a time and caused chaos in the lives of countless civilians. Interestingly, a child he fathered while abusing his powers grew up to become the Canadian hero Persuasion, but

I would be hard-pressed to find any other good that has come from him. Once, we believed his threat had ended when the more ambitious Dr. Doom used Killgrave's powers to enslave the world, only to have those plans end with Killgrave's seeming death, but it seems his corruptive influence could survive even burial. Recently, Killgrave found himself manipulated by Baron Zemo, who at the time believed he was working for the greater good, but Killgrave has been left to his own devices again.

TREATMENT: Recommend securest possible incarceration, far away from populated areas or potential victims; ideally such arrangements could be maintained indefinitely.

CLASSIFICATION	MUTATE
GOALS	WEALTH & FAME
SCOPE	NATIONAL
MEANS	LEADERSHIP

RAGNAROK

AFFILIATIONS: Unknown

ENEMIES: Thor, Asgardians, Initiative, Goliath

Perhaps the superhuman civil war's darkest legacy, Tony Stark's scientists created Ragnarok using a combination of Thor's DNA (as Thor was dead at the time) and advanced cybernetic technology. I witnessed Ragnarok's destructive power firsthand when he killed my friend and ally Goliath during a confrontation between Tony's pro-registration forces and my resistance movement, and I think it became evident even to Tony at that moment that Ragnarok's creation was a mistake. Prior to our movement's surrender to the government, Hercules severely damaged the cybernetic clone, and his remains were transported to Camp Hammond under the care of Initiative scientist Baron von Blitzschlag. However,

a rehabilitated Ragnarok escaped and laid waste to Camp Hammond before setting his sights on Thor and his fellow Asgardian gods, whom Ragnarok believed were false gods created in his image. As Ragnarok was symbolic of the dark period that befell our nation following the civil war, it is fitting that Thor destroyed him prior to our ushering in of what the media has dubbed a new "heroic age."

TREATMENT: Our scientists are currently debating how to best dispose of Ragnarok's remains; as he was reactivated following his seeming destruction at Hercules' hands, we must take precautions to ensure history does not repeat itself following his destruction by Thor.

CLASSIFICATION	CYBORG
GOALS	CONQUEST
SCOPE	NATIONAL
MEANS	FOLLOWER

RAZOR-FIST

AFFILIATIONS: Hood, Crossfire, Shockwave, Maximillian Zaran

ENEMIES: Shang-Chi, Toxin, Avengers, Spider-Man, Cat

Douglas Scott was originally paired with his brother, both men dubbed "Razor-Fist" after an earlier blade-for-hire. Each brother was missing one hand, so they replaced their missing appendages with steel blades. After his brother's death, Razor-Fist had his good hand replaced as well. Losing both his hands doesn't seem to have troubled him; he's been outfitted with prosthetic hands while in custody, but each time he's replaced them with blades after gaining his freedom. His love for cutting others is what I find most disturbing, and I think it puts Wolverine's

behavior into perspective; however I may feel about his propensity to maim opponents, Wolverine has never suggested he "gets off" on it. Razor-Fist has hired out his services for years, but the Hood may have commanded him longer than anyone. With the Hood out of business, I expect Razor-Fist will look overseas for clientele; Hydra, Maggia, Triads, Yakuza, they'd all have uses for him. Razor-Fist is low-powered enough that almost any experienced hero could capture him, but he's dangerous enough that no law enforcement agents should engage him.

TREATMENT: Recommend long-term incarceration, until and unless psychiatric aid can break his vicious habits.

CLASSIFICATION	HUMAN
GOALS	NIHILISM
SCOPE	INTERNATIONAL
MEANS	MERCENARY

RED SKULL

AFFILIATIONS: Arnim Zola, Dr. Faustus, Sin, Skeleton Crew, Third Reich

ENEMIES: Avengers, Captain America, SHIELD

Since World War II Johann Shmidt, the Red Skull has haunted me, constantly finding ways to threaten the world. Personally chosen by Adolf Hitler to be the perfect Nazi, the Red Skull survived the war's end in suspended animation, reawakening in the modern era. A constant reminder to me of the evils of the war, thus far my fellow heroes and I have always managed to stop him in his schemes wether he traveled through time, used giant robots created during the war or allied with a variety of mercenaries and racists. Shockingly he also managed to rise into the highest echelons of our

soceity under differing aliases, and has used powerful objects including the Cosmic Cube in plots to conquer the world. Obsessed with me, he recently plotted to pose as me by stealing my body, and we destroyed him while his mind was trapped in a robotic body. He had nowhere else to go, but it's hard to accept he's truly gone for good after he returned so many previous times. If Shmidt turns up again, I will track him down, personally put him in prison and make sure he never gets out again.

TREATMENT: Recommend life-long incarceration; the International Criminal Court is eager to put him on trial, although I fear he would rather enjoy the exposure.

CLASSIFICATION	HUMAN
GOALS	CONQUEST
SCOPE	INTERNATIONAL
MEANS	LEADERSHIP

REDEEMER

AFFILIATIONS: Doctor Everything, Dementoid, Eleven, Hippo, General Wolfram

ENEMIES: Venom

Like Dr. Shep Gunderson, I believe that criminals, even super-criminals, can be rehabilitated. I disagree with him, however, that the correct way of doing so is to pull on a skull mask, recruit a team of vengeful super-villains, and attack another super-villain in the hopes of rehabilitating him, as he did with Venom. Unsurprisingly, this resulted in the deaths of several of his patients, as well as Venom eating all four of Gunderson's limbs. Understandably distraught by this, Gunderson gathered his remaining allies and went after Venom again. This too ended poorly for Gunderson, and he was arrested. Gunderson's naiveté makes him a danger to himself and others. Not everyone can be redeemed; certainly Venom can't. But I think Gunderson can be. Having to deal with his former employer J. Jonah Jameson, and Norman Osborn's pet symbiote, would be enough to drive a lot of men mad; Gunderson is still a world-class psychologist, and it would be a shame to let Gunderson's talents go to waste in prison.

TREATMENT: Recommend transfer to the Thunderbolts program. While I don't think putting Gunderson in a supervisory role is in anyone's best interest, his expertise could be useful in a consulting position.

CLASSIFICATION	HUMAN
GOALS	CHALLENGES
SCOPE	LOCAL
MEANS	SCIENCE

SOVEL REDHAND

AFFILIATIONS: Glitter, Horse, Jat

ENEMIES: Charles Xavier, Gambit, Rogue, Danger

Sovel Redhand, a Shi'ar ship captain who retrieves scrap and resells it, brought his ship, Tath En'ruh (or the Boneyard Dog), to Earth to salvage a rogue sentient Shi'ar technology called Danger. According to Wolverine, years ago Charles Xavier enslaved this technology to act as a training facility for his X-Men; years later, the technology escaped and attacked the X-Men, resulting in the death of at least one of their students. When Redhand's crew landed in Australia, where Xavier, Gambit, and Rogue were, they got caught up in a complex holographic environment that could have killed all of them. Redhand's ship somehow took away Danger's free will, compounding the situation until they stopped the program. Redhand and his crew then promptly turned on the X-Men, planning on taking Danger and Xavier back to the Shi'ar for rewards. When the conflict got too difficult, Redhand teleported his crew to the ship and retreated. I doubt Redhand will return to Earth, and if he does it will likely be as an enemy of the X-Men (who fight the Shi'ar frequently).

TREATMENT: Contact Abigail Brand from SWORD and let her handle Redhand's crew as she sees fit. (Beast assures me she is trustworthy).

CLASSIFICATION	EXTRATERRESTRIAL
GOALS	WEALTH & FAME
SCOPE	INTERPLANETARY
MEANS	MERCENARY

RHINO

AFFILIATIONS: The Leader, Sinister Syndicate, the Abomination, Exterminators, Egghead, Justin Hammer

ENEMIES: Spider-Man, Hulk, Defenders, Doc Samson

The Rhino is a sad example of a man who acquired superhuman power but lacked the intelligence or emotional capacity to handle it. Originally a small-time member of the Russian Mafia, he submitted to treatments by a foreign spy agency, endowing him with superhuman strength. Its scientists bonded to his skin a highly durable costume modeled after the hide of a rhinoceros, complete with a horn. But despite the Rhino's sheer power, he has no talent for battle strategy, and Spider-Man outwitted and outmaneuvered him. The Rhino has since repeatedly battled Spider-Man and the Hulk, and worked with other criminals, such as the Leader and the Sinister Syndicate. But the price he paid for his power was his inability for years to remove his Rhino costume. Recently, the Rhino gave up his life of crime and married a woman named Oksana. But another criminal took on the role of the Rhino and attacked them. When Oksana was killed, the original Rhino gave in to rage and murdered his would-be successor.

TREATMENT: The Rhino has proved in the past he is capable of reform and longs for a peaceful life. But after he killed the new Rhino, it is unclear whether he can truly be rehabilitated.

CLASSIFICATION	MUTATE
GOALS	WEALTH & FAME
SCOPE	NATIONAL
MEANS	ROBBERY

RINGER

AFFILIATIONS: Justin Hammer, Norman Osborn

ENEMIES: Moon Knight, Avengers Resistance, Pantheon

No matter how frustrated I get with criminals who are repeat offenders, I have to admire their tenacity and stick-to-it attitude that keeps them trying to score big despite multiple defeats. Small-time hood Keith Kraft donned the Ringer suit after the original Ringer, Anthony Davis, was believed killed by the Scourge organization. Kraft, despite having expensive and deadly technology at his disposal, has been defeated time and again, by Moon Knight, She-Hulk, me, and others. He must have felt like he'd scored the jackpot when Osborn recruited him to serve in the Initiative. Though many of his peers (including Johnny Guitar and Slaughter Boy) were killed in battle, Ringer stayed true to Osborn until the last bitter battle, and he now sits in jail. Although Kraft has never done anything truly heinous that I'm aware of, I have little hope he will rehabilitate unless he shows more initiative. It is best to simply take his suit away and let him pay for his crimes. If we can't convince him to tread the straight and narrow, his continued involvement in battles with super-powered heroes and villains will in time assuredly lead to his death.

TREATMENT: Long-term incarceration, with opportunities at rehabilitation after his release.

CLASSIFICATION	HUMAN
GOALS	WEALTH & FAME
SCOPE	LOCAL
MEANS	ROBBERY

ROMULUS

AFFILIATIONS: Wild Child, Sabretooth, Omega Red

ENEMIES: Wolverine, Cyber, Skaar, Cloak

For more than a century, Romulus has been obsessed with creating a perfect weapon, toying with the lives of men and the destinies of countries in order to achieve his goals. Romulus considers himself the perfect predator, and he has spent decades building a power base so he can devise a weapon that will eventually kill him and take his place. Behind the scenes and using political contacts, torture, kidnapping, and blackmail, Romulus has funded wars across the world and worked to make men as violent and deadly as possible. He saved the future Cyber from execution for mass murder and made him a trainer at his camps. Finally finding his perfect weapon in Wolverine, Romulus sent the man into multiple wars and government organizations, making him a hardened weapon and repeatedly manipulating his memories. Any time Wolverine came close to finding peace, Romulus shattered that happiness, generally by sending Sabretooth or others to kill someone Wolverine cared about. He saw Wolverine's skeleton encased in Adamantium, and raised Daken similarly as a weapon. Wolverine assures me Romulus is taken care of for now, though he won't tell me where Romulus is. I have to trust he knows what is best.

TREATMENT: If he reappears, consult with Wolverine, but this time provide oversight to ensure his definite capture.

CLASSIFICATION	MUTATE
GOALS	CONQUEST
SCOPE	INTERNATIONAL
MEANS	LEADERSHIP

ROSE

AFFILIATIONS: Boomerang, Armadillo

ENEMIES: Spider-Man, Jackpot

After an accident exposed the dangerous conditions in his lab, scientist Dr. Philip Hayes turned to crime, reverse-engineering the Corruptor's mutated sweat glands to produce a potent street drug. To garner respect, he took on the dormant identity of the Rose. I don't understand what's so compelling about a well-dressed crimelord in a leather mask, and yet, Hayes is one of a long line of Roses – the Kingpin's son Richard Fisk, vengeful cop Sgt. Blume, and embittered journalist Jacob Conover. They're all dead or rotting in jail, so why take on the identity of a three-time loser? Nevertheless, Hayes is a gifted scientist, and while he may not be much of a crimelord, he arranged the murder of an innocent man and put a dangerous drug out on the streets. Hayes is the worst kind of criminal – he's not motivated by madness, misguided ambition, or even passion. He's just a selfish, petty man.

TREATMENT: Recommend long-term incarceration. Ensure that Hayes is kept away from any substances beyond his food and toiletries; chemists have a nasty habit of blowing their way through prison walls with bombs made out of floor polish and drain cleaner.

CLASSIFICATION	HUMAN
GOALS	CONQUEST
SCOPE	NATIONAL
MEANS	LEADERSHIP

R. ROTTWELL

AFFILIATIONS: Charlie Chainsaws, Nurse Fester

ENEMIES: Wolverine, Marshall Swinson, Nightcrawler, Psylocke

Wolverine describes "Dr. Algernon Rottwell" (though I doubt that is his real name) as one of the most evil men he's ever encountered, and that is saying something in today's day and age. By his own account, Rottwell started committing murders as a child and discussed openly how he loved watching others die. He became a patient at Dunwich Sanatorium, which I understand brainwashed and trained assassins for hire. Rottwell eventually overthrew the head doctor, Marshall Swinson, and took over the facility, building brain machines to pacify and control everyone. Rottwell specially created several serial killers, which he loosed on the public, and he brutally experimented on Wolverine when he came to investigate. In time, Wolverine and his X-Men allies shut down Dunwich Sanatorium, but not before Rottwell escaped, using a brain-bomb of sorts (reminds me of the Mad Bomb) to erase the memory of his escape from the minds of the others. He later contacted Wolverine, promising some sort of sick revenge. Rottwell is a mass murderer with no regard for life in any form, and he must be apprehended immediately.

TREATMENT: Keep flagged on watchlists, secure the best psychiatric personnel to treat him.

CLASSIFICATION	HUMAN
GOALS	CHALLENGES
SCOPE	LOCAL
MEANS	SCIENCE

ROXXON

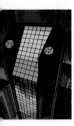

AFFILIATIONS: Brand Corporation, Serpent Squad, Killer Shrike, Magma, Stratosfire, Sunturion, Windshear

ENEMIES: Captain America, Iron Man, Sub-Mariner, Black Panther, Nick Fury, SHIELD, Ka-Zar, Shanna the She-Devil, Thing, Spider-Man, US Department of Justice

The Roxxon Energy Corporation is probably the largest, most powerful oil company on Earth, with wealth that dwarfs most nations. Roxxon's advertising slogan says, "Roxxon: your energy friend." But Roxxon has ruthlessly pursued the goal of gaining a monopoly on energy sources and eliminating competition, whether from private businesses or governments. I first learned of Roxxon's dark side in my encounters with its president Hugh Jones, who wielded the ancient power object called the Serpent Crown. But while executives like Jones may fall from power, Roxxon's corporate culture remains corrupt. Its original owner, Republic Oil, even had Tony Stark's parents killed. Roxxon has tried to seize control of the Savage Land's natural resources and empowered numerous superhuman criminal operatives. Roxxon heedlessly create environmental disasters, such as when its tanker Velasquez spilled millions of gallons of oil into the ocean. Recently, Aleksander Lukin's Kronas Corporation bought Roxxon, but with Lukin gone, I suspect Roxxon now controls Kronas.

TREATMENT: Roxxon has shielded itself from the law with its lawyers, public relations staff, and, I'm sorry to say, allies in government who receive Roxxon's financial "contributions." However, the Justice Department has shown admirable persistence in trying to prosecute Roxxon for its many crimes.

CLASSIFICATION	GROUP
GOALS	WEALTH & FAME
SCOPE	INTERNATIONAL
MEANS	BUSINESS

RUBY THURSDAY

AFFILIATIONS: Headmen, the Answer

ENEMIES: Wolverine, Romulus, the Defenders, AIM, Heroes for Hire, Bullseye

There are all kinds of insanity out there, and I don't claim to understand many of them. I will never understand, however, what would drive an educated woman like Thursday Rubinstein to replace her head with an organic computer able to change shape and release kinetic energy attacks. Ruby has been killed more than once, but always has a back-up head handy, making her more cyborg than human. My understanding of her motivations, and her ongoing association with the Headmen, is that she wants to replace the heads of all humans with similar computers. Wolverine recently crossed paths with Ruby, using her in his ongoing plot against Romulus, and she proved entirely untrustworthy (though it seems she may have a daughter, something she has kept well hidden). Her villainous campaigns have included several attempts to rule the world, generally through subtle means, and she has been incarcerated multiple times, though she seems to get away frequently. Ruby's methods and motivations are entirely self-serving.

TREATMENT: Recommend long-term incarceration with extensive therapy. She could be a potential candidate for Luke's Thunderbolts program.

CLASSIFICATION	CYBORG
GOALS	CHALLENGES
SCOPE	NATIONAL
MEANS	SCIENCE

SAVAGE LAND MUTATES

AFFILIATIONS: Sauron, Magneto, Zaladane

ENEMIES: X-Men, Avengers, Ka-Zar, Spider-Man

In the Savage Land, Antarctica's strange tropical realm, mutant terrorist Magneto experimented on natives, altering their DNA to transform them into the original Savage Land Mutates, whom he sent to combat the X-Men and the Savage Land's protector Ka-Zar. The original roster included the froglike Amphibius; Barbarus, who has four super-strong arms; the superhuman genius Brainchild; the vertigo-inducing Equilibrius; Gaza, blind but possessing superhuman strength and a radar sense; Lorelei, whose voice can hypnotize men; the wolf-controlling Lupo; and Piper, who mentally controls animals by playing his flute. Later recruits include Leash, who can capture a victim's astral self; animal-controlling Lupa; Vertigo, who lives up to her name; Whiteout, able to emit a temporarily blinding light; and the mind-controlling Worm. Besides Magneto, the Mutates have served the sorceress Zaladane and Sauron, human scientist who transforms into a being resembling a pterodactyl. At other times Brainchild commands his fellow Mutates. They seem primarily interested in conquering the Savage Land, not in the outside world.

TREATMENT: If the Savage Land Mutates are captured, it may be wise to try to find a way to permanently reverse the artificial mutations, returning them to their human states.

CLASSIFICATION	GROU
GOALS	CONQUES
SCOPE	INTERNATIONA
MEANS	MERCENARIE

SCARECROW

AFFILIATIONS: Blackheart, Ghost Rider Assassination League, the Hood

ENEMIES: Steve Rogers, Ghost Riders, Spider-Man, Iron Man

When I first crossed paths with the Scarecrow, a strange costumed man with trained crows and a talent for contortion, I never could have guessed how deeply depraved and twisted a soul he is. Had I known, I would have done everything in my power to ensure he got the treatment and incarceration needed to prevent him ever being loosed on the public again. Ebenezer Laughton had a very tortured past filled with abuse and neglect, and he has grown to become one of the world's most despicable serial killers, using crows, pitchforks, and his occasional powers over fear to feed his addictions and hungers. Despite serious injuries, lengthy incarceration, and even death, the Scarecrow keeps finding ways to return and inflict his inner pains on others, leaving a trail of bodies in his path. His recent association with the Hood concern me; I'm accustomed to the Scarecrow being a rather isolated villain.

TREATMENT: Requires extensive exploration of his damaged psyche and his unusual powers. Recommend consult with Dr. Voodoo.

CLASSIFICATION	MUTAT
GOALS	NIHILIS
SCOPE	LOCA
MEANS	MERCENAR

SCOURGE

AFFILIATIONS: Thunderbolts, Kingpin

ENEMIES: Captain America, Daredevil, Wolverine

Scourge is none other than the super-soldier Nuke, who was brainwashed, drugged and physically altered to become a merciless killing machine. I first ran into him during his assault on Hell's Kitchen a few years back. I felt guilty at the time because I thought Nuke was an attempt to recreate me and beat him into submission. Shot from a helicopter Nuke seemingly died that day, but unknown to me the government retrieved his body and saved him only to turn him into a being more machine than human. They sent him after Wolverine and I was sent in to clean up the mess caused by them. It was devastating for me to see what the government had done to Nuke and how they used him and it still got worse when Norman Osborn turned Nuke into the Thunderbolts' field leader Scourge. During his tenure with the Thunderbolts brutally injured USAgent during the siege of Asgard. I can only wish for a way to permanently shut down this soulless killing machine. I honestly think it would be the right thing to do at this point.

TREATMENT: Recommend complete and permanent shut down of all his systems. He is nothing more than a mad puppet anyway these days, so we should treat him that way before someone else uses him as their personal killing machine including our government.

CLASSIFICATION	CYBOR
GOALS	SERVANTHOO
SCOPE	INTERNATIONA
MEANS	FOLLOWE

SECRET EMPIRE

AFFILIATIONS: William Taurey, Hydra, Professor Power, Red Skull, Viper

ENEMIES: Captain America, SHIELD, Falcon, Thunderbolts, X-Men, Nomad, Young Avengers

Originally the subversive Secret Empire cabal was one of Hydra's many arms until SHIELD agent Gabe Jones infiltrated it and wiped out most of its ruling council. A new "Number One" reorganized the Empire, who, through their front organization, the Committee to Regain America's Principles, framed me for murder. Finally, Number One publicly demanded America's surrender on the White House lawn. Finally, Number One publicly demanded America's surrender on the White House lawn, but I forced Number One to unmask, discovering to my shock that he was [[PRESIDENT'S EYES ONLY]], shaking my faith in America. Recently, my old enemy William Taurey has renamed his Royalist Forces of America as the new Secret Empire. Taurey intends to undo the American Revolution, not to restore British rule, but to turn our democracy into an empire controlled by an aristocratic elite headed by himself. Taurey's "Imperial Forces" include his own army, the Shocktroopers, and superhuman operatives, making him a particularly dangerous threat. The Empire employed Professor Power to brainwash high school students into a riot, but Nomad and the Young Avengers fortunately halted this.

TREATMENT: William Taurey has turned the Secret Empire into a political movement, which can best be defeated by courageous politicians and other citizens willing to speak out against them.

CLASSIFICATION	GROUP
GOALS	CONQUEST
SCOPE	INTERNATIONAL
MEANS	TERRORISM

SHADOW COUNCIL

AFFILIATIONS: Roxxon

ENEMIES: Secret Avengers

While I was Captain America, I frequently fought the subversive Secret Empire, but as far as domestic terror groups went, their tactics were fairly conventional, and their grandiose plots always foiled by traditional super heroicss. In this new era, however, the threats posed by our enemies have become exponentially larger in scope and scale. Traditional super heroics won't always save the day, which is why I recruited a team of Avengers specializing in stealth tactics and preemptive intervention. It was on our first mission that we encountered the mysterious Shadow Empire. Although similar in name to the Secret Empire, the Shadow Empire seems to have far more resources (including the ability to travel through folds in space-time) at its disposal. It seems to be run by a board of directors known as the "Shadow Council" who employ an international network of espionage agents. Our most reliable intelligence indicates they were instrumental in granting the Roxxon oil company mining rights on the planet Mars. Sources also often cite a common name: Aloysius Thorndrake.

TREATMENT: Recommendations for treatment at this juncture are premature and speculative until we determine the identity and nature of the individuals involved in the Shadow Empire.

CLASSIFICATION	GROUP
GOALS	CONQUEST
SCOPE	INTERPLANETARY
MEANS	WARFARE

SHI'AR

AFFILIATIONS: Kree, Imperial Guard, Shi'ar Death Commandos

ENEMIES: X-Men, Avengers, Skrulls, "Cancerverse"

The Shi'ar control an intergalactic empire across the vast reaches of space, affecting thousands of worlds and billions of sentient creatures. Though Earth is small in the cosmic scheme of things (at least according to most of the aliens I have crossed paths with), we, as a planet, somehow stay involved with the Shi'ar. Charles Xavier was once married to the Majestrix Lilandra, who has been assassinated, and Darkhawk framed for the crime; the Imperial Guard has been active on Earth multiple times; the Shi'ar Death Commandos wiped out Jean Grey's entire extended family; Vulcan (Gabriel Summers) married Deathbird and commanded the empire for a time; the entire Empire is ruled over by the Inhumans now (as they also control the Kree); they have abducted humans (Cyclops' parents included), and have sent agents to Earth (including Davan Shakari and Cerise). I crossed paths with the Imperial Guard during the Kree/Shi'ar war, and the Avengers tried settling the conflict, somewhat unsuccessfully. The Shi'ar Empire has been through serious upheavals in recent months, and it is my hope their affairs will stay far from Earth in the coming years.

TREATMENT: I need to sit down with Abigail Brand of SWORD to discuss containment and avoidance strategies.

CLASSIFICATION	EXTRATERRESTRIALS
GOALS	CONQUEST
SCOPE	INTERPLANETARY
MEANS	WARFARE

SIN

AFFILIATIONS: Red Skull, Crossbones, Sisters of Sin, Serpent Squad

ENEMIES: Steve Rogers, Captain America

Of all the heinous crimes Johann Shmidt, the Red Skull, has committed over the years, outside of mass murder and attempted genocide, his brutal treatment of his daughter, Sinthea, ranks right at the top, even more than his ongoing attempts to destroy me personally and professionally. As I understand it, the Red Skull never wanted a daughter, but he raised her to be cruel, sadistic, and mentally unstable. Calling her Mother Superior, and later Sin, the Red Skull employed his daughter in various plots of destruction, torture, and world domination. Sin may be beyond redemption now, and she has become a deadly mass murderer in her own right. For a time, Sin worked with doctors to stabilize her mental health issues, and she led a brief happy life in another identity, but Sin needs to pay for her crimes, and a life behind bars is the best place for her at this point. In our most recent encounter, her face was tragically scarred, leaving her looking more like her father. I don't know what to expect from Sin next.

TREATMENT: Her entire life has been a therapist's nightmare; requires extensive therapy and maximum security.

CLASSIFICATION	HUMAN
GOALS	NIHILISM
SCOPE	NATIONAL
MEANS	TERRORISM

SKELETON KI

AFFILIATIONS: Advanced Idea Mechanics (A.I.M.), Blastaar

ENEMIES: Iron Fist

For three-and-a-half decades, Uzbeki national Alisher Sham has operated as the mysterious "Skeleton Ki," a notorious master thief known the world over for his ability to pick any lock via self-taught mysticism. Able to circumvent even the most advanced electronic security systems and dual-control combination locks, Skeleton Ki's luck finally ran out when he was captured by US authorities and transferred to Negative Zone Prison 42 following the superhuman civil war. But when the Negative Zone despot Blastaar laid siege to Prison 42, Skeleton Ki was one of the criminals who rose to prominence, betraying his fellow inmates and granting Blastaar's forces entrance into Prison 42 in exchange for his life. Blastaar's forces were finally defeate after the arrival of Initiative troops from Norman Osborn's Camp HAMMER. Skeleton Ki was returned to custody and is now incarcerated in the Raft.

TREATMENT: Willing to switch sides at the drop of a hat so long as it serves his purposes, Skeleton Ki could most likely be persuaded to join the Thunderbolts program if made to believe doing so would lead to bigger and better opportunities down the road. His unique combination of mysticism and espionage skills would be a valuable asset to any team, though his duplicitous nature is a drawback.

CLASSIFICATION	HUMAN
GOALS	CHALLENGES
SCOPE	LOCAL
MEANS	MERCENARY

SPECTRUM

AFFILIATIONS: Morgan Ridgway

ENEMIES: Spider-Man

When someone shows up in public wearing a costume and creating mass panic with their powers, for a super-hero it's second nature to leap into the fray and start punching them in the face. In Spectrum's case, however, that would have been an overreaction. Gifted with the ability to alter others' perception of light, Spectrum decided not to use these powers to commit crime, but to entertain, giving his clients a hallucinogenic experience with none of the side-effects of illegal drugs; a wise choice on his part, given the beating he'd likely receive the first time he ran into Daredevil. Unfortunately, he decided to advertise his services by giving unannounced and unexplained demonstrations, leading Spider-Man to believe he was a super-villain for some time. Although he eventually cleared the air with the web-head, it doesn't speak well for his judgment; I'm concerned that some enterprising criminal might exploit his naiveté and hire hi as a distraction for an actual crime. Conversely, we could use him if we ever need a distraction. Provided he sticks to private parties and the like, and avoids easily-panicked crowds, I think he's not worth bothering with; at worst, he a harmless annoyance.

TREATMENT: Send him a warning about disturbing the peace.

CLASSIFICATION	HUMAN
GOALS	NIHILISM
SCOPE	LOCAL
MEANS	NUISANCE

SPHINX

AFFILIATIONS: None

ENEMIES: Nova, New Warriors, Fantastic Four, Galactus

Anath-Na Mut discovered the legendary and extremely powerful Ka Stone in ancient Egypt thousands of years ago, and he has been manipulating the barriers of time and reality ever since. I believe the Sphinx is a threat on the same level of Kang and Immortus (so far as time travel), Morgan Le Fey (in regard to the construction of alternate realities), the Grandmaster (in manipulating heroes for his own gains), and Galactus (in increasing power levels that threaten the world). Nova reports that after the opening of the Fault in space, the Sphinx got a second Ka stone by defeating a future version of himself, and he literally almost remade the universe in his image. Nova managed to defeat the Sphinx, with the help of some heroes from other time periods, and assures me the Sphinx won't be returning. But how many times have the Avengers said that about Kang, and Ultron, and Dr. Doom? I doubt the world has seen the last of the Sphinx.

TREATMENT: Some sort of permanent containment, or incarceration after the removal of the Ka Stone, though that is likely the only thing keeping the Sphinx alive.

CLASSIFICATION	MUTATE
GOALS	CONQUEST
SCOPE	UNIVERSAL
MEANS	LEADERSHIP

SPIRAL

AFFILIATIONS: Mojo, Freedom Force, the Reavers, Sisterhood of Evil Mutants

ENEMIES: X-Men, Longshot, Avengers

In a bizarre series of extra-temporal and extra-dimensional events, Rita Wayword, a one-time stuntwoman, became the six-armed sorceress Spiral. Loyal primarily to Mojo, who has plagued the X-Men repeatedly to get greater "ratings" in his own dimension, Spiral has joined various villainous factions on Earth, using her magic in support of evil. According to Wolverine, Spiral has a genetic-altering facility in another dimension that she calls her Body Shoppe, and she has used it to alter operatives such as Psylocke, the Reavers, and Lady Deathstrike. Spiral has at times seemingly switched sides and motivations, battling on behalf of the heroes or against a common threat. She has strange connections to Longshot and Shatterstar of X-Factor, and her true motivations remain beyond me. Whatever it is that drives this woman, she is a clear and present danger. Ultimately, she'll need help finding her lost humanity and recovering from her terrible ordeals. As one who has been lost in time and frozen in an iceberg, I can sympathize with her confusion and madness at trying to hold on to a life that sometimes seems to slip away.

TREATMENT: Recommend long-term incarceration with extensive therapy. There must be some way to undo what Mojo did to poor Rita.

CLASSIFICATION	MUTATE
GOALS	NIHILISM
SCOPE	INTERPLANETARY
MEANS	MERCENARY

SPOT

AFFILIATIONS: Kingpin, MODOK, the Hood

ENEMIES: Spider-Man, Tombstone, Black Cat

Johnathon Ohnn was a brilliant research scientist with a Ph.D. in engineering before he was recruited by the Kingpin; a scientific accident left him a permanent conduit to a strange dimension loosely associated with the Darkforce (I've heard this dimension called "Spotworld," though that term was likely used by the Spot himself). As the Spot, Ohnn has had a fairly tragic career as a villain, suffering defeats on his own and as part of the Spider-Man Revenge Squad; both Tombstone and the Hand seemingly slew him on separate occasions, though neither "death" stuck. Spot recently went on a murder spree, killing a group of gangsters, and has been affiliated with the Hood and Mr. Negative. Ohnn can no longer be considered harmless, and he appears to be mentally unstable. It has recently come to light the Spot has a son, Wyatt, who could be in danger by association.

TREATMENT: Ohnn needs to be apprehended, and quickly. Containing a living conduit to another dimension may prove difficult; I'll have to check if Hank Pym or ARMOR's Charles Little Sky have any ideas. Until his powers can be understood and neutralized, imprisonment seems doubtful.

CLASSIFICATION	MUTATE
GOALS	CURE
SCOPE	LOCAL
MEANS	MERCENARY

SPYMASTER

AFFILIATIONS: Greta Abbott, Ghost, Living Laser, Karim Wahwash Najeeb

ENEMIES: Ghost, Happy Hogan, Iron Man, Spymaster (Lemon)

Sinclair Abbott is a wealthy entrepreneur and CEO of the Abbott Foundation who is a firm believer in traditional villainy. Upon learning Tony Stark was Iron Man, Sinclair became the new Spymaster, but not before having his contacts in prison murder the previous Spymaster, Nathan Lemon. Adopting the Spymaster identity, Sinclair began plotting Iron Man's destruction while antagonizing Stark at social events in hopes of pushing him over the edge psychologically. Spymaster teamed with Ghost to help Living Laser escape prison and convinced him to help destroy Iron Man.

Sinclair's wife, Greta Abbott, was apparently killed during the battle between Spymaster, Living Laser, and Iron Man. With nothing to live for, Sinclair seemingly became devoted to destroying Iron Man while giving up his life as a CEO and becoming an assassin and saboteur. Spymaster was contracted by Karim Mahwash Najeeb, chairman of the World Islamic Peace Coalition, to kill Tony Stark, but instead ended up killing Happy Hogan, who interfered in his attempt to kill Stark.

TREATMENT: Recommend life-long incarceration.

CLASSIFICATION	HUMAN
GOALS	WEALTH & FAME
SCOPE	INTERNATIONAL
MEANS	MERCENARY

SQUID

AFFILIATIONS: Hood, Ms. Fortune, Wicked Brigade

ENEMIES: Spider-Man, Punisher, Mr. Negative, Hammerhead

Like too many teenagers, Don Callahan and his girlfriend Laura escaped troubled home lives by turning to crime; unlike most, they also allowed themselves to be mutated into superhumans. With their comrades in the Wicked Brigade, Don and Laura, now the Squid and Ms. Fortune, respectively, embarked on an extremely undistinguished criminal career. After one brief humiliating fight with Spider-Man, both Laura and his employers turned on him, and the Squid set out on his own, eventually finding a place in the Hood's criminal syndicate. The Squid may have been the lucky one; Ms. Fortune's

dropped off our radar, and the rest of the Wicked Brigade was killed by a zombie virus in the Caribbean. Despite his limited ambition and competence, the Squid seems to have held his own with the more experienced members of the Hood's gang until he was recently captured. The Squid may not be wholly irredeemable; in my opinion, he'd be a strong candidate for the Thunderbolts program if he can muster the courage to volunteer.

TREATMENT: Recommend incarceration; make sure the pipes in his cell have fine grating in them to prevent escape.

CLASSIFICATION	MUTATE
GOALS	WEALTH & FAME
SCOPE	LOCAL
MEANS	ROBBERY

GABRIEL STACY

AFFILIATIONS: Norman Osborn

ENEMIES: Spider-Man, Harry Osborn, Sarah Stacy

Our information on Gabriel Stacy is limited; most of what we know comes from Spider-Man, and he's been somewhat reluctant to give us the full story. Stacy is the illegitimate son of Norman Osborn; although he was born less than ten years ago, Osborn's Goblin-serum-damaged DNA rapidly aged Stacy to adulthood. Manipulated by Osborn into believing Spider-Man had killed his mother, Stacy injected himself with Osborn's serum, arresting his aging but driving him insane. After a brief stint as the "Gray Goblin," Stacy had another encounter with Spider-Man in France and dropped off the radar. He's recently resurfaced in America, having apparently been a test subject for Osborn's attempts to

combine the Goblin formula with the super-soldier serum. It makes me sick to see the way Dr. Erskine's work has been corrupted over the years — and especially to see it used on a man like Stacy, whose entire life has been shaped by a lunatic like Osborn. It looks as if Stacy may have stolen the American Son armor intended for his half brother, Harry Osborn, and is using it to act as a vigilante; while the world always needs more heroes, Stacy is too unstable to be trusted.

TREATMENT: Recommend long-term psychological care.

CLASSIFICATION	MUTATE
GOALS	REVENGE
SCOPE	LOCAL
MEANS	MERCENARY

MORGAN STARK

AFFILIATIONS: Count Nefaria, Maggia, Mordecai Midas, Madame Masque

ENEMIES: Iron Man, War Machine

Tony Stark's cousin Morgan is not a hardened criminal but suffers from a weak moral character. Shirking responsibility for his failures in life, Morgan prefers to blame his brilliant, successful cousin. Like Tony, Morgan has an addictive personality, but whereas Tony fought to overcome his alcoholism, Morgan succumbed to gambling, piling up debts he tried to escape by conspiring with Tony's enemies such as the Maggia and Mordecai Midas against him. Each time Tony kept Morgan out of prison; perhaps this is foolish, but if Morgan were my relative, I might do the same. When Fujikawa Industries bought Stark Enterprises, they put Morgan in charge of North American operations, and for a time he did a reasonably good job. But Morgan erred in attempting to utilize the colossal alien robot Ultimo as a power source. Recently, Morgan ingested Ultimo's neural net and was transformed into a gigantic version of Ultimo. War Machine induced Ultimo to separate itself from Morgan, who returned to normal human form.

TREATMENT: If Morgan Stark is given a job he can handle, as he was at Stark-Fujikawa, he will have less motivation for plotting against his cousin Tony. But Morgan must always be watched, to keep him both from gambling and from making horrific errors.

CLASSIFICATION	HUMAN
GOALS	WEALTH & FAME
SCOPE	INTERNATIONAL
MEANS	BUSINESS

STEGRON

AFFILIATIONS: Ka-Zar, dinosaurs

ENEMIES: Roxxon, Spider-Man

Using tissue samples of dinosaurs living in Antarctica's hidden Savage Land, scientist Vincent Stegron repeated the process that transformed Dr. Curt Connors into the murderous Lizard to become a self-proclaimed "Dinosaur Man." Unlike Connors, Stegron deliberately chose to alter himself and rarely returns to human form. He tried to conquer the world with dinosaur armies a couple of times, running afoul of Spider-Man, the Savage Land's jungle lord Ka-Zar, and others, but eventually took up semi-permanent residence in the Savage Land. Though he has occasionally ventured forth to make a pest of himself, he now primarily acts as defender of the Land's dinosaurs. Despite remaining contemptuous of humanity, Stegron found common ground with his old foe Ka-Zar in jointly defending the Savage Land from exploitation, and a realization that Ka-Zar deters at least some incursions has maintained their uneasy truce. Stegron has even demonstrated an altruistic side; when SHIELD had the ape-like Moon-Boy abducted for research, leaving the unique saurian Devil Dinosaur pining close to death for his missing friend, Stegron let himself be captured in a ploy to free Moon-Boy.

TREATMENT: So long as he remains content to defend the Savage Land's dinosaurs from outsiders, Stegron's threat is minimal. Return him to the Savage Land, but monitor his actions.

CLASSIFICATION	MUTATE
GOALS	SAURIAN SUPREMACY
SCOPE	INTERNATIONAL
MEANS	SCIENCE

STRIKEFORCE X

AFFILIATIONS: Roxxon, Blackguard

ENEMIES: Wolverine

I understand why governments want to create super-soldiers. But putting a super hero in the employ of a political body contains so many inherent problems that the chance for success is far outweighed by the chance for failure — disastrous failure. Weapon X was one such program, producing a number of superhumans, including modification on Wolverine. When Blackguard, a subsidiary of Roxxon, tried to recreate Weapon X for the private sector, in essence creating a group of corporate mercenaries, the result was Strikeforce X: a group of twelve dishonorably discharged men, convicted of crimes ranging from rape to murder, given artificial healing factors, laser claws, enhanced senses, and Adamantium bones. Wolverine obviously took this one to heart, and he personally saw these monstrosities destroyed; though I don't always agree with his methods, he gets the job done. His reporter friend, Melita Garner of the Post, aided him in turning the US government against Blackguard as well. Roxxon's ability to perpetuate criminal acts like Strikeforce X without tarnishing their reputation amazes me.

TREATMENT: Executive involvement to ensure Blackguard never re-forms or continues its experimentation. Containment and/or destruction of the Weapon X files.

CLASSIFICATION	GANG
GOALS	SERVANTHOOD
SCOPE	INTERNATIONAL
MEANS	FOLLOWERS

SWARM

AFFILIATIONS: Exterminators

ENEMIES: Avengers, Champions, Alyosha Kraven, Spider-Man, Thunderbolts

Evading capture at WWII's end, Nazi scientist Fritz von Meyer set up in South America to develop chemical weapons from insect toxins, but an attack by killer bees mutated by meteor radiation transformed him into Swarm, a psychic entity focused around his skeletal remains, with a body formed from the bees that had slain him. Los Angeles' Champions stopped him from turning the city into an enormous hive, and since then Swarm has been revived and dispersed several times, usually by separating him from his queen bee or skeleton. He hates humanity in general, but harbors a special antipathy for Spider-Man, viewing arachnids as apoidea's natural foes; the only time he's worked with others has been to attack Spidey. It used to be possible to capture Swarm by locking von Meyer's skeleton away from any bees, but Venom recently devoured that skeleton unintentionally freeing Swarm of that weakness; his mind now centers on any suitable queen bee.

TREATMENT: We should consult Reed Richards and Charles Xavier to see if it's possible to contain von Meyer's psyche. Until they come up with something, the best we can probably hope to do is locate and destroy his queen bee, dispersing his swarm, each time he manifests.

CLASSIFICATION	MUTATE
GOALS	CONQUEST
SCOPE	INTERNATIONAL
MEANS	LEADERSHIP

TABOO

AFFILIATIONS: Mole Man

ENEMIES: Avengers, Beast, Hulk, Nova, Thing, Wasp

Taboo hails from an unidentified extraterrestrial race. We do know Taboo's people consider him a retrograde; his desire to conquer others is what led him to our world, but his ability has never matched his ambition. Taboo's body appears to be a gelatinous substance, a thick, oozing slime. So long as even a fragment of his form persists, he can regain his full body. He can expand his size and smother humans in his grasp, yet his unearthly appearance is the veritable knot in his hose. He has a sly penchant for trickery, but being (by human standards) a horrible monster in both body and spirit, no one has fallen for his schemes for very long. Unable to conquer by mind or might or even walk amongst humans unnoticed, Taboo threw in his lot with the Mole Man's army of monsters. No doubt this would-be conqueror from the stars chafes at being a mere subordinate, trapped underground.

TREATMENT: Confer with Nova about possibility of contacting Taboo's people and transferring him to their custody. If Taboo is "ill," perhaps their psychiatric resources can aid or even cure him.

CLASSIFICATION	EXTRATERRESTRIAL
GOALS	CONQUEST
SCOPE	LOCAL
MEANS	WARFARE

TASKMASTER

AFFILIATIONS: Albino, Agency-X, Batroc's Brigade, Cabal, Copycat, Constrictor, Deadpool, Dr. Octopus, Grim Reaper, Justin Hammer, Norman Osborn, Outlaw, Red Skull, Spymaster, Wizard, Org

ENEMIES: AIM, Black Choppers, Black Swan, Captain America, Cyber Ninjas, Daredevil, Deadpool, Dr. Doom, Elektra, Hydra, Inquisition, Legions of the Living Lightning, Militiamen, Mr. X, Moon Knight, Org, Secret Empire, Sons of the Serpent, Spider-Man, Sunset Bain, Tombstone, Trenchcoat Mafia, ULTIMATUM

Taskmaster is an exceptionally skilled, prodigious savant of mnemonic talents, otherwise known as photographic reflexes, which enable him to watch another person's physical movements and duplicate them without practice, no matter how complex. Over the years he has not only trained innumerable criminals and super villains, but has also reduced evaded prison in exchange for working for the government training heroes like USAgent and Initiative recruits. Taskmaster avoids direct confrontations when possible, making him one of the more difficult villains to capture as he is more apt to retreat than take a chance at being captured.

TREATMENT: Recommend hiring him as Avengers staff member to train heroes of both this and the next generation, but keep under permanent house arrest.

CLASSIFICATION	HUMAN
GOALS	WEALTH & FAME
SCOPE	INTERNATIONAL
MEANS	MERCENARY

TEMUJIN

AFFILIATIONS: Agents of Atlas, Mandarin

ENEMIES: Iron Man, Ultra Adaptoid, MODOK

It's difficult to predict the effect that having a super villain as a parent will have on a child's psyche. There is a vast gulf between those who follow the route of Ezekiel Stane and those who are Fury's Secret Warriors. Fortunately, Temujin was raised at a remote monastery in China, far away from the influence of his father, the megalomaniacal Mandarin. Upon his father's seeming death, Temujin inherited his powerful alien rings and was pressured by his attendants to continue his father's vendetta against Iron Man. However, after several unfulfilling altercations with Iron Man, Temujin resolved to use his father's resources to bring tranquility rather than terror to the world. After disposing of his father's rings, Temujin was chosen by the Atlas Foundation to serve as Atlas leader Jimmy Woo's understudy and eventual successor. Although their relationship got off to a contentious start, Temujin and Woo developed a mutual respect, and Temujin was apparently appointed to oversee the Atlas Foundation's former rivals — the Great Wall.

TREATMENT: Even though he appears to be on the straight and narrow, we should keep an eye on Temujin's activities in Asia. Although he believes he has attained spiritual purity by channeling all his anger into martial arts and other disciplines, he is also known to be headstrong and stubborn.

CLASSIFICATION	HUMAN
GOALS	CONQUEST
SCOPE	INTERNATIONAL
MEANS	LEADERSHIP

THANOS

AFFILIATIONS: Death, Reptyl, Infinity Watch

ENEMIES: Avengers, Drax the Destroyer, Silver Surfer, Magus, Goddess, Tyrant, Nebula, Walker, Hunger

The mad Titan Thanos has committed greater atrocities than anyone else in these files, and yet his case also presents the greatest conundrum. The brother of my fellow Avenger Starfox, Thanos is one of the Eternals of Titan, a race that dwells on Saturn's moon of that name. Born with a monstrous appearance, Thanos felt an outcast, and fell obsessively in love with Death, which appeared to him in female form. Enraged at being exiled from Titan, Thanos massacred most of its population in a nuclear attack, including his mother. Since then, Thanos has sought and sometimes achieved virtual omnipotence. Once he used the Infinity Gauntlet to wipe out half the population of the universe; thankfully, that horrific act was reversed. Yet Thanos has also allied with his nemesis Adam Warlock and other heroes to combat threats to the universe. In the past, he has attempted to reform and once even retired to lead a peaceful life as a farmer. But Thanos remains mentally unstable, and in seeking his life's purpose is likely to create devastation on a cosmic scale.

TREATMENT: Earth has no means of imprisoning or killing Thanos. He has sought redemption in the past and with help from allies like Warlock may be capable of achieving it.

CLASSIFICATION	EXTRATERRESTRIAL
GOALS	NIHILISM
SCOPE	UNIVERSAL
MEANS	WARFARE

TITAN

AFFILIATIONS: John Cartwright

ENEMIES: Avengers, GRAMPA

A so-called "Amphibian from Atlantis," Titan seems to represent an unidentified aquatic species. Given his immense size, it's a wonder so few sightings of his kind have been recorded. Titan claims to be from Atlantis; perhaps he's a one-of-a-kind, one of Namor's people transformed into a sea monster. Regardless, Titan's only desire seems to be conquest of the surface world. I can't imagine the oceans could be that restrictive, even to a being of his size. In his first identified sighting, Titan promised a fortune to whoever would share Earth's defense secrets with him; US auto magnate John Cartwright accepted his terms and disappeared with Titan beneath the ocean; Cartwright is missing, presumed dead. Strangely, it was decades before Titan returned, this time assaulting the coast of France. Thankfully, Pym's Avengers and the GRAMPA agency swiftly ended the attack.

TREATMENT: Query Namor about Titan's origins and usual haunts. Titan may be susceptible to Atlantis' Horn of Proteus, which could be used to force him into an underwater prison. Alternatively, Hank's Pym Particles could shrink him down to a more manageable size for confinement on US soil. Perhaps he'll prove reasonable when he has to look us in the eye.

CLASSIFICATION	SUB-SPECIES
GOALS	CONQUEST
SCOPE	INTERNATIONAL
MEANS	WARFARE

TOLTEC

AFFILIATIONS: Unknown

ENEMIES: Moon Knight

It's unknown how long the vigilante Toltec has been meting out his violent brand of justice in the back alleys of Mexico City and countryside of central-eastern Mexico. Although I'm aware Moon Knight had a run-in with him, he speaks very little of their encounter. From what I can piece together from Policía Federal reports, Toltec believes he is avenging the poor and disadvantaged residents of Mexico by stalking and brutally dismembering the criminals who would prey upon them. With a name and appearance inspired by Aztec lore, Thor has speculated Toltec may be a demigod affiliated with the Aztec pantheon, or even an agent empowered by and acting on behalf of Tezcatlipoca, the brutal god of war and vengeance. The residents of Mexico City's poorest colonias would tend to agree, as Toltec has attained a legendary, almost mythical, status among the lower class, law enforcement agents, and criminals alike. Whatever his nature and origin, I hope Toltec keeps his activities south of the border for the foreseeable future — the last thing w need is a vigilante as lethal as the Punisher combined with the populist appeal of Robin Hood.

TREATMENT: Frankly, not enough is known about Toltec to recommend a course of treatment upon incarceration. Is he merely mortal? Or, as many in the Distrito Federal believe, is he a divine agent of the Aztec pantheon?

CLASSIFICATION	HUMAN
GOALS	REVENGE
SCOPE	NATIONAL
MEANS	VIGILANTE

TRULL

AFFILIATIONS: Big Wheel, possibly Blackout, Scarecrow, Madcap, others

ENEMIES: Ghost Riders

I've encountered some pretty strange and crazy things in my years as Captain America. From being turned into a werewolf to fighting the Asthma Monster, there have been few things that made me look twice. Then there's Trull, or as he prefers, Trull the Unhuman or Trull the Mighty. Trull is a steam shovel, albeit an alien-possessed one. As best we can piece together, Trull's body was destroyed when his spacecraft crashed on Earth, but his ability to transfer his essence to anything mechanical led to his taking over the vehicle. Believed destroyed, Trull has turned up again recently, though the details are sketchy. Daimon Hellstrom claims Trull was part of a group brought together to destroy both Ghost Riders and conquer heaven, failing in both, but with Daimon, one must take everything with a grain of salt. Trull's ability to transfer his essence to any mechanical item must be considered in any confrontation.

TREATMENT: Recommend containment in a form he can't leave and possible extradition to his planet's authorities.

CLASSIFICATION	EXTRATERRESTRIAL
GOALS	CONQUEST
SCOPE	LOCAL
MEANS	MERCENARY

DAMIAN TRYP

AFFILIATIONS: Cortex, Singularity Investigations

ENEMIES: X-Factor

Damian Tryp says he is a killcrop, someone born with superhuman powers evident from birth; it's uncertain whether this is a separate genus from mutants, or just his name for one mutant subtype. Jamie Madrox believes Tryp murdered Madrox's parents, but he mostly stayed off the official radar until setting up Singularity Investigations. Supposedly a father and son company, both Tryp Sr. and Jr. were actually the same man, thanks to some temporal shenanigans, and there was a third, even older Tryp, behind the scenes. Tryp claimed X-Factor's investigation into M-Day's cause might lead to mutant repowering and a future he'd experienced where mutants exterminated mankind. If true, then his motivation was good, but Singularity planned to unleash a lethal virus targeted at the surviving mutant population, until a rogue Madrox duplicate blew up Singularity's headquarters, apparently slaying Tryp Jr. and Sr. However the eldest Tryp survived as some kind of temporal ghost, and Madrox reports Tryp (presumably the ghost, but maybe it was one of the younger Tryps; it's hard to be sure with time travelers) was later behind the Cortex assassinations.

TREATMENT: While I don't agree with his genocidal methods, we must prevent a future where mankind is destroyed. We need to assess the validity of Tryp's story.

CLASSIFICATION	MUTANT?
GOALS	REVENGE
SCOPE	NATIONAL
MEANS	LEADERSHIP

U-FOES

AFFILIATIONS: Hood, Initiative, Leader, Master of the World, Norman Osborn

ENEMIES: Avengers, Crossfire's gang, Hulk, Oracle Inc.'s Heroes for Hire, Portal, Puma

A would-be business rival to Tony Stark, industrialist Simon Utrecht sought to reproduce Reed Richards' rocket flight, hoping to be reborn a superhuman like the Fantastic Four; he and his crew — his lover Ann Darnell, her brother, Jimmy Darnell, and the ship's designer and pilot Mike Steel — were mutated by cosmic rays, transforming them into the telekinetic Vector, gaseous Vapor, radioactive X-Ray and metallic behemoth Ironclad, respectively. Dubbing themselves the U-Foes, the group went on to be lackeys for one criminal mastermind after another.

Recently, as part of the Hood's organization, they joined Osborn's corrupted Initiative, were assigned to be North Carolina's state team — I presume the Tar Heel state had annoyed Osborn somehow — and struck the first blow in what became the Siege of Asgard. Though the U-Foes have the potential to be truly dangerous, they are dogged by a constant problem — Utrecht lacks the vision of either Stark or Richards, and without that the U-Foes are condemned to be at best pale imitators and goons for hire.

TREATMENT: Each of the U-Foes is a ruthless killer, though Vector has occasionally shown signs of regret. Utrecht may be a Thunderbolts candidate; others recommended for lengthy incarceration.

CLASSIFICATION	GROUP
GOALS	CHALLENGES
SCOPE	NATIONAL
MEANS	MERCENARIES

ULTIMATUM

AFFILIATIONS: Flag-Smasher, Red Skull, Sabretooth, Marduk

ENEMIES: Captain America, SHIELD, Domino, Punisher, Moon Knight, Silver Sable, Spider-Man, USAgent, V-Battalion

Many terrorist organizations are driven by fanatical nationalist fervor, but not ULTIMATUM. Founded by my old enemy Flag-Smasher, ULTIMATUM (Underground Liberated Totally Integrated Mobile Army To Unite Mankind) follows his belief that nationalism — patriotism — divides the people of the world and must be abolished. They intend to use terrorism to overthrow every government in the world, and target symbols of patriotism, including our National Archives and Captain America: ULTIMATUM once took the passengers of an airplane hostage and demanded me in exchange. At one point the Red Skull took over ULTIMATUM, but Flag-Smasher reasserted control. Reportedly the mutant Domino assassinated the original Flag-Smasher (though many of my foes have returned from seeming death before), and another ULTIMATUM agent has become the new Flag-Smasher. ULTIMATUM has access to highly advanced weaponry, and most of its agents have had intensive military training, making their terrorist army particularly formidable. ULTIMATUM even briefly took control of the nation of Rumekistan.

TREATMENT: Some crimefighters have had success against individuals like Flag-Smasher, but the forces of SHIELD are best suited to combating ULTIMATUM as a whole. ULTIMATUM members are dangerous fanatics and should be put on trial and imprisoned.

CLASSIFICATION	GROUP
GOALS	CONQUEST
SCOPE	INTERNATIONAL
MEANS	TERRORISM

ULTIMO

AFFILIATIONS: "Team War Machine," Mandarin

ENEMIES: Armory, Avengers, Golden-Blade, Iron Man, Rajaki, War Machine

Ultimo was created as a doomsday machine to destroy whole civilizations throughout the galaxy. Since arriving on Earth, Ultimo became a pawn of the Mandarin, who regularly used him against Iron Man and the Avengers. He was nearly destroyed on several occasions, but always proved more resilient than we thought. He was disassembled after Armory and the Avengers took him down in San Francisco, but due to questionable decisions Ultimo's technology was sold to private organizations resulting in the creation of a highly contagious virus used by Eaglestar International in Aqiria. Ultimo created a new body for itself, but War Machine and his team foiled its plan to destroy humanity and even convinced Ultimo to purge its genocidal programming. War Machine left cybernetic genius Suzi Endo in charge of turning Ultimo into a benevolent technological being. Though Ultimo seems under control, parts of the malevolent version are most likely still in the possession of Roxxon and other organizations that worked with Ultimo-tech.

TREATMENT: Recommend leaving Ultimo in Suzi Endo's custody. Search and destroy any remains of Ultimo's original form.

CLASSIFICATION	ROBOT
GOALS	SERVANTHOOD
SCOPE	INTERNATIONAL
MEANS	FOLLOWER

X

ULTRON

AFFILIATIONS: Grim Reaper, Alkhema, Dr. Doom, Jocasta, Masters of Evil, the Phalanx

ENEMIES: Wasp, Avengers, Machine Man, Daredevil, Mechadoom, Nova, Warlock

The greatest mistake my friend and colleague Henry Pym ever made was creating the mad sentient robot Ultron. Experimenting with artificial intelligence, Hank based Ultron's mind on his own brain patterns. But Hank was not then aware of his own growing mental instability, and I'm sorry to say safely designing such a complex artificial brain was beyond even his skills. The result was that Ultron developed a maniacal Oedipus complex and determined to destroy not only his "father" Pym, but also his allies, the Avengers, and the entire human race. Ultron has been reconstructed and upgraded numerous times, usually in a robotic body made of Adamantium. He has even developed the ability to mentally control hundreds of robotic bodies at once, becoming a nearly unstoppable army. Ultron committed his greatest atrocity against humanity when he massacred the entire population of the European nation of Slorenia, but even that pales against the billions of Kree who perished at the hands of the Phalanx under his leadership.

TREATMENT: I suspect it may be impossible to destroy Ultron permanently: even if his Adamantium body is obliterated, his consciousness can survive. Perhaps scientists could find a way to reprogram Ultron to correct the mistakes Henry Pym made in designing his mind.

CLASSIFICATION	ROBOT
GOALS	CONQUEST
SCOPE	INTERPLANETARY
MEANS	WARFARE

GENERAL ULYSSES

AFFILIATIONS: General Combest, Dr. Nacht

ENEMIES: New Mutants, X-Men

Years ago, in one of the X-Men's most complicated battles, demons struck New York City and inanimate objects came to life everywhere. As I understand it from Wolverine and Beast, several mutant infants were used to power a gateway between Earth and limbo. It has now come to light that after this conflict concluded, an anti-mutant military group, including two American generals, Ulysses and Combest (though Combest is dead, at last report), took custody of those babies. The generals oversaw a military base's construction in limbo, where time passes at an accelerated rate, and Ulysses and his men spent several years there. They also apparently trained and weaponized the mutant children. Ulysses and his men recently kidnapped the X-Man Pixie, and is yet another group seeking to destroy the world's remaining mutants. The entire world has been through a terrible ordeal in recent years, but none have been hit harder than the X-Men, who continue to suffer casualties. Wolverine assures me the situation with Gen. Ulysses is "under control," but I have offered my support and that of the Avengers to the X-Men.

TREATMENT: General Ulysses has to be brought in and made accountable to a military tribunal; what he's done is tantamount to training child soldiers.

CLASSIFICATION	HUMAN
GOALS	CONQUEST
SCOPE	INTERDIMENSIONAL
MEANS	WARFARE

UNSPOKEN

AFFILIATIONS: Inhumans, Alpha Primitives

ENEMIES: Inhumans, Avengers, People's Defense Force, GRAMPA

Quicksilver tells me the Unspoken is something of a bogeyman to the Inhumans, a monster discussed only in fearful whispers. He was Inhuman king, but was deposed after stealing the ancient Slave Engine from Attilan. The engine generates Xerigen, a crystalline substance that transforms humans into Alpha Primitives, the simple-minded laborers of Inhuman society. Even without this doomsday device, the Unspoken is extremely powerful. He claims he can access any Inhuman ability, a frightening thought. The Unspoken remained exiled in a cave for decades, but re-emerged following a war between the US and Attilan. Apparently he once tried to save humanity from the doomsday device, but now believes we are not worth saving. The Wasp's Avengers defeated him, restoring those transformed into Alpha Primitives and turning the Unspoken into a helpless senile man. The Chinese government apparently agreed with the Wasp's recommendation to let the Unspoken return to his cave to die in peace.

TREATMENT: Wasp's decisions are not usually made in haste, but perhaps the Unspoken should be located and contained. An individual with his powers and knowledge of Xerigen Crystals could be an even greater threat should he ever regain his faculties.

CLASSIFICATION	SUB-SPECIES
GOALS	CONQUEST
SCOPE	INTERNATIONAL
MEANS	LEADERSHIP

VALI HALFLING

AFFILIATIONS: The Pantheon

ENEMIES: Hulk, Thor, Amadeus Cho

As a youth, Vali was taken as an apprentice in sorcery by his father, Asgardian god of mischief Loki; but when Loki caught Vali stealing from him, he cursed his son to remain an adolescent for eternity. Vali fled Asgard to Earth, where he adopted the name "Agamemnon" and assembled the Pantheon, a think tank dedicated to detecting and averting calamities. Over the centuries, Vali gathered many of his descendants to act as the Pantheon's inner circle; but in recent times a bargain Vali struck with the extraterrestrial Troyjans wherein he allowed them their pick of his descendants in exchange for genetic manipulation secrets was exposed. Vali was ousted from the Pantheon and perished. But when Thor resurrected the Asgardians following the latest Ragnarok, Vali was reborn with a new goal: to attain omniscience and overthrow the Council of Godheads, whom he viewed as corrupt and ineffective. Having reasserted himself as leader of the Pantheon, Vali's plans were thwarted by Thor and Olympus Group CEO Amadeus Cho.

TREATMENT: Vali Halfling was last seen stranded in Duat, the nether realm of the Heliopolitan gods of Egypt. Should he ever resurface in the mortal realm, he should be apprehended and transferred to Asgardian custody. I fear he's too crafty and possesses too many loyal followers on Earth to incarcerate in the Raft.

CLASSIFICATION	MAGICAL BEING
GOALS	CONQUEST
SCOPE	INTERPLANETARY
MEANS	MAGIC

VAMPIRES

AFFILIATIONS: Dracula, Baron Blood, Lilith, Nina Price, Xarus

ENEMIES: Blade, Doctor Strange, Frank Drake, Hannibal King, Elsa Bloodstone

I never imagined when I was a young boy watching Bela Lugosi in the new "Dracula" movie that a decade later I would be battling actual vampires. It was in 1942 that I first fought Baron Blood of Hitler's Third Reich. Possessing superhuman strength, hypnotic powers, and the ability to transform into bats or mist, any vampire is a formidable opponent. They spread their plague by causing their slain victims to rise again as "undead" vampires; driven by their lust to feed on human blood, most vampires become ruthless predators. The most powerful and dangerous of all vampires is their leader, Dracula himself, who is all too real. A brilliant strategist, Dracula even recently sought to conquer Britain and his children have engineered a plot to create new vampires en masse, using suicide bombers whose blood infects innocent bystanders. Although I and other costumed heroes have had successes fighting vampires, vampire hunting is best left to specialists like Blade and Elsa Bloodstone.

TREATMENT: It is extremely rare to find a vampire like Hannibal King who has the will to resist preying on humans. Most vampires must be destroyed. However, experience has shown that it is nearly impossible to destroy the most powerful vampires permanently.

CLASSIFICATION	MAGICAL BEINGS
GOALS	SURVIVAL
SCOPE	INTERNATIONAL
MEANS	CONSUMPTION

VENOM

AFFILIATIONS: Norman Osborn, the Masters of Evil, the Thunderbolts

ENEMIES: Spider-Man, J. Jonah Jameson, the Avengers

Years ago, Spider-Man returned from an extraterrestrial sojourn wearing a new costume that proved to be an alien Symbiote. Though he escaped becoming its permanent host, it has afflicted Earth ever since, subsequently empowering Venom, while its offspring turned hosts into Carnage, Toxin and others. There was even a large scale Symbiote invasion, with the creatures possessing dozens of infected humans. The newest Venom is Mac Gargan, who was trapped in the Scorpion suit for years. I faced Scorpion years back, when he teamed with Mr. Hyde, and he was a particularly nasty opponent. After multiple revenge schemes against Spider-Man and J. Jonah Jameson and joining a few teams over the years, Gargan eventually adopted the Venom suit. As a criminal, as part of the Thunderbolts, and as part of the Avengers (posing as Spider-Man, ironically), Venom has struggled with mental illness, extreme ferocity, and brutally disgusting responses in combat (including biting off Steel Spider's arm and eating several Skrulls).

TREATMENT: Gargan needs to be stripped of the Symbiote suit, and that monstrosity needs to be destroyed once and for all. Spider-Man shares little hope of rehabilitation for Gargan.

CLASSIFICATION	MUTATE
GOALS	NIHILISM
SCOPE	NATIONAL
MEANS	MERCENARY

VULTURE

AFFILIATIONS: Electro

ENEMIES: Spider-Man, the Maggia

"Vulture" appears to be a popular name in the criminal community: I battled a few "Vultures" back in the 1940s. One of Spider-Man's longtime adversaries is another Vulture, Adrian Toomes. But as the decades pass, criminals seem to this old soldier to be getting more vicious. Now there is a new, younger Vulture who plagues Spider-Man. Like Toomes, this new Vulture can fly, but he seems to have been grotesquely mutated, and can spit acid at his victims. While Toomes is primarily a thief, the new Vulture purports to be a vigilante, but he is hardly a hero. Not only does he murder criminals, but he even devours their remains, like the bird who is his namesake. I am appalled that even a costumed criminal could stoop to such horrific behavior. Vulture attacked New York's mayor, J. Jonah Jameson, thinking him responsible for transforming him into this vile creature, but Spider-Man saved him. Next, Vulture became convinced it was the Maggia who turned him into a monster. Whoever was to blame, I hold the Vulture responsible for this cannibalism and hope Spider-Man or the authorities can bring him to justice.

TREATMENT: The new Vulture must be captured and safely imprisoned. I hope scientists can find a way to reverse his mutation and, if possible, eliminate his taste for human flesh.

CLASSIFICATION	MUTATE
GOALS	REVENGE
SCOPE	LOCAL
MEANS	VIGILANTE

WATCHDOGS

AFFILIATIONS: Red Skull, Captain America (Burnside)

ENEMIES: Steve Rogers, Captain America (Barnes), USAgent, Falcon, Battlestar

"I solemnly vow to walk the virtuous path, to safeguard society from the forces that would corrupt it, and to destroy the enemies of decency, morality, and the values upon which our country was founded." This is the oath of the Watchdogs, a domestic terrorist group devoted to enforcing their vision of a perfect America through any means necessary. Their vision, however, is a country that is white, heterosexual, and strictly moral. After my recent "death," the Watchdogs dedicated themselves to my memory — imagine a group started by the Red Skull that commit murders and kidnappings, aligning themselves with me. Needless to say, my ideas about what the American dream is do not limit the choices and diversity of our country. The Watchdogs consist of hundreds of members across the country. In their most recent venture, they tried blowing up Hoover Dam, and this battle led to the death of the 1950s Captain America (who had taken over leadership of the faction) at the hands of the current Cap. I would not deny the Watchdogs the opportunity to speak publicly about their views, but they cannot commit crimes to force their views upon others.

TREATMENT: Incarceration for members with criminal convictions; seize all armaments and keep frequented sites under observation.

CLASSIFICATION	TERRORISTS
GOALS	CONQUEST
SCOPE	NATIONAL
MEANS	TERRORISM

WHITE RABBIT

AFFILIATIONS: Hood, Arcade, White Rabbit Gang, Terrible Two

ENEMIES: Black Cat, Frog-Man, Gibbon, Grizzly, Spider-Man, Wolverine

White Rabbit is a bored billionaire widow, who finances her own criminal endeavors and dresses up in a costume influenced by Lewis Carrol's *Alice in Wonderland* novels. She is definitely not sane, but looking back at her career she can't be taken seriously despite her expensive gadgets, including jet-boots, a blimp, a giant rabbit robot and her infamous Bunnymobile. She even financed the creation of genetically altered killer bunnies. Until her recent alliance with the Hood, her allies were mostly inept criminals like the Walrus or actors she paid to pose as her partners. For some time she seriously regarded Frog-Man as her nemesis, and none other than Gibbon and Grizzly stopped one of her most thoroughly thought-out schemes. She also had a short fling with Arcade that ended with her trapped in the Savage Land. It's shocking how ruthless she has become in recent times. She definitely needs all the psychiatric help she can get.

TREATMENT: Recommend placing her on disability and committing her to a mental hospital. Maybe taking away any trace from her life of crime helps her to remember what a wonderful life she once had.

CLASSIFICATION	HUMAN
GOALS	WEALTH & FAME
SCOPE	LOCAL
MEANS	ROBBERY

WITCHFIRE

AFFILIATIONS: Alpha Flight, Belasco

ENEMIES: X-Men, Magik, Llan the Sorcerer, the Hardliners

Ananym is the alleged daughter of the demon Belasco, a deadly sorcerer who has faced the X-Men and Ka-Zar in battle, and who was responsible for the kidnapping and aging of young Illyana Rasputin into Magik. Apparently hailing from limbo, Ananym was one of many superhuman operatives recruited into Canada's Department H program, which divided its recruits into Alpha, Beta, and Gamma Flights. Struggling with not having memories of her past and an underlying evil nature, Ananym took the name Witchfire and went on several missions alongside her teammates, succumbing to the evil in her more than once. When the Goddess attacked the Earth, Witchfire gave into her demonic side and was only narrowly defeated. In recent months, she has tried claiming her father's realm for herself, and she had a battle with the X-Men that nearly ended in the death of more than one of them. Wielding her vastly powerful magics, Witchfire is a deadly threat to all on Earth, and the Avengers stand ready to stop her at any time. I should consult with Hank Pym and Charles Little Sky about permanently closing off limbo from Earth.

TREATMENT: Recommend containment at ARMOR facility.

CLASSIFICATION	MAGICAL BEING
GOALS	CONQUEST
SCOPE	INTERDIMENSIONAL
MEANS	MAGIC

XRAVEN

AFFILIATIONS: Mr. Sinister

ENEMIES: Spider-Man, X-Men

Xraven is apparently one of the maniacal geneticist Mr. Sinister's creations, a clone of Kraven the Hunter infused with the powers of the original X-Men — Cyclops, Angel, Beast, Jean Grey, and Iceman — and armed with Vibranium weaponry. Sinister sent Xraven to exterminate inferior mutants and collect samples from others, eventually bringing him into conflict with Spider-Man and the X-Men. They eventually turned him against Sinister, but if he shares any of the original Kraven's personality, then he's extremely dangerous and is likely operating on his own agenda now; we need to learn what that agenda is. Just because he was created by an evil man for evil purposes doesn't mean he's a monster — the Vision and Jocasta are proof of that. That said, he's committed at least one murder, so we need to bring him in.

TREATMENT: Xraven should be incarcerated quickly, before the Kraven family can locate him; given their recent killing spree, which they accomplished with little more than spears and knives, I shudder to think what might happen if they had access to Xraven.

CLASSIFICATION	MUTATE
GOALS	SURVIVAL
SCOPE	LOCAL
MEANS	VIGILANTE

YMIR

AFFILIATIONS: Giants of Jotunheim

ENEMIES: Thor, Odin, Asgardians, Surtur, Avengers

Although Thor and Valkyrie often tell me myths are only stories the listener ascribes meaning to, mythology still boggles my simple, mortal mind at times. Case in point: Norse myth maintains the giant Ymir (or "Aurgelmir," as Thor sometimes calls him) was slain by Thor's father and uncles — his flesh creating the earth, his blood creating the seas, his bones creating the mountains, and his hair creating the trees. Yet Ymir, very much alive, has returned on several occasions to threaten the very world his deceased body allegedly gave form to millennia earlier. Ymir sired the entire race of giants inhabiting the realm of Jotunheim prior to Odin imprisoning him and his army in the fiery realm of Muspelheim. Ymir recently attacked New York City, and it took several teams of Avengers to occupy him until the Olympian god Ares obtained the Twilight Sword, an artifact capable of banishing Ymir from the Earth realm.

TREATMENT: Standing over 1000 feet tall and possessing incalculable physical strength as well as a body constantly generating intense cold, there's no question Ymir can't be incarcerated by mere mortals — there isn't a prison in existence to restrain him. Rather, the Twilight Sword should be kept available in order to send the ice giant to another dimension should he ever return.

CLASSIFICATION	MAGICAL BEING
GOALS	CONQUEST
SCOPE	INTERDIMENSIONAL
MEANS	WARFARE

YOUNG MASTERS

AFFILIATIONS: Loki (allegedly)

ENEMIES: Young Avengers, Princess Python, Hydra

Groups like the Young Masters are the reason my job exists. They are young, powerful individuals lacking direction and guidance. Their leader, the new Melter, is wanted in connection with several gruesome deaths, but wants to be an Avenger. Each member is similarly conflicted. Coat of Arms wants to play hero, but is willing to act the villain. Executioner wants to punish the guilty, but isn't bothered by collateral damage. Big Zero and Egghead are geniuses who signed up to do good, but continually espouse the language of hate. Enchantress fancies herself an Asgardian warrior, but has shown none of their honor. This group rejected help from the Young Avengers and recruitment by Norman Osborn, they do not seem set on a path of good or evil — yet. Th[e] need help. Hopefully they find it before it's too late.

TREATMENT: After any necessary trials and punishment for previous crimes, the Young Masters could benefit from a rehabilitation program similar to Thunderbolts, or a deterrence program like Avengers Academy.

CLASSIFICATION	GROUP
GOALS	WEALTH & FAME
SCOPE	LOCAL
MEANS	VIGILANTES

ZADKIEL

AFFILIATIONS: Big Wheel, Blackout, Deacon, Death Ninja, Doghead, Lucifer, Madcap, Master Pandemonium, Orb, Scarecrow, Verminus Rex, Vengeance, Trull

ENEMIES: Caretaker, Johnny Blaze, Jaine Cutter, Heaven, Daimon Hellstrom, Danny Ketch, Kid Blackheart, Sisters of the Holy Sepulcher, Spirits of Vengeance

Zadkiel (aka Sachiel, Zedekiel, Zadakiel, Tzadkiel, Zedekul and Hesediel), is an alleged rogue angel of mercy. While I do not completely understand the realm of the supernatural, Zadkiel manipulated the Spirits of Vengeance, better known as Ghost Riders, into helping him overthrow heaven while attempting to murder the Antichrist Kid Blackheart to prevent biblical prophecies from coming true. Zadkiel leeched the powers of various Spirits of Vengeance to obtain enough power to complete his goal. However, the sibling Ghost Riders — Johnny Blaze and Danny Ketch — defeated Zadkiel with the help of Caretaker, Jaine Cutter, Daimon Hellstrrm and an army of Spirits of Vengeance and restored heaven. Blaze and Ketch told me Zadkiel now resides in hell as punishment for his misdeeds.

TREATMENT: If Blaze and Ketch are to be believed, no further action warranted.

CLASSIFICATION	MAGICAL BEING
GOALS	CONQUEST
SCOPE	INTERDIMENSIONAL
MEANS	MAGIC

ZAPATA BROTHERS

AFFILIATIONS: Moon Knight, Deadpool, Punisher

ENEMIES: Toltec, Mickey Dobbs, Pablo Espinoza, Gilberto Alcantara

Rigo and Gustavo Zapata, who have been described as the luchadore hitmen, are relative newcomers to the world of super heroes, though, from what I know, they have no powers themselves. Using impressive offensive weaponry and their fighting prowess, these two masked men (who, as I understand it, never remove their masks) have operated through Mexico, where they were recently offered a reality series. With deadly force, access to technology, and a habit of double-crossing their employers for greater profit, the Zapata Brothers have gained vast fan followings on social networking sites, most well-known for their habits of high-fiving during fights, their exchange of witty banter, and their frequent usage of the word 'bro.' Moon Knight assures me these men only target criminals (much like the Punisher does), but I could never condone murder-for-hire. The Zapata Brothers nearly killed Moon Knight during his brief stay in Mexico, and they later got involved in a deadly battle involving the Punisher, the monstrous Toltec, and Gilberto Alcantara and his gang; more recently, they were involved with Deadpool. I don't understand how their actions can be glorified by their country.

TREATMENT: Should they cross into the USA, these men need to be arrested and deported immediately.

CLASSIFICATION	HUMANS
GOALS	WEALTH & FAME
SCOPE	LOCAL
MEANS	MERCENARY

ZODIAC

AFFILIATIONS: Death Reaper, Clown, Trapster, Manslaughter Marsdale, possibly others

ENEMIES: Fantastic Four, Norman Osborn, previous Zodiacs

The man calling himself Zodiac is a disturbing and troubling individual. As best we can tell, he considers himself an anarchist, reveling in the chaos his actions sow. He has assaulted heroes and villains alike, murdering the entire previous Zodiac team, sabotaging Norman Osborn's operations and viciously beating the Human Torch before blowing up the hospital the Torch was taken to. We now believe he possesses the Zodiac Key as well. His allies consist of a group of misfits, several of whom we have as little information about as we do their leader. In the wake of defeating Osborn and the Hood, I want to take this psychopath down as quickly as possible before he does more damage, but he seems to stay one step ahead of us. Sooner rather than later, though, we have to find him before his actions cost more lives.

TREATMENT: Zodiac is clever at evading our customary espionage procedures; perhaps an unconventional analyst like T'Challa or Shroud can helps us make an arrest.

CLASSIFICATION	HUMAN
GOALS	NIHILISM
SCOPE	NATIONAL
MEANS	TERRORISM

ARNIM ZOLA

AFFILIATIONS: Red Skull, Hate-Monger/ Adolf Hitler, Doughboy, Primus, Dr. Faustus, Secret Empire

ENEMIES: Captain America, Thunderbolts, Deadpool, Cable, Wolverine, Thor

A pioneer in genetic engineering, Arnim Zola is unquestionably a genius. Although he was born in Switzerland, Zola served Adolf Hitler during World War II, providing him with potential immortality by transferring his consciousness into cloned bodies. Thus Hitler survived death at the war's end, becoming the Hate-Monger. In recent times, Zola has worked primarily for the Red Skull, enabling him to survive death too. Zola once attempted to transplant Hitler's brain into my body and later succeeded in transferring the Red Skull's consciousness into a cloned duplicate of myself! But Zola's most startling creation may be himself. He has constructed new bodies for himself, housing his brain within his chest. In place of a head he has an "ESP box" he uses to mentally control his genetic creations. This inhuman form seems symbolic of how Zola has renounced his humanity. Zola has aptly been dubbed the "Bio-Fanatic," turning humans into victims of his experiments.

TREATMENT: Recommend incarceration. But Zola does not seem to be a true Nazi ideologue. His main interest is his research, so perhaps his talents could be used in legal genetic engineering projects. However, Zola would have to be stopped from experimenting on unwilling human subjects.

CLASSIFICATION	MUTATE
GOALS	CHALLENGES
SCOPE	INTERNATIONAL
MEANS	SCIENCE

ZOMBIE-VERSE

AFFILIATIONS: None

ENEMIES: Midnight Sons, ARMOR, Fantastic Four

I've seen my fair share of alternate realities, dystopian futures and bizarre otherwordly realms, but few have unnerved me as much as the one ARMOR Director Charles Little Sky has sent me reports of dubbed the "Zombie-verse." Officially designated Earth-2149 by ARMOR, this world was overrun by a mysterious virus that turned most of its superhuman population into flesh-devouring ghouls. Depleting their own world, they were soon looking for new ones to consume, including ours. Thankfully, ARMOR's Michael Morbius and his Midnight Sons team contained the virus, but we must not only be vigilant for future invasions, but in finding a cure for the virus as well. I believe at least one resident of this world, their version of Deadpool, still exists here; we must find him and contain him before he spreads the virus further. It is imperative that any encounter with these creatures does not involve contact.

TREATMENT: Cure for virus is not just recommended, but a priority, as is shutting off access to and from the "Zombie-verse" reality. Containment of all infected regardless of cure is essential. ARMOR cooperation is required and will be requested.

CLASSIFICATION	ALIEN DIMENSION
GOALS	SURVIVAL
SCOPE	UNIVERSAL
MEANS	CONSUMPTION

HEROIC AGE: X-MEN

HEROIC AGE
X-MEN

Head Writer/Coordinator
MICHAEL HOSKIN

Writers
CHAD ANDERSON, MIKE O'SULLIVAN, PETER SANDERSON, MARKUS RAYMOND, ANTHONY FLAMINI, KEVIN GARCIA, STUART VANDAL, JACOB ROUGEMONT & MADISON CARTER

OHotMU Overseers
JEFF CHRISTIANSEN WITH STUART VANDAL

Cover Artists
JAE LEE WITH JUNE CHUNG
Book Design
RODOLFO MURAGUCHI

Editor
JEFF YOUNGQUIST
Editors, Special Projects
JENNIFER GRÜNWALD & MARK D. BEAZLEY
Assistant Editors
ALEX STARBUCK & NELSON RIBEIRO
Editorial Assistants
JAMES EMMETT & JOE HOCHSTEIN
Copy Editor
THEODORE W. KUTT
Senior Vice President of Sales
DAVID GABRIEL

Editor in Chief
JOE QUESADA
Publisher
DAN BUCKLEY
Executive Producer
ALAN FINE

Special thanks to **TOM BREVOORT, WWW.G-MART.COM** and the guys at **THE APPENDIX (WWW.MARVUNAPP.COM)**.

JOURNAL OF STEVE ROGERS

JUNE 17

Since assuming my responsibilities as commander of my nation's superhuman forces, the status of mutants has preyed upon my conscience. It seems as though I've never had the time to deal with the issues as I would have liked, but I lead a life of interrupted vigilance. Many of the difficulties with mutants didn't arise in public until the past 15 years, when the number of mutant births vastly increased. In spite of the recent reduction in births to almost none, the persecution of mutants continues unabated.

In the War, I regularly fought alongside two great mutants: Prince Namor the Sub-Mariner, one of my most valued comrades; and Toro, a promising youth only recently returned to us from seeming death. In those days, the existence of mutants was largely unknown to the general population, and they were considered similar to humans who had gained powers through some experiment or accident. Unfortunately, the climate shifted during the decades I spent frozen in ice, and I've never ascertained when or how things went wrong.

Suffice to say, mutants frighten most normal humans. The terror, I think, stems from the idea that mutants are "the other," but they come from within, hidden among the ranks of our own children. When the mutant birth rate was in the millions, it seemed as though mutants might replace humans. This has led to the prejudice, violence and in-fighting that has afflicted mutants ever since. Worse yet, opportunists have tried to spin these tragedies for their benefit, making mutants into puppet soldiers, slaves or simply scapegoats.

Fortunately, there are men like Charles Xavier, whose belief that humans and mutants can coexist peacefully is, by far, the most comforting solution. Xavier's X-Men have fought the enemies of human and mutantkind, saving scores of lives even on other worlds and teaching new generations of mutants to be proud of their identities and to use their abilities responsibly. The X-Men are not as cohesive today as they once were, likely because Xavier has become isolated from his own movement, but they remain the most able group at effecting change in our society.

For my part, I helped mentor Magneto's children, Quicksilver and the Scarlet Witch, into members of the Avengers. I can't say I'm entirely pleased with how either sibling has turned out, but I remain ever optimistic for their futures. It was particularly through Wanda and her romance with the Vision that I experienced anti-mutant bigotry first-hand, as their love brought crowds of protestors and even suicide bombers to the doors of Avengers Mansion. The horrors of such protests remind me all too well of the Nazi regime, the very evil Captain America was created to fight.

I've done my part to combat the likes of the Brotherhood of Mutants and the Resistants, tried to save lives in the Genoshan civil wars, and recently awarded the Presidential Medal of Freedom to Cyclops for holding the line against Norman Osborn. I have spoken against anti-mutant hysteria, but my words seem to carry little weight on this issue. "The mutant question" remains a hot topic on the political stage, one every politician dreads to be queried on. Given my new role in the government, I cannot feign ignorance on the status of mutants today. This is why I have taken on this project to research the mutant condition as it currently exists. It is my hope that with a greater understanding of the issues that face mutants today and a better comprehension of what mutants aspire to achieve, I can better serve them, the larger population of the United States, and above all, the American dream.

JUNE 18

Word has reached me that previously unrecognized mutants are beginning to emerge across the globe; more than ever, we need to make our world ready to receive them, and that work begins in our hearts and minds.

X-MEN

CLASSIFICATION: Mutants (humans)

LATEST SIGHTING: Utopia

The X-Men were initially a small group of teenaged mutants gathered by Charles Xavier, with intents to teach them how to use their innate powers and train them to protect the world from mutants who would use their powers for evil. Since their founding, the X-Men have grown from their humble beginnings as a small, private school into a sprawling, massive operation with many members and one of the broadest power bases in the superhuman community. While widely misunderstood by the public, the X-Men have always acted with the world's best interests in mind and have saved the world (and reality) countless times, mostly without credit and often blamed for the threat in the first place. Yet, despite the endless hatred directed toward them, they endlessly persist in their fight for peaceful human/mutant co-existence. I've never known an X-Man to quit in a fight...I doubt I ever will.

The X-Men have endured dark times in recent years, having seen unprecedented levels of mutant culture and community acceptance during the period when Xavier publicly revealed himself to be a mutant and vastly expanded the school's roster. Even that event was tarnished by the devastation of Genosha at the hands of Sentinels, but incidents since then have been consistently violent. There was Xorn's occupation of Manhattan where hundreds were put to death and ultimately cost Jean Grey's life to bring to an end; Xavier ostracized from the very team he created after several revelations of past misdeeds were made; the tragedy of "M-Day" where mutants who lost their powers died as their bodies failed to adapt; the dismal decision to transform the Xavier Institute into a refugee camp for the 198 and the government's ultimately ineffective attempts to police the remaining the mutants, treating the X-Men and their charges as though they were inmates; Kitty Pryde's personal sacrifice to save Earth from an extraterrestrial bullet fired from the planet Breakworld; the slaughter of nearly an entire town by the groups competing to find the first mutant born since M-Day, the infant Hope; the San Francisco anti-mutant riots fanned by Simon Trask; the X-Men's retreat from San Francisco to an isolated island; Selene's resurrection of deceased mutants

as an army she could sacrifice in an effort to become a goddess; and Bastion's last-ditch effort to destroy Hope herself.

Many of the fallen mutants were relatively unknown to the public, their loss eliciting a muted response from the world at large. More recently, prominent members of the X-Men's own ranks — namely Cable and Nightcrawler — are amongst the dead. The team has become fractured by internal strife, from those who take issue with Emma Frost and Cyclops' leadership to those who have never been able to accept Wolverine's willingness to kill. These disagreements spurred Beast to leave the X-Men, which was certainly to my gain. Still, the majority of the X-Men have fallen into line and accepted the changing face of mutantkind.

There have certainly been occasional reasons for optimism; by gaining my old friend Namor as an ally, the X-Men have essentially forged a pact with the undersea kingdom of Atlantis. Kitty Pryde has been found and rescued and the formerly-deceased Cypher has returned. Now that the X-Men's homes and identities are nearly all public, there has been an increased effort from the X-Men's ranks to coordinate with local law and order officials. Former enemies such as Danger and Magneto have become significant allies of the X-Men, leaving old vendettas to the past. For my part, I helped Cyclops obtain the Presidential Medal of Freedom and heartily endorsed reintegrating the X-Men with the outside world.

At present, the X-Men are organized into a number of loosely-identified squads, with Dazzler and Northstar overseeing most of the group's activities in San Francisco, Cannonball leading many of his fellow former New Mutants in their own team, Rogue working with an ever-shifting team comprised of members from the student body (notably the "Five Lights" recruited by Hope) and the main team headlined by Cyclops and Emma Frost. The X-Men's major associates of X-Factor Investigations are currently based out of Manhattan and have little coordination with the Utopia-based teams.

QUOTE: "We have been, and always will be, sworn to protect a world that hates and despises us."

ARCHANGEL

CLASSIFICATION:
Mutant (human)

LATEST SIGHTING:
Utopia

Wealthy socialite. President of Worthington Industries. High-flying mutant hero. Public figure. Warren Worthington has been many things since he sprouted feathered wings from his back

at puberty. Through it all, despite his sometimes foppish behavior, he has consistently landed on the side of the angels, using his vast abilities and resources to benefit humanity and protect mutantkind as the Angel. But after his wings were badly damaged and amputated, and he was genetically altered by Apocalypse, Worthington manifested a dark personality that matched his razor-sharp metal wings, becoming the lethal Archangel. With the help of the X-Men, he was able to reclaim his humanity, and eventually, his original feathered wings grew back. However, Worthington has recently been seen manifesting his metal wings and dark side periodically. What this means for him, I don't know — I just hope that whatever is taking place, he is surrounded by those that can help him hold on to his core goodness.

QUOTE: "No matter how twisted you've made me...there's still mercy deep within me. There's still humanity somewhere inside me."

ARMOR

CLASSIFICATION:
Mutant (human)

LATEST SIGHTING:
Utopia

Hisako Ichiki enrolled at the Xavier Institute to better learn to utilize her psionic exoskeleton armor and made no secret of her ambition and desire to become a member of Xavier's

heroic X-Men. However, after M-Day, when the majority of mutants were stripped of their abilities, Hisako (as Armor) retained her powers and participated in a match to determine who would become an X-Man-in-training, but failed to make the cut. Not long afterward, though, she was abducted to an alien planet alongside the X-Men, and during that mission, she proved her mettle and was inducted to the team. Wolverine tells me she has a wicked, sarcastic sense of humor, which she uses to cope with the difficulties she has faced, not least of which were the suicide of a close friend at Xavier's and being terrorized by artificial intelligence Danger and the demonic Belasco. Armor has tremendous power and ambition and if shaped properly could easily become a pillar of the superhuman and mutant communities.

QUOTE: "I know who I am. Hisako Ichiki. Armor. Mutant. Not a problem."

COLOSSUS

CLASSIFICATION:
Mutant (human)

LATEST SIGHTING:
Utopia

Huge power-houses are not uncommon in this line of work. Men and women with unbelievable strength generally have the personalities to match their power. Then there's Colossus.

Russian-born Piotr (Peter) Rasputin is a genuinely peaceful soul, an artistic gentle giant who has been thrust into a dichotomous role of the muscled enforcer. From what I know of Peter's life, he's been through more than his fair share of tragedy as an X-Man: his family murdered, his brother becoming an unstable threat, losing his sister to the Legacy virus, dying and being resurrected himself, believing the love of his life gone forever...the poor guy has been through the wringer. Yet, despite all this, Peter still stands for what he believes in, still stands with the X-Men. And what's amazing to me is that while he has a deeper intensity than he did before going through what he has, he still maintains the gentleness that defines him. Truly one of the pillars of the X-Men, a genuine Colossus.

QUOTE: "This is why I joined the X-Men — to combat evil, to stand by those without the power or strength to defend themselves."

CYCLOPS

CLASSIFICATION:
Mutant (human)

LATEST SIGHTING:
Utopia

It's hard to believe the intense, take-charge leader Scott Summers once was the skinny, timid, soft-spoken boy that used to quietly obey Charles Xavier's orders without

question. But I've watched his development with my own eyes (I've interacted with Cyclops periodically since his teens), and clearly see how he's become what he is. Scott's carried more than his fair share of the burden for protecting mutants his whole life, and as one of the leaders of the X-Men, he's been forced into some horrible situations and had to make some very tough choices. No less so than now, with mutantkind in a most precarious position, Scott's got the survival of an entire race to consider. I suspect he's had to make some questionable decisions to ensure that survival, and I have a feeling that those choices have caused him no little agony. I don't envy the situation he's in, and I hope he's got the proper people surrounding him that will support and strengthen him until mutants can come through these dark times. I pray they do.

QUOTE: "We've saved the world — worlds even — time and again. That's the truth. That's what we do."

DAZZLER

CLASSIFICATION:
Mutant (human)

LATEST SIGHTING:
Utopia

More famous for her career before the X-Men than after, Alison Blaire is one of the more high-profile mutants for reasons that have nothing to do with combat. Dazzler was a promising

pop singer before a lover revealed her mutant nature to the world, devastating her career. Now thrown into the mutant struggle, Dazzler found herself drawn inexorably to the X-Men. Although she has tried to reclaim her fame more than once, she has not shied away from the responsibilities of a hero. She has found numerous uses for her deceptively simple power to turn sound into light, achieving effects as varied as blinding flares, cutting lasers and "solid" photon weapons. She has also volunteered herself to causes that had nothing to do with her, like rebellions in the Mojoverse and the well-being of the strange creatures known as the X-Babies. For the greater good she has even accepted roles that frighten others, including helping Galactus on one occasion. Any team would be lucky to have her, and the X-Men are no exception.

QUOTE: "If other people really can't feel sounds the way I do, I feel sorry for them!"

EMMA FROST

CLASSIFICATION:
Mutant (human)

LATEST SIGHTING:
Utopia

I'd be a hypocrite to say those that used to walk on the wrong side of the tracks can't be redeemed. I'm surrounded by incredible men and women that once were villains: one of my closest

friends and trusted compatriots is Hawkeye, for crying out loud. So, it'd be wrong for me to not offer Emma Frost the same benefit of the doubt. However, as a hero, Frost seems to have as much disdain for others as she did as the White Queen of the Hellfire Club. While her efforts with the X-Men to protect mutants seem genuine (as does her romance with X-Men leader Cyclops), I just can't seem to relax at the thought of her. There's no denying her power is a great boon to the X-Men: her tremendous telepathy and solid diamond form are unbelievable assets. I just have some concerns about how far removed she truly is from her nebulous history. I suspect a number of X-Men have similar fears. Her acquaintance with Avengers Iron Man and Namor offers me some comfort, as well. I earnestly hope I'm wrong in these concerns.

QUOTE: "The world is watching. We must be nothing less than fabulous."

GAMBIT

CLASSIFICATION:
Mutant (human)

LATEST SIGHTING:
Utopia

I'm repeatedly promised that Gambit is on the side of the angels, and he's completely dedicated to the causes of the X-Men and the welfare of mutants. If the X-Men vouch for him, then I'm inclined to give him some leeway. But the scuttlebutt in the community is he's done some pretty questionable things, even since joining the X-Men. I've heard he's maintained ties with his New Orleans Thieves Guild all these years, and there have been occasions of him willingly serving the would-be conqueror Apocalypse and the murderous Mr. Sinister. Granted, I don't know all the specifics of these instances, and maybe he's keeping his nose clean through it all. Maybe. But it's enough for me to be wary of him. However, I know he's a valuable member of the X-Men, his explosive energy and acrobatic abilities are useful in a fight, and while I'm reluctant to admit it, his phenomenal skills as a thief would come in handy on any clandestine operation. Long story short: if the X-Men trust him, that's good. Personally, I wouldn't want him on my team.

QUOTE: "Playin' for keeps is still playin', Mon Ami, so take a card...any card!"

ICEMAN

CLASSIFICATION:
Mutant (human)

LATEST SIGHTING:
Utopia

I'm very familiar with heroes that use humor and light-heartedness in their efforts. I've spent so much time around Hawkeye and Spider-Man, I've grown accustomed to their antics. Heck, even Beast keeps me on my toes in this regard, too. Iceman, though? He's raised immaturity and clownish behavior to an art form. For so long the youngest X-Man, I think he created this side of his personality as a method for gaining attention initially, but in later years, as the stakes got much higher for mutants and the X-Men, I think it became his method for compensating for his insecurities about himself, his powers and his role on the team. The ironic thing is he's got great potential. Potential that only he is keeping himself from reaching. His ice-manipulation powers could be used on a level he can (currently) only dream of, but his fears are holding him from that. However, I don't want to paint him in the wrong light. Bobby Drake is an X-Man with great experience, great ability, and one that can be relied upon at all times, even when he's playing the class clown.

QUOTE: "Me? Shut up? Sheesh! You think I can't talk and freeze stuff at the same time?"

MAGNETO

CLASSIFICATION:
Mutant (human)

LATEST SIGHTING:
Utopia

I have no definitive statement of Magneto's true name, but he commonly goes by "Magnus." As a young Jew in the 1940s, Magnus suffered horribly under the Nazi regime, losing his entire family to the concentration camps. When the world learned of the Final Solution they declared "never again;" Magnus has lived his life by this philosophy, wielding his magnetic powers in a righteous cause for the betterment of mutantkind — but his rigid rhetoric and violence have threatened to make him a monster as despicable as those who persecuted him. Magnus has occasionally flirted with fighting for his cause on the X-Men's side and has just recently rejoined their ranks on Utopia, humbly submitting to Cyclops' leadership. I'd rather not have Magnus for an enemy so I hope his claims are genuine. With the tumult surrounding his daughter, the Scarlet Witch, Magneto could play a positive role in finding and rehabilitating her. Overall, Magneto needs to understand that the majority of humanity shares his feelings, but doesn't condone his methods.

QUOTE: "Without the protection from psychics my helmet provides my mind is an open book to you all. I have nothing to hide. Keep it, destroy it, I don't care. Look at it as a gesture: my sword... laid at your feet."

NAMOR THE SUB-MARINER

CLASSIFICATION:
Mutant (human-Atlantean hybrid)

LATEST SIGHTING:
Atlantic Ocean

Namor was one of the first mutants to capture the public's attention. Yes, mutants have been around for several thousand years, but they were often explained through magic or folk beliefs. Namor was different. He was a creature of science, born of two worlds while possessing abilities neither parent could have dreamt of. Namor gave little consideration to this for years, but his first meeting with Magneto helped him understand and appreciate his mutant nature. Although he has always put Atlantis at the top of his priorities, he has had more than a passing interest in mutant affairs. Perhaps he felt they were kindred spirits; the X-Men were maligned on land, and he was an outcast in the sea. Recently, Namor has cemented this friendship, officially joining the X-Men's ranks as they moved to the island of Utopia, and his people suffered from diaspora. If this partnership lasts, both mutants and Atlanteans may begin to recover from recent losses.

QUOTE: "These 'mutants' are an ungainly bunch. Children, fools…cowards who seem to be oppressing themselves."

NIGHTCRAWLER

CLASSIFICATION:
Mutant (human)

LATEST SIGHTING:
Utopia

Kurt Wagner enriched the lives of all who knew him. He possessed a strong, loving heart with compassion for all, mutant or otherwise. He was an accomplished combatant, but kept a light spirit to resist fear. He was a natural leader, an excellent medic and a good friend. It would be tempting to call him the moral backbone of the X-Men; the loss of Nightcrawler certainly seems to leave the team with less zest, more gloom. The world is poorer for his absence, but he lived a life of courage, knowing that he could die any day and that there were plenty of people who wanted him dead based solely on his genes. Nightcrawler couldn't have known that Bastion would be the one to kill him, but I suspect he knew his day would come; one of his cinema heroes Douglas Fairbanks, swashbuckled to the climax of all his pictures without dying except in one — *The Iron Mask*. It seems that Kurt Wagner has finally played his death scene.

QUOTE: "I have made this far, have I not? And I expect to continue on, so long as it remains God's will."

NORTHSTAR

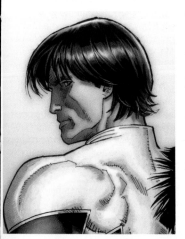

CLASSIFICATION:
Mutant (human)

LATEST SIGHTING:
Utopia

The mutant ability to travel at superhuman speed; a close relationship to a sister who suffers from repeated mental traumas; time spent in a terrorist group during his formative years; an abrasive, arrogant individual who shuns most people's company; I might have been talking about Quicksilver, but I'm actually referring to Jean-Paul Beaubier. Northstar is best known for his time spent in Canada's Alpha Flight, but for years now has been an occasional member of the X-Men and instructor to their pupils. Most recently he's worked closely with Dazzler to provide superhuman defense in San Francisco. Northstar may be the most prominent hero from Canada — moreso than Wolverine — because of his willingness to engage the public about his past terrorism, his homosexuality and his part in mutant affairs. Northstar's openness has certainly made it easier to form dialogues between mutants and normal humans; besides that, his super-fast flight powers grant the X-Men an ability they had previously lacked in their team rosters. It's easy to see why Cyclops wants him at Utopia.

QUOTE: "Kiss my Quebecois butt."

PIXIE

CLASSIFICATION:
Mutant (human/faerie)

LATEST SIGHTING:
Utopia

Pixie is apparently the daughter of a faerie and a mutant terrorist, but grew up unaware of her background while being raised by her Welsh grandparents

(who she thought were her parents). After Pixie's mutant nature (fairy wings, hallucination-inducing "pixie dust") manifested at puberty, she accepted a scholarship to Charles Xavier's school so she could study amongst other mutant youth. While at Xavier's, Pixie joined one of the training squads to better learn how to use her wings and protect herself and others. When the demonic Belasco assaulted the students, Pixie was drastically changed, coming back from limbo able to recite a teleportation spell and summon a "soul dagger" from her soul. While embittered at what happened there (and furious at X-Man Magik, limbo's ruler), Pixie eventually joined the X-Men when they relocated to San Francisco, where she's become a valued member and a solid link between the X-Men and their trainees, Pixie's former teammates.

QUOTE: "Pixie dust! Viola!"

KITTY PRYDE

CLASSIFICATION:
Mutant (human)

LATEST SIGHTING:
Utopia

I think a lot of people are guilty of underestimating Kitty Pryde. People still see her as the doe-eyed kid sister-type of the X-Men, the cute girl everyone babies and

watches out for. Granted, the diminutive "Kitty" and the passive phasing power probably encourage those thoughts to a certain extent. That mindset may have been true at one time...but now? Now, it couldn't be further from the truth. Kitty has grown to be a young woman of immense capability, strength and determination. A genius-level intellect with a stunning mastery over computers. It's no exaggeration that the X-Men have saved countless lives time and again, but Kitty herself saved the entire human race when she prevented a 10-mile-long bullet from shattering Earth, an act that left her lost in space, then physically intangible once finally rescued. I hope the damage to her body can be reversed somehow, because the world is much safer with a fully functional Kitty around to protect it. God knows there's no way I could ever underestimate her again.

QUOTE: "Weird is relative. You're talking to someone who's been regarded as dinner by space aliens more often then you've had fresh air in your lungs."

PSYLOCKE

CLASSIFICATION:
Mutant (human)

LATEST SIGHTING:
Utopia

Betsy Braddock always wanted to be an adventurer. When her telepathic powers emerged she was approached by British agency STRIKE, and jumped at the chance to join their Psi-Division. When STRIKE was infiltrated, the Psi-Division, whose powers risked exposing that infiltration, were targeted for

assassination. Betsy not only watched, but telepathically experienced, many of her closest friends' deaths, before her brother Brian, Captain Britain, stopped the killer, Slaymaster. Later, when Betsy temporarily became Captain Britain, she faced Slaymaster herself; he didn't just beat her, he brutally gouged the eyes out her head. Though cybernetics eventually restored her sight, after that Betsy didn't want to be an adventurer any more; she wanted to be a warrior, able to defend those she loved. She joined the X-Men and reinvented herself as Psylocke. You could even say, quite literally, that she lost the woman she once was in her quest to become a perfect fighting machine — her original body is dead, and Psylocke's mind now resides within a Japanese ninja's form. She achieved her goal, but I can't help wondering if the price was too high.

QUOTE: "This challenge is to the death, remember? So how 'bout we see just how good you really are?"

ROGUE

CLASSIFICATION:
Mutant (human)

LATEST SIGHTING:
Utopia

Everyone knows Rogue made an early public appearance by beating the tar out of me. You'd think I should hold a grudge, but I can't. In all the time since those days with the Brotherhood of Evil Mutants, Rogue has gone on to redeem herself dozens of times over. I've seen her make sacrifices the most stalwart hero would balk at, yet she perseveres. She's a hero in the truest sense of the word, and only because she made the choice to be. That's impressive. Thankfully, the days of Rogue being insane because of her uncontrollable powers seem to be behind her. Somehow, her psyche and power absorption abilities are finally under her control. And from what I've heard, she's using them at phenomenal skill levels. In addition, she's taken on a mentor-type role to the young mutants and X-Men-in-training on Utopia, rather than serving on an active battle roster. I think this is ideal. No one else has a better grasp on the difficulties of fitting in and adjusting to mutanthood than Rogue.

QUOTE: "Truth is, sugar…once you've had three or four personalities at a time runnin' in yer skull…altered states of reality become second nature."

STORM

CLASSIFICATION:
Mutant (human)

LATEST SIGHTING:
Wakanda

Storm truly is a force of nature. Even if she didn't have total control of all weather, her skills as a thief, her unbelievably strong will and her dedication to mutant causes make her an invaluable X-Man, and after years of serving as one of their leaders, Storm has become an expert strategist, often thinking steps ahead of the team's enemies. I have to admit I was extremely pleased to finally see my teammate and friend the Black Panther take a queen, and doubly so when I learned his queen was Ororo. She is simply magnificent — a phenomenal person and a passionate protector of those she loves. Her very presence is commanding. She makes a superb partner for T'Challa. However, I know that while she embraces her role as Wakanda's queen, being away from the X-Men pains Storm. She's torn between her responsibilities to both worlds, both kingdoms. I know she splits her time between them, striving to fulfill all expectations of her. If she can't do it, no one can.

QUOTE: "I suggest, gentlemen, that you renounce your evil ways. If you do not, I shall learn of it…and be very angry."

WOLVERINE

CLASSIFICATION:
Mutant (human)

LATEST SIGHTING:
Utopia

What can I say about Wolverine that hasn't been said already? He's been heard to say that he's the best there is at what he does. That about sums it up. Wolverine is ferocious, highly-trained, instinctual, loyal, and unfortunately, deadly. While I don't like the fact that he is willing to kill at times, I have come to appreciate Logan as a teammate. When you need something accomplished, send Wolverine. He'll always come back. While he's spread very thin, serving as both a member of the X-Men and the Avengers, he still manages to give his all to both organizations and both causes. Especially the X-Men. They're his family, the only ones that have stood by him through thick and thin. I worry he'll ever be forced to choose between the two. Hopefully, that will never happen. His unbreakable skin and claws, fast-healing abilities, espionage training and military background make him an invaluable resource. While I loathe lethal practices, and hate having that represented in the Avengers, the good Wolverine brings to the mix is undeniable. I'm positive the X-Men would completely agree on this point.

QUOTE: "Go ahead. Pull the trigger. But after you do, bub… then you're mine."

NEW MUTANTS

CLASSIFICATION: Mutants (humans/extraterrestrial)

LATEST SIGHTING: Utopia

The New Mutants were once a group of mutant youth gathered by Charles Xavier so he could train them in the use of their powers and abilities and educate them to survive in a world that commonly feared and hated them. Well, the New Mutants aren't children anymore, and most definitely not students needing protection. After growing up together — and years of difficulty and struggle — this group has become a tight-knit surrogate family within the X-Men, one that operates with the efficiency and comraderie that comes from intense shared life experiences. While under the X-Men "umbrella," the former New Mutants are led by Cannonball, who reports directly to Cyclops, and serve as a cohesive unit for various missions. This team (like all the X-Men) took heavy hits in recent assaults by Selene, Bastion and in missions to the demonic limbo. Despite this, they seem to thrive in adversity and bounce back from defeat twice as strong. I'd expect no less from those raised by the X-Men.

QUOTE: "These kids were raised in Xavier's dream. We'll need that dream again someday."

CANNONBALL

CLASSIFICATION: Mutant (human)

LATEST SIGHTING: Utopia

While I've not often directly associated with Sam Guthrie over the years, my few encounters with Charles Xavier's younger students have let me watch him grow from a timid, soft-spoken boy to a confident, composed man of great capabilities. I've had my concerns regarding Cannonball, especially during the time he was involved with Cable's X-Force, a group of angry young mutants that generally shot first and never bothered to ask questions. However, it seems Sam grew out of this brash stage with a level head and what seems to be a healthy balance between Cable's aggressive mentoring and Xavier's pacifistic approach. Family is important to Sam, and as the oldest of a large number of siblings, it's no wonder that he's become the protective leader of his generation of Xavier's former students, shepherding them through the extreme challenges mutants face today, serving as a big-brother figure for this surrogate family. With proper guidance, Sam will no doubt be one of the leaders who will help mutantkind flourish, despite the forces against them.

QUOTE: "This is my team, and I'm taking it seriously."

CYPHER

CLASSIFICATION: Mutant (human)

LATEST SIGHTING: Utopia

Individuals like Doug Ramsey are why the Initiative was flawed: not everyone with powers should fight crime. In a perfect world, a world that isn't beset by alien invasions or power-mad megalomaniacs, someone with Doug's amazingly useful ability to communicate in any language would be the most important person on Earth. Unfortunately, we do not live in that world. Because of his distinction as a mutant, Doug was inducted into a life protecting people who fear and hate him. The Technarch alien Warlock kept him safe at first, and Doug kept Warlock grounded, but it was just a matter of time before Doug's inadequacy in battle caught up to him. He was shot and killed by the lunatic Ani-Mator. That would've been it had it not been for a blessing in disguise. The ancient mutant Selene resurrected dead mutants, including Doug, in a recent bid for power. Brought back fully by his old teammates, Doug again helps fight for mutant rights, though hopefully he will do so from behind the scenes.

QUOTE: "It's like, the only people I can trust as friends — the only ones I'm allowed to even know — are in this school."

KARMA

CLASSIFICATION:
Mutant (human)

LATEST SIGHTING:
Utopia

Life has not
been easy for
Xi'an "Shan"
Coy Manh.
She grew up in
Southeast Asia
during one of the
many conflicts
there, losing all
she had many
times over due
to her crimelord

uncle. Eventually, her family escaped communist Vietnam
after her father was killed, only to lose her mother on the
journey, then was forced to kill her twin brother when he
used his mind-control power for cruel purposes. Luckily,
the Fantastic Four's Reed Richards thought to put Karma
in touch with Charles Xavier, the resulting affiliation
helping Karma become a confident woman and hero. Her
trials continued even after joining Xavier's flock, though —
losing her young brother and sister for an extended period,
and recently losing her leg in a war against anti-mutant
forces. As expected, her friends and surrogate family —
the now grown New Mutants — have rallied around her,
helping her adjust to her bionic leg. While Karma's spirit
and innate goodness have kept her from the dark path of
some of her family, thank God for Xavier's clan providing
her with even more direction and good works.

QUOTE: "I pride myself on being in constant control. Of
everything around me. It's part of who I am."

MAGIK

CLASSIFICATION:
Mutant/sorcerer
(human)

LATEST SIGHTING:
Utopia

Magik is another
example of a
mutant kid
who lost their
childhood, going
from young child
to mid-teens
"overnight" by
growing up in
another dimension. Unfortunately, in Magik's case, that
other dimension was a demon-infested limbo ruled by the

malign sorcerer Belasco, who made Magik his protégé and
corrupted her soul. After escaping him Magik joined the
X-Men's "junior team," the New Mutants, proving time and
again she could be a true hero, but she was also constantly
fighting that demonic taint within her. Though only a
handful of us recall it, she was pivotal in saving Manhattan
a number of years back when another sorcerer transformed
it into a barbarian nightmare, and I'm informed that she
later sacrificed herself to end the demon invasion of New
York that took place a few years back. Like many deaths
in the superhuman community, it didn't last, and Beast
tells me she rejoined the New Mutants, now a subdivision
of the overall X-Men group, some months ago. Sadly, he
also informs me that the demonic aspect is stronger than
ever. If she succumbs to her dark side, we'll have a major
problem on our hands.

QUOTE: "Belasco took apart my soul piece by piece.
He took my innocent soul and twisted it, to use it as a
sacrifice to the elder gods."

MAGMA

CLASSIFICATION:
Mutant (human)

LATEST SIGHTING:
Utopia

Amara Aquilla
is the daughter
of one of the
ancestors of an
original citizen
of Nova Roma,
a colony of the
Roman Republic
founded in 44
BC that remained
hidden within
the Brazilian

Amazon, never advancing past the Roman era. Discovered
by Xavier's New Mutant students around the same time
her fire, magma and tectonic manipulation mutation
manifested, Amara was sent to the modern world to
learn how to control her powers and study within modern
civilization. As Magma, Amara studied under Xavier,
Magneto, and then with Emma Frost's Hellions before
returning to Nova Roma for a time. However, she and
the other Nova Romans were led to believe they were
brainwashed victims of a complex hoax and Nova Roma
never truly existed. After a time of aimless anger and
frustration, Amara regained her true identity and eventually
returned to Xavier's fold, where she seems to have returned
to a level of stability. Amara tends to be level-headed, but
when provoked, her anger can be as fiery and red-hot as
her skin becomes as Magma. I think being surrounded by
beloved friends is the best place for Amara to be.

QUOTE: "I've been reborn — made one with the molten
heart of Mother Earth herself!"

MOONSTAR

CLASSIFICATION:
Human
(ex-mutant)

LATEST SIGHTING:
Utopia

When Danielle Moonstar's mutant power to fashion illusions of a person's greatest fear became evident during her teenage years, she was sent to Charles Xavier, a friend of her father's. Becoming one of the founding New Mutants, she often used the codename Mirage and became one of the group's de facto leaders. While visiting Asgard, Moonstar took custody of Brightwind, a winged stallion of the Valkyrie; this led to her receiving the powers of a Valkyrie and although she later lost this status, she still possesses Brightwind. Moonstar matured into the role of instructor at the Xavier Institute, leading an all-new class of New Mutants, but when she lost her powers on "M-Day" she was unceremoniously released from the Institute. After a brief period serving the Initiative, Moonstar has returned to the X-Men's side, using her extensive combat experience to substitute for her lack of superhuman ability. As a fellow non-powered person who has fought alongside gods, I understand Danielle's drive to prove her right as a hero; fortunately, it seems that her friends understand her too.

QUOTE: "I learned a long time ago to face my fears. To fight them! To fight them with every ounce of my being!"

SUNSPOT

CLASSIFICATION:
Mutant (human)

LATEST SIGHTING:
Utopia

Roberto Da Costa can absorb solar energy and convert it into phenomenal strength; basically, a human solar energy battery. However, his durability does not simultaneously increase with his strength, so his body can't always match what his incredible strength can do. For example, he may be able to knock down a skyscraper, but if it falls on him, he'll be killed. Sort of an unusual problem for a strongman. But Sunspot's power doesn't lie just with his mutant gift. He's also a savvy businessman and is highly accomplished in running multi-faceted corporations. Believe it or not, if applied properly, these transferable skills could greatly benefit the X-Men, whose operations have become quite diverse, with numerous personnel and theaters of operation to maintain. Hopefully, he's able to offer that skill set to the team, and Cyclops finds ways to incorporate him into team management. Roberto is especially close with the sub-team of the X-Men that was once the New Mutants, especially team leader Cannonball, as they've grown up together. His hot-tempered personality often causes friction amongst them, but like any family, disagreements can be forgiven quickly and the bond easily re-established.

QUOTE: "I thought being the hot-headed jerk was my job."

WARLOCK

CLASSIFICATION:
Mutant
(Technarch)

LATEST SIGHTING:
Utopia

Warlock is the heir apparent to the ruling line of a shape-shifting alien race bent on universal domination. His mutant nature allowed him to experience emotions foreign to other Technarchy and has led him on an unlikely journey. Discovering Earth while escaping from his father, Magus, Warlock was adopted by Xavier's New Mutants. They helped protect and guide him through his journey of discovery, particularly Cypher. Sadly, both Cypher and Warlock met untimely deaths while fighting anti-mutant bigotry, though both have since recovered. Warlock recently returned to Earth after helping another young Technarch, Tyro, spread a peaceful way of life for their people. Nova informs me he was a tremendous help in turning the tide of war against Ultron's forces in the Kree galaxy. Though he still acts slightly strange by human standards, Warlock is back with the New Mutants and the recently resurrected Cypher, once more using his amazing ability to transform into anything he can imagine for the protection of Earth.

QUOTE: "The Technarchy is self's species. But self never really fit in. Self's Siredam did not approve of self's lifestyle choices."

BANSHEE

CLASSIFICATION:
Mutant (human)

LATEST SIGHTING:
Manhattan,
New York City

The daughter of former Interpol agent and longtime member and ally of the X-Men Banshee, Siryn recently adopted her father's code name after accepting that her father was killed trying to save civilians from Vulcan. Banshee has been active in the US, Ireland, and on Muir Island for years. Siryn served on Cable's X-Force for a time fighting in multiple public battles and suffering several personal tragedies (including being trapped in a mental institution and temporarily having her vocal cords severed). More recently, she has been active with X-Factor, Madrox's private investigation team, during which she has lost both her father and her newborn son (who turned out to be a dupe of Madrox), and she was kidnapped and nearly killed until Rictor saved her. A recovering alcoholic, Banshee has had several complex relationships with men, including Madrox, Warpath, and Deadpool. Banshee has a proud family legacy to live up to, but has experienced more loss and trauma than most of the heroes I know. Her continuation as a hero and an investigator is a testament to her true character.

QUOTE: "Tragically, some of us don't have that luxury. Your vocal indulgence is my weapon of mass destruction... I'd rather focus on what brings me happiness, thank you ever so."

DARWIN

CLASSIFICATION:
Mutant (human)

LATEST SIGHTING:
Manhattan,
New York City

After a lifetime of being manipulated by others, it seems Darwin is coming into his own. As I understand it from the Beast, when Xavier formed his new X-Men team to rescue the originals from Krakoa, one group of new recruits tragically met their end, and Xavier kept it a secret from his students. Two of these students, Darwin and Vulcan, survived for years using Darwin's ability to evolve to endure any circumstances. Since his revival, Darwin has aided the X-Men in their mission to the Shi'ar empire, was nearly recruited by the Skrulls for help in their invasion, has been kidnapped and experimented on by the Karma Project, and has been betrayed by his birth father. Now that he is a part of X-Factor, he's finding his voice, making decisions for himself, and has even enrolled in some college classes. I know what it is like to lose years of your life due to tragic circumstances and to find yourself in a world years later that you don't understand. I empathize with Darwin, and commend him on the new life he is making for himself.

QUOTE: "I survived a jump through space holding onto the roof of your ship...if you think that blaster is going to hurt me, you're dreaming."

LONGSHOT

CLASSIFICATION:
Mutant
(Mojoverse native)

LATEST SIGHTING:
Manhattan,
New York City

Hailing from the extra-dimensional Mojoverse (or Wildways, as it's also been known), the probability-influencing Longshot led a rebellion against his dimension's tyrannical ruler, Mojo, before his memory was erased, and he was deposited on Earth. Longshot aided the X-Men (then transformed into "X-Babies") against Mojo, subsequently joining their ranks before returning to the Mojoverse to continue his rebellion. Believed dead for a time, Longshot was captured by Mojo, but was freed by the reality-hopping Exiles. Joining them, Longshot was apparently instrumental in saving multiple realities and British news footage shows Longshot aided in the downfall of the reality-altering "Mad Jim" Jaspers before reuniting with his estranged wife, the mutant Dazzler. He has since joined X-Factor Investigations, which specializes in superhuman-related cases. While I've only seen Longshot in passing, I sense a strong nobility in him, and his track record seems to speak for itself. He has been known to risk his life for the sake of a planet not his own and, despite falling into numerous dangerous situations on a daily basis, luck always seems to be on his side.

QUOTE: "I cannot remain vigilant if I'm distracted. For your own safety, please try to keep your hands off me."

CLASSIFICATION:
Mutant (human)

LATEST SIGHTING:
Manhattan,
New York City

Monet St. Croix is described as both insufferable and perfect by most who know her. She is super-strong, super-intelligent, telepathic, and can fly as well as being incredibly

beautiful. I'm told she describes herself this way as well. Such cocky self-assuredness belies a dark past. Her brother, Emplate, has sought the subjugation of mutantkind for his own ends, once imprisoning her in the mute body of Penance. Her twin sisters merged to impersonate her, freeing her after they learned what happened. Despite her history and superiority complex, M has remained on the straight and narrow. After Generation X disbanded, she joined her former teacher Banshee in the paramilitary X-Corps and now assists Jamie Madrox in X-Factor Investigations. She remains loyal to her co-workers, but holds a high standard for her friends. All indications are, M will continue to mature into a well-meaning, if hot-headed hero, but she should be closely monitored. Self-confidence is important, but overconfidence has been the downfall of far too many people.

QUOTE: "I'm sick and tired of people like you trying to tell people like us how to live. Trust me, you would be best served by just leaving us be."

JAMIE MADROX

CLASSIFICATION:
Mutant (human)

LATEST SIGHTING:
Manhattan,
New York City

Jamie Madrox was considered the government's X-Factor's team clown. Something has changed since then. Perhaps it was the death of one of his bodies, possibly

even the "real" Jamie, from the Legacy virus. Maybe it was watching so many of his fellow mutants being depowered, and ongoing attempts by organized bigots to exterminate what remained. Certainly the tragic loss of his "son," Sean, weighs on him. But I think most of it is the burden of leadership. In charge of his own X-Factor now, a detective agency, I think he feels aggrieved that if he's having to grow up and be responsible for his team and community, he's not going to put up with any authority figure he feels isn't living up to their obligations — he spoke out against registration very publicly, and he's made it clear how unimpressed he's been with Cyclops' Utopia. While Cyclops tries to forge surviving mutants into a nation and army, Jamie, quite unintentionally, has created an alternative, a growing, and yes, somewhat dysfunctional, family. Somehow, without ever intending to, he seems to be evolving into one of mutantkind's greatest leaders.

QUOTE: "Believe me, if there's one thing I know about, it's company."

LAYLA MILLER

CLASSIFICATION:
Mutant (human)

LATEST SIGHTING:
Manhattan,
New York City

Everyone who has met Layla Miller describes her as... disconcerting at best. Quicksilver seriously dislikes her, though to be fair, Pietro isn't fond of too many people at the best

of times. A young girl in her early teens, Layla turned up at X-Factor Investigations shortly after M-Day and inserted herself into their lives. It's unclear whether she is a mutant, either currently or formerly, but, as she is fond of pointing out, she "knows stuff." It seems to be more than precognition; reports suggest an... awareness of events that reminds me of Starhawk (another "one who knows"), coupled with a cynicism more commonly found in far older individuals. Beast tells me that Layla accompanied Madrox into the future for a while back, but apparently X-Factor and the Fantastic Four ran into her in Latveria recently, now a full grown adult, and socializing with Dr. Doom. The change in her age I'd put down to yet another kid growing up fast thanks to time travel, but I'm far more concerned with the company she is keeping. Though latest reports suggest she has rejoined X-Factor, my concerns remain: If she and Doom are now allies, it bodes ill for all of us.

QUOTE: "I'm Layla Miller. I know stuff."

RICTOR

CLASSIFICATION:
Human
(ex-mutant)

LATEST SIGHTING:
Manhattan,
New York City

Growing up
largely unaware
of his family's
criminal
background, Julio
Esteban Richter
saw his father
killed by Stryfe,
a clone of the mutant Cable. After his seismic powers
manifested, and he destroyed three city blocks, Julio was

captured by the anti-mutant Right organization and dubbed
Rictor. Records show he was taken in by the government-
sponsored X-Factor group, where he was trained in the use
of his powers, then with the X-Terminators, and later as one
of the New Mutants. Shortly after Cable reorganized the
New Mutants into X-Force, Rictor joined with the SHIELD-
sponsored Weapon: PRIME to bring Cable down, mistakenly
thinking Cable to be his father's murderer. Upon learning
the truth, Rictor joined X-Force, becoming involved with
teammate Shatterstar before joining the Paris branch of the
X-Corporation. Unfortunately, Rictor was one of the mutants
depowered during the "M-Day" event but was subsequently
offered a place in Jamie Madrox's X-Factor Investigations
detective agency. Accepting, Rictor has continued helping
those who seek the agency's aid, and I'm told he has also
reunited with Shatterstar.

QUOTE: "Yeah, well...I used to be able to make the ground
shake. You gotta learn to change with the times."

SHATTERSTAR

CLASSIFICATION:
Mutant
(Mojoverse native)

LATEST SIGHTING:
Manhattan,
New York City

There is little
information
regarding
Shatterstar's
background, as
very few records
exist and all
begin with his
arrival on Earth. Rumored to be the son of the X-Men's
Longshot, Shatterstar arrived on Earth from the Mojoverse

seeking aid for a rebellion against his world's dictator, Mojo
V. The mutant Cable agreed to help on the condition that
Shatterstar join his reorganized New Mutants team, which
shortly after became X-Force. With X-Force, Shatterstar
attempted to acclimate himself to Earth culture while
secretly becoming involved with teammate Rictor. The
O*N*E's file on Shatterstar states he was once physically
merged with mutant criminal Benjamin Russell, and
he sees no problem in murder, his violent tendencies
verified by the Avenger Firestar, who teamed up with
X-Force during her days with the New Warriors. Given
these tendencies, I would be tempted to place Shatterstar
into custody, but his time with James Madrox's X-Factor
Investigations detective agency and his past associations
with other heroic mutants make me reconsider. After all,
the Avengers have given their fair share of second chances
to others in the past.

QUOTE: "It's better to die in a worthy fashion than live in
an unworthy one."

STRONG GUY

CLASSIFICATION:
Mutant (human)

LATEST SIGHTING:
Manhattan,
New York City

Some costumed
adventurers
fight to protect
the weak and
innocent or
for what they
perceive is the
greater good.
Some are driven
by personal
tragedies,

seeking revenge or redemption. A few do it for profit. But
with Strong Guy, though I have no doubt he is morally
upstanding and can be trusted to do the right thing, I get
the impression he just fell into it. He'd been a bodyguard
and music tour manager and shown no real inclination
to fight crime before Val Cooper convinced him to enter
government service as part of X-Factor. He served with
distinction, never hesitating to fight the good fight even
when it endangered his own life, but it was always just a
job, albeit working alongside people he genuinely liked.
Since going back into the private sector he's just been
hanging out with his friends and trying to make a living;
if, as part of that, he runs into evil doers, then he's happy
enough to pulverize them, but he's not out actively seeking
to save the world. And I can't help but wonder if that
makes him smarter and saner than most of us, myself
included.

QUOTE: "We prefer the term 'Genetically Challenged.' Or
'GeeCees' for short."

HOPE

CLASSIFICATION:
Mutant (human)

LATEST SIGHTING:
Utopia

The day mutantkind's ranks were decimated and virtually eliminated was one of the most horrible days I've ever witnessed. Then came Hope. A lot of people are pinning a lot

of pressure and expectation on this child, the first mutant born since the mutant genome was all but erased. And frankly, I don't know how she can withstand it. Being told by so many people that you're the "messiah" of an entire race? That's daunting for anyone, let alone a teenage girl. I feel bad for her — raised in dystopian future after dystopian future. Not given any semblance of a normal childhood: no school dances, no movie nights, no birthday parties...just war and survival. That she's as well-adjusted as she is says volumes about Cable, her lifelong father figure. That she's recently dedicated her life to helping mutants says volumes about her. She's not running from the pressure. She's not being selfish with her amazing gift and her unwanted role. She's turning into it and meeting i face-first. That's an X-Man for you. Hope, indeed.

QUOTE: "We're not witches or monsters or abominations or anything, okay? You — me — we're miracles."

GABRIEL COHUELO

CLASSIFICATION:
Mutant (human)

LATEST SIGHTING:
Utopia

Prior to being identified as one of the "Five Lights," Gabriel lived a fairly privileged life in Mexico City where he was brought up by a wealthy family. When Gabriels's mutant power

of superhuman speed first manifested, he moved so fast he couldn't be seen. Hope rescued him and brought his powers down to a less harmful level. Gabriel is terribly devoted to Hope for saving him, but there's no guarantee that his power won't return to its previous state. I understand from Quasar that the speed-loving Makkari the Eternal once had a similar difficulty synching himself to normal time when his powers advanced past his ability to control them; he might be a fit mentor. Of course, it would be obvious to bring in Quicksilver to train Gabriel and I hope he's on the X-Men's list; I would be willing to authorize Gabriel access to the Infinite Avengers Mansion if he's interested. It might actually be good for Pietro to meet another mutant whose speed powers set him apart from the, ah, "herd," as he puts it.

QUOTE: "I am oh so very, very quick."

IDIE OKONKWO

CLASSIFICATION:
Mutant (human)

LATEST SIGHTING:
Utopia

Hailing from a village in Delta State, Nigeria, 12 year old Idie's mutant powers only recently surfaced, identifying her as one of the "Five Lights." Idie can manipulate heat energy,

giving her some control of fire and ice. As a God-fearing young woman, Idie was frightened of her powers at first; worse still, she accidentally killed people with her powers, causing a mob to form against her. Hope and Storm intervened in time to save Idie and Hope brought Idie's powers under control. Idie remains faithful to Hope, but she is so young and grew up in such an isolated environment that I wonder how capable she is of dealing with such sudden changes in her life. To have gone from poverty to privilege and from the everyday to the extraordinary, it's no mean feat for any adult to adapt, much less someone in her early teens. For now, she seems content to assist Hope and the other "Lights" in exploring their abilities. Perhaps Idie is destined for greatness and will be a key player in the next generation of X-Men; time will tell.

QUOTE: "I am the girl who wouldn't burn... but she says I'm a light."

TEON SAVKO

CLASSIFICATION:
Mutant (human)

LATEST SIGHTING:
Utopia

First sighted in the Ukraine, Teon's mutation has rendered him the ultimate predator, in every sense of the word. Extremely fast, strong and agile, Teon has thus far demonstrated an animal-like personality. Driven by animal instinct, Teon went hunting for potential mates, but Hope was able to bring him to heel (literally). Teon is seemingly utterly devoted to Hope, like a dog to its master. Presumably, Hope is encouraging this relationship to keep Teon in line until a permanent solution can be found. If there is a normal human mind within Teon, it is hidden beneath layers of feral programming. It would be startling to see Teon up against Daken, another mutant predator; would Teon's instincts identify Daken as a rival, or a friend? I don't know what the X-Men's expectations for Teon are, but presumably they will try to overcome his predatory instincts and release the man within; they've certainly seen some success with Logan and similarly I know Valerie Cooper had some luck deprogramming Wild Child. Personally, I would like to see Tigra brought in for a consultation; she has a high degree of empathy and has similarly wrestled in her soul against her human and animal personalities.

QUOTE: "Matematematemate."

LAURIE TROMETTE

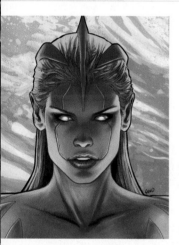

CLASSIFICATION:
Mutant (human)

LATEST SIGHTING:
Utopia

Laurie was living in Vancouver when her powers emerged, identifying her as one of the "Five Lights." Although so far her only obvious power is her ability of flight, her entire body has been specially adapted to render her form aerodynamic, with the side effect of transforming her skin blue. I'm told that Laurie is still having difficulty reconciling her altered form and to living amongst other mutants, but so far her devotion to and trust in Hope has kept her relatively calm. She may not be equipped for a life of action and danger, but such is the lot of all mutants, it seems. CSIS has sent polite inquiries to me regarding her status; no doubt they're still smarting over the depleted ranks of Alpha Flight. I'll send a reminder to Scott to see that the X-Men stay on friendly terms with the Canadian government — there's no need to repeat their unfortunate altercations after Wolverine joined the team.

QUOTE: "I'm a light. Which makes sense: they always said I was bright. But I was never sure if I was bright because I *was* bright... or because I made sure I burned so hard."

KENJI UEDO

CLASSIFICATION:
Mutant (human)

LATEST SIGHTING:
Utopia

The last of the "Five Lights" to be encountered by the X-Men, Kenji Uedo was an artist in Tokyo, Japan, when he manifested the mutant power to telekinetically create objects of flesh and metal. Using his artistic temperament, Kenji can create almost any form, altering reality as he might have touched up a painting on his easel. Unfortunately, Kenji's mind seems to have snapped at some point in his power's activation. Suffering from an existential crisis, Kenji seems unable to discern the difference between reality and fantasy and unleashes his power against others with no regard for their lives, as though they were smears on his canvas. So far, Hope has been exceptionally capable at captivating the hearts and minds of the Lights; as before, I fear it will rest upon her to bring Kenji's powers under control and ease his troubled psyche. If Hope cannot save Kenji from himself, then it will remain for others to provide a solution; regrettably, preventing Kenji from altering reality may call for drastic measures.

QUOTE: "I am becoming art. Art is ideas. Ideas aren't real. Therefore..."

ADAM-X

CLASSIFICATION:
Mutant (Shi'ar/
human hybrid)

LATEST SIGHTING:
San Francisco,
California

Adam-X — or
X-Treme — is
a wanderer with
little direction.
According to our
late ally Captain
Marvel, Adam
is the son of
former Shi'ar
Emperor D'ken

and a human mother. Raised without knowledge of his
royal heritage on a farm, he made his way to Earth, where
he was briefly employed by Martin Henry Strong as a
Bloodhound hunting down other mutants. At some point,
the geneticist Mr. Sinister became aware of him and
began trying to capture him to study, for reasons I can
only theorize may have something to do with Sinister's
fascination with the Summers family bloodline and Adam's
supposed connection. He later showed up in the X-Men's
San Francisco safe haven and was part of a small group
that clashed with Norman Osborn's "Avengers." SWORD
took him into custody afterward due to his alien nature,
but he escaped thanks to the Beast's aid. If we can find
him again, I think there's a lot of potential in this young
man. Perhaps we can help him answer some of the
questions he has about himself.

QUOTE: "I am an outcast...I always have been. Of
everywhere and nowhere my whole life. A part of everything
around me, but also apart from everyone I know."

ALCHEMY

CLASSIFICATION:
Mutant (human)

LATEST SIGHTING:
Xavier Institute,
Westchester,
New York

Thomas Jones
was in high
school when he
developed the
mutant power
to manipulate
the molecular
structure of
anything into
elements on

the periodic table. Not long after, he was kidnapped by
trolls, who wanted him to create massive amounts of gold
to destabilize the global economy. He was rescued by the
original X-Men (X-Factor at the time), and when the trolls
threatened him again later, the X-Men and their British
counterpart, Excalibur, defeated them once more. Despite
offers to join various mutant hero groups, Thomas has
consistently refused, preferring to focus on his education
and developing his powers to their full potential, but
briefly joined the remnants of Earth's mutants at the Xavier
Institute for protection following M-Day. Beast tells me
he's an incredible young man, focused on education and
science. However, with power like his, he's going to remain
a target for many seeking power, and abilities like Thomas'
could prove deadly in the wrong hands.

QUOTE: "I have some of the elements memorized already,
you see. Now all I have to do is memorize the rest, and
study, and practice..."

ANOLE

CLASSIFICATION:
Mutant (human)

LATEST SIGHTING:
Utopia

Beast tells me
the young mutant
Anole led a fairly
charmed life,
even with his
green-hued lizard-
like appearance,
camouflage
ability, and
prehensile
tongue, and he
was accepted

by his family and city before he was recruited at Xavier's.
Anole found comfort in the Alpha Squadron, a team of
students led by Northstar, in whom Anole could confide
his sexual preference. After Northstar was killed (though
later revived), a series of tragedies beset the students,
each worse than the last. M-Day deprived many of their
powers, many of Anole's friends were killed, and multiple
attacks leveled the school, all before Anole lost an arm
in a torturous adventure in limbo. His arm regenerated,
but Anole's innocent soul seems not to have recovered as
yet, and the recent increased attacks on the X-Men by the
Nimrods, the Predators X, and vampires can't be helping
the young man. Beast surmised, and I agree, that Anole
has been required to grow up far too fast.

QUOTE: "We're not even X-Men-in-training. We're...we're
cannon fodder. This is why I didn't want to come back. Us?
The junior team? The young X-Men? All we do—the only
thing we do—is die."

BEAST

CLASSIFICATION:
Mutant (human)

LATEST SIGHTING:
Manhattan,
New York City

Henry McCoy is dichotomous in nearly every sense: one of the most brilliant, genius minds I've ever encountered, yet one of the silliest, goofiest men I've ever met. He's a brawling, ferocious animal on the battlefield, yet a genteel scientist sipping tea in his laboratory while investigating the molecular structure of the universe. Over the years, Hank has become a valued teammate and adviser and someone I trust implicitly. I believe Hank struggles with his paradox from time-to-time: as an Avenger he's at the forefront of public accolades, yet as a mutant X-Man he's always skirting the edges of prejudice and hatred directed toward him. So, he throws himself into his scientific work and a devil-may-care persona, both of which help him cope with the intense, conflicting emotion he has inside. Despite all this, Hank is a proven faction and a resource of great depth. I'm proud to serve by his side and even more proud to call him my friend.

QUOTE: "For my part, I intend to die standing up. And singing the Marseillaise."

BLACKWING

CLASSIFICATION:
Human
(ex-mutant)

LATEST SIGHTING:
Manhattan,
New York City

Beast describes a special affinity for young Blackwing (formerly Beak), and says he can relate to trying to fit into society for who you are and not what you look like. As an avian-mutant who could fly, Beak had difficult beginnings at Xavier's school, subject to mind control (by Cassandra Nova and the Stepford Cuckoos) that forced him to hurt his teachers (the Beast and Emma Frost). In an unexpected turn, Beak became romantically involved with new student Angel, and they soon had several winged children. Beak was forcibly recruited into the reality-hopping Exiles for a time, though he eventually made it back home to his family. After M-Day, Beak and most of his family lost their mutant powers, but he donned a flight and strength-enhancing suit and joined the teenage rebels the New Warriors as Blackwing, while Angel became Tempest. After a series of disasters, including the deaths of three of their teammates and a difficult mission in an alternate future, Blackwing and Tempest have gone home to focus on raising their family.

QUOTE: "You learn to accept these things at Xavier's. You learn to love people for their differences. I never expected any of this...to be a daddy...to be with a woman like Angel...to have so much."

BLINDFOLD

CLASSIFICATION:
Mutant (human)

LATEST SIGHTING:
Utopia

One talent we have never emphasized, utilized, or recruited among the Avengers is precognition. While I can see some militaristic value in this skill, I could never see it as reliable, what with the myriad of potential futures — besides, I can see my operatives slacking off in the field if they felt the outcome of a battle was predetermined. Despite the Avengers' experiences with Kang, the Gatherers, Immortus, and more, the X-Men have the monopoly on complicated time-travel adventures. Among mutants, there have been a surprising number of precogs, though I believe the only one left living is Blindfold, a young woman with no eyes and a bizarre speech pattern. Blindfold comes from tragedy, her mother dying mysteriously while protecting her from her brother (identities remain unknown at this time), and she has predicted no small amount of tragedy among the team in recent months. Most recently, she was possessed by a revived Proteus and nearly destroyed several of her friends, but Proteus was defeated in the end.

QUOTE: "I know someone dies, I saw it, but I can't make it clear to him. How can I make it clear to him when I can't make it clear to myself?"

BLING!

CLASSIFICATION:
Mutant (human)

LATEST SIGHTING:
Utopia

The daughter of famous musicians, young Bling! is among the world's few remaining mutants. Possessing diamond-hard skin (encompassing 90% of her body) that she can fire from her body like shrapnel (Diamondback would be jealous), Bling! has tended to avoid combat among the X-Men, seeking only to train in the use of her powers and stay alive. Despite these intentions, however, I understand she's been involved in fights with the Sentinels and Mystique, and she was among Belasco's captives taken to limbo. More recently, Bling! was kidnapped by the vampiric Emplate, who fed on her mutant body in another dimension (something he did to the mutant Penance for years before he was stopped) before Rogue was able to rescue her. Beast tells me Bling! has expressed inappropriate romantic feelings for some of her mentors among the X-Men, including both Gambit and Rogue. Despite the tragedies she has faced in her difficult upbringing and as a mutant, Beast tells me Bling! is a resilient soul with great potential.

QUOTE: "Okay. Come and get it. 'It' being the mother and father of all smackdowns!"

BOOM-BOOM

CLASSIFICATION:
Mutant (human)

LATEST SIGHTING:
Utopia

Even if she didn't have the ability to create plasma bombs, Tabitha Smith would be an explosive person. Despite, or perhaps because of, humble beginnings, Tabitha demanded more from life after her mutant abilities surfaced. Her distinctive personality has drawn her to the incalculably powerful Beyonder, the untrustworthy Vanisher and the unstable Dirk Anger. Any of these associations could have a profound effect on a weaker mind, but Tabitha's chipper personality belies a strong character. In fact, it was her belief in the inherent good of others that led her to give Sabretooth a chance when no one else would. Although she was wrong about Sabretooth, she has always stood for what she believes is right. She stuck with other idealistic mutants as they searched for their places in the world, helped fight terrorism with the Nextwave Squad and stood up against the clandestine Weapon X program. Tabitha is someone who could easily be overlooked for bigger names or fancier powers, but she is someone I'd be glad to have in my corner.

QUOTE: "This isn't about anything other than one thing: Giving somebody a second chance."

CABLE

CLASSIFICATION:
Mutant/techno-organic (human)

LATEST SIGHTING:
San Francisco, California

After a life of intense tragedy, warfare, and self-sacrifice, Cable recently perished at the conclusion of the battle with Bastion, sacrificing himself to the techno-organic virus that plagued him since infancy in order to save several of his teammates. The son of Cyclops and a clone of Jean Grey, Cable was raised in a war-torn far future ruled by Apocalypse. Entrenched in warfare for decades, Cable sacrificed his wife, his son, and his loved ones over and over again in both the future and the past in an effort to save the world from a myriad of threats. Though Cable often employed methods I would never use, including lethal force, he was very effective at getting the job done, and I had great respect for him. After the birth of the young mutant messiah, Cable spent over a decade traveling through time with Hope in order to raise her. In the end, he got her back to the X-Men safely, bringing all of them renewed hope. I can't imagine the pain Cyclops is in over Cable's loss.

QUOTE: "You'll feel it, Hope. Like nothing you've ever felt before. It'll be like a switch turned on inside you. Like a fire. And once that fire's lit, everything will change. I have. The moment I first held you."

ATIANA

CLASSIFICATION:
Mutant (human)

LATEST SIGHTING:
Manhattan,
New York City

According to
her O*N*E file,
Tatiana Caban
has always had
an affinity for
animals, which
might explain
the nature of her
mutant powers'
rst manifestation. While trying to save the life of a dog
hat had been struck by a car, Tatiana came into contact

with its blood, which later caused her to uncontrollably
transform into a dog-like humanoid during a high school
class. Cornered in an alley by an anti-mutant mob, Caban
transformed into a feline form by killing a cat and touching
its blood, scaring off the mob before mutant runaways
Kiden Nixon and X-23 found her. Soon after, she aided
her newfound friends against New York pimp Zebra Daddy.
Tatiana later learned she could assume forms other than
animals when she and her friends were led into a trap by
an unidentified power player. Surviving capture and torture
by the power player's daughter, the so-called "Sniper
Chick," Tatiana Caban is reportedly growing more and more
tired of living on the streets. I suggest we give her someone
to turn to. If not myself, then I believe that Cyclops would
be more than willing to provide sanctuary and even training
in the use of her unpredictable abilities.

QUOTE: "You kidnapped us. You want to use us. That's not
freedom—that's not any kind of survival that sounds good
to me."

ILA CHENEY

CLASSIFICATION:
Mutant (human)

LATEST SIGHTING:
Westchester
County, New York

An internationally
and intergalacti-
cally renowned
singer and
performer, Lila
Cheney has few
connections to
Earth and seems
to spend the bulk
f her time on other planets. Able to teleport herself and
thers across interstellar distances, Lila is a renowned

thief, using her powers to benefit her own greed, but also a
recognized hero. Wolverine says she has helped the X-Men
and New Mutants teams on multiple occasions, including
helping thwart wars between the Skrulls and the Shi'ar,
and between the Jorken and the Krant. Raised off-planet
and sold into slavery for a time, Lila has few friends on
Earth, though she has frequently been romantically linked
to Cannonball, and Dazzler toured with her for a time.
Strong Guy, who was part of the government-sponsored
X-Factor for a time, served as Lila's bodyguard for an extended period as well. Wolverine tells me it is lucky Lila is
currently off-planet as the world's remaining mutant teleporters (Magik, Vanisher, Ariel, and Nightcrawler, though
not Pixie) were all targeted by Bastion for death during his
recent attack on the X-Men.

QUOTE: "Oh, come here, you big goof! I guess I can see
why you'd be a little suspicious...I was sneaking around,
and I am used to my space...how about we forgive each
other?"

CIPHER

CLASSIFICATION:
Mutant (human)

LATEST SIGHTING:
Utopia

An intensely
private mutant,
the young woman
known as Cipher
has the power
to remain truly
undetectable,
both intangible
and invisible and
with seeming
immunities to
psychic and

sensory detection as well. During an anti-mutant attack,
Cipher revealed herself to Cyclops and Jean Grey, asking
for a home among the X-Men, and they agreed to keep her
existence a secret. Jean Grey was eventually killed, leaving
Cipher all the more isolated, but she formed a close
friendship with Blindfold, standing by her during multiple
attacks against the mutants and going to California with
her when the X-Men moved. Cipher kept a close eye on
the team when Donald Pierce posed as Cyclops, seeking
to manipulate a group of young X-Men into murdering
their seniors, and she aided the team when things got
bad, finally revealing herself when Danielle Moonstar was
almost killed by the Y-Men. Beast confided in me that
Cipher is intensely afraid of a mysterious individual, but
she no longer wants to hide, instead embracing her new
life as one of the X-Men on Utopia. I'll trust the X-Men to
take good care of her.

QUOTE: "If he finds out I'm still alive, he'll come for me.
But I suppose I'll just have to get over my fear, won't I?"

DECIBEL

CLASSIFICATION:
Human
(ex-mutant)

LATEST SIGHTING:
Manhattan,
New York City

Mutants generally manifest their powers in adolescence, and for many this is a truly tragic experience. For the young man who would become Chamber, it was life-defining as he became a living energy well that caused him to lose half his face and many of his internal organs. Chamber was a valuable member of Generation X and the X-Men, finding love and even going on covert missions, and Beast describes him as a man of incredible strength and tenacity who faced down Emplate and Omega Red on two of his earliest missions. Chamber helped expose the Neverland extermination camp a few years ago. After losing his powers on M-Day, one of Apocalypse's followers restored Chamber's devastated face and organs, and some of his powers. He joined Night Thrasher's New Warrior teenage rebels, calling himself Decibel and using Klaw's sound technology in combat. The Warriors, despite an impressive track record, simply didn't have the training to survive; they lost three members in battle, and Decibel has been known to be suicidal. Beast expresses concern over Decibel's whereabouts now.

QUOTE: "I can create now. I'm not just a being of bloody destruction. You can't imagine how good that feels. It's all about rebirth, luv."

DOMINO

CLASSIFICATION:
Mutant (human)

LATEST SIGHTING:
Utopia

With ambiguous origins and ambiguous mutant powers (something about causing "luck" to work in her favor), Domino has had a deadly history of acting as a mercenary for decades. Mercenary may be too soft a term; she is likely considered a terrorist and an assassin by many of the world's governments. I don't know how to gage this esoteric woman. She recently assisted X-Force in the mass murders of mutant-hunting groups like the Purifiers and the Right and was even in an altercation with the Red Hulk. With the right incentive, it seems Domino can be reined in for specific missions, as seen when she joined G.W. Bridge's task force against the Punisher. But when it comes right down to it, I don't, and I can't, trust her. She's an unknown quantity, and I can't figure out what drives her: not money, not family, not loyalty. Beast doesn't seem to trust her either, though he said she's good in a pinch.

QUOTE: "I nearly shot my own left nipple off, but sanity and a steady eye won in the end."

DOOP

CLASSIFICATION:
Artificial being

LATEST SIGHTING:
Utopia

I do not know how to describe the Doop. A relic of the Cold War, he was created as a super-weapon but has proved too powerful and unstable. Wolverine has worked with the Doop and seems to trust him, but I would be concerned if his power went unchecked. I was wary of the X-Statix (formerly X-Force), from the start — celebrity and super heroics rarely mix well — but their association with Project Doop made them an international incident waiting to happen. After Russian terrorists captured and lobotomized the Doop, the Avengers and X-Statix were put at each other's throats to solve the situation. Even catatonic, the Doop was a serious threat to both teams. We allowed the X-Statix to restore the Doop, only to learn the team was slaughtered shortly afterward. True to its enigmatic nature, the Doop seems to have survived. The small, green, floating amorphous thing, with ill-defined powers over time and space seems to operate with motives known only to itself. All reported sightings should be treated with the utmost sincerity and addressed immediately.

QUOTE: "ℑ°ϛϛ ᚐ⌑ ℮ℐ ℏ℗℧ℐℚ ⅆℚᚐ ℧⍙ℝ ℴⅆℚ ϛ⌑℟℗ℼ ℈ℚ."

DUST

CLASSIFICATION:
Mutant (human)

LATEST SIGHTING:
Utopia

Up until recent years, I remained largely unaware of Middle Eastern culture, except as it related to America's war conflicts. As I understand it from Beast, young Dust, who can transform into a deadly sentient dust cloud (and subsequently propel and re-form herself) has been no stranger to intolerance and hatred. As a woman and mutant in her own culture and in larger society and as a Muslim in American society, Dust has constantly felt like an outsider. Wolverine recounted his rescue of Dust from a slave camp and informed me that her mother has been missing in Afghanistan for some time, though Dust was briefly reunited with her before she went missing again. As a student of Xavier's, Dust has faced multiple threats, including the demons of limbo, Apocalypse, the Purifiers, Donald Pierce, and the Predators X. She has witnessed the death of many of her friends and recently faced death herself, though she was narrowly saved by her teammate Ink.

QUOTE: "I enjoy talking to you, Mr. Pierce. Your unbridled prejudice and hate, to say nothing of your tragic misunderstanding of Mohammed's teachings…it reminds me of home."

ELIXIR

CLASSIFICATION: Mutant (human)

LATEST SIGHTING: Utopia

Based on his upbringing, one would not suspect Joshua Foley to have a dark side. Growing up with a typical home life, Josh eventually fell into anti-mutant bigotry, joining the cyborg Donald Pierce's Reavers before Foley's own mutant powers manifested while saving the mutant Wallflower. Shunned by his parents and his friends, Josh was made a ward of the Xavier Institute's Danielle Moonstar and soon joined the Institute's New Mutants training squad as Elixir. Despite a brief fling with his teacher, Wolfsbane, Elixir competed with fellow student Wither over the affections of their teammate Wallflower. When Wallflower was killed in front of him by Rev. William Stryker's Purifiers, Elixir turned his full powers against the anti-mutant Stryker, apparently killing Stryker via complete cellular degeneration. After having Beast's medical knowledge telepathically downloaded into his brain, Foley became the X-Men's resident medic and while I don't approve of his recent association with Wolverine's black ops X-Force team, I have to trust Wolverine to keep Foley out of danger. While I'm mildly suspicious of his anti-mutant past and his possibly deadly temper, I remain confident that Elixir's heart is in the right place.

QUOTE: "Listen to me. I…I didn't want to be involved in this, I didn't want to know, or even come. But now I know why I'm here. To save you. I will never let another friend of mine die again."

GATEWAY

CLASSIFICATION:
Mutant (human)

LATEST SIGHTING:
Great Victoria Desert (somewhere between Laverton & Neale Junction), Australia

It's widely believed the elderly, Aboriginal mutant known only as Gateway has lived in the Australian outback for decades, though his precise age and place of birth remain elusive. He first encountered the X-Men in the outback when he was working under duress for the band of cybernetic criminals known as the Reavers, who threatened to destroy a place of spiritual significance to Gateway if he failed to comply. When the Reavers abandoned their outback base, it was inhabited by the X-Men, who were assisted by Gateway's teleportation powers. Beast tells me that he is unsure of the full extent of Gateway's mutant abilities; while his ability to teleport himself and others definitely seems mutant in nature, Beast is not so certain with respect to Gateway's telepathic, remote viewing, precognitive, and postcognitive powers. Thor suggests another source for these powers: that they are derived from Gateway's connection to the Dreamtime — the infinite spiritual cycle which gave rise to Altjira and the Aboriginal gods.

QUOTE UNAVAILABLE

GENTLE

CLASSIFICATION:
Mutant (human)

LATEST SIGHTING:
Utopia

Half-Russian, half-Wakandan, Gentle grew up in Wakanda with his mother and was ostracized for his heritage. When his mutant powers manifested, things grew worse. Gentle can increase his size and bulk to massive levels, rivaling Colossus' strength, but each time he does it has a detrimental effect on his health, with only Vibranium tattoos keeping him alive. A pacifist, Gentle has witnesse the deaths of dozens of his friends and has battled Nimrods, Sentinels, Predator X, and the demons of Limbo. Though he originally went to Xavier's school at Storm's request, he returned to Wakanda after the school disbanded and experienced isolation among his people, a feeling the Shadow King used against him when he mind-controlled Gentle into killing the mystic B'Chaku. Now back among the X-Men, T'Challa and Storm assure me Gentle is being well taken care of, and he has found a home among his fellow mutants. I can't help but be concerned, though, about how so gentle a soul will thrive among such violence.

QUOTE: "All my life, I have only ever wanted to be accepte by my people. I have always been an outsider...and now this...I will never be accepted now..."

GRAYMALKIN

CLASSIFICATION:
Mutant (human)

LATEST SIGHTING:
Utopia

I know what it is to be a man out of time. After my years in the war, I was left adrift in an iceberg for decades, surviving against all odds to be brought forth in the modern day. And more recently, after my "death," I was lost in time until my restoration. Coming into the world was vastly difficult as I no longer understood the culture, politics, or technology, and I could never have acclimated without friends. It is my hope Graymalkin is getting similar support. Reportedly a distant relative of Charles Xavier's from over 200 years ago, Graymalkin, who shares a last name with the street Xavier's school was built on, awakened after the destruction of the X-Mansion (potentially buried underneath?) and followed the X-Men to California, where he befriended the enigmatic Cipher and aided a young X-Men team against various threats, most notably Donald Pierce. Beast tells me Graymalkin is a complete mystery, and he is completely protective of his history, though they have discovered his strength is enhanced in the darkness. Despite his many mysteries, Graymalkin seems to have a home among the X-Men.

QUOTE: "Turncoat! Brigand! I know you. I know who you are, deceiver. Eventually, everything always comes to light...in the dark."

HAVOK

CLASSIFICATION:
Mutant (human)

LATEST SIGHTING:
Shi'ar Empire, M-31 galaxy

Your heart just goes out to Alex Summers. He reminds me of young men drafted into the war, whether they wanted to be or not. Alex is a reluctant X-Man, a reluctant mutant, a reluctant hero. I think if he had his druthers, he'd be content as an academic. But life's circumstances thrust him into the X-Men, and he's struggled to find his place ever since. I think he second-guesses himself often, which is natural, considering he's the younger brother of Cyclops, who is possibly the model X-Man. Add that he's got more power than any one man should have (he's basically a human star, for lack of a better explanation), he's constantly unsure when using it, afraid of the destruction he could cause. I wish Havok could see his worth and strengths and come to embrace them. I hear he's done better in recent years and an extended period fighting a rebellion in space has chastened him. I hope so. It's time for him to claim his rightful place as a leader of the mutant community.

QUOTE: "The professor told me that I may never know the upper limit of my power. He never thought to throw me into a star."

MOLLY HAYES

CLASSIFICATION:
Mutant (human)

LATEST SIGHTING:
Los Angeles,
California

Molly Hayes is
one of those
cases where the
Avengers and
myself have
tried to steer
youngsters in a
better direction
than superheroics
yet they refuse
to yield. I first

met young Ms. Hayes almost immediately after her mutant
supervillain parents were killed along with the rest of the
criminal Pride cabal. After placing her in an X-Corporation
school, I was confidant that she was on the right track until
Molly and the other children of the Pride ran away from
their respective new lives to live on the streets battling
those who would fill the Pride's void. I've thankfully had
the opportunity to keep an eye on her on occasion, such
as when Molly and the other Runaways chanced upon the
Avengers as we were searching for what ended up being
a criminal posing as Cloak. Despite being a super-strong
mutant, Molly still needs discipline. Beast tells me that he
recently saw Ms. Hayes at the La Brea Tar Pits and assures
me that the other children of the Pride are educating
Molly, but I can't help but think that a proper education
and training in the use of her powers would benefit her
more.

QUOTE: "It's not fair. We do so much for everybody all the
time. Why are we being punished for it?"

HELLION

CLASSIFICATION:
Mutant (human)

LATEST SIGHTING:
Utopia

Young Julian
Keller grew up
in a billionaire's
home in
California.
His parents,
potentially
through
business with
the criminally

connected Kingmaker, achieved vast fortune and spared
no expense for their two sons. Julian, after discovering

his proficient mutant talent at telekinesis, enrolled in
Xavier's school, where he led the Hellions squad (adopting
the name Hellion himself) to fame and frequent victory,
despite isolating himself from nearly every other mutant
due to his brash and arrogant nature. Hellion has known
vast amounts of tragedy in recent months, however,
including his parents disinheriting him, a public outing in
a newspaper titling him a "mutant menace," the deaths
of many friends after M-Day, and, most recently, the loss
of both his hands in battle with the Nimrods. Beast and
Wolverine both have very positive things to say about
Hellion, however, and feel he is one of the brightest young
mutants they have associated with. Emma Frost has taken
a special interest in the young man as well, though only
time will tell where that will lead. I have concerns about
Hellion's tendency to step outside the law, however.

QUOTE: "That's right. My name's Julian Keller. No secrets
here. I'm a Los Angeleno, born and bred, and I just wanted
to chip in, you know?"

HUSK

CLASSIFICATION:
Mutant (human)

LATEST SIGHTING:
Utopia

I'll never quite
approve of
Xavier's penchant
for training
young mutants
as soldiers, but I
can't argue with
the results. The
Initiative was
trying to do just

that, and I have been working with the Young Avengers in
similar capacities. It seems that if our youth are going to

have powers, they ought to be trained in how to use them.
The mutant woman known as Husk has one of the most
complex skill sets I've ever come across as a tactician,
though I suppose it isn't all that different from the
Absorbing Man (and is nowhere near as complex as that of
the Scarlet Witch). She rips off her own skin and changes
the chemical composition of her body beneath, altering
herself from stone to diamond or anything in between.
Beast tells me that Husk has used her powers bravely on
multiple missions among various teams, including the
X-Men, Generation X, the X-Corps, and the Mutantes Sans
Frontieres, a group she helped found with Angel. Closely
connected to her brother Cannonball, and romantically
connected to both Decibel and Angel, Husk has seen no
small amount of tragedy in her young life, most recently
the savage murder of her brother Jay.

QUOTE: "Good thing about carrying your wardrobe on the
inside is that you always have something that fits the
occasion."

INDRA

CLASSIFICATION:
Mutant (human)

LATEST SIGHTING:
Utopia

Of all Xavier's former students, Wolverine tells me Indra is among those who least want to be a member of the X-Men combat teams. As I understand it, Indra's family are Jains, a religious sect tracing its roots to India that teaches non-violence to all living things and the consistent bearing witness of truth. Indra, a peaceful soul, can armor himself with a powerful exoskeleton and named himself for the Indian god of war. Recently forced into combat when attacked by HAMMER agents, Indra defended himself and has suffered a crisis of conscience since. After a recent furlough to India, Wolverine tells me (as reported by Rogue) Indra has confronted his difficulties and seems to have embraced his future as a hero and an X-Man, but he had a difficult confrontation with his biological family and a prearranged marriage that fell apart. Wolverine states Indra has extreme potential as both a defensive and offensive opponent, but I doubt he would ever say that to Indra. After all the tragedy in his young life, I hope Indra finds happiness among his kind.

QUOTE: "You can't take this burden from me, Rogue. The sin was mine, so the karma has to be mine. That's how it works."

MADISON JEFFRIES

CLASSIFICATION:
Mutant (human)

LATEST SIGHTING:
Utopia

Madison Jeffries is one of two mutant children born to a Canadian family — Madison could sculpt metal and inanimate objects, while his brother could manipulate organics. During a Southeast Asian conflict, Madison was forced to subdue his brother after he went insane while trying to revive dead soldiers. Madison eventually was recruited into the Canadian equivalent of the Avengers, Alpha Flight, where he served as the robotic Box for a lengthy time before retiring to marry fellow Alphan Diamond Lil. Things get murky after that: Madison is said to have been brainwashed into the service of a Zodiac terrorist group, then Weapon X, a shady organization that has often capitalized on mutants for its own subversive goals. Although now apparently mentally damaged from the years of manipulation, Madison has joined the X-Men. Not long after finally reuniting after an extended separation, Madison's wife, Lil, was killed during an assault on the X-Men by the immortal sorceress Selene. How this will affect his already (somewhat) tenuous grasp on sanity remains to be seen. If anyone can help him though, it's the X-Men.

QUOTE: "I can create. That's my gift. I can make anything I can imagine. Out of metal. Glass. You name it."

MARTHA JOHANSSON

CLASSIFICATION:
Mutant (human)

LATEST SIGHTING:
Utopia

Appearances can be deceiving. Admittedly, when I first saw Martha Johansson's file photo, I immediately thought of Werner Schmidt — the Nazi scientist better known as "Brain Drain," whom I battled alongside the Invaders during World War II. Although Johansson and Schmidt both exist as disembodied human brains and are adept at manipulating the minds of others, their morals and virtues could not be any further apart. While Werner faithfully served the Führer's cause during World War II and still sought to destroy European unity even after forsaking Nazi ideology in modern times, Johansson (despite her physical limitations) has selflessly put her life on the line on several occasions to rescue her fellow students at the Xavier Institute, where the young runaway has lived since having her brain removed from her body by the villainous John Sublime and his U-Men. Despite her lack of a physical body, Beast tells me Johansson aspires to one day use her telepathic abilities as well as her power to broadcast psychic distortion as a super hero. Given Johansson's bravery and determination, I doubt any barrier can stand in the way of her goals.

QUOTE UNAVAILABLE

JUBILEE

CLASSIFICATION:
Vampire (human, ex-mutant)

LATEST SIGHTING:
San Francisco, California

Jubilation Lee grew up privileged in LA only to lose her parents in an act of violence. Alone and adjusting to her plasma "fireworks" mutant ability,

Jubilee snuck into the X-Men's hidden base, earning Wolverine's respect several times over, and later making a name for herself as a member of Generation X. Even as others underestimated her powers, she refused to show weakness. After M-Day, when most mutants lost their abilities, Jubilee was alone and powerless once more. Undeterred, she used stolen technology to compensate for her missing powers; calling herself Wondra, she joined the current Night Thrasher in rebuilding the New Warriors. While her time with that team has ended, she remains in the thick of mutant events, as she was recently one of the first infected in the vampire-mutant war. Whether or not she retains her vampiric powers, I have no doubt she will find a way to continue operating in the hero community. In fact, I wouldn't be surprised if she were an Avenger some day.

QUOTE: "Me? I don't ask for nothin' ever…from nobody… and that way, I don't get let down."

KYLUN

CLASSIFICATION:
Mutant (human)

LATEST SIGHTING:
Edinburgh, Scotland

There's a bizarre trend, unique to mutants it seems, of children who go to other worlds and times for years and then return moments after originally leaving (from our perspective) as adults. From what Brian Braddock tells me, Kylun was a Scottish school boy with

a visibly obvious mutation that led to his kidnapping; he escaped his abductors through a portal to another world, an alternate Earth dominated by magic, grew up to be his new home's greatest hero, then returned to this world less than a year later as a man in his twenties. Ironically, his mutant power is relatively unimpressive — he can perfectly mimic any sound he hears — so kidnappers who hoped to exploit it would have gained very little from their crime. However, between the fighting skills he picked up on his barbarian world, and the magical swords he wields, which Brian says can slice through anything sorcerous, he's a formidable combatant. Kylun adventured with Excalibur for a while until he tracked down his parents. Since then he's kept below the radar, but I presume Wisdom will have found work for him with MI13. Britain's been under demonic siege since repelling the Skrulls, and Kylun is uniquely suited to fight black magic.

QUOTE: "If I am to die, I will die fighting. And I will not die easily."

LEECH

CLASSIFICATION:
Mutant (human)

LATEST SIGHTING:
Manhattan, New York City

Young Leech spent his earliest years among the Morlocks, a group of outcast mutants. Feared by humans for his unusual appearance and green skin and by mutants for

his ability to disable their powers, Leech was constantly ostracized. Eventually, X-Factor accepted responsibility for him, and he became best friends with a similarly unfortunate young mutant, Artie Maddicks. The pair have been inseparable ever since, working with slightly older mutants in the X-Terminators and with Generation X, who allowed Leech to live in a tree house for a time. The X-Men lost track of Leech when he was captured and tortured by the rogue military program Weapon X, who weaponized Leech, turning him against imprisoned mutants. Eventually he escaped, and retaining his powers after M-Day, returned to the X-Men. Reed Richards has since welcomed Leech and Artie to the Baxter Building, educating them alongside his own children, Franklin and Valeria, and giving them anything they might need. This seems like the most beneficial environment Leech has ever lived in. He has shown no interest in fighting, so I wish him a peaceful life.

QUOTE: "Lost. Lonely. Scared."

LIFEGUARD

CLASSIFICATION:
Mutant (human, possibly part extraterrestrial)

LATEST SIGHTING:
The Xavier Institute, Salem Center, New York

Over the years, many mutants have had difficulty coping with their powers and the fact they are different from baseline humans.

Heather Cameron, a young Australian woman, is a case in point. She has a particularly astonishing mutant power: the apparent ability to manifest whatever superhuman power is necessary to save someone's life. At first she used this talent secretly in her job as a lifeguard, which inspired her code name when she joined Storm's X-Men. I would be fascinated to see how far her ability extends: what would happen if she wanted to save someone from Galactus? But so far she seems to have no conscious control over which specific powers she develops, and she seems only able to manifest them for defensive purposes. Moreover, on one mission she took on physical features of the alien Shi'ar race, and it has been speculated she and her brother, Davis, alias the mutant Slipstream, are part Shi'ar, perhaps even the children of Deathbird. She clearly needs help discovering more about her powers and true identity, but her current whereabouts are a mystery.

QUOTE: "I'm Heather Cameron. At least...I used to be."

LOA

CLASSIFICATION:
Mutant (human)

LATEST SIGHTING:
Utopia

There are many variances of powers and abilities. I've been associated, for example, with many that possess super-strength; some, such as the

Hulk, sacrifice intelligence for strength while Namor needs water to recharge, and the Thing is trapped in a monstrous

appearance. Loa has a variation of the phasing power (much like Vision, Shadowcat, Moonstone, and Ghost, to name a few), but whatever she passes through dissolves. This was violently demonstrated during Selene's attack on Utopia, when Deadpool manipulated her into crumbling the three reanimated Acolytes who attacked her. Loa, like all young mutants these days, has suffered untold amounts of tragedy, including the murders of dozens of classmates and a frightening trip to limbo. Beast and Wolverine have both told me her laid-back Hawaiian nature has helped to calm her teammates, who rely on Loa for strength and friendship during trying times. Loa was instrumental in helping young Elixir recover from his crisis of conscience after the death of William Stryker, and the two have since begun a romantic relationship.

QUOTE: "Josh? Hi. I've...I've been doing a lot of thinking lately. With everything we've been through, and thinking that it's going to get worse...and I was wondering...I wondered...Do you want to make out?"

ARTIE MADDICKS

CLASSIFICATION:
Human (ex-mutant)

LATEST SIGHTING:
Manhattan, New York City

Artie Maddicks is a sad example of what happens when people try too hard to fix the "mutant problem." In a desperate attempt to return his son to normal, Dr. Carl Maddicks experimented on both Artie and the Beast, only to die

before the Beast could reason with him. Artie then moved from caretaker to caretaker, living for a time with the mutant team X-Factor, in traditional care at St. Simons School, serving with the teenage group X-Terminators and staying in a tree house at Generation X's Massachusetts Academy. Fortunately, through most of that time he has had the constant support of his friend Leech. Despite his bright pink skin, lesions and inability to verbally communicate, Artie connects with the world through his psionic projections and Leech's interpretations of his desires. This was greatly disrupted during "M-Day" when Artie, like many other mutants, lost his powers. The Fantastic Four have since found Leech and Artie, taking them under their roof and providing them with an advanced education. Reed Richards created a helmet that simulates Artie's old powers and has recently discovered the child to be a savant, excelling in Richards' Future Foundation for advanced children.

QUOTE: ";)"

MARVEL GIRL

CLASSIFICATION:
Mutant (human, extra-temporal)

LATEST SIGHTING:
Shi'ar Empire, M-31 galaxy

Evidently born to Scott Summers and Jean Grey in an alternate future, Rachel (using both Summers and Grey as her surnames) has been a woman

out of her element, living amongst younger versions of the X-Men she knew from infancy. I understand it was trying for her to see that our reality is not precisely the one she hails from, with an assortment of minor alterations. Sharing her mother's affinity for the Phoenix Force, Rachel has often wielded it for good and attained a deep understanding of its celestial origins and source of power. At last word, she had lost the Phoenix's power, but her mutant telekinetic abilities are certainly formidable on their own. Rachel took the name "Marvel Girl" in honor of her mother, the recently-deceased Jean Grey; currently serving in the Starjammers under the leadership of her uncle Havok, I hope she's found a place in our reality; when the Phoenix emerges again, we definitely want her around to help control the situation.

QUOTE: "I'm not my mom. I'm not the Phoenix. I'm my own woman. And by the time I'm done... they'll wish I *was* the Phoenix."

MATCH

CLASSIFICATION:
Mutant (human)

LATEST SIGHTING:
Utopia

A young mutant who burned his city's park when his powers manifested, Match, as Wolverine describes him, is a hot head in more ways than one. Match controls flame, and his head is constantly on fire, but he also has a quick temper and is prone to rash

action with little thought for consequences. Though he has been among Xavier's students for a while, Match has not seen a lot of combat, outside of the students' battle with Belasco, as he tends to be in the background in many conflicts, something that likely has kept him alive. Voted by his class as having the shortest temper, Match recently got into trouble by violently protesting Osborn's attempts at corralling the mutant population; after battling Osborn's X-Men, Match was briefly taken into custody, and he's since stayed in the background once again. A mutant version of the Human Torch, it seems, Match could use some training and mentoring in the use of his powers and appropriate ways to involve himself in combat situations. Hot-headedness is no excuse for improper action.

QUOTE: "If we wait here long enough, some horrible thing is going to happen to us. Some random, snarling monster is going to crash through that window or something and kill us all. This is what our lives are now."

MERCURY

CLASSIFICATION:
Mutant (human)

LATEST SIGHTING:
Utopia

The young woman known as Mercury has experienced rejection and discontent nearly her entire life. Rejected and kept at arm's length by her parents after her body metamorphed

into liquid metal, she enrolled in Xavier's school and sought to be included among her teammates, constantly struggling to fit in and appear as human as she could. Beast reports Mercury developed a crush on teammate Wither, who ultimately became a villain and was killed; it is unknown how this impacted her. She's lost multiple teammates to death and has faced a number of deadly threats, including from the Skrulls, Apocalypse, and the Purifiers. Mercury's sincerity was solely responsible for the Hulk stopping his attack on the X-Men. In addition, Mercury and her father were manipulated by Osborn in the public eye in recent days in a complex debacle involving Deadpool. It is my hope this young woman has brighter and happier days in store.

QUOTE: "You want to talk about suffering? Look around you…Don't tell me we haven't suffered like you. And don't ever tell us not to fight for what we have left! You're trying to do to us exactly what your enemies did to you. Destroy what happiness we've managed to find in a world that hates us."

MICROMAX

CLASSIFICATION:
Mutant (human)

LATEST SIGHTING:
London, UK

Reports suggest that Micromax is potentially one of the British Secret Service's more powerful and versatile operatives. He fought bravely alongside some of my fellow Avengers during Kang's invasion, and as far as I can ascertain, he's been tied to one or other UK paranormal response agency for his entire costumed career. Able to alter his own body, he's potentially a spy who can shrink out of sight or change his appearance, but who can also become a super-dense giant with immense strength and durability — think James Bond crossed with Ant-Man crossed with Mystique crossed with Giant-Man crossed with the Vision. What stops this happening is his slipshod attitude — when Britain lent him to O*N*E to help recapture errant members of the 198 mutant group, his treating his mission as one big adventure nearly cost him his life. Since then I've heard whispers that he got more serious and involved with a black ops group, Vanguard, but I've been stonewalled each time I try to dig up more about them. He's kept a low profile since, though I suspect Wisdom has him working covertly somewhere for MI13.

QUOTE: "I have a sound system built into the suit. Action scenes should always have a soundtrack."

KIDEN NIXON

CLASSIFICATION:
Mutant (human)

LATEST SIGHTING:
Manhattan,
New York City

While I haven't met the time-shifting Ms. Nixon myself, the O*N*E's file on her informs me that she has spent months, if not years, living on the streets after a troubled adolescence. Wolverine also tells me that despite her anti-authoritarian demeanor, she is fiercely loyal to her friends and will risk her own life to save those she cares about. Apparently led by visions of her deceased father, Kiden has twice saved the life of her former teacher, Cameron Palmer, and has also opposed the forces of the now-deceased New York pimp, Zebra Daddy. I've been told she has considerable survival skills, having recently survived being captured and tortured, along with her friends, by an unidentified power player. One has to wonder how these traumatic events in her life has affected her mental state and living on the streets seems to have only exacerbated her already volatile personality. Despite her occasional acts of heroism, it remains to be seen on which side of the fence she will fall.

QUOTE: "I've spent years trying to kill myself... slowly, in different ways. Because of my father. Because he died. And then I got better. I made a new life. I had friends who trusted me. I moved on."

LEON NUNEZ

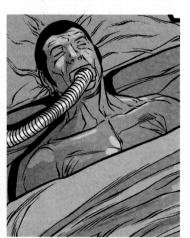

CLASSIFICATION:
Mutant (human)

LATEST SIGHTING:
San Francisco,
California

A San Francisco-based tattoo artist, mutant Leon Nunez managed to stay off the grid, completely unknown to the X-Men until just months ago. Nunez discovered his bizarre ability to bestow super-powers on others via tattoos quite some time ago. When he got into debt with some California gangs, he began paying it off by giving tattoos to local thugs and criminals, including Julio and Carlos Rodriguez, who later facilitated a jailbreak at Pelican Bay. Nunez caused Ink to believe he was a mutant, but the X-Men later sorted out the truth, though not before battling 99 tattooed criminals who called themselves the Y-Men. The Y-Men were later defeated at the La Jolla paintball arena when Ink received a tattoo representing the powerful Phoenix Force over his eye, and he used it to negate the powers of the others. Nunez has since been in a coma and protected by the X-Men, who have learned every tattoo he creates sap his will and mutant potential. Nunez is a very dangerous man with purely selfish motivations.

QUOTE: "Look, I don't know what kinda tat I could put on you that'd make you smarter...but how about something like this?"

NUWA

CLASSIFICATION:
Mutant (human)

LATEST SIGHTING:
San Francisco,
California

Over the years, I've watched some of the world's mutants do truly terrible things to their own populations. Political strategies for the militarization, containment, research, experimentation, and, worst of all, extermination of mutants have been utilized from the US to Russia. In China, the woman called Nuwa helped her government design tracking and containment protocols for mutants. Later disgusted with herself after seeing the true plight of her people, Nuwa, alongside fellow mutants the Jade Dragon and the Collective Man, formed 3-Peace, and the group worked to foment mutant revolution in their country. Involving themselves with US-based terrorists the Mutant Liberation Front (during the time when Danielle Moonstar was a spy for SHIELD), 3-Peace turned against their government, but they were ultimately betrayed by the MLF and had to go into hiding. Now one of the world's few remaining mutants, Nuwa has used her powers to create tranquility waves, which put others to sleep (the full extent of which are likely unrealized), to turn to crime in California.

QUOTE: "And in your mind then, the ends will totally justify the means? When all is said and done, Danielle Moonstar, and you stand triumphant, when you look around you — you will see that in truth, you won nothing!"

PHASER

CLASSIFICATION:
Human
(ex-mutant)

LATEST SIGHTING:
Manhattan,
New York City

The New Warrior known as Phaser was, before M-Day, a mutant named Radian, who generated light blasts during a riot on the day the X-Men opened their school to human students. Beast feels Radian was influenced by his sister, then known as Tattoo, into participating in these crimes. After M-Day, the siblings lost their powers and joined the rebellious teenage New Warriors. Phaser, using technology to develop force blasts and fields, was horrified when his sister (now called Longstrike, using Stilt-Man's technology) was killed in battle with the Zodiac. Phaser stayed with the Warriors, however, and participated rather successfully in fights with Machinesmith, the Skrulls, the Dread Dealers, and SHIELD. The New Warriors were not well trained, however, and they lost Skybolt and Ripcord in battle. (It saddens me how much the New Warriors name has come to be associated with tragedy). After a brief trip to an alternate future, Phaser is back in the present and is not trying to be a hero. This angry young man could use some direction.

QUOTE: "She was my sister, Angel! I don't want to take my mind off her! For a long time, it was only me and her. And now…"

POLARIS

CLASSIFICATION:
Mutant (human)

LATEST SIGHTING:
Shi'ar Empire,
M-31 galaxy

Lorna Dane was raised by foster parents, leaving her unaware of her genetic heritage. However, once she manifested her mutant power of magnetism it became clear — she was connected to Magneto. Eventually she was identified as Magneto's daughter, making her a sibling to Quicksilver and the Scarlet Witch. Polaris has been an occasional member of the X-Men and X-Factor but has suffered repeated instances where enemies (such as the Marauders' Malice) placed her under their mental control. Lorna has found it difficult to cope with the assaults upon her psyche and has demonstrated some erratic behavior, occasionally lashing out with violence against her own teammates. I think her romantic relationship with Havok has helped to stabilize her. At last report, she was with Havok as one of the Starjammers, helping to hold the Shi'ar Empire together. I hope that time spent away from Earth will help her regain her sense of identity, that she might one day return stronger for her ordeals.

QUOTE: "Why do I have to call myself an X-Man? It's pretty ridiculous. I'm not a man. Why aren't we called X-People? Why can't I call myself an X-Woman?"

PRODIGY

CLASSIFICATION:
Human
(ex-mutant)

LATEST SIGHTING:
Utopia

While still empowered, Prodigy possessed perhaps the most dangerous power I've ever heard of. When in close proximity, he could absorb and contain any person's knowledge and abilities, including Beast's scientific skills and Wolverine's fighting talents.

Biochemistry, robotics, warfare, nothing would be beyond him, and there would be no secret he couldn't obtain. But you put all that knowledge into the mind of someone who hasn't spent years studying it, has no regulatory board governing his practice, and without the emotional capacity to handle such advanced issues, and the result would likely be disaster. For a time, Prodigy could only retain the skills while in the subject's proximity, but he later had a mental block removed that allowed him to retain the information. Prodigy lost his powers on M-Day, but the Stepford Cuckoos restored all the knowledge he'd had prior to losing his ability. Prodigy works closely with the X-Men in several capacities, but according to Beast he seems to have distanced himself from his peers, in particular his romantic connection to Surge.

QUOTE: "I saw the worst I could do, and it was awful. But I'd cured all disease, ended poverty...I also saw the potential. I don't know...one day, when I'm ready, maybe I can..."

PROFESSOR X

CLASSIFICATION:
Mutant (human)

LATEST SIGHTING:
Utopia

Charles Xavier has often been regarded as the Martin Luther King of mutants — the man whose vision has helped shape countless people's thoughts and efforts toward equality

for mutants. His tireless work has accomplished an immeasurable amount of good for all, however, I'm positive he doesn't see it that way. No matter who he helps, all he focuses upon are those he hasn't reached yet. The man's drive is unbelievable and intense. Xavier spent much time in a wheelchair, but fairly recently regained the use of his legs. He also lost his telepathy on the calamitous "M-Day," but it was somehow restored while he was off-planet. I'm sure it's odd for Xavier to watch the remaining mutants gather together as never before (including his archnemesis, Magneto), especially as he's apparently not taking an active role in leadership. However, those he personally groomed for this — namely Cyclops — have stepped into that role, and I'm sure are doing Xavier proud.

QUOTE: "Violence and destruction always seem to come so easily to even the best among us. But together, we found a better way."

PULSE

CLASSIFICATION:
Mutant (human)

LATEST SIGHTING:
Westchester County, New York

Otherwise known as Augustus, the Pulse came to the government's attention when he was brought to the X-Men by Mystique (although affiliated with Mystique, there

is no evidence Augustus has been involved in terrorist activity). The Pulse can generate pulses of energy that short out electronic devices and inhibit the effects of most superhuman powers. It seems Mystique hoped to make him one of the X-Men so he could be a romantic partner to her daughter, Rogue. This was motivated in part because Mystique disapproved of Rogue's relationship with Gambit. However, Augustus is an unassuming, hesitant person, slow to take initiative and not fond of violence. Although he aided the X-Men in battle with Apocalypse, he departed the Xavier Institute shortly afterward, evidently failing to make the connection with Rogue that Mystique had wished for. Because of his abilities, surveillance has been spotty at best, and Augustus has vanished off O*N*E's radar. From what I know of him, I think the Pulse has the makings of a hero, but he has to want it for himself first.

QUOTE: "It's a little difficult to know if my pulse would work with him...until I got really close and...well...the thing is...I'm a bit of a coward, really."

QUICKSILVER

CLASSIFICATION:
Mutant (human)

LATEST SIGHTING:
Avengers Infinite
Mansion

I have known
Pietro Maximoff
longer than I've
known most
Avengers. I trust
him implicitly,
but he can be a
difficult friend.
He is arrogant,
elf-righteous, impatient and occasionally violent. That
aid, he has always come through for teammates in

need and is fiercely loyal to his family. I am particularly
worried about recent events in his life. Although there
were extenuating circumstances — mind control or Skrull
interference — Quicksilver was involved in many of the
worst tragedies to befall mutants of late. He influenced
the mutant-dominated "House of M" reality, which in turn
ignited "M-Day," when the majority of mutants, including
Quicksilver, lost power. He attempted to reverse the
damage by using stolen Terrigen Crystals to awaken mutant
abilities; unfortunately the results were tragic, more
often than not. Publicly, Quicksilver has been absolved
of many these situations, but privately he has a long
road to redemption ahead of him. I have faith Quicksilver
will ultimately recover, and mutantkind as a whole will
rebound. Hopefully his position with Avengers Academy
will facilitate this.

QUOTE: "Not everyone can raise arrogance to the level of an
art form."

RENASCENCE

CLASSIFICATION:
Human
(ex-mutant)

LATEST SIGHTING:
Manhattan,
New York City

Raised in
Argentina, the
young woman
who would
become Wind
Dancer could
manipulate the
winds until she
ecame a human on M-Day. After the death of her mother,
Vind Dancer was taken in by her reluctant father, a wealthy

businessman who rejected her mutant heritage, until she
enrolled at Xavier's school. Wind Dancer thrived alongside
her fellow students, leading the New Mutants squad
supervised by Danielle Moonstar (of SHIELD) and forming
close connections to her teammates and entertaining a
lengthy flirtation with rival student Hellion. It seems Wind
Dancer left the school in time to stay alive, as the Purifiers'
attack came soon after her departure. After working as
a waitress in New York City for a time, Wind Dancer was
recruited into Night Thrasher's New Warriors, a group of
former mutants using technology to grant them powers.
Wind Dancer took the name Renascence and donned a suit
with extra arms (like Doctor Octopus) that emit electricity
and a personal force field. The New Warriors lost several
members in battle, but somehow Renascence pulled
through. It is my hope she'll return to a safe civilian life.

QUOTE: "I mean, even without mutant powers, I'm still
hanging out with a group of super heroes. I can't tell you
how much I missed it all."

CECILIA REYES

CLASSIFICATION:
Mutant (human)

LATEST SIGHTING:
Chinatown,
New York City,
New York

Dr. Cecilia Reyes
is a clear case
of someone
always putting
others before
themselves.
Losing her father
in a drive-by
hooting at age six, Cecilia devoted her life to saving
thers. Unfortunately, the anti-mutant Bastion's Operation:

Zero Tolerance outed her as a mutant and publicly ruined
her medical career after she was attacked by a Prime
Sentinel. Despite uneasily joining the X-Men, Reyes found
friends amongst their ranks, and Beast tells me she even
saved Cyclops' life when he had been implanted with a
nanotech bomb. She has made a few attempts to restart
her medical career following her time with the X-Men,
but her mutant status always seems to haunt her. After
overcoming a brief addiction to the drug Rave and capture
in the subversive Weapon X organization's "Neverland"
mutant concentration camp, Reyes returned to her medical
practice by setting up in homeless shelters and her
apartment when necessary. Focusing on helping those who
are unable to help themselves, Dr. Reyes continues to aid
those in need of medical help with no questions asked,
and I'm confident any who seek her out are in good hands.

QUOTE: "Choices, children. We all make...choices.
And mine...made sense, at the time."

ROCKSLIDE

CLASSIFICATION:
Mutant (human)

LATEST SIGHTING:
Utopia

Rockslide, who can shatter and reform his stony body (with accompanying super strength, of course) initially joined the X-Men, according to Beast, with the goal of becoming a professional athlete or super hero. Like his fellow students, however, multiple traumas have forced this light-hearted soul to grow up far too quickly. Rockslide enjoyed a popular reign among his fellow students in the Hellions, Emma Frost's training squad at Xavier's school, and he even got to live out his dream as a wrestler briefly (due to a deal with the Kingmaker) but the events of M-Day changed everything for him. He watched dozens of friends get killed by the Purifiers, was nearly killed in limbo by the demon sorcerer Belasco, and stood by during battles with the Hulk and Apocalypse. Most recently, he was manipulated by Donald Pierce into fighting the New Mutants, and saw his friend Wolf Cub killed at Pierce's hands. Wolverine has high hopes for Rockslide's future as an X-Man, and Beast assures me Rockslide has many friends, but I am saddened by the frequent losses he's been through.

QUOTE: "You're telling me there's a new group of X-Men. And I'll be one of 'em. And I'll be kicking the holy crap outta bad guys and stuff. This is the coolest thing ever."

SAGE

CLASSIFICATION:
Mutant (human)

LATEST SIGHTING:
The Panoptichron (Crystal Palace)

When the young Charles Xavier first encountered the alien invader who called himself Lucifer in Asia, the alien dropped an enormous stone block on him, crushing his legs. It was a young girl, known as Tessa (though I do not know if this is her original name), who "heard" his telepathic call for help and rescued Xavier. She proved to be a mutant with telepathic abilities and a computer-like mind. She has a seemingly unlimited photographic memory, can analyze information at speeds rivaling computers, and is the ultimate multitasker, capable of several different simultaneous thought processes. She became the personal aide to Sebastian Shaw, the Hellfire Club's Black King, to spy on him for Xavier. Later, under her new name "Sage," she joined Storm's X-Treme Sanction Executive X-Men team and Excalibur. I admire her mental abilities and her skill in undercover work, although I am concerned her later undercover identity, Diana Fox, turned into her alternate personality. Reportedly, Sage has joined the dimension-traveling Exiles and has merged with their computer, the Panoptichron.

QUOTE: "Analyzing…"

SKIDS

CLASSIFICATION:
Mutant (human)

LATEST SIGHTING:
Lindisfarne (underground in New York City area)

Unless young mutants receive proper guidance, their young lives can easily become a series of misfortunes. Sally Blevins, alias Skids, is a case in point. She first manifested her ability to generate a force field to protect herself from her abusive father. Unable to control her power, she went to live underground among the Morlocks. By helping another teenage mutant, Rusty Collins, with whom she fell in love, Sally became, like him, a target for Mystique's Freedom Force. Her luck changed for the better when the original X-Factor gave them refuge, she learned to control her power, and joined the New Mutants. But Freedom Force captured Sally and Rusty, who were later freed and brainwashed by Stryfe's terrorist Mutant Liberation Front. When Magneto restored Sally and Rusty's free will, they felt obliged to join his Acolytes. After Rusty was killed, Sally tried to lead a normal life as a college student, but became involved with X-Force and the X-Men. Recently, Skids joined SHIELD, which assigned her to infiltrate the Morlocks. I applaud Skids for surviving the turmoil of her past and finding new purpose, but I am not the first to wonder what her true motives and loyalties now are.

QUOTE: "This darn force field! It's stuck on. . .Bad things skid off me. . . but good things do, too."

BOBBY SOUL

CLASSIFICATION:
Mutant (human)

LATEST SIGHTING:
Manhattan,
New York City

Despite his
unspecified
history with New
York pimp Zebra
Daddy, the body-
possessing Bobby
Soul (aka Felon)'s
main priority
is his autistic,
mutant younger
brother. Taking

whatever risks necessary to care for his brother, Soul has used his mutant abilities for numerous criminal jobs at the risk of his mind, as the more Soul uses his abilities, the longer he suffers from temporary amnesia upon returning to his body. After seeing the danger he put others in following a job for Zebra Daddy, Soul relented and led the runaways Kiden Nixon, Tatiana Caban and Cameron Palmer to safety. Shortly thereafter, I'm told Bobby and his brother were captured and tortured, along with Nixon and Caban, by an unidentified power player. Following their escape, reports show Bobby wants a stable life for his brother more than ever. Last seen contemplating a move to Las Vegas, one has to wonder when and if Bobby Soul will once again resort to crime to make ends meet. Perhaps I should contact him before it comes to that.

QUOTE: "My brother is home. All of us, together... home. I don't need this city to feel that way. But I do need to do more than just... survive."

STEPFORD CUCKOOS

CLASSIFICATION:
Mutants
(humans)

LATEST SIGHTING:
Utopia

The so-called
Stepford Cuckoos
were developed
by the Weapon
Plus program
in the World
facility, using
ova harvested
from Emma
Frost. Rapidly grown to adolescence, the original five
Stepfords left the World to become Frost's pupils. Although

two of the girls fell by the wayside, the remaining three — Celeste, Mindee and Phoebe — carry on amongst the X-Men. Like Frost, they have prodigious telepathic powers which increase in strength from their shared mind link. The effect of their group mind can be eerie to communicate with, but what's truly frightening is their link to the Phoenix Force. After discovering they could harness the Phoenix's powers, the girls used Frost's diamond form power to seal the Phoenix within their own hearts, although they eventually set the Phoenix free. The girls showed tremendous willpower in rejecting the Phoenix's power, but I fear for them as those with an affinity for the Phoenix seem to court tragedy. Although the Stepfords function as a remote, aloof group mind when dealing with others, I'm told that they demonstrate differences of personality and opinion while conversing amongst themselves.

QUOTE: "Our hearts are diamond now. Permanently. We'll never feel anything ever again. But the Phoenix will never escape."

SUNFIRE

CLASSIFICATION:
Mutant (human)

LATEST SIGHTING:
Muir Island,
Scotland

Shiro Yoshida,
alias Sunfire,
seems like the
living embodiment
of the atomic
bomb blast that
devastated the
Japanese city of
Hiroshima at the end of World War II. Shiro's mother was
exposed to radiation, causing him to be born a mutant with
the power to convert matter into its super-heated plasma

form. A highly formidable warrior, Sunfire can unleash intense heat and flame and fly. Influenced by his fanatical uncle, Sunfire became a terrorist and tried to destroy the US Capitol in retaliation for Japan's wartime defeat. He was disgraced in Japan but to his credit redeemed himself, becoming Japan's leading costumed champion. He once joined the X-Men for a single mission, but his first loyalty was to Japan. For a while he even headed the nation's super-hero team, Big Hero 6. Sunfire has always been notorious for his super-heated temper, which I suspect results from emotional instability. When Lady Deathstrike severed his legs, Sunfire must have undergone a horrible psychological shock. He let his enemy Apocalypse restore his legs in exchange for being transformed into the Horseman Famine. Since then, Sunfire has joined the criminal Marauders, and it remains to be seen whether he will redeem himself from this latest dishonor and return to the role of Japan's heroic protector.

QUOTE: "My duty is to my country and my emperor!"

SURGE

CLASSIFICATION:
Mutant (human)

LATEST SIGHTING:
Utopia

A Japanese runaway that got stranded as a vagrant in New York, for years Surge struggled to control her mutant abilities, which allow her to absorb electrical energies and discharge them, however a strong build-up causes her to think and react at super-speed. Initially, Surge could not control these abilities and turned to sedatives to maintain her sanity, though she would sometimes harm others. I have never been quiet about my disapproval of drugs; things like Ice and MGH should be off our streets completely. Eventually, Surge got specially designed gauntlets (first via Beast, then by Forge) to help with her abilities. Now her problems seem more emotional than physical in nature. Beast describes Surge as a brave young woman with natural leadership skills. Back to back battles with the Hulk, Belasco, the Purifiers, Predator X, and others have left Surge in a consistent state of trauma, which was not helped when Surge was recently kidnapped by the Sapien League and nearly killed by an injection of the Legacy virus.

QUOTE: "This has to end. We have to end it. Forty-seven of us are dead…The X-Men can't save us…and the Avengers don't care. It's up to us. The X-Men are half a world away. We can't wait for them."

TEMPEST

CLASSIFICATION:
Human
(ex-mutant)

LATEST SIGHTING:
Manhattan,
New York City

Originally a sassy, winged mutant with acidic vomit, young Angel was saved by Wolverine from the organ-harvesting U-Men (and he says she thanked him by tossing a beverage in his face). Angel didn't seem to fit in with the X-Men's students, but she formed an unlikely relationship with the bird-like Beak, and the two of them had several mutant children after Angel laid eggs. After M-Day, Angel, Beak, and most of their children lost their powers, but Angel and Beak joined the rebellious teenage New Warriors as Tempest and Blackwing. Angel used appropriated super-villain technology to manipulate cold, heat, and intangibility in battle against a number of villains, including Grey Gargoyle, the Rhino, Zodiac, the Skrulls, and the Dread Dealers. After an ill-fated trip to the future and the death of three of her teammates, Angel and Blackwing seem to be focused on raising their family. I understand the drive to be a hero, and I wasn't in support of the Initiative in theory, but I question Angel and Beak's decisions to operate outside the law when they have children to protect. Luke Cage and I have had similar discussions about his daughter.

QUOTE: "This is your so-called safe house? There's nude guys running out the door screaming."

THUNDERBIRD

CLASSIFICATION:
Mutant (human)

LATEST SIGHTING:
Singapore

Neal Shaara was the second X-Man to call himself Thunderbird, after the infamous death of John Proudstar. Hailing from India, his power to generate flame made him a welcome addition during one of the periods when Xavier was absent from the team. Neal served most of his time as an X-Man alongside Storm's team who hunted for Destiny's diaries, hoping to avert future crises identified in those pages. Thunderbird was romantically involved with Psylocke at first, but later grew attached to Lifeguard. Neal eventually retired from active duty as an X-Man to aid Lifeguard in finding her errant brother Slipstream and the duo served in Singapore's X-Corporation office until the organization was dismantled as a result of "M-Day." Neal has retained his mutant powers but so far has not returned to the X-Men's ranks; presumably he and Lifeguard are still on the trail of Slipstream.

QUOTE: "Xavier founded the X-Men. His dream of a world where all of humanity — mutants or otherwise — live together in peace is the guiding light that brought us all together! Yet our very actions cry out that we don't trust him. We're walking away from our own history!"

TRANCE

CLASSIFICATION:
Mutant (human)

LATEST SIGHTING:
Utopia

I sometimes question if all mutants should live together in one place; with so much hatred and prejudice directed toward them, it would seem that makes mutants an easier target for hate

crimes. However, when young Trance went home after the closing of Xavier's school, her house was destroyed and her parents the victims of attacks by Nanny and the Orphan-Maker. Trance was only narrowly saved by Wolverine, though he reported she later saved him in turn from a massive bomb. Though barely trained in the use of her powers, Trance has been instrumental in the recent battle against Emplate (her astral powers allowed the X-Men access to his private dimension), and she has been a brave and willing participant in fights with Osborn's Avengers and HAMMER agents and against the reanimated Proteus on Muir Island. Trance seems to have developed a special bond with Rogue, according to Wolverine, and Rogue has taken a mentoring role with several mutants of the younger generation. Trance's astral, energy-wielding form leaves her human body defenseless, which Wolverine deems a liability in battle, but he's underestimated young women before.

QUOTE: "I totally saved us! Maybe I can do this! ...Do I get my own costume?"

LORELEI TRAVIS

CLASSIFICATION:
Mutant (human)

LATEST SIGHTING:
San Francisco, California

Though I've never been entirely comfortable with people, women in particular, who sell their bodies, dance for money, engage in criminal activities, or even dress provocatively, my association with a number of heroines in general, and with Diamondback

in particular, has really helped me be more accepting of others and the decisions they make. One of the world's few remaining mutants, Lorelei used her prehensile hair (with a level of control similar to Medusa of the Inhumans, and ironically with the same hair color) as a professional dancer at a club in Mutant Town until the club was burned down. After being attacked by the anti-mutant group Purity, who chopped off all her hair, Lorelei joined the 198 in the X-Men's camp. The supremely powerful Mr. M healed her, and the two began a romantic relationship before he was tragically killed by Johnny Dee, a villain Lorelei crossed paths with again during the Civil War. She has since relocated to San Francisco with the X-Men, where she took a public stand against Osborn's Avengers. Lorelei seems to have few connections among mutants.

QUOTE: "I've spent my entire adult life pleasing men. It's the closest thing I have to a vocation. The point is, I'm very good at it. And I'd like to stay with you tonight. Please."

WARPATH

CLASSIFICATION:
Mutant (human)

LATEST SIGHTING:
Utopia

James Proudstar is the younger brother of Thunderbird, an X-Man who was killed in combat, leaving the team traumatized. James took his idolized brother's death extremely hard.

It embittered him for a time, and he blamed X-Men founder Charles Xavier, vowing revenge. He attended a school owned and operated by Emma Frost when she was a part of the vile Hellfire Club. But even with the bad influence of the Club, James managed to escape with his integrity intact, eventually realizing Xavier wasn't responsible for his brother's death, coming into the X-Men's fold, first in the pseudo-military X-Force, the mutant rights protecting X-Corporation, then ultimately, the X-Men. He's a great warrior, using his enhanced strength, speed, endurance and durability in the X-Men's missions. Wolverine has told me James is a chip off his brother's block — respect, honor, tradition and integrity are important to him, and recent decisions he's been forced to make have shaken him. Hopefully not enough for him to lose his focus and vision for doing good.

QUOTE: "My name is James Proudstar. I don't want to be a killer. But now I have no choice."

EVANGELINE WHEDON

CLASSIFICATION:
Mutant (human)

LATEST SIGHTING:
Washington, DC

In many ways, Ms. Whedon is the epitome of what Charles Xavier has sought — mutants who integrate themselves into human society as equals. Evangeline can transform into an immense red winged dragon, an ability that manifests uncontrollably when she's injured. However, she does not use this power to win fights, instead relying on her savvy as a lawyer. This power cost her career as a prosecutor, her fiancé's love and the support of her family, but she's become a major figure in the battle for mutant rights, serving in the Mutant Rights League and offering counsel to the X-Men on many occasions. She has also taken the former anti-mutant activist Marie D'ancanto under her wing, helping to change Miss D'ancanto's perspective on mutants. Ms. Whedon has made remarkable strides for mutant advancement in the courtroom and is to be commended for her demonstration of self-restraint and peaceful coexistence. She is a model for other mutants to follow.

QUOTE: "With my power I could go totally Godzilla and smash the world to bits. But I found a better way that allows me to build and not destroy."

WOLFSBANE

CLASSIFICATION:
Mutant (human)

LATEST SIGHTING:
Manhattan,
New York City

Charles Xavier's dream to found a school to teach young mutants how to cope with their powers, and to promote peace between mutants and normal humans, went wrong thanks to hostile anti-mutant forces outside his control. Xavier's school became a barracks, his students an army. More than most, Wolfsbane should never have needed to become a soldier. A bigoted, bible-thumping foster father, the Reverend Craig, had already blighted her youth and mentally scarred her with threats of hellfire. When her powers emerged she feared it was proof of her eternal damnation. Xavier's should have been a haven; it gave her close friends for the first time in her life, but time and again she's seen those friends, and even her adoptive mother, Moira MacTaggert, murdered. The Genoshans tortured and experimented on her. And sadly Beast tells me the pattern continues — Craig recently helped the Purifiers brainwash her to be their killing machine. Though she's been rescued and deprogrammed, I can't help wondering how much more she can possibly endure before something inside her breaks forever. Pregnant, she's recently rejoined X-Factor, to be with her child's alleged father, Rictor; I hope this will provide the stability she dearly needs.

QUOTE: "I don't feel evil, but I wonder sometimes, deep in my secret soul, if perhaps I am."

X-23

CLASSIFICATION:
Mutant (human, clone)

LATEST SIGHTING:
Utopia

Every murder X-23 commits, every personal tragedy that besets her, it all falls on my shoulders. A clone of Wolverine with similar powers, X-23 was developed by the Facility as a weapon; X-23 was raised in the most gruesome way imaginable, tortured and brutalized and utilized as an assassin to the highest bidders. In one of her first public trials, X-23 killed dozens, including a political figure and his family, but when I investigated, I thought she was the only survivor of the deadly attack. It turned out she was the assassin. And I let her go. I tried years later to track down X-23 and learned of her upbringing. It is clear she has a soul and truly seeks to learn about herself and how to make herself a better individual, and Wolverine assures me she is well on the path. But SHIELD and HAMMER investigated X-23 as well, and the killing hasn't stopped. I don't know what to do about her. My guilt is enormous.

QUOTE: "I am used to kill. I am used for death. Even to the X-Men, sometimes I think that is all I am worth. But I have a choice. I could leave. Even if I know nothing else. Even if I have no one else."

WILLIAM CONOVER

CLASSIFICATION:
Human

LATEST SIGHTING:
Sturgis, South
Dakota

Anti-mutant
groups have
made it seem
that Christianity
and mutantkind
are at odds, often
to cloak their own
motivations for
mutant hate.
As counter-
evidence,

I submit Reverend Conover, who has fought doggedly to
spread his (non-denominational) message of peace to
humans and mutants across the US. Like Xavier, Conover
believes in human-mutant equality and sees no division
between mutants and God except for the barriers set up by
groups like the Church of Humanity and Purifiers. In fact,
Conover has at times publicly expressed how he would
have liked to be born a mutant. Conover has suffered
hardship, notably when his wife, Hannah, was infected by
the Brood. He has won the enmity of anti-mutant groups
such as Humanity's Last Stand, but he hasn't backed
down on his message. With the events of "M-Day," Conover
has helped reintegrate ex-mutants into human society and
counsels them regarding the loss of their powers.

QUOTE: "We are — all of us — God's children, both Homo
Sapiens and Homo Superior. We were all given the gift of
immortal souls, which makes us all brothers and sisters in
God's eyes."

VALERIE COOPER

CLASSIFICATION:
Human

LATEST SIGHTING:
Manhattan,
New York City

Ever since the
decimation, when
nearly all the
world's mutants
were depowered,
Valerie Cooper
and the Office
of National

Emergency (O*N*E) have been actively involved protecting
the remaining mutants. Initially, they attempted setting
up Sentinels around the Xavier Institute, but that turned

out to be disastrous; Valerie had to brutally interrogate the
traitorous General Lazer before he was killed by Johnny
Dee, and the Sentinels were used to attack the mutants.
Valerie has more recently been concerned with X-Factor, a
group of mutants outside the X-Men's influence, and even
attempted to recruit them after Mutant Town was burned
down. After passing them work in Detroit, she stayed
closely associated with them in New York, even though
she was shot in one conflict. Despite no small amount of
personal tragedy, I have always known Valerie Cooper to
be an honorable woman. She has served with distinction
for the Commission on Super Human Activities and, for
the most part, she did great work among the Freedom
Force and X-Factor programs, both teams of mutants
under the government's employ. Despite manipulations by
Mystique and the Shadow King, Valerie has repeatedly done
impressive work for the government in the hero community.

QUOTE: "We mere humans are getting good at handling
emergencies. Lord knows we've had plenty of practice."

MARIE D'ANCANTO

CLASSIFICATION:
Human

LATEST SIGHTING:
Washington, DC

Marie D'ancanto
is a rare example
of anti-mutant
bigotry being
turned into
something
positive. She lost
her brother and
parents when
reckless mutants

forced their car off a highway. Losing an eye and suffering
horrific burns, the teenaged Marie was further bedeviled

when the mutant Elias Bogan arranged to drive her from
her family's home, inflaming her hatred of mutants. Miss
D'ancanto became affiliated with the hate group Purity
and attempted to suicide bomb the mutant community of
Valle Soleada, an act prevented by the X-Men. Now in the
custody of mutant lawyer Evangeline Whedon, Marie has
gradually learned tolerance for mutants and become an aid
to the Mutant Rights League, even living on the grounds
of the Xavier Institute for a time. Although mutants are
still wary of her, I think Marie is one of their best friends
— because in spite of suffering horribly at the hands of
mutants, she has learned how to forgive. There's hope for
human-mutant relations so long as people like Marie exist.

QUOTE: "Mutants killed my family...I learned my lesson —
but how many others are there like me who haven't?"

DANGER

CLASSIFICATION:
Mutant (artificial intelligence)

LATEST SIGHTING:
Utopia

I've had my share of experience with artificial intelligence over the years: some good (Vision & Jocasta — to name the most obvious) and some not so good (Ultron, Supreme Intelligence), so the concept doesn't frighten me. That th[e] X-Men have an artificial intelligence as their warden and teammate makes perfect sense. Danger can do the job efficiently and competently. What offers me some pause is Danger's origins: designed to be a training room for the X-Men, studying their weaknesses, then trying to exploit them in a controlled environment so the X-Men could strengthen themselves. Now, that room is sentient and autonomous, with extensive files on how to kill the X-Men and, I worry, the rest of mutantkind. While it seems to be on the side of the angels now, what happens if it revolts, or someone gains control of it? It worries me to think the X-Men have a potential extinction-level threat within their own midst.

QUOTE: "Freeing my control center gave me limits. I am separate now. Like you. I needed that. To feel this the way you feel it. Because you see, I don't want to kill you. I wan[t] to beat you to death."

DEADPOOL

CLASSIFICATION:
Mutate (human)

LATEST SIGHTING:
Las Vegas, Madripoor, England, Mexico, Hell, somewhere in space, alternate Earths (he is everywhere these days)

Let the X-Men deal with him. Deadpool thinks he is one of them anyway. I really don't know what else to say about him. I never had an encounter with him that ended well and he is clinically insane. There were times when he actually did help people and he is good at what he does, but what he does is most of the time plain evil. He is a mercenary and an assassin with a healing factor given to him by the infamous Weapon X program. He is not a mutant, but that never stopped him from causing them the most trouble. Wolverine and Cable seem to be able to deal with him pretty well and women can temporarily distract this chauvinistic pig (who often acts like a caveman around them) from killing people as well. I have to admit that at least his taste in women is good and Bea Arthur, a woman Deadpool admires, was indeed an attractive woman, but that is probably the only thing we have in common.

QUOTE: "Rochambeau. See? I told you it was easy, I win."

DOCTOR NEMESIS

CLASSIFICATION:
Mutant/cyborg (human)

LATEST SIGHTING:
Utopia

When I first met Dr. James Bradley, he was a traitor and terrorist. Despite his reputation as a robotics genius and burgeoning career as the super hero Dr. Nemesis, he allowed pride to overtake him. He became Dr. Death and recruited other disenfranchised heroes to his Nazi-collaborating Battle-Axis team. They say time heals all wounds, and Bradley has spent the last several decades making amends for his mistake. Artificially extending his life through the use of his mutant intellect and once again calling himself Dr. Nemesis, he uses his own brand of pseudoscience to hunt down Nazis and other modern terrorists. Before World War II, Bradley co-created the original Human Torch and the electronic man Volton, now he is trying to solve the problems of his fellow mutants. Working with the Beast's "X-Club," Bradley and other scientists are working to unravel the mysteries of M-Day, when most mutants lost their powers, and maintain the X-Men's new home on Utopia. His record will always be marred by Nazism; hopefully that won't overshadow the good he's done.

QUOTE: "I don't believe in magic. I believe in science. And I believe in applying it harshly to any problem life presents."

FANTOMEX

CLASSIFICATION:
Mutate/cyborg (human)

LATEST SIGHTING:
Utopia

Although often associated with the X-Men, Fantomex is not technically a mutant. He actually has more in common with me, as we are both allegedly products f the Weapon Plus Program. While I was designated Weapon I" near the time of the program's inception n the 1940s, Fantomex was created decades later as

"Weapon XIII." Needless to say, technology had advanced significantly by the time of Fantomex's creation, and he was the product of a "mating" between his human mother and a machine. His nervous system was extracted by the Program's scientists and mutated into an autonomous, shape-changing entity named "EVA." Although he was trained to serve mankind in a future war against humans and mutants, Fantomex escaped and sought asylum with Charles Xavier's X-Corporation under the pretense that he was a mutant thief. He has since affiliated with the X-Men on several occasions, such as when the rogue mutant Kuan-Yin Xorn besieged Manhattan under the guise of Magneto. Possessing multiple brains for independent parallel processing and an external nervous system in the form of EVA to which he is telepathically and symbiotically linked, Fantomex is truly a unique specimen among the X-Men.

QUOTE: "Why, it appears you have me at a disadvantage, monsieur. However, as with most things regarding me… appearances can be deceiving."

FBI MUTANT CIVIL RIGHTS TASK FORCE

CLASSIFICATION:
Humans

LATEST SIGHTING:
Washington DC

During the period where Xavier had "outed" his school, Mutantown was in full bloom and the likes of X-Statix had become international celebrities, the FBI assigned

agents Catherine Gray and Aaron Kearse to its Mutant Civil Rights Task Force. Both agents have strong feelings on mutant issues: Gray's infant daughter accidentally killed herself when her powers emerged uncontrollably; Kearse lost his right arm to a mutant terrorist and his deep Christian values left him confused about mutant rights. Ultimately, the duo exposed and halted an FBI plot to have the Xavier Institute bombed. For his actions, Kearse became director of the MCRTF and he continues to offer aid to mutants. Although the MCRTF has had less work since the events of "M-Day," they attempted to defuse the confrontation between the X-Men and Osborn in San Francisco, only to be shut out by HAMMER officials.

QUOTE: "Some have suggested that the MCRTF is nothing but a politically-driven empty gesture. We are eager to prove those cynics wrong." — Aaron Kearse

HEPZIBAH

CLASSIFICATION:
Extraterrestrial (Mephitisoid)

LATEST SIGHTING:
San Francisco, California

Under tragic circumstances, Hepzibah came to live with the X-Men on Earth. After years of freedom-fighting among the Starjammers, a team she helped form after she escaped from the Shi'ar slave pits, Hepzibah lost her life-mate

Corsair (the father of Cyclops, Havok, and Vulcan) and relocated to Earth. She has been a founding member of Wolverine's new X-Force, though she quickly stopped associating with that team for unknown reasons, and has aided the X-Men against a number of deadly threats, including the Morlocks and the Sentinels. Hepzibah was recently apprehended by SWORD agents when Gyrich tried to take all aliens off Earth, but that was short-lived. I do have some concerns about Hepzibah's alien heritage, the Avengers once fought a deadly battle with a member of their race, but it is unfair to hold her accountable for the actions of the Mephitisoid. Wolverine tells me Hepzibah is good in a scrap, and she has tightly bonded with the mutant Warpath. Where her journey on Earth will take her remains to be seen, but I hope she does not show the same thirst for savagery she did in her battles in space.

QUOTE: (to Warpath) "There is nothing left there for me… nothing but death. And I'm tired of seeking revenge, James…it buys nothing but blood."

INK

CLASSIFICATION:
Mutate (human)

LATEST SIGHTING:
Utopia

After receiving a series of tattoos from California-based tattoo artist Leon Nunez, the young man who became Ink believed he was a mutant, with the symbolic tattoos granting him special abilities.

A tattoo of wings on his back let him fly; a Colossus-like metal forming tattoo gave him superior strength; a hazmat sign allowed him to make others ill; and two lightning bolts on his shaved head allowed him to read minds. It was eventually discovered Ink wasn't the mutant at all, but Nunez was. After a rocky beginning with a young X-Men team that was initially manipulated by Donald Pierce, formerly of the Hellfire Club, Cyclops convinced him to stay and aid the team against various threats, though Ink was constantly at odds with the others. After receiving additional tattoos to heal and an approximation of the Phoenix Force, Ink ultimately sacrificed himself to save Dust from death. The young man, as well as Nunez, is currently comatose.

QUOTE: "Hate to be the one to tell you this, guys, but the only reason I hooked up with you all is I figured the safest place for a mutant to be was with other mutants. Looks like I don't have that problem anymore."

LOCKHEED

CLASSIFICATION:
Extraterrestrial (Flock)

LATEST SIGHTING:
SWORD orbital headquarters (the Peak)

Kitty Pryde first came into contact with Lockheed, the dragon-like extraterrestrial, when she was in outer space battling the parasitic Brood.

Lockheed had been exiled from his race, the Flock, and had been terrorizing the Brood (which is no easy feat. The Brood are not easily scared of anything). After helping Pryde in space, Lockheed stowed away on the X-Men's transport back to Earth, where he and Pryde became inseparable. He has been her constant companion ever since, only separated by brief periods when one thought the other dead. Sometime in the recent past, Lockheed was approached by SWORD, the extraterrestrial monitoring agency, and became a mole in the X-Men, monitoring their activities in exchange for SWORD assistance with problems on his homeworld. Not long after this revelation caused a bit of a rift between Pryde and Lockheed, Pryde was lost in deep space for an extended time, the two unable to reconcile (if they even need reconciliation). With Pryde on Earth once more, I doubt it'll be too long before Lockheed is back amongst the X-Men.

QUOTE: "CooOOOoo"

OMEGA SENTINEL

CLASSIFICATION:
Mutate/cyborg (human)

LATEST SIGHTING:
San Francisco, California

Sentinels have come in many forms over the years, from giant robots to ever bigger Master Molds down to nano-size. One of the most frightening forms, to me, is the human/Sentinel hybrid. Hailing from India, Karima Shapandar was a talented detective-inspector whose

association with the mutant Thunderbird led her to be targeted by Bastion during Operation: Zero Tolerance (one of the most disgusting things our government has sanctioned since my revival). Bastion, who was recently revived and defeated by the X-Men, turned Shapandar into one of these Prime Sentinels, giving her extensive offensive and defensive weaponry, though you can't tell by looking at her. Karima has been a longtime ally of the X-Men on Genosha and Utopia, and she actually joined their team for a time, aiding them against deadly threats such as Pandemic, the Children of the Vault, and the Hecatomb. Karima was allied against her will with the Marauders, yet her later association with the Acolytes helped unite this rival team with the X-Men on Utopia. I have sincere concerns about Sentinel tech living among the X-Men, but Wolverine assures me, as always, it is a mutant problem, and they'll handle it.

QUOTE: (about Xavier) "Whatever humanity I still have, it's down to this man. I can't harm him. Or stand by and see him harmed."

KAVITA RAO

CLASSIFICATION:
Human

LATEST SIGHTING:
Utopia

Kavita Rao began her career in Calcutta, India, and traveled to England and America in the pursuit of advanced degrees in genetics. Backed by the alien Ord of Breakworld (who also had a questionable arrangement with SWORD), and a company called Benetech, Rao developed a "cure" to the mutant condition she called the Hope Serum. Believing being a mutant was simply a genetic mistake, or a disease, Rao experimented on mutants and corpses until she perfected the serum. She eventually came to see the error of her ways, realizing she almost committed genocide on a species, and has since joined the X-Men as a valuable ally. Along with Dr. Nemesis and Madison Jeffries, as well as others, Rao has worked in the other direction, seeking a way to cure the mutant gene. In this pursuit, she has helped transform Asteroid M into Utopia and even time-traveled to the early 1900s. Rao's cleverness stopped Graydon Creed and Bastion from getting their hands on the Hope Serum. Rao maintains her idealism that through her work she may leave a positive mark on the world.

QUOTE: "I am obsolete now, Hank. Surely you realize that. My field of research is soon to be an exercise in archeology. Who needs a mutant geneticist when there are no more mutants?"

STARJAMMERS

CLASSIFICATION:
Humans/
Extraterrestrials

LATEST SIGHTING:
The Shi'ar Empire

When a group of slaves escaped from the Shi'ar, no one could have predicted they would go on to battle injustice across the galaxy. Led by Corsair, an Earthman, the group fought against Shi'ar atrocities for several years, always against superior firepower and overwhelming odds. Aboard their ship the Starjammer, the group was frequently at odds with the massively powerful Imperial Guard, entire fleets of enemy ships, and various alien entities. The Starjammers have frequently visited Earth over the years as well; on one such visit, they lied and manipulated the Avengers, which makes me question their motivations now. One can't sacrifice integrity for personal gain and maintain alliances with heroes. Despite my doubts, though, Ms. Marvel, who served among them as Binary, assures me they are honorable and valuable allies. In recent months, the Starjammers have been held captive, utilized in mass war efforts, and, now, are widely accepted by the Shi'ar with Gladiator on the throne. I am very accustomed to the waging of war, and I must admit the Starjammers have done well in theirs.

QUOTE: "Only so fast can we run. Only so many places to hide. Only ourselves to trust. Odds turning more and more against us." — Hepzibah

SWORD

CLASSIFICATION:
Espionage agency

LATEST SIGHTING:
The Peak,
Earth orbit

Sentient Worlds Observation and Response Department (SWORD) is a top secret espionage agency handling extraterrestrial affairs for Earth. Led by Abigail Brand, a human-extraterrestrial hybrid, SWORD made an alliance with Breakworld's Ord to protect his homeworld from a prophecy that saw Breakworld destroyed by an X-Men. Ord, authorized by SWORD to eliminate the mutant genome, but eventually saw himself imprisoned by them for abusing his privileges. SWORD kept monitoring the X-Men through bugs and Lockheed. To protect Earth from Breakworld's fleet SWORD eventually brought Colossus, who was revealed to be the prohesized destroyer, to Breakworld and worked together with the mutants to avert the prophecy and save Earth from a gigantic bullet shot at our planet. SWORD's base the Peak was later destroyed during a Skrull invasion. Rebuilt after the invasion SWORD stayed autonomous under Osborn's regime and averted an invasion attempt by the Drenx, a crisis caused by Metroliths and a variety of other extraterrestrial threats since then. Employing Spider-Woman to hunt down remaining Skrull invaders SWORD also intensified their working relationship with mutants especially Beast, who worked closely with Brand on several missions.

QUOTE: "I've got to save the world." — Abigail Brand

ACOLYTES

CLASSIFICATION:
Mutants
(humans)

LATEST SIGHTING:
San Francisco,
California

Not only did
the mutants
called the
Acolytes idolize
Magneto, sharing
his belief that
mutants should
rule humanity,
but many of
them literally

worshiped him as a mutant messiah. Magneto gave sanctuary to the original Acolytes, led by Fabian Cortez. However, Cortez treacherously attempted to kill Magneto and then, claiming to be his "last disciple," become leader of mutantkind. But Magneto survived, enlisted the mutant Exodus, and reclaimed control of the Acolytes. When Magneto has been incapacitated or absent, Exodus has commanded the Acolytes. The team has had a long, varied roster, including Charles Xavier's former lover Amelia Voght, and even, briefly, Colossus and Skids. Besides their various powers, the Acolytes' fanatical fervor makes them formidable opponents. Many Acolytes have died, some were later resurrected as techno-organic beings by Selene, and others lost their mutant powers on "M-Day." Exodus recently disbanded the remaining Acolytes, but I expect that another team using that name will eventually arise, whether under Magneto's leadership or someone else's.

QUOTE: "We're the Acolytes, Flatscan. The Vanguard of the mutant race." — Frenzy

APOCALYPSE

CLASSIFICATION:
Mutant (human)

LATEST SIGHTING:
Blue Area of
the Moon

Possessing vast
powers and a
sinister genius for
battle strategy,
Apocalypse rivals
Magneto as
potentially the
most dangerous
mutant to threaten the planet. Reportedly born in Egypt 5000 years ago, Apocalypse was originally known by a name that translates into modern Arabic as "En Sabah

Nur," or "The First One," and he boasts he is the first superhuman mutant. (Actually, Selene predates him by at least 5000 years.) Apocalypse has elevated his obsession with power into a fanatical ideology that only the strong are fit to survive and dominate. Unsurprisingly, Apocalypse thinks of mutants as the strong and himself as the strongest. He glories in fomenting warfare to winnow out the supposed weak. A shape-shifter with control over his body's molecular structure, Apocalypse can give himself virtually any super-power. Through a combination of his mutation, his "regeneration" chambers, and taking over host bodies, he is effectively immortal. The X-Men and the Avengers have thwarted him, but we may never be truly rid of this menace. In one alternate timeline (Earth-295) he even ruled over America.

QUOTE: "As long as man has existed, I, Apocalypse, have stalked among them. I have had other names...But wherever there was cruelty and death, there was my face worshipped."

AVALANCHE

CLASSSIFICATION:
Mutant (human)

LATEST SIGHTING:
Utopia

With his mutant
ability to generate
powerful waves
of vibrations,
Dominic Petros,
alias Avalanche,
can trigger
avalanches and
even earthquakes.
If he is this
powerful, why did
he need to belong

to Mystique's Brotherhood of Evil Mutants? Once, on his own, Avalanche tried to extort millions from the state of California by threatening to cause a major quake. But when Avalanche turned his power against the Hulk, the feedback broke his own arms. Perhaps that understandably discouraged him from solo missions. I cannot approve of Petros' loyalty to the terrorist Mystique, but I admire his character for pursuing a cure for the Legacy virus to save his friend Pyro. To his credit, Avalanche has sought to give up crime and he opened his own bar in San Francisco. Recently Petros even fought alongside the X-Men against Bastion's forces. I hope that Petros can be encouraged to remain an honest citizen. Should he ever return to terrorist activity, he could possibly devastate entire cities. Even in a best case scenario, Avalanche will remain under surveillance for the rest of his life.

QUOTE: "Would you prefer your drink shaken or stirred?"

ISHOP

CLASSIFICATION:
Mutant (human, extra-temporal)

LATEST SIGHTING:
Reportedly stranded in an alternate future circa 6700 AD

Although the public is unaware, Lucas Bishop says he comes from a future timeline in which he grew up in a concentration camp for mutants. After their Sentinel rulers were overthrown, Bishop joined

the XSE (Xavier's Security Enforcers), a mutant police force that fought criminal mutants. The XSE was inspired by the memory of Charles Xavier, so, after Bishop traveled to our time in pursuit of a criminal, he was thrilled to meet the X-Men and join their legendary team. He was a valuable member of the X-Men with his mutant power to absorb kinetic energy, using it to project force blasts or amplify his strength. Having served as a New York police officer myself, I am particularly interested in the period when Bishop joined the FBI and helped police District X (Mutant Town), a mutant ghetto in New York. Lately, however, Bishop has betrayed the X-Men, first when he sided with pro-registration forces in the Civil War, and then by attempting to prevent his dystopian future by killing the infant mutant "messiah" Hope Summers. I am saddened Bishop seems to have succumbed to a murderous fanaticism, even inadvertently nearly killing his hero Xavier and losing his eye, his arm, and his moral compass.

QUOTE: "Talk about deja vu all over again."

BLACK WOMB

CLASSIFICATION:
Mutant (human)

LATEST SIGHTING:
Manhattan, New York City

One of this era's earliest mutants, Black Womb is immortal, though her body ages. Born in the late 1800s, she received her code name due to her inability to carry a child to full-term pregnancy, always losing them before birth (though I understand

she later gave birth to a few). Black Womb teamed with several prominent figures of the time, including Brian Xavier (father of Charles), Kurt Marko (father of Juggernaut), Destiny (later of Freedom Force), Alexander Ryking (father of Hazard), and Mister Sinister researching mutants in Alamogordo, New Mexico. There they dissected, experimented upon, and tortured many mutants, affecting the next generation in unforeseen ways. Black Womb stayed relatively isolated until months ago when, after Sinister's death, she sought to resurrect his form in her body so she'd have greater powers. Sinister had created a fail-safe in certain mutants that would allow him to control their forms in the event of his death. Black Womb was ultimately defeated, but Sinister was later resurrected as Miss Sinister, possessing telepathic powers; it is unknown if Black Womb is connected to this resurrection.

QUOTE: "You chose children, of course, because they'd be more likely to survive until you needed them. What about me, Nathaniel? Did you forget that I'd survive, too?"

BLINK

CLASSIFICATION:
Mutant (human)

LATEST SIGHTING:
Genosha

Clarice Ferguson has had to endure nothing but suffering from the day her mutant powers emerged. I'm told that when her powers first manifested, she awoke in a pool of blood, as her teleportation abilities tear apart anything she teleports. Shortly thereafter, she was captured

along with many other young mutants by the techno-organic Phalanx. During the subsequent battle against the Phalanx member Harvest, Clarice reportedly used her powers to rip Harvest into shreds, apparently killing Clarice herself. Despite confusing reports from Hercules that she was seen in the Olympian underworld, Clarice was, in fact, never truly dead. Instead, Wolverine tells me that she had teleported herself along with Harvest and spent years being physically tortured by her own uncontrollable powers. Recently, the long-lived sorceress Selene returned Blink to this plane of existence, healing her scars and manipulating Clarice into her service. Following Selene's apparent death in Genosha at the hands of Wolverine's X-Force black ops group, Blink disappeared. I can only hope that when she turns up next she will have seen through Selene's manipulations or else we will have a deadly enemy on our hands.

QUOTE: "No one hurts me! You never hurt me, do you hear me? I'm going to teleport your heart out of your body, do you hear me?!"

CHIMERA

CLASSIFICATION:
Mutate (human, extradimensional)

LATEST SIGHTING:
Westchester County, New York

Chimera is a known terrorist throughout realities wielding telekinetic energy dragons as weapons. Extradimensional firm Landau, Luckman, and

Lake were after her for some time, but never got their hands on her. She ran afoul Wolverine on our Earth after Genesis (Tyler Dayspring) hired her and has since then repeatedly returned to our Earth through her Warp Chambers forming alliances with the likes of the mutant Emplate and the Red Queen (Madelyne Pryor). With Red Queen's Sisterhood Chimera faced off with the X-Men in a failed attempt to transfer Pryor's mind into the late Jean Grey's body. She didn't fare well against the X-Men and fled with the Sisterhood after Pryor was seemingly destroyed. It would be interesting to know if Chimera stayed in our reality by will or if she is stuck here. With her current whereabouts unknown we can't do anything about her, but I heard Beast and his scientist friends have invented some technology countering teleportation, so Chimera and her friends shouldn't be too hard to catch if they face off with the X-Men again.

QUOTE: "Come to Chimera and offer us your throat."

COLLECTIVE MAN

CLASSIFICATION:
Mutants (humans)

LATEST SIGHTING:
San Francisco, California

Sun, Chang, Ho, Lin and Han Tao-Yu are quintuplet mutant siblings. Although they usually wield their power to merge all five of their bodies into a single, formidable form, they can also draw upon the strength of (supposedly) every being in China — hence, "Collective Man." I

first met them during the Grandmaster's "Contest of Champions," when they were pit against my forces in a match played in South America (they won). The Tao-Yus are usually ardent supporters of China's Communist regime amidst the many changes to their nation and mutantkind itself. After "M-Day" they joined the 198 refugee camp at Xavier's for mutual protection, but when the 198 were allowed to disperse by the O*N*E, the Tao-Yus returned to service in the Chinese government, recently serving on the People's Defense Force. I was shocked to learn that in the past few weeks the Tao-Yus have been patrolling San Francisco's Chinatown districts, working as enforcers in what amounts to a protection racket. I could respect the five brothers when they were patriots, but it seems they've been reduced to little more than thugs.

QUOTE: "There's one of me. With the strength of five."

DAKEN

CLASSIFICATION:
Mutant (human)

LATEST SIGHTING:
Japan

Recently, Daken has been increasingly in the public eye. After being trained in secret for decades by Romulus, he joined Osborn's Avengers as a brown-costumed Wolverine and participated in

very public fights with the Fantastic Four, the Molecule Man, the Asgardians and others. A loose cannon with claws, a healing factor, and the ability to manipulate the emotions of others, Daken seems to serve only his own agenda, and it is a deadly one with little to no regard for human life. Daken has, of late, repeatedly crossed paths with his father, Wolverine, as well as the Punisher. He is a frightening man who should be locked away, but Wolverine won't hear of it, saying Daken must be given a chance to prove himself, given a chance to be a hero. Wolverine assures me he has the Daken situation under control, but Wolverine himself barely seems in control some of the time; the situations with Daken and X-23 are in need of much closer monitoring. The Avengers stand ready when things get out of hand, and I'm sure they will.

QUOTE: "There's a Buddhist saying…you can explore the universe looking for somebody more deserving of love than yourself and you will not find that person. A perfect truth. No one deserves anything. You have to take what you want."

DARK BEAST

CLASSIFICATION:
Mutant (human, extradimensional)

LATEST SIGHTING:
Manhattan, New York

When you're in the business of super heroics, it's not uncommon to run into one of your counterparts from a divergent reality. From my briefings with ARMOR, I know some of my alternate-reality counterparts have been real gems, like the zombified "Colonel America" from Earth-2149 and the Mexican government's "Captain Mexica" from Earth-1519. But while ARMOR has been able to keep most of my extradimensional doppelgangers confined to their universes of origin, they were not as successful in the case of Hank McCoy's counterpart — aptly named the "Dark Beast." Dark Beast hails from Earth-295, a world in which the ancient mutant despot Apocalypse rose to power. Dark Beast became one of Apocalypse's top geneticists, subjecting other mutants to sadistic, inhumane experiments within his prison-like breeding pens. When Dark Beast sensed the end of Apocalypse's reign of terror was near, he teleported to our reality via the M'kraan Crystal, where he secretly continued his experiments. Most recently, he allied with Norman Osborn and served as one of his "Dark X-Men," although he has evaded capture following Osborn's defeat.

QUOTE: "Cutting into the flesh, altering the genetic code, twisting and changing…it's enough to make your mouth water, wouldn't you agree?"

DRAGONESS

CLASSIFICATION:
Mutant (human)

LATEST SIGHTING:
Utopia

Tamara Kurtz's mutant bioelectric abilities stem from her ancestors' having been affected by the bombing of Hiroshima. Growing up with a heart bursting with anger, she turned to terrorism and fell under the sway of time-traveling madman Stryfe. As part of his Mutant Liberation Front, Kurtz was equipped with mechanical wings and given the codename Dragoness. She fell off the radar for a while after Stryfe's seeming demise, but recently turned up amongst the crowds seeking sanctuary with the X-Men on Utopia, proving to be one of the few MLF members to retain their powers after "M-Day." As is her nature, she briefly joined other dissidents there in a failed attempt to hold the water supply hostage. Dragoness isn't a noticeable threat only because she feels comfortable following others. Even under the X-Men's protection, she bears watching, as she is definitely powerful enough to be a true threat should she decide to be. Hopefully, the team's influence will persuade her to try a new path in life.

QUOTE: "My family's genes were twisted in the fires of Hiroshima… a curse that has freed me to take my revenge upon mankind!"

EMPATH

CLASSIFICATION:
Mutant (human)

LATEST SIGHTING:
Utopia

Manuel de la Rocha is a prime example of how arrogance can twist a person. Constantly bombarded by others' conflicting emotions after his emotion-manipulating mutant powers first manifested, Manuel chose to ease his pain by ensuring those around him shared a single emotion towards him: hatred. After joining Emma Frost's Hellions, Empath repeatedly clashed with Charles Xavier's New Mutants training team and Firestar has told me of how Empath took special pleasure in manipulating her emotions. Despite his traumatization of Xavier's staff members Tom Corsi and Sharon Friedlander, the New Mutant Magma fell for Empath following her transferral to the Hellions and the two visited her homeland Nova Roma, where they shared a romance. After parting ways with Magma, Manuel briefly worked for the X-Corporation before falling under the influence of first the telepathic Elias Bogan and the drug "Kick," and later the clone Madelyne Pryor. Under Pryor's influence, Empath manipulated the emotions of the anti-mutant Hellfire Cult and battled the X-Men before being imprisoned. I can only hope that his time in the X-Men's custody will prompt him to change his ways for good but given his past history, it seems unlikely.

QUOTE: "A little bit of attention and a little psychic push and they'll do anything I ask."

EMPLATE

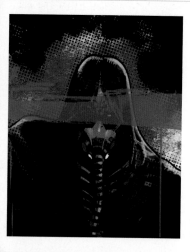

CLASSIFICATION:
Mutant (human)

LATEST SIGHTING:
Unidentified alien dimension

Like a perverted derivative of a vampire, Marius St. Croix must feed on the bone marrow of mutants in order to survive. He also duplicates the abilities of the mutants he dines upon; he's also been able to transform his victims into weird creatures similar to himself. His sisters — who formerly comprised Generation X's M — exiled him to an alien dimension, but with the assistance of his flunky DOA he's made periodic attempts to rematerialize on Earth and claim fresh victims. Due to "M-Day," Marius' menu has dwindled in size. He recently infiltrated Utopia and took Bling! back to his realm for sustenance, but Rogue led a successful rescue team and left Emplate stranded in his realm. With the efforts of Dr. Nemesis, Emplate's imprisonment may now be a permanent one. Still, as I've learned from my repeated battles with Baron Blood, vampires of any ilk will find new ways to thrive.

QUOTE: "Don't be afraid, my dear. There's nothing that need frighten you. Except for agony, enslavement and eventual death. And since you'll endure those things in the service of my survival and comfort — they're all most necessary, right and fitting."

EXODUS

CLASSIFICATION:
Mutant (human)

LATEST SIGHTING:
New Avalon

If fate had taken a different turn, the mutant known as Exodus could have been a champion for justice. Born in the 13th century, Bennet du Paris was the friend and ally of Eobar Garrington, the heroic Black Knight of that time. But on an expedition in Egypt, Bennet encountered Apocalypse, who activated the Frenchman's mutant powers and dubbed him "Exodus." Bennet rebelled against Apocalypse, who imprisoned him in the Alps for centuries. Perhaps that experience drove him mad. Exodus became fanatically devoted to his eventual rescuer, Magneto. After Xavier shut down Magneto's mind, Exodus took over his Acolytes and insanely believed he could hear his master speak to him. Exodus once tried to force the mutates of Genosha to exterminate the nation's non-mutant humans. He has allied himself with Mister Sinister and the Marauders. No one seems to know the limits of Exodus's vast powers of telepathy and telekinesis; he may even be able to raise the dead. Charles Xavier has tried to persuade Exodus to find a peaceful way to protect mutantkind, but Exodus's mental instability and disregard for non-mutant human lives make him a dire potential threat to Earth.

QUOTE: "I am Exodus—and I am slave to neither man—nor a false god the likes of you."

GAMESMASTER

CLASSIFICATION:
Mutant (human)

LATEST SIGHTING:
Manhattan, New York City

The omnipath known as the Gamesmaster reminds me somewhat of the Avengers' old foe, the Grandmaster. The X-Men have reported that the Gamesmaster's telepathic abilities are so strong that he constantly hears the voices of every mind on the planet and, in an effort to keep his mind focused, plays mental games with those he finds interesting. First gaining notoriety as the brains behind the young mutant Upstarts' game of killing mutants, the Gamesmaster masterminded the killing of Emma Frost's Hellions students as well as the attempted murders of Magneto, Cyclops, Storm, Professor X and the Hellfire Club's Sebastian Shaw. After apparently tiring of games of death, the Gamesmaster manipulated X-Force's Shatterstar into believing he was human Benjamin Russell and later tested the X-Men by altering their worldly perceptions. Wolverine tells me that most recently, the Gamesmaster, acting apparently out of loneliness, manipulated the female Wolverine clone X-23, hoping to find peace from his telepathic bombardment. Supposedly promising to return, the Gamesmaster may turn up anywhere and anytime. I suggest we be ready for him.

QUOTE: "We are all alone. Even me. Listening to every mind in the world. Every mind, weeping and loving and screaming and dying. And it never quits. Oh, God. Please. I wish it would quiet."

GLOB HERMAN

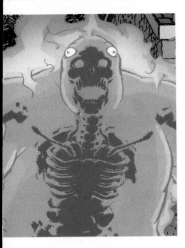

CLASSIFICATION:
Mutant (human)

LATEST SIGHTING:
San Francisco, California

Glob Herman, who appears to be a human skeleton with eyes floating in a body-form of living wax (or "bio-paraffin"), is one of the world's few remaining mutants. Beast states Glob has never shown much heroic potential and instead seems to have a tendency for rioting. Before M-Day, Xavier's school had a multitude of mutants attending, and they considered opening the doors to human students as well. A group of students, led by Kid Omega, charged themselves up on a drug called Kick and created quite a ruckus at the school. Beast told me he personally had to chase Glob, who had lit himself on fire and was chasing a bus full of students, and bury him in cement to subdue him. Kid Omega was stopped and the riot quelled, and Glob stayed relatively quiet until the mutant riots in California that led to Norman Osborn's Avengers intervening. What a mess that was. Glob Herman is an unlikely hero, assuredly. If he weren't contained by the X-Men, I might recommend him for Pym's Avengers Academy program.

QUOTE: "Wow. So now what happens when the X-Men turn up to kick our asses, Quentin?"

GORGON

CLASSIFICATION:
Mutant (human)

LATEST SIGHTING:
Unverified sightings in New Zealand

Magneto. Apocalypse. The Living Monolith. In any list of the world's most dangerous mutants, it would be foolish not to include Tomi Shishido, aka the Gorgon, near the top. After all, he is one of a very few beings in existence who can accurately profess to have "killed" Wolverine. But Gorgon's lethality is not what sets him apart from the average mutant; rather, it's his versatility. Born in Kyoto, Japan, by all accounts Gorgon was a child prodigy — gifted both physically and intellectually. But Gorgon was also an extremely disturbed individual, attempting suicide multiple times during his childhood and joining a mutant death cult known as "Dawn of the White Light" after his mutant powers manifested. By age 18, he killed his family and committed suicide to prove his loyalty to the Hand ninja cult, which mystically resurrected him to serve as their assassin. Although he was later killed by Wolverine, Gorgon was again resurrected, this time by the Hydra terrorist organization to serve as one of Baron Strucker's lieutenants. Besides his primary mutant ability to petrify people upon eye contact, Gorgon possesses superhuman speed and strength, telepathy, and a healing factor. He is also adept in the art of ninjutsu as well as the supernatural arts and is a mathematical and artistic genius.

QUOTE: "The Gorgon is that fast. The Gorgon is this silent."

HELLFIRE CLUB

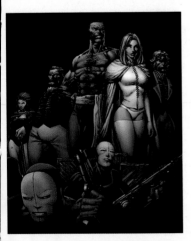

CLASSIFICATION:
Mutants/humans

LATEST SIGHTING:
New York City; London; Paris; Hong Kong

Founded in 18th-century England, the Hellfire Club has grown into a worldwide social organization for the elite in high society, politics, and business, best known for its lavish parties. The New York City branch is just a few blocks down Fifth Avenue from Avengers Mansion. Tony Stark and Warren Worthington are members, as is Norman Osborn. But, unknown to most members, each branch of the Club has an Inner Circle committed to amassing political and economic power by illicit means. In recent years, New York's Inner Circle has been dominated by its Black King, Sebastian Shaw, and his mutant allies, formerly including Emma Frost, aka the White Queen. They first came into direct conflict with the X-Men when they mentally enslaved Jean Grey as their new Black Queen; later, the mutant Selene took over that role. Roberto Da Costa, alias Sunspot of the New Mutants, lately became Lord Imperial, head of all the Club's branches. I had hoped Da Costa could restrain the Inner Circles from further criminal activity, but he was not able to stop Selene's recent conquest of Genosha.

QUOTE: "Fais ce que te voudras" ("Do what thou wilt") — club motto.

JOHNNY DEE

CLASSIFICATION:
Mutant (human)

LATEST SIGHTING:
Manhattan,
New York City

The criminal
mutant Johnny
Dee has an
intensely
complicated
power set.
Though appearing
like a normal
human, Dee
has a sentient entity growing on his abdomen, really
just a mouth with teeth, eyes, and tentacles, though it

does seem to have its own digestive system. Incapable
of speech, the entity can utilize the genetic material of a
known superhuman in the creation of an egg, which later
hatches a small living puppet through which Johnny can
control the person the puppet is formed after. Using these
powers, Dee, whose motivations are entirely self-serving,
killed the mutant Jazz, broke the neck of O*N*E General
Lazer, and forced Magma to kill the powerful Mr. M. Dee
manipulated the X-Men, as well as the government and the
198, during times of tremendous political stress. When the
198 were being contained by the O*N*E, Dee deliberately
heightened tensions in the camp. And during the Civil War,
Dee, nearly caused all the world's mutants to be killed.
What a relief he is behind bars.

QUOTE: "I'm not a mutant. He's the mutant. Two separate
brains. Two different personalities. It's a drooling idiot. It
doesn't need a name. And it can't talk. You need something,
talk to me. I'll make him do it — if I feel like it."

LADY MASTERMIND

CLASSIFICATION:
Mutant (human)

LATEST SIGHTING:
San Francisco,
California

Regan Wyngarde,
alias Lady
Mastermind,
is the blonde
daughter of
the late Jason
Wyngarde,
the original
Mastermind, and
inherited his
mutant power

to cast illusions. She and her half-sister, Martinique, who
calls herself the new Mastermind, seem locked in an
intense sibling rivalry, presumably over who has a better
right to carry on their father's name. This is hardly a noble
tradition; the original Mastermind was a contemptible man
who invaded and twisted Jean Grey's psyche, inadvertently
triggering her emergence as Dark Phoenix. Rogue made
a serious mistake by trusting Regan enough to induct
her into the X-Men; the treacherous Regan proved to be
working with their enemies, the Marauders. A brilliant,
murderous sociopath, she takes perverse joy in her
criminal acts. Recently, the two Wyngarde sisters worked
together, if not amicably, in the Red Queen's Sisterhood.
Surprisingly, it is rumored both Regan and Martinique are
sisters of Pixie, a new member of the X-Men, but the truth
has yet to be confirmed.

QUOTE: (to her half-sister Mastermind) "Bimbo!"

LEGION

CLASSIFICATION:
Mutant (human)

LATEST SIGHTING:
Utopia

David Charles
Haller is
perhaps the
most dangerous
mutant alive,
mostly due to his
unpredictable
nature. The son
of Professor
Charles Xavier
and Israeli diplomat Gabrielle Haller, Haller suffers from
multiple personality disorder wherein each personality

within David manifests a different mutant power that
Legion can utilize while that personality is dominant.
Kept hidden from Xavier, Legion was placed in the care
of Dr. Moira MacTaggert on Muir Island, where he battled
Xavier's New Mutants after he uncontrollably absorbed
the psyches of two of Xavier's associates. Returned to a
temporary semblance of normalcy, Legion was now aware of
his father and later sought to slay Xavier's enemy Magneto,
ultimately resulting in a brief temporal warp. His mind
shattered into thousands of personalities from the event,
Legion sought out the New Mutants and was taken into
X-Men custody, where he recently aided the X-Men against
Bastion's Sentinels with the help of Xavier. Despite my
concerns about his fragile mental state, Beast tells me that
the X-Men's scientists have contained 53% of Legion's
personalities and with time, may be able to use Legion to
cause spontaneous mutations in an effort to reignite the
depowered mutant population.

QUOTE: "No no no...I've been bad again, haven't I?"

MARAUDERS

CLASSIFICATION:
Mutants
(humans, clones)

LATEST SIGHTING:
Kitakyushu,
Japan

While the Right
and other anti-
mutant groups
have turned even
more vicious of
late, mutantkind
has a group just
as lethal: the
aptly named
Marauders.

Often working for Mr. Sinister, this team of murderers has
utilized their unique powers for little more than targeting
and killing other mutants. They made their first mark when
they massacred nearly the entire Morlock community, and
have returned time and again, leaving untold numbers
of bodies in their wake. A number of Marauders have
been killed in action only to turn up later; presumably,
this is due to Sinister's cloning expertise. Not one of
these assassins can be taken lightly, from the marksman
Scalphunter to the unassuming, ability-disrupting
Scrambler. Joined by Exodus' Acolytes, they took part in
the hunt for Hope Summers when she was first discovered,
with more casualties added to their body count in the
process. Each and every one of these butchers must be
found and apprehended before they can kill again. They
are not to be underestimated under any circumstances.

QUOTE: "We kill mutants. Who's next?" — Scalphunter

MASTERMIND

CLASSIFICATION:
Mutant (human)

LATEST SIGHTING:
San Francisco,
California

The mutant
known as
Mastermind is
the dark-haired
daughter of
the late Jason
Wyngarde,
the original
Mastermind, and
shares his ability
to cast illusions.

Although she was born Martinique Wyngarde, she calls
herself Martinique Jason, perhaps in order to distinguish
herself from her half-sister, Regan Wyngarde, alias Lady
Mastermind, whom she detests. Before he succumbed to
the Legacy virus, their father was a longtime foe of the
X-Men. The new Mastermind seems to be following in his
footsteps, first trying to take revenge on Wolverine and later
joining Mystique's Brotherhood; recently, both Wyngarde
daughters joined the Red Queen's Sisterhood. Martinique
is arguably the most powerful and malevolent member of
the Wyngarde family. She seems to have developed strong
telepathic abilities, once casting illusions affecting the
entire city of San Francisco, and aided Mystique in her
devastating terrorist assault on Paris.

QUOTE: (to her half-sister, Lady Mastermind) "Remedial
mathlete!"

MENTALLO

CLASSIFICATION:
Mutant (human)

LATEST SIGHTING:
New York City

The criminal
telepath Mentallo
is a perennial
underachiever.
Indeed, as Marvin
Flumm, he once
seemed content
to work as a shoe
salesman, despite
his powers.
SHIELD recruited
him into its ESP

Division, where Flumm mastered his abilities and started
his criminal career. It seems that Flumm usually needs
teammates or a partner to pursue a plan, and so he teamed
up with Norbert Ebersol, the criminal inventor called the
Fixer. Backed by Hydra, Mentallo and the Fixer almost took
over SHIELD's New York headquarters but were thwarted
by Nick Fury. Later, they attempted to mentally control
the President of the United States, but were stopped by
the Fantastic Four. After splitting with the Fixer, Mentallo
joined the mutant Resistants under the alias Think-Tank.
It's ironic that Fixer has seemingly gone straight while his
friend Mentallo still pursues a third-rate criminal career.
Over the years Mentallo has also worked for the Red Skull,
MODOK and the Hood. His powers may not be as great as
Charles Xavier's but are still formidable enough. We should
be grateful that he hasn't figured out how to use them
more effectively.

QUOTE: "Not even ESP can accurately predict a person's
shoe size."

MISTER X

CLASSIFICATION:
Mutant (human)

LATEST SIGHTING:
Madripoor

The mutant low-level telepath only known as Mr. X is a merciless killer from parts unknown. According to Wolverine X experienced death for the first time as a child when a woman died after a car accident. He became addicted to the feeling and trained to become what he is today after destroying all records on his true identity. We know each scar on his body is a mark for a murder and he has plenty of scars. Trained in several forms of martial arts and armed combat X's ability to anticipate his opponent's every move turns any confrontation with him into an uneven fight. Only few were ever able to beat him either due to their feral rage (Wolverine) or speed (Quicksilver). He has many enemies, but has no need of protection and honestly has no right to get one either in my opinion after the countless murders he committed, even though he is part of an endangered species. X avoided legal ramifications and fled to Madripoor after his recent alliance with Norman Osborn. Wolverine beat him several times and would probably be best suited to catch X and hand him over to US authorities.

QUOTE: "Finally a suitable challenge!"

MORLOCKS

CLASSIFICATION:
Mutants (humans)

LATEST SIGHTING:
The Alley and other tunnels beneath New York City

Aptly named after the subterranean dwellers in H. G. Wells' "The Time Machine," the Morlocks are another example of the sad fate so many mutants have experienced. Their mutations made most of them look so inhuman that they became outcasts in mainstream society. So instead they formed a community in the network of abandoned tunnels beneath New York City, founded by their original leader Callisto. Although the Morlocks would steal food and other necessities from the surface world, they were no serious threat. Nevertheless Mr. Sinister sent his assassination squad, the Marauders, to massacre the Morlocks. Many survivors later returned as Gene Nation, terrorists taking revenge on humanity. Most Gene Nation members (except Marrow) have been killed, and many other surviving Morlocks lost their mutant powers on "M-Day." Masque, one of those to retain their powers, leads a small Morlock band that SHIELD regards as a potential menace. Though the New York Morlocks are so radically reduced in number, similar underground mutant communities have been discovered in Chicago and London. I would not be surprised if major cities around the globe had their own Morlocks.

QUOTE: "Heh... Maybe yer a hunter where you come from, kid... but this's our territory, an' we got an edge you don't even know." — Masque

MORTIS

CLASSIFICATION:
Mutant (human)

LATEST SIGHTING:
Utopia

Lois London, the mutant Dazzler's half-sister, possesses a matter-decaying touch capable of causing instant death. While living with her half-sister her powers first manifested, and she accidentally killed a derelict. Blackmailed by a detective, who was sent after her by her father, Lois was cleared of the murder charges when the detective's pictures didn't depict her powers. The detective was arrested, and Lois returned to her father to use his money to protect herself. Though she parted on good terms with Dazzler, Lois' hatred toward her grew when she remembered how her father always preferred Dazzler. After killing her father, she joined former Hellfire Club Black Queen Selene's Inner Circle as Mortis. After Selene's defeat at the hands of the combined forces of X-Force and the X-Men, Mortis joined forces with Murderworld creator Arcade and sonic-powered Ulysses Klaw to destroy Dazzler. Unaffected by Lois' touch, Dazzler defeated her and took Lois to Utopia, where she is now under the X-Men's care. In light of her recent actions, I would've preferred Lois to be handed over to the proper authorities.

QUOTE: "I wanted to kill every one of us! We're abominations!"

MYSTIQUE

CLASSIFICATION:
Mutant (human)

LATEST SIGHTING:
New York City

Of all known terrorists, Mystique is the most difficult to find and stop. A mutant shape-shifter, who is also a consummate actress, she is apable of impersonating anyone, male or female. She even nfiltrated the US Department of Defense, becoming a high official under what appears to be her real name, Raven Darkholme. She first came to public attention when she led her own Brotherhood of Evil Mutants in an assassination attempt on the late Senator Robert Kelly. Mystique was sincerely devoted to her partner, Destiny, and their adopted daughter, Rogue, but she also tried to kill her son, Nightcrawler, in infancy. When circumstances dictated, she has led Freedom Force for the US government, joined X-Factor and operated as Charles Xavier's agent. But Mystique seems to be mentally unstable, reportedly planned to use a variation of the Legacy virus to wipe out non-mutant humanity, made a terrorist attack on Paris, killed Dr. Moira MacTaggert, and served in Norman Osborn's Dark X-Men. The X-Men once inducted her as a member, but of course she betrayed them. Mystique should never be trusted: she is never what she appears to be.

QUOTE: "I am Mystique! My colleagues and I comprise the Brotherhood of Evil Mutants. We are your future, humans. Resist us at your peril."

NEKRA

CLASSIFICATION:
Mutant (human)

LATEST SIGHTING:
San Francisco

Nekra Sinclair can increase her strength and durability through hate and other violent emotions. Born an albino to African-American Gemma Sinclair, she befriended fellow mutant Mandrill during their teens and affected by Mandrill's pheromones didn't hate him. For years they tormented the world with terrorist plots to overthrow nations and governments but parted ways when Mandrill left her behind to be captured. Nekra worked solo awhile, but soon found a new partner and lover in Grim Reaper (Eric Williams), whom she brought back to life with voodoo when he fell to his death in a fight against the Avengers. Grim Reaper showed no sympathy for her actions and sacrificed himself to stop her from harming his brother, Wonder Man, Vision and the Scarlet Witch. Not learning her lesson, Nekra revived Grim Reaper again, and he killed her. Resurrected by the Son of Satan Hellstorm, Nekra eventually reunited with Grim Reaper, whom she still loved. They formed a new incarnation of the Lethal Legion to oppose Norman Osborn. When the Reaper's gang folded, Nekra wound up incarcerated at the Raft, but was later released and wound up in San Francisco.

QUOTE: "I cannot be conquered, for mine is the living power of hate!"

NEO

CLASSIFICATION:
Mutants

LATEST SIGHTING:
San Francisco, California

Led by Domina, the Neo are comprised of "warclans," who honor hunting and killing. Their mutations seem to reflect this, having developed powers such as turning parts of their bodies into firearms or generating bladed weapons. Just as some mutant supremacists look down on humans as "Flatscans," the Neo have little regard for other mutants, dubbing non-Neo as "Spikes." The Neo have been secluded in their culture for most of their history, but exploded into the public eye after the High Evolutionary briefly removed the powers of all mutants on Earth, inadvertently killing several Neo. The Neo have clashed repeatedly with the X-Men, at first thinking them responsible for their depowerment. Given this, one wonders how widely they were affected by "M-Day." In their most recent assault on the X-Men in San Francisco, they were driven off by the X-Men's youthful trainees. The Neo have no known allies outside their own ranks; although they profess to be a long-lived culture of warriors, they will surely dwindle in stature unless they come to terms with human and mutant values.

QUOTE: "There is much to admire about them. Were circumstances different, I might have welcomed them as friends. But this is war and friendship is a risk we dare not take." — Domina

OMEGA

CLASSIFICATION:
Mutant (human)

LATEST SIGHTING:
Manhattan,
New York City

On M-Day, millions of mutants lost their powers, and all their energy was gathered by a being called the Collective, which possessed a new mutant with the ability to absorb other mutants' energies and turn them into concussive force. The Collective destroyed the town of North Pole, Alaska, killing thousands, and then killed most of Alpha Flight, before it was finally defeated by the Avengers. The mutant who had been possessed later joined Omega Flight as Weapon Omega, seeking penance for his crimes by protecting the Canadian people in the Guardian armor. The Canadian government captured dozens of criminals and used them to experiment on Weapon Omega's absorption capabilities, lying to the Americans along the way. Weapon Omega left there addicted to power and highly insane. Now calling himself Omega, he joined Osborn's X-Men team and grew even more addicted to power absorption and criminal activity. Iron Man and USAgent both assure me Omega has a noble soul, but this man has shown weakness over strength thus far.

QUOTE: "I remember now...what he did to Alpha Flight...to my home...my family. I did, you know? Didn't remember. Not at first. But that thing — the Collective — it's still in there. A little bit is still inside of me...and it remembers."

ONSLAUGHT

CLASSIFICATION:
Energy manifestation of mutants

LATEST SIGHTING:
The Negative Zone

Charles Xavier is one of the wisest persons I have ever known, yet even he is capable of grave error. In combat with his nemesis Magneto, Xavier felt it necessary to telepathically shut down Magneto's mind. Unwittingly, Xavier absorbed the negative side of Magneto's psyche, which combined with the darker impulses that existed deep within Xavier's own mind. Together they gave rise to a separate entity that manifested itself as Onslaught. Determined to bring about Xavier's dream of a safe world for mutants through Magneto's goal of conquering the Earth, Onslaught took over Manhattan. Capturing Franklin Richards and Nate Grey, Onslaught added their powers to its own, enabling it to remake reality at will. Ultimately, Onslaught decided to exterminate both mutants and non-mutants. The Fantastic Four, the Avengers and I plunged into Onslaught's psionic form to destroy it. We too would have been destroyed had Franklin not used his vast powers to create an alternate world as our temporary refuge. Nonetheless, Onslaught was recently reborn, only to be exiled into the Negative Zone, I hope, permanently.

QUOTE: "Homo sapiens — hear the words of Onslaught! From this day forward, the humans shall no longer inherit the Earth! No more shall mutantkind be so savagely oppressed — for today marks the ultimate ascendance of the Homo Superior race!"

RED QUEEN

CLASSIFICATION:
Mutant (human, clone)

LATEST SIGHTING:
Westchester County, New York

The family tree extending from Cyclops and Phoenix is one of the most complex and convoluted I can imagine. Determining that their genetic stock would produce a powerful mutant, Mr. Sinister cloned Jean Grey, creating Madelyne Pryor, who briefly married Cyclops and conceived a son, Nathan, who grew to adulthood in the future and eventually returned as Cable (when you mix in the Phoenix Force, alternate reality versions of Jean and Madelyne, and Cyclops and Jean's children from alternate timelines, Marvel Girl and Nate Grey, things get even more confusing). Madelyne, a trained pilot, entered a lengthy association with the X-Men during their days in Australia. In a complex series of events, Madelyne became the Goblin Queen and tried to murder her son before she died tragically. Recently, Beast tells me, Madelyne returned as the Red Queen, an intensely powerful psychic ghost, and formed the Sisterhood of Evil Mutants and the Hellfire Cult in an attempt to resurrect Jean and inhabit her body. The X-Men defeated her at Jean's grave, but I doubt this powerful spirit will stay at rest.

QUOTE: "Let you help me? Don't make me laugh, you child. You could never help me. Not as a hero — not as a man — and certainly not as a husband. Madelyne Pryor never loved you."

SCARLET WITCH

CLASSIFICATION:
Mutant (human)

LATEST SIGHTING:
Unknown

I look at my early days with the Avengers and my media-dubbed "Kooky Quartet" as some of my finest memories. Hawkeye (who'd fought Iron Man), with Quicksilver and the Scarlet Witch (formerly of the Brotherhood of Evil Mutants) quickly became my close friends and allies,

and I've watched all three go through powerful changes throughout the years. The Scarlet Witch learned magic at the hands of Agatha Harkness, married the Vision (a synthetic man), bore twin sons and later lost them, and grew to lead the Avengers. Unfortunately, Scarlet Witch also went insane for a time, and none of us realized how badly that would come back to haunt us. She tampered with reality itself, lashing out at her own friends and family in her hysteria. She murdered Ant-Man, the Vision, Hawkeye, and Jack of Hearts. Scarlet Witch's powers over probability did irrevocable damage to our world. I can't help but wonder if I could have done something, anything, to stop things from going so far. But as well as I knew the Scarlet Witch, or thought I knew her, I couldn't have predicted this. I don't even know if she's dead now.

QUOTE: "You are the oldest, Pietro, and I shall do as you say! But, I thought we had vowed never again to use our super-powers for others!"

SELENE

CLASSIFICATION:
Mutant (human)

LATEST SIGHTING:
Genosha

I have known the evil that is Selene for quite some time now, ever since she collapsed the Hellfire Club's ceiling on Diamondback and I years back. A bizarre and complicated

woman, Selene is immortal, an energy vampire, and has multiple psychic abilities, including changing her shape and commanding matter. Selene is thousands of years old and seems to be content at times to wait decades, manipulating powerful figures and being involved in politics, such as she did in ancient Rome, Nova Roma, and the Hellfire Club. At other times, she is megalomaniacal and covets thousands or even millions of souls for her own sustenance, proclaiming this will ascend her to godhood. Selene is directly behind the event the X-Men are calling Necrosha, and she resurrected millions of deceased mutants and former mutants all so she could kill them again and drain their energy. Selene was narrowly defeated on Genosha by Wolverine's X-Force team, but I have no doubt she'll return, as Apocalypse does repeatedly. The Avengers need to be ready.

QUOTE: "Do you understand the power of a living soul? It is like nothing you have ever experienced, my children. To consume such a thing…it is ecstasy."

SEBASTIAN SHAW

CLASSIFICATION:
Mutant (human)

LATEST SIGHTING:
Utopia

Charismatic, cunning, and highly ambitious, Sebastian Shaw made a fortune while still in his 20s as head of Shaw Industries. Like his ancestors, he joined the Hellfire Club, and he became a member of the New York branch's secret Council of the Chosen. Shaw was

secretly a mutant, with the ability (resembling Bishop's) to absorb kinetic energy to amplify his physical strength. In alliance with fellow mutant Emma Frost, Shaw engineered the death of Council leader Edward Buckman and took command as its Black King, renaming it the Inner Circle. Since then, Shaw has worked through the Inner Circle to amass power by ruthless and covert means. Ironically, he has even manufactured Sentinels for the federal government, presumably in order to use them against his enemies, like the X-Men. Shaw has clashed with them repeatedly, starting when he used the original Mastermind to mentally enslave Jean Grey. A formidable adversary, Shaw has survived attempts to overthrow him, even an assassination attempt by his son Shinobi, and always returns to power. Recently the X-Men took him prisoner at their new haven, Utopia, but I suspect his mutant abilities make it hard to keep him incarcerated for long.

QUOTE: (to Magneto) "The world cannot be bound by physical power, Magnus. Even power such as yours!"

SILVER SAMURAI

CLASSIFICATION:
Mutant (human)

LATEST SIGHTING:
Agrashima, Japan

The allegiances and dealings of the Silver Samurai are as complicated and ambiguous as the history of his familial clan, the Yashida. The powerful Clan Yashida was one of many samurai clans founded in ancient Japan to protect their members from those who would oppress and exploit them. However, by the time of my first arrival in Japan during World War II, many of the clans had degenerated into modern-day Yakuza gangs. For instance, Silver Samurai's father, Lord Shingen Harada, spent decades transforming Clan Yashida into an illegal heroin-smuggling operation. The bushido-trained Silver Samurai inherited control of Clan Yashida following the deaths of his father and half-sister, Mariko Yashida. As oyabun, he has worked to divest Clan Yashida of its extensive criminal holdings to atone for his past crimes and even briefly served as field leader of Japan's premier super-team, Big Hero 6, before finding employment as the captain of the Japanese Prime Minister's personal security cadre. Nonetheless, the general populace still fears the Silver Samurai, despite his efforts to reform. He was last sighted in the clan's ancestral castle in the port city of Agrashima, Miyago Prefecture, defending Clan Yashida's assets from those seeking to seize them.

QUOTE: "I have no time to waste on you, gaijin. Your lack of discipline is obvious to all!"

SKEIN

CLASSIFICATION:
Mutant (human)

LATEST SIGHTING:
Broxton, Oklahoma

Skein, formerly known as the criminal Gypsy Moth, is a Romanian mutant who can manipulate fabrics and levitate. When she suspected her boyfriend, to an American actor, of cheating on her she became Gypsy Moth. After he died of natural causes, she inherited his fortune and became leader of a hedonistic cult in Los Angeles. She ran afoul of Spider-Woman on several occasions and worked with many criminal groups including Night Shift, the Femizons and the Masters of Evil. She also formed a small business empire by founding an adult club chain. She turned away from crime when Hawkeye offered her membership in the Thunderbolts for ulterior reasons. Reimagining herself as Skein, she worked with them for a short time, but eventually quit the team. Norman Osborn later hired her for the Initiative as a member of Delaware's Women Warriors and participated in Osborn's assault on Asgard. Skein isn't a criminal at heart, but she lives an amoral lifestyle, willingly allies with criminals and never shows much loyalty to others beside herself.

QUOTE: "I never did it with a hero before...I wonder if they like to keep their costumes on?"

STINGER

CLASSIFICATION:
Mutant (human)

LATEST SIGHTING:
Utopia

I recently looked up the criminal record of Wendy Sherman, known as Stinger, learning she served a long prison term for her role in a group called the Alliance of Evil alongside Frenzy (of the Acolytes), Tower (now deceased), and Timeshadow (completely off the grid). The Alliance remained united for a lengthy period, fighting for various purposes. Originally working for the megalomaniacal Apocalypse, during which time Wendy grew addicted to deceased mutant Michael Nowlan's power enhancing abilities, they later fought X-Factor a few times. The Alliance later re-formed to make a public statement after the passing of the brief Mutant Registration Act. The Alliance then briefly worked for a strangely powered terrorist called Harness. After M-Day, Stinger, who can emit electrical discharges from her hands, was one of the world's few remaining mutants and felt she had no choice but to live among her kind on Utopia. I understand from Beast she recently panicked, feeling isolated and like she had no friends among her kind. She kidnapped Kavita Rao, but Iceman was able to calm her. I'll trust Cyclops to keep Ms. Sherman contained.

QUOTE: "You're an X-Man. One of the originals. You're a hero. I just...I just needed to know...that everything was going to be okay."

SUGAR MAN

CLASSIFICATION:
Mutant (human, extradimensional)

LATEST SIGHTING:
Genosha

According to information gathered by the X-Men and their allies, the Sugar Man seemingly hails from an alternate Earth and at some point traveled to our Earth's past where he helped turn the island nation Genosha into an industrial giant with future technology. He was responsible for the creation of the mutate slave population and has to be considered behind all atrocities committed on Genosha over the last 20 years. Though his activities were exposed, he escaped captivity and survived a violent encounter with X-Men ally Callisto and a Sentinel attack that nearly wiped out Genosha's whole population. Beast assured me of his survival, as Sugar Man was among the scientists he contacted to find a way to save mutantkind. The greedy abomination refused to help due to Beast not offering him any payment. Sugar Man can alter his size and mass, ruthlessly kills enemies with his extendable tongue and is as ugly on the inside as he is on the outside. Sugar Man's whereabouts are unknown, though he could still be on Genosha, having survived the recent rise of the dead on the devastated island nation.

QUOTE: "I've kept my secret for 20 years. You won't catch the Sugar Man unprepared."

TOAD

CLASSIFICATION:
Mutant (human)

LATEST SIGHTING:
San Francisco, California

Though he is considerably more dangerous than he may seem at first glance, Mortimer Toynbee, alias the Toad, has long struck my colleagues as more pathetic than truly evil. Abandoned by his parents, Toynbee grew up in an orphanage, where other children tormented him, considering him a freak. Toynbee became so introverted he was mistakenly thought to be mentally challenged, and he was desperately lonely. Possessing superhuman leaping ability, Toynbee was recruited into the original Brotherhood of Evil Mutants and became slavishly devoted to his "master" Magneto, who treated him with contempt. Toynbee's rage at this abuse grew, and he finally rebelled against Magneto. But since then Toynbee has drifted, sometimes trying to kill his supposed enemies, and once even joining a super-hero team, the Misfits. He tried forming his own short-lived criminal Brotherhood, later joined other mutant Brotherhoods, and even reverted to his sad loyalty to Magneto. What the Toad needs is a mentor in the mutant community to give him a positive direction in life, away from empty criminality.

QUOTE: "Nothing can stop you, Magneto!! You were born to rule!"

TYPHOID MARY

CLASSIFICATION:
Mutant (human)

LATEST SIGHTING:
Manhattan, New York City

While I have never encountered Typhoid Mary, I am confidant she is one of the most dangerous women alive.

Suffering from dissociative personality disorder, Mary can access telepathy, telekinesis and pyrokinesis, the levels of which vary by her dominant personality. Typhoid began her criminal career working with mercenary T-Ray before she came to the attention of the Kingpin. While working for the Kingpin, Typhoid romanced and attempted to ruin Daredevil, who had her committed. Typhoid escaped and was employed by Wolverine to help free mutant empath Jessie Drake, during which time her misandric Bloody Mary persona and later her generally well-balanced Walker identity became dominant. Typhoid eventually joined the Initiative, who pardoned her and integrated her personalities into the coldly efficient Mutant Zero. Shortly after Norman Osborn took over the Initiative, Mary's Typhoid identity re-emerged, and she aided her Shadow Initiative teammates against Hydra before departing the team. Why Henry Gyrich thought Typhoid would be a good candidate for the Initiative is anyone's guess, especially given her track record at containing her various personalities. She has recently been active in Shadowland as one of Daredevil's lieutenants, just one of many signs pointing to Daredevil's corruption by the Hand.

QUOTE: "I have four different personalities. I've tried controlling them...tried closing them off. Nothing worked."

VANISHER

CLASSIFICATION:
Mutant (human)

LATEST SIGHTING:
Utopia

I understand the need for a teleporter in a superhuman combat unit, as they are a distinct tactical benefit. I also understand the desire to keep mutants together, as the dwindling population makes "strength in numbers" a necessity more than just a cliché. But it disgusts me the Vanisher is one of the mutants the X-Men have come to rely on. He's utterly irredeemable. He is a blackmailer, a would-be terrorist, a thieves' gang leader, a drug cartel lord; a slimy, nasty individual that has brought the world more harm than good. Many villains have become heroes of great standing (Hawkeye, Rogue), but I suspect that even though Vanisher has worked with the X-Men recently, it's been more for self-serving reasons, and he never stopped his shady underworld activities. I trust Cyclops, and even Wolverine, to keep him somewhat in check, but as I said, redemption is beyond Vanisher's grasp, as far as I'm concerned. Vanisher's current status is unconfirmed, as he was one of the teleporters targeted by Bastion in his recent campaign against mutants.

QUOTE: "God, you idiots love your drama."

WHIRLWIND

CLASSIFICATION:
Mutant (human)

LATEST SIGHTING:
Denver, Colorado

David Cannon is one of the Avengers' most recurring enemies. Starting his criminal career as the Human Top, Cannon battled Giant-Man (Hank Pym) and the Wasp, beginning his obsession with Janet Van Dyne. After changing his criminal identity to Whirlwind, David posed as the Wasp's chauffeur to briefly capture Pym (then as Goliath) and Wasp before joining Ultron's Masters of Evil to battle the Avengers. Whirlwind later joined an incarnation of the Lethal Legion, where his powers were briefly amplified before being absorbed by Count Nefaria. Rejoining the Masters of Evil under Egghead, Whirlwind attacked the Wasp unauthorized, leading to the Masters' capture. Shortly thereafter, Whirlwind added deadly wrist blades to his costume. Over time, Whirlwind's obsession with the Wasp seems to have affected his mental stability. Whirlwind has even resorted to murdering prostitutes whom he dressed as the Wasp. Whirlwind later teamed with Mr. Hyde, Boomerang and Tiger Shark to blackmail Norman Osborn. With Osborn now behind bars, Whirlwind most recently turned up in Manhattan, seemingly more deranged than ever, where he publicly battled Pym's Avengers Academy students.

QUOTE: "I'm not crazy. I'm just a man in love. And sometimes, Wasp, love doesn't just hurt. It kills."

X-CELL

CLASSIFICATION:
Humans
(ex-mutants)

LATEST SIGHTING:
Manhattan,
New York City

After M-Day, most of the world's mutants were left powerless. Many integrated into regular society with no problems, many were thrilled to no longer have powers, but still many others were dead because their malformed bodies could no longer survive without their powers. One group of former mutants formed the criminal X-Cell and, based in Mutant Town, began attacking government officials and military representatives, believing they were behind the decimation. X-Cell was primarily made up of former mutant criminals, including the Blob, Callisto, Fatale, Marrow, Abyss, Reaper, and Elijah Cross. When a group of them received facsimiles of their powers from a Terrigen Crystal-powered Quicksilver (or a Skrull posing as Quicksilver, as I understand it), they engaged in a very public battle with X-Factor on the streets. As their powers burnt out, unable to be contained in their now-human bodies, the X-Cell disappeared with a teleporting Abyss. This situation grew out of control too quickly. Criminals, mutant or not, need to be locked up, and the idea of re-powerment through alternative sources is too dangerous to be contemplated. Far too many lives have been lost.

QUOTE: "We're the good guys here! That's why people like Callisto and Marrow joined up! We should all be working together to build a future!"

ANTI-MUTANT SENTIMENT

"...I have created a defense for mankind! Whether I win or lose this debate does not matter...for the mutants will never take over the human race now! Not while my new army of Sentinels live!"

With those words Bolivar Trask ushered his Sentinels into the world, and anti-mutant hysteria reached new heights. The launch of the first wave of Sentinels was accompanied by rioting across the country, and its impact can still be felt to this day. It is not simply that Trask introduced the Sentinels — which, to be sure, have proliferated considerably — but he legitimatized the beliefs of anti-mutant bigots across the globe and demonstrated that humans could fight back against the "mutant menace."

Mutant hate groups have come in many stripes beyond the obvious Sentinel programs. They have included: William Stryker's Purifiers, who justified their hatred through their twisted religious beliefs; Donald Pierce's Reavers, a gang of cybernetic mutant-haters; Cameron Hodge's Right, whose members claimed to be mutants to sway the public; Graydon Creed's Friends of Humanity, which had significant political support in their attempts to put Creed in the White House; Simon Trask's Humanity's Last Stand, which impersonated the Mutant Liberation Front to mask their actions; Bastion's Operation: Zero Tolerance, the briefly sanctioned outfit that tried to imprison our nation's mutants; John Sublime's U-Men, who harvest mutants for their organs to become "post-human"; Purity, a largely Internet-driven movement with large followings amongst teens and college-aged people; the Church of Humanity, another religion-based cult that brutalized mutants; and post-"M-Day" groups including the Leper Queen's Sapien League, the violent Hellfire Cult gang and Simon Trask's Humanity Now! Coalition, which have tried to strike down the few mutants who remain.

Perhaps the single most dangerous enemy to mutantkind is Mr. Sinister, despite having employed many mutants to his cause. Sinister is linked to more than 1000 mutant deaths, but considering his activity reaches back more than 120 years, that figure may be well into the hundreds of thousands.

Of course, the government has played a considerable role in this sad state of affairs. Not only has most of the research into Sentinels been paid for with government funds through the likes of Project: Wideawake, but it has instituted Mutant Registration, allowed maniacs like Norman Osborn to terrorize the mutant community and turned a blind eye to the horrors of the Neverland concentration camp, the struggles of the 198 and the misery of the Morlocks. Further, conspiracies in virtually every intelligence department from the FBI to CIA to O*N*E have sought to have mutants exterminated.

However, persecution of mutants occurs across the globe. The USSR instituted a brutal practice of conscripting mutants for national service, killing those who failed to comply, and Cuba possessed its own Sentinel program. Of course, all examples pale next to that of Genosha, which was host to four monstrous exhibitions within a matter of years: first, the Genoshan regime stripped mutants of their free will and forced them to serve the state as "mutate" slaves, viewing them as a mere natural resource to be exploited; second, the fall of that regime, which led to mutate uprisings and civil war; third, Magneto's rise to power and the militarization of mutants that nearly exploded into full-out war; and fourth, the destruction of Genosha by Cassandra Nova's Sentinels, at the time the largest loss of mutant life in history.

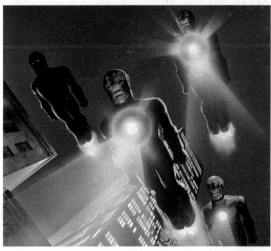

But perhaps the most unfortunate aspect of anti-mutant rhetoric is that mutants themselves come to believe it. Not only can you find self-loathing mutants who also hate their "community," but you find good men like Cyclops authorizing an assassination squad, believing there were no other options to deal with their enemies. X-Force, along with terrorist groups like the Acolytes and Mutant Liberation Front, have only further swayed public opinion against the mutants and made the zealots more dogged in their hopes of exterminating them. Then you have the regrettable period when Warren Worthington's X-Factor posed as mutant hunters, the mutant Stryfe unleashed the Legacy virus, and the Hellfire Club's Inner Circle persecuted fellow mutants for their own profit. Tragically, many of the mutants depowered on "M-Day" found themselves rejected by the mutant communities they had always called home, an attitude no better than mutant supremacy. Sadly, we are all too human, as these incidents attest.

BASTION

CLASSIFICATION:
Techno-organic

LATEST SIGHTING:
San Francisco, California

Bastion is the worst sort of anti-mutant being I've encountered, in part because of his unfeeling, robotic nature. According to SHIELD files, Bastion exists as a strange combination of two robotic X-Men foes: the mutant-hunting Sentinel Master Mold and the futuristic, alternate reality Nimrod. Having assembled the international strike force Operation: Zero Tolerance, Bastion was thought destroyed following a battle with Cable and Machine Man. Unfortunately, his head remained intact and the anti-mutant religious sect known as the Purifiers grafted it onto the body of an inert, earlier form of Nimrod, effectively resurrecting Bastion. Upon his return, I'm told Bastion used an offshoot of the techno-organic Magus to resurrect several anti-mutant humans and used them to facilitate a war on all mutants. After endangering the entire city of San Francisco to further his plans, many of the Avengers were called in to aid the X-Men against Bastion and his agents. Unfortunately, Bastion destroyed the Golden Gate Bridge before being apparently destroyed himself by the emerging mutant Hope Summers. Given that Bastion has returned from seeming destruction a few times before, I remain skeptical that he is truly gone for good.

QUOTE: "We have created a terrestrial solution to the X-Men and the global mutant threat. The first stage is complete. From here, we expand."

FACILITY

CLASSIFICATION:
Humans

LATEST SIGHTING:
Air space above Pennsylvania

I have learned sometimes the most evil of men can hide behind the simplest of titles and groups; the Corporation and the Facility come to mind rather quickly. The Facility spent years trying to recreate the Weapon X process to clone Wolverine. Their 23rd attempt resulted in X-23, and they brutally tortured and raised her to be nothing more than a weapon. I spent some time learning about X-23's past, and I was truly horrified. Despite the deaths of the men responsible, the Facility has continued, creating deadly assassins like Kimura and genetic monsters like the Predators X. Their clients range from the Kingpin to the Purifiers, and the men of the Facility seem to have absolutely no conscience. In their field test of X-23, she slaughtered a group of innocents, and I let her go without realizing what she was. In ways, every sin the Facility has committed since then comes back on me now. They must be stopped.

QUOTE: "The Facility I work for is a business, Miss Kincaid. We provide our clients with weapons. In fact, your friend X-23 is one of our best creations. Our current client wanted us to create a very specific item, to do a very specific job. He left it to us as to how to proceed."

HELLFIRE CULT

CLASSIFICATION:
Humans

LATEST SIGHTING:
San Francisco, California

For years, the Hellfire Club has operated internationally (with prominent branches in New York and London), perpetuating bizarre rituals among its members, such as dressing women in revealing garb and adorning their guards in a frightening mask. Firestar tells me, however, during her time with the Hellfire Club she learned at least some of those men were honorable; Wolverine disagrees completely. Recently, those same masks have been utilized by the Hellfire Cult, a group of California-based anti-mutant practitioners. Formed by the Red Queen and pushed into a fervor by Empath, the Hellfire Cult targeted mutants that relocated with the X-Men to San Francisco, violently attacking Pixie and later staging attacks on Mercury and others. Compared to other anti-mutant groups, the Hellfire Cult is relatively small in scope and notoriety; it was not considered by Bastion to be one of the groups he recruited to wipe out mutants worldwide. But their hate crimes have been truly horrific, and any who have participated deserve to be prosecuted to the law's fullest extent.

QUOTE: "We're pros now — so act like it. That mutie won't think twice before gutting you if you give it half a chance. So let's get out there and win one for humankind and let these muties know...the Hellfire Cult owns these streets."

CAMERON HODGE

CLASSIFICATION:
Techno-organic/
human hybrid
(formerly human)

LATEST SIGHTING:
The Xavier
Institute, Salem
Center, New York

I can think of no
personal betrayal
worse than what
Cameron Hodge
did to Warren
Worthington,
the Angel. They were friends and roommates at boarding
school and years later came up with the idea for the

original X-Factor. But Hodge now obsessively hated Warren,
for reasons I will leave to psychiatrists to analyze, and
all mutants. He had Warren's wings amputated, tried to
kill him, and used Warren's fortune to start a paramilitary
anti-mutant organization, the Right. Later Hodge murdered
Warren's girlfriend Candy Southern. As Archangel, Warren
used his new wings to behead Hodge. But Hodge's head
was immortal, due to a deal he had made with the demon
N'astirh. As a cyborg, Hodge allied himself with the
Genoshan government to combat the X-Men and their
mutant allies. Next Hodge became a "techno-organic"
member of the alien Phalanx. Recently revived by Bastion,
Hodge was drained of life energy by the techno-organic
alien Warlock, though I suspect Hodge, being immortal,
was merely deactivated. Hodge saw mutants as monsters,
and yet his maniacal vendetta against them has literally
turned Hodge into the true monster.

QUOTE: "I had those wings cut off. I hoped it would drive
him mad. I set him up to die."

STEVEN LANG

CLASSIFICATION:
Techno-organic/
human hybrid
(formerly human)

LATEST SIGHTING:
San Francisco,
California

Originally Dr.
Stephen Lang was
a brilliant human
scientist driven
by a fanatical,
visceral hatred of
mutants. Gaining
financial backing from Edward Buckman, leader of the
Hellfire Club's "Council of the Chosen," Lang constructed

a new series of Sentinel robots, based on Bolivar Trask's
original designs. In a tremendous battle between the X-Men
and the Sentinels aboard his space station base, Lang nearly
perished, and was left in a coma. Lang had programmed
the surviving "Master Mold" Sentinel with his own brain
patterns; later it became the mutant hunter called Bastion.
The real Lang was transformed into a "techno-organic" being
by the alien Phalanx, enabling him to change shape and
infect other people with the techno-organic virus. His ally
against mutantkind, Cameron Hodge, turned against Lang
and killed him. Ironically, Bastion, who was partly Lang's
creation, resurrected Lang to serve him. Hope Summers, the
so-called "Mutant Messiah," recently killed Lang again. But
since Lang is now more organic machine than man, I doubt
that his latest death will prove to be permanent.

QUOTE: "I'm a man, Cyclops—which is more than you'll
ever be, you mutant swine! D'you hear me, homo-so-called-
superior? A man! I'm better than any of you! Better than
all of you!"

MISS SINISTER

CLASSIFICATION:
Mutate (human,
clone)

LATEST SIGHTING:
Manhattan,
New York City

Over a century
ago, during a
brief awakening
of his centuries-
long sleep,
the Darwinist-
obsessed Apocalypse mutated a young scientist named
Nathaniel Essex into the deadly Mr. Sinister. (Wolverine
tells me Cyclops and Jean Grey were present at the
time, in some bizarre way). Ever since, Sinister has been

manipulating and experimenting upon mutants with no
regard to human life. Sinister was directly responsible
for the formation of the Marauders, who slaughtered the
Morlocks; he was involved in Neverland, the death camp
where thousands of mutants were slaughtered; and he has
cloned the world's mutants repeatedly. As I understand
it, Sinister was killed during the massive battle over the
newly born mutant Hope and was later reborn in a cloned
female body. As the telepathic Miss Sinister, he — er,
she — has toyed with Daken and the Hellfire Club. Though
reportedly dead, I can only hope we've seen the last of
this self-serving, megalomaniacal monster. Sinister is like
Arnim Zola and the Red Skull combined in one form; a
master plotter, an evil geneticist, extremely long-lived, and
obsessed with the lives of heroes.

QUOTE: "There's something real nasty in there. You
wouldn't want Claudine to hurt herself, would you?
Not when there's a way to hurt someone a little more
expendable."

MUTANT RESPONSE DIVISION

CLASSIFICATION: Humans

LATEST SIGHTING: Manhattan, New York City

A United Nations military unit that responds to mutant acts of terrorism, the Mutant Response Division, under the lead of Colonel Moran, was recently manipulated into seeking the extermination of X-Factor, the mutant private investigators who recently relocated to New York City. When Bolivar Trask, the creator of the Sentinels, returned from the dead and obtained a seat of political power, few people seemed to question his return, but he was being controlled by the deadly Bastion, who was seeking to wipe out mutants for good. The MRD used the ruse of having the Absorbing Man hire X-Factor, luring them into an isolated area from which to attack them, while subsequently attacking operatives in South America (where they also battled Baron Mordo, of all people) and Ireland. X-Factor took down the MRD, despite the unit's massive firepower, by freeing Trask from Bastion's mental control. The Avengers shared a lengthy association with the UN; I am appalled a UN military unit was manipulated in such a fashion. I need to raise my concerns publicly.

QUOTE: "The problem is, Colonel Moran, that X-Factor has situated itself squarely in the middle of a populated area in order to use humans as shields against attack. How can that cynicism not fill you with outrage?"

DONALD PIERCE

CLASSIFICATION: Cyborg (human)

LATEST SIGHTING: San Francisco, California

Donald Pierce's family has been affiliated with the Hellfire Club and their power-hungry Inner Circle for generations. Donald was recruited as the White Bishop after he'd already proved himself in battle against Cable and Iron Man, a fight Pierce only survived through the aid of cybernetic enhancements. Pierce has continually upgraded these enhancements and now seems to be more robot than man. Pierce has committed horrific atrocities over the past decade, killing many innocents and torturing others. Of all his crimes, none seems worse than his formation of the Reavers, who have murdered multiple civilians. Pierce has fought the X-Men on several continents and has consistently sought to murder or exploit mutants for his own purposes. Most recently, Pierce was infected by the techno-organic virus and controlled by Bastion. He murdered Wolf Cub before spending months as a seeming captive, secretly relaying information to Bastion about the surviving mutants and their California headquarters. Pierce was killed, and I can't help but be relieved he is no longer free to murder others.

QUOTE: "Look at you. In your prime. Healthy and hardy. Yet the news tells us your time, my time, is running out. They say we are being replaced on the evolutionary ladder by Homo Superior. Mutants. I'd say we are wrong."

PREDATOR X

CLASSIFICATION: Artificial being

LATEST SIGHTING: Manhattan, New York City

Seeking to put a complex series of events in place that would influence future events in his favor, Reverend William Stryker hired the Facility to genetically engineer a number of monsters that would hunger for mutant flesh. Calling each beast Predator X, the Facility kidnapped the mutant Mercury, took portions of her living flesh, and enhanced the beasts further. Only one Predator survived the initial battle with Hellion, Mercury, and X-23, and it went on to consume several mutants, including Mammomax, Peepers, and Vertigo, as well as the corpses of some mutants, before finally meeting defeat on Muir Island; Wolverine describes a less than glamorous battle as the creature had to eat him before it finally died. Another Predator X was nearly sold to Hydra on Madripoor, and it may have been later altered to target the Punisher. Most recently, John Sublime altered several Predators and staged a brazen attack on Utopia, but the X-Men were specifically trained to defeat the beasts, and they are all dead now. It disgusts me creatures like this exist in our world.

QUOTE UNAVAILABLE

URIFIERS

CLASSIFICATION:
Humans

LATEST SIGHTING:
Near Loyalsock
State Forest,
Pennsylvania

While I fully
believe in
freedom of
speech, religion,
and assembly,
I know those
rights can only
extend so far as
arm is not coming to another person. The Purifiers, who
ere organized by the militant Reverend William Stryker,

have committed multiple horrors in the name of their god.
Many of these atrocities have been silenced by politicians
being members of, or associated with, the Purifiers. Among
these terrorist acts were the callous murders of over 40
of Xavier's students (all former mutants who lost their
powers after M-Day), and the slaughter of other mutants,
including Icarus, the brother of Cannonball and Husk.
Most horrifying, however, was their slaughter of children in
Cooperstown, Alaska, in an attempt to stop a mutant birth.
The Purifiers have had reported access to future knowledge
from the robot Nimrod. They were also responsible for
the resurrection of Bastion, the creation of the deadly
winged Choir, and the development of the techno-organic
virus Selene used in her plots, as well as the hiring of the
Facility to create the Predators X.

QUOTE: "Fortunately for your friend, I am a man of God
and decided to show her mercy not deserving of your kind.
But I am only human. So surrender now or she begins her
eternal suffering in hell tonight."

EAVERS

LASSIFICATION: Cyborgs (human)

ATEST SIGHTING: Alberta, Canada

No one seems to know how the original Reavers became
cyborgs: part human and part machine. When they first
appeared they comprised a large gang of thieves, based in
the Australian outback, but staging robberies all over the
world. The X-Men not only bested them but took over their
base. Only three Reavers escaped: Bonebreaker, Pretty
Boy, and Skullbuster. Then Donald Pierce, the renegade
cyborg from the Hellfire Club's Inner Circle, took command
of the Reavers, adding four cyborg foes of Wolverine,
notably Lady Deathstrike. Yet another anti-mutant bigot,
Pierce used the Reavers as a strike force to try to battle
and kill the X-Men and other mutants. He later formed a
new team of Reavers that fought a new generation of the
New Mutants. However, the most recent Reavers team was
led by Lady Deathstrike. Typically, Reaver cyborgs have
superhuman strength and speed, and carry formidable
weaponry. They typically also rely on brute force rather
than skill. Lady Deathstrike, though, is a formidable
martial artist and swordswoman.

HE RIGHT

CLASSIFICATION:
Humans

LATEST SIGHTING:
St. Louis,
Missouri

One of several
anti-mutant
terrorist groups,
the Right was
formed by
Cameron Hodge
and funded
with money
appropriated
from Warren
Worthington,

who was employing Hodge at the time in a position of
trust. Equipped with eerie smile-faced armor and extensive
offensive weaponry, the Right soldiers participated in
several atrocities, including the kidnapping of a number of
young mutants, the torture of young Rictor, and the murder
of Candy Southern, girlfriend of the Angel. Villains the
Nanny and the Animator trace their origins to the Right as
well. After making their primary foes the original X-Factor,
the Right disbanded as Hodge pursued other plans. They
reformed under Hodge recently, at Bastion's instruction,
and fought the New Mutants in a battle that led to Karma
losing her leg. I must see to it this group is permanently
shut down.

QUOTE: "Mutants do not give orders! They obey...or
they die! Test that truth at your peril! War! A state of
martial law...has been declared! Mutants — by their very
existence. You have been created as tools, as slaves of
humanity. It's time you realized it...and ceased questioning
your better!" — Cameron Hodge

SAPIEN LEAGUE

CLASSIFICATION: Humans

LATEST SIGHTING: Westchester County, New York

When the woman called the Leper Queen gave birth to a mutant who later died tragically (scarring her face in turn), she vowed revenge on all mutants and began systematically killing all who she came in contact with.

She gathered other mutant-hating humans and formed the Sapien League, and the group brazenly attacked Xavier's school after M-Day, even when it was surrounded by Sentinels and the O*N*E. Despite being arrested and put on death row for murder, the Leper Queen (who would kill anyone who saw her unmasked face), was saved by Bastion. She re-formed the Sapien League and killed mutants Beautiful Dreamer and Fever Pitch, taking hundreds of humans with them. The Leper Queen was later killed after kidnapping Boom Boom, Surge, and Hellion, but the Sapien League was still deployed against Hope and Cable. Now that Bastion has been defeated, I hope this group has seen its last. Organized terror groups like the Sapien League, the Right, the Watchdogs, and the Resistants have the right to freely speak on issues, even if their message carries hatred, but murder is never justified.

QUOTE: "This is it! This is where we put a bullet in the mutants' heads! All of them! This is where the Sapien League takes back the planet for humanity!"

SENTINELS

CLASSIFICATION: Robots

LATEST SIGHTING: Xavier Institute, Salem Center, Westchester County, New York

The world first learned about the Sentinels when Dr. Bolivar Trask introduced his creations during a live television debate on the so-called "mutant menace." Fanatically obsessed with the idea that mutants would enslave humanity, Trask devised these robot warriors to capture or exterminate all mutants. But Trask fatally underestimated the power of their implacable logic. To put an end to mutants and mutation, the Sentinels will attempt to conquer or even sterilize humanity. Nevertheless, misguided individuals — even our own government — have repeatedly tried to use the Sentinels for their own ends. Sentinels now come in forms ranging from the skyscraper-sized "Wild Sentinels" that devastated Genosha to microscopic "nano-Sentinels"; there are even cyborg "Prime Sentinels," part human, part robot. The government's "Sentinel Squad O*N*E" were controlled by human pilots, but even these robots were taken over by nano-Sentinels. Kang, Onslaught and Cassandra Nova have all usurped control of Sentinels as lethal weapons. The government should destroy all Sentinels; they are simply too dangerous to exist.

QUOTE: "Our programming is specific and binding, mutant — all who resist us must be destroyed!"

U-MEN

CLASSIFICATION: Mutates (human)

LATEST SIGHTING: Westchester County, New York

I have faced thousands of villains, soldiers, and militant groups over the years and should be accustomed to every type of evil in the world. Yet I continue to be horrified by the reports I hear, especially in regard to groups like the U-Men, a group of organ harvesters who have been known to kidnap mutants, steal their organs, and transplant them into their human forms. Many members, thus, have abilities, such as enhanced sight, wings, or electric blood, each culled from a living person! The U-Men cover themselves in containment suits that keep them free from what they consider a tainted world. The U-Men were formed by John Sublime, who Beast describes as a sentient bacterial life form who claims to have had his hand in the super-soldier projects that led to the creation of Wolverine, me and many others. Sublime kept a camp mutant prisoners, removed Martha Johansson's brain from her body, is directly tied to the death of Jean Grey, and is responsible for loosing several Predator X's on Utopia. This bizarre threat needs to be contained immediately.

QUOTE: "For today is the day of the Recycled Man! The third species eternal! Homo perfectus! Let the harvest begin."

REAKWORLD

CLASSIFICATION:
Planet

Breakworld is home to a warrior culture defined by combat. Deprived of any contempt for the weak and suffering most citizens craved for more bloodshed, but the former gladiatrix Aghanne plotted to end her people's suffering once and for all. Creating a false prophecy Aghanne had her loyal augurs foretell Breakworld's destruction at the hands of an X-Man from Earth, starting a decades long contest won by Ord to bring a declaration of war to Earth. SWORD allied with Ord to deactivate the mutant genome, but when Colossus, the mutant Ord resurrected for his work, was revealed to be Breakworld's destroyer, Ord tried to kill him. SWORD took Colossus and Ord to Breakworld where its ruler Powerlord Kruun already planned Breakworld's retaliation on Earth in case of Breakworld's destruction. When Aghanne tried to force Colossus to fulfill the prohecy and destroy Breakworld by causing a chain reaction inside the reactor's energy sphere beneath Kruun's palace, Colossus killed her. Though Breakworld was saved Kruun had already shot a gigantic bullet at Earth, which mutant Kitty Pryde phased through our planet to save our world.

QUOTE: "To kill the weak is the honored path."
— Powerlord Kruun

ENOSHA

CLASSIFICATION: Island nation

TEST SIGHTING: Off the east coast of Africa, near adagascar, approximately 4° S, 55° E

enosha's past is the most tragic story in the history of cial tension between mutants and non-mutant humans. utsiders long thought of Genosha as a paradise, one of e most prosperous and technologically advanced nations on Earth. But Genosha's success was built on the backs of slaves. When Genoshan children turned 13, the government subjected them to genetic tests. Any children possessing mutant genes were stripped of their rights as citizens. Genoshan scientists then turned the children into mutate slaves. The X-Men and other mutant heroes overthrew the government, but periods of civil war between non-mutant humans and mutates followed. Then the United Nations shamefully attempted to appease Magneto by imposing him on the Genoshans as their ruler; Magneto predictably turned the nation into a base from which to conquer the world. Later, Cassandra Nova dispatched Sentinels that devastated the country, obliterating most of its population. Recently, Selene reportedly somehow resurrected the population of Genosha, most of them without their mutate powers, renaming the island "Necrosha." This seems like a dark miracle, but I suspect the suffering of the people of this tormented nation is far from over.

QUOTE: "A green and pleasant land" — national motto.

UTANT TOWN

WELCOME TO
MUTANTTOWN
POPULATION - 743

CLASSIFICATION:
City district

LATEST SIGHTING:
New York City,
New York

It wasn't long ago mutants numbered in the millions instead of the tens. For a time, mutants found relative peace in a few communities.

ne section of New York City, now called the Middle East ide, actually became known as Mutant Town (though sometimes called District X) for a time, and it was heavily populated by mutants and mutant supporters. When a number of bizarre cases plagued the citizens there, such as the serial killer called the Worm and the outbreak of the deadly drug Toad Juice, Detectives Ismael Ortega and Bishop, of the X-Men, did their best to police matters. After M-Day, Mutant Town slowly emptied, even after X-Factor Investigations made its home there and declared themselves Mutant Town's protectors. Citizens have divided into PANs (former mutants seeking to "pass as normal" humans) and REMs (former mutants who still have altered appearances), and some have even formed mutant gangs, like the X/Ms. Large portions of Mutant Town were destroyed by Arcade, and the Purifiers have targeted former mutants there. Many citizens have vacated, leaving Mutant Town just another city borough.

QUOTE: "District X used to be a thriving mutant community. A place where mutants could live among their own kind, feel like they belonged. Now it's just another ghetto."

UTOPIA

CLASSIFICATION: Private island

LATEST SIGHTING: Off the coast of San Francisco, California

I'm not a huge fan of segregation, but with the constant prejudice, persecution and violence directed toward mutants, grouping together seems a necessity. Utopia was

Cyclops' final move in a series of conflicts with the corrupt Norman Osborn when Osborn targeted mutants in his effort to dominate the superhuman community. Cyclops recovered X-Men archenemy Magneto's fallen Asteroid M from the ocean's depths, and built a city upon it off California's coast, declaring it a mutant haven named Utopia. While I don't think secession is the only option mutants have, the island has thrived — the remaining mutants of the world creating a community there. However, I have my concerns. Is this "country" meant to be a nation unto itself? What are the legal ramifications of that? Also, having all mutants gathered creates a tempting target for enemies, as shown by recent attacks by Selene and Bastion. Hopefully, the X-Men are able to protect those that live on Utopia and a healthy mutant community and population can spring forth from it.

QUOTE: "This ground — this city that we live in, just off your shores — this fortress we occupy…this ground is sacred. No mutant or their family will be harmed here." — Cyclops

THE WORLD

CLASSIFICATION: Genetic weapons facility

LATEST SIGHTING: Undisclosed; in the hands of Fantomex

I have literally heard dozens of theories about the origins of the super-soldier project that granted me my powers. One such theory is the Weapon Plus program, a decades-old complex government implementation, has sought to create the perfect human weapon. According to this theory,

I was the first successful weapon, and other weapons have included Nuke, Wolverine, and Fantomex. If this theory holds true, there are dozens more men who have been failures of this project, including Protocide, the Grand Director, and Deadpool. Regardless of where the truth lies, Wolverine assures me the World, a now-sentient facility that creates ever-evolving weapons (like the Ultimaton and the Allgod) as well as various mutates and tech monsters as its anti-bodies (rather like Ego the Living Planet), is in safe hands; I'm hard-pressed to believe him. When Osborn recently tried to seize the World as his own, Wolverine and Fantomex, with the help of my new ally the Protector (the Marvel Boy), stopped him.

QUOTE: "The World was built to breed and supply artificially-evolved super-soldiers. Part man, part machine — bio-engineered to win the imminent war between man and mutant…The human species is dying. Their only hope lies in machine fusion and a program of sustained mutant extermination. Genetic war is coming." — Fantomex

XAVIER INSTITUTE

CLASSIFICATION: Educational institution

LATEST SIGHTING: 1407 Graymalkin Lane, Salem Center, Westchester County, New York

Years ago, Charles Xavier turned his ancestral mansion in New York's Westchester County into "Professor Xavier's School for Gifted Youngsters," where he personally instructed his five pupils in high school and college level courses. But Xavier's students were secretly mutants, the original X-Men, whom he trained both to master their powers and to use them to combat mutants that menaced the public. Xavier's second team of X-Men and the New Mutants were likewise based at the school. Combat training took place in the "Danger Room," which was equipped with alien Shi'ar technology that could use hard-light holograms to duplicate any environment. Eventually, since most of the X-Men were adults, Xavier renamed the school "the Xavier Institute for Higher Learning." After Xavier was publicly revealed to be a mutant, he greatly expanded the student body, enlisting other mutants as teachers. Unfortunately, over the years Xavier's mansion has been repeatedly destroyed by the X-Men's enemies and then rebuilt. However, after the mansion was recently demolished by Sentinels, the Xavier Institute ceased to exist, and the X-Men relocated to San Francisco. Nevertheless, I suspect tradition will someday demand Xavier's mansion to rise once more.

QUOTE: "Mutatis mutandis" (Latin for "with the necessary changes having been made") — school motto.